Visual Basic
Algorithms

A Developer's Sourcebook of

Ready-to-Run Code

ROD STEPHENS

John Wiley & Sons, Inc.

New York • Chichester • Brisbane • Toronto • Singapore

Publisher: Katherine Schowalter
Editor: Phil Sutherland
Managing Editor: Susan Curtin
Technical Reviewer: Deepak Agrawal of DAConsulting, Inc., Chicago, IL
Text Design & Composition: North Market Street Graphics

Designations used by companies to distinguish their products are often claimed as trademarks. In all instances where John Wiley & Sons, Inc. is aware of a claim, the product names appear in initial capital or all capital letters. Readers, however, should contact the appropriate companies for more complete information regarding trademarks and registration.
Some of the material presented in this book has previously appeared in a slightly different form in *Visual Basic Developer* by Pinnacle Publishing, Inc.

This text is printed on acid-free paper.

This publication is designed to provide accurate and authoritative information in regard to the subject matter covered. It is sold with the understanding that the publisher is not engaged in rendering legal, accounting, or other professional service. If legal advice or other expert assistance is required, the services of a competent professional person should be sought.

Library of Congress Cataloging-in-Publication Data:

Stephens, Rod
    Visual basic algorithms : a developer's sourcebook of ready-to-run
  code / Rod Stephens.
      p.   cm.
    Includes index.
    ISBN 0-471-13418-X (pbk. : alk. paper)
    1. BASIC (Computer program language)   2. Microsoft Visual BASIC.
  I. Title.
  QA76.73.B3S834   1996
  005.26'2—dc20   95-45546
                                                          CIP

Printed in the United States of America
10 9 8 7 6 5 4 3 2 1

To Kenneth R. Stephens, 1938–1992

C O N T E N T S

I N T R O D U C T I O N

Programming for Windows has always been a daunting task. The Windows Application Programming Interface (API) provides a powerful set of tools for building Windows applications, but this power comes with the price of added difficulty and danger. In that respect the API is a bit like a bulldozer: if you use it properly you can build amazing things, but without the proper skills and care you will probably create only havoc and destruction.

Even if you avoid making catastrophic mistakes, errors in Windows programs can be subtle and difficult to find. Sometimes an error can remain hidden until a user presses just the right combination of keys and mouse buttons and only while certain other Windows events are occurring.

Visual Basic has changed all that. Using a point-and-click interface, Visual Basic allows you to quickly build complete applications without ever dealing directly with the Windows API. In fact, using Visual Basic you can write and test sophisticated Windows applications without knowing a thing about the API or even knowing that it exists. This means you no longer need to learn the complexities of the API and you are safe from its many dangers. By freeing you from API worries, Visual Basic lets you concentrate on the details of your application.

While Visual Basic makes building a program's user interface much easier, you must write the rest of the application yourself. You must write the code that takes input from the interface, processes it, and presents the results. That is where algorithms come in.

Algorithms are formal instructions for performing complicated tasks on a computer. A searching algorithm, for example, might describe how to locate a particular customer record in a 10 million record database. The quality of the algorithms you use can make the difference between locating needed data in seconds, hours, or not at all.

This book describes algorithms, their implementations, and their uses in the Visual Basic programming language. It contains many interesting and useful algorithms, completely implemented in Visual Basic. It analyzes techniques for managing data structures such as lists, stacks, queues, and trees. It also describes algorithms to perform common programming tasks like sorting, searching, hashing, and shortest path calculation.

To use these algorithms successfully, you must do more than copy the code into your program and press F5. You also need to understand how different algorithms behave under different circumstances. You need to determine which circumstances apply in your situation. Finally, you must use that information to select the algorithm that best fits your needs.

In this book each algorithm is described in plain English to give you a feel for the behavior of the algorithm. This will allow you to decide when the algorithm is appropriate and how best to use it in your programs.

Each algorithm is also explained in detail. The algorithm's typical and worst-case behaviors are discussed so you will know what to expect when you use it in your programs. This will also allow you to recognize worst-case behavior when it occurs so you will know that an algorithm is failing and must be rewritten or replaced.

Finally, each algorithm is implemented in ready-to-run Visual Basic source code which you can easily plug into your programs. The code is provided on the accompanying disk along with example applications. These examples not only show how the algorithms can be incorporated into programs, but they also demonstrate important characteristics of the algorithms themselves. By changing input parameters in the example programs, you can see the effects on the algorithms' performance. Many of the examples allow you to study the algorithms' expected and worst-case behaviors.

What This Package Includes

This book and disk package will provide you with:

- A solid introduction to algorithms. After reading the book and running the example programs, you will be able to use sophisticated algorithms in your Visual Basic projects. You will also have all the background you need to understand and evaluate new algorithms written by yourself or others.
- A library of 45 algorithm modules, ready for you to plug into your programs. Each is written as generally as possible so you can use it in a wide variety of circumstances. The book provides instructions for modifying the algorithms to fit your particular needs.
- 62 complete, ready-to-run example programs that allow you to test each of the algorithms. Using these programs you will be able to see the average and worst-case behaviors of many of the algorithms so you can gain a deeper understanding of how they work. The disk contains source code for all of the examples. You can modify the algorithms to learn even more about them, or you can use them as a basis for building your own programs.

Intended Audience

This book covers advanced Visual Basic programming topics. It does not teach Visual Basic itself. If you have a good understanding of the fundamentals of Visual Basic, you will be able to concentrate on the algorithms themselves rather than becoming bogged down in the details of the language.

This book will teach you important programming concepts that you can generalize and use to solve new problems. The algorithms discussed use powerful programming techniques such as recursion, binary subdivision, dynamic memory allocation, and network data structures that you can apply to your unique situation.

Even if you have not yet mastered Visual Basic, you will be able to run the example programs and compare the performance of different algorithms. Most importantly, you will be able to select the correct algorithms for your needs and add them to your Visual Basic projects.

Equipment You Will Need

To read the book and understand the algorithms, you need no special equipment. To run the example programs and see the algorithms in action, you need a PC that is reasonably able to run Visual Basic. A 386-based computer running Microsoft Windows 3.0 or later will work.

If you also want to examine and modify the source code provided on the disk, you will need to run Visual Basic 3.0 or later.

The algorithms will run at different speeds on different computers with different configurations, but they will all work. If you own a 90 megahertz Pentium with 16Mb of memory, you will be able to handle much larger problems than you could if you owned a 386-based computer with 4Mb of memory. Both machines will be able to run the example programs, just at different speeds and with problems of different sizes. You will quickly learn the limits of your hardware.

Visual Basic Version Compatibility

All of the programs contained on the disk have been tested using Visual Basic 3.0 and Visual Basic 4.0. Though the programs will look slightly different in the two environments, they will perform in roughly the same manner.

If you install the executable programs, the programs are installed as Visual Basic 3.0 executables. If you are currently running Visual Basic 4.0, you will notice differences in appearance between the executable programs and the programs as you run them from within the Visual Basic programming environment.

Some of the lines of code in the text are too long to fit all on one line. In these cases the line ends with and underscore and the code is continued on the next line. Visual Basic 4.0 allows you to break lines in this way but Visual Basic 3.0 does not. If you enter this code in Visual Basic 3.0, be sure you remove the underscores and combine broken lines into a single line.

Long lines are not broken in the source code on the disk, so you don't need to worry about this when using code from the disk.

Chapter Overview

Chapter 1 covers background material that you should be familiar with before you begin to analyze complex algorithms. This chapter covers some of the mathematical concepts necessary to theoretically analyze the complexity of algorithms. Some algorithms that perform well in theory may not do as well in practice, however, so this chapter also deals with practical programming considerations like paging.

Chapter 2 builds on the background presented in Chapter 1 by describing several important techniques for creating dynamic data structures. This chapter explains how you can build linked lists and stacks. You will find these data structures useful in your programs and they are used throughout the rest of the book to implement more complicated algorithms. Chapter 2 also describes how to generalize the pointer faking techniques used by linked lists to build other, more complicated data structures such as trees and networks.

Chapter 3 continues the discussion of dynamic data structures by presenting queues and dynamic arrays. Queues are used in many algorithms including several that are described later in the book, like the shortest path algorithms in Chapter 11. Irregular and sparse arrays allow you to create flexible array structures while reducing your program's memory usage.

Chapter 4 discusses the topic of recursion. For many, recursion is a confusing subject, but when used correctly it can be a powerful tool for building algorithms. Recursion can also be dangerous in some cases. Chapter 4 explains when this is the case and shows how you can remove recursion from your programs when necessary. This chapter demonstrates recursion removal for several examples of different complexities.

Chapter 5 uses many of the techniques presented earlier, such as recursion and linked lists, to examine the more complicated topic of trees. This chapter covers different tree representations like the *fat node, forward star,* and *linked sibling* representations, several important tree algorithms such as tree traversal, and finally two special purpose trees: *tries,* which are used to store text data, and *quadtrees,* which are useful for performing spatial operations.

Chapter 6 continues the discussion of trees by examining the more advanced topic of *balanced trees,* which have certain properties that keep them evenly balanced and efficient. These algorithms are surprisingly simple to describe but quite difficult to implement. This chapter uses one of the most powerful of these structures, a *B+tree,* to build a sophisticated relational database. Many commercial databases use B+trees and understanding how they work will give you some insight into these databases. You can also use the example program as the beginning of your own database application.

Chapter 7 introduces *decision trees.* Many problems can be described as searching for a solution within a decision tree. Even for small problems these trees can become enormous, so searching them as efficiently as possible is absolutely necessary. This chapter compares different techniques that can make searching for solutions manageable. These techniques include exhaustive searching, branch and bound, and several heuristic strategies that do not guarantee a perfect solution but which often find good solutions to difficult problems.

Chapter 8 deals with sorting, probably the most heavily studied topic in algorithms. Sorting algorithms are interesting for several reasons. First, sorting is a common task in programming. Second, different sorting algorithms have their own strengths and weaknesses, so no single algorithm works best in all situations. Finally, sorting algorithms demonstrate a wide variety of important algorithmic techniques such as recursion, list merging, linked lists, trees, heaps, and the use of random numbers to minimize worst-case behavior.

Chapter 9 examines searching, a topic closely related to sorting. Once a list has been sorted, your program may need to locate items within the list. This chapter compares several methods for locating items in sorted lists including exhaustive searching, searching linked lists, binary searching, and interpolative searching.

Chapter 10 introduces *hashing*, a technique for storing and locating items even more quickly than is possible using trees or sorting and searching. The chapter covers several hashing techniques including chaining, buckets, and many different kinds of open addressing. These techniques are particularly useful for storing extremely large lists that must be stored on a hard disk or other slow storage device.

Chapter 11 describes network algorithms. Some of these algorithms, like shortest path calculations, apply directly to networks like street, telephone, or power networks. The algorithms can also be used indirectly to solve other problems that may initially seem unrelated to the algorithm. For example, shortest path algorithms can be used to divide a network into districts or to identify critical tasks in a project schedule.

How to Use This Book

Chapter 1 gives background material used later throughout the book so you should start there. This chapter also explains how to add algorithms to your programs and how to modify them to suit your needs. You should read this material even if you do not need an in-depth understanding of the algorithms right away.

Chapters 2, 3, and 4 deal with the fundamental topics of dynamic memory allocation, data structures, and recursion. The tools developed in these chapters are used extensively in later parts of the book, so you should understand them before continuing.

Chapter 5 discusses material that is used heavily in Chapters 6, 7, and 11. It is also used to some extent in Chapters 8 and 9. While you can probably read Chapters 8 and 9 before Chapter 5, it may be easier to read Chapter 5 first.

Table I.1 Chapter Dependencies

Chapter	Strongly Recommended	Recommended
1		
2	1	
3	1, 2	
4	1, 2	
5	1, 2, 3, 4	
6	1, 2, 3, 4, 5	
7	1, 2, 3, 4, 5	
8	1, 2, 3, 4	5
9	1, 2, 3, 4	5, 8
10	1, 2, 3, 4	
11	1, 2, 3, 4, 5	

You can read the remaining chapters in any order. Table I.1 summarizes the dependencies between the chapters and shows which chapters you should read first before you move on to other chapters.

Table I.2 shows three possible plans of study that you can use depending on how broad you want your introduction to algorithms to be. The plan in the left column covers basic techniques and data structures that you will find helpful in your programs. The middle column also describes fundamental algorithms, like sorting and searching algorithms, which you may need to build more advanced programs.

The plan in the right column shows one order in which you could cover the whole book. While Chapters 6 and 7 follow logically from Chapter 5, they are more difficult than some of the later chapters so in this plan they are studied a little later. Chapters 6 and 11 are probably the most difficult chapters in the book so they are left for last. Of course, you can also read the book in order from the front cover to the back cover if you like.

Table 1.2 Plans of Study

Basic Techniques	*Fundamental Algorithms*	*In-depth Coverage*
1	1	1
2	2	2
3	3	3
4	4	4
	5	5
	8	8
	9	9
		10
		7
		11
		6

Why Visual Basic?

One of the most common complaints about Visual Basic is that it is slow. Pascal, C, C++, and many other compiled languages are faster, more flexible, and more powerful than Visual Basic. With this in mind it is natural to ask, "Why should I implement complex algorithms in Visual Basic? Wouldn't it be better to write complex applications in C? Or at least to build algorithms in C and make them available to Visual Basic programs through libraries?"

There are several reasons why implementing algorithms in Visual Basic makes sense.

First, Visual Basic provides a powerful environment for developing graphical user interfaces. Building a complete application in C or C++ is much more difficult and dangerous. If your program does not handle all of the details of Windows programming correctly, your application, the development environment, and possibly all of Windows will come crashing down around your ears.

Second, building a C library for use by Visual Basic involves many of the same dangers as writing a Windows application in C. While the mechanics are simple, the details can be tricky. If your library and Visual Basic program do not cooperate in just the right way, you will again crash your program, probably the Visual Basic environment, and maybe Windows as well.

Third, many algorithms are efficient enough to give good performance even in a slower language like Visual Basic. For example, countingsort in Visual Basic can sort 32,000 items in about two seconds on a 50 megahertz 486-based PC. You might be able to make the algorithm run a little faster using a C library, but the Visual Basic version is fast enough for most applications.

Fourth, if Visual Basic was your first programming language, there is no need for you to wait until you have mastered Pascal or C before you study algorithms. While some techniques are a bit easier to handle in other languages, all of the algorithms can be implemented in Visual Basic. Using Visual Basic will also save you the expense of buying a new compiler.

Finally, by implementing algorithms in *any* programming language, you will learn more about that language, and about programming and algorithms in general. As you study the algorithms, you will learn techniques that you can use in other parts of your programs. Once you have mastered an algorithm in Visual Basic, it will be much easier for you to reimplement it in Pascal or C if you find it absolutely necessary.

Installing the Source Disk

The disk that accompanies this book contains the Visual Basic source code for most of the algorithms discussed in the book. It also contains the source code and executable files for the example programs that demonstrate the algorithms.

Since these files add up to be fairly large, they come in a compressed format. The SETUP program on the disk allows you to decompress the files and install some or all of them on your system. To run the SETUP program follow these steps:

1. Insert the Visual Basic Algorithms disk in your floppy drive.
2. From the Windows Program Manager or the Windows File Manager, select the Run . . . command from the File pull-down menu.
   Enter the command to execute the SETUP program on your floppy drive. If your floppy drive is drive A, the command is "A:\SETUP".
   Press the **Enter** key or the OK button.
3. When the SETUP program prompts you, enter the directory where you would like the files installed. The default is C:\VB_ALGS.
4. The SETUP program will then allow you to install any or all of the following:

   - Algorithm library code.
   - Example program source code.
   - Executable example programs.

   Select the components you want to install.
5. When you have finished making selections, press the Continue button and the SETUP program will finish the installation. If you decide that you want to add more items later, you can use the SETUP program again to install them. Be sure to make copies of any files you have modified before you reinstall them, or the new versions will remove any changes you have made.

The SETUP program creates three subdirectories called LIB, SRC, and EXE. These contain the files for the algorithm library source code, example program source code, and the executable example programs. These directories are further divided into subdirectories named after the chapter in which the material appears. The actual files have names reflecting their contents. For example, if you decide to install the files in the default location C:\VB_ALGS, then the library source code for the quicksort sorting routine described in Chapter 8 will be placed in C:\VB_ALGS\LIB\CH8\QUICK.BAS.

Running the Example Programs

One of the most useful ways to run the example programs is using Visual Basic's debugging capabilities. Load the source code into Visual Basic. Then using breakpoints, watches, and other debugging commands, you can watch the internals of the algorithms in action. This can be particularly helpful for understanding more complicated algorithms like the balanced trees presented in Chapter 6 and the network algorithms presented in Chapter 11.

If you install the executable example programs from the disk, you can run them in all of the usual ways in Windows. Perhaps the easiest way is to double click on the name of the example program in the File Manager.

If you install the executables, the SETUP program places the RUN_EXE.EXE application in the EXE\CH1 subdirectory. It also creates a "Visual Basic Algorithms" program group with an icon that starts this application. You can double click on this icon to start the program. RUN_EXE.EXE presents the names of the other example programs, grouped by chapter, along with a one sentence description of each. If you select a program and press the Run button, RUN_EXES will start the program you have selected.

Some of the example programs create data or temporary scratch files. These programs will automatically place the files in an appropriate directory. Some of the sorting programs presented in Chapter 8, for instance, create data files in the CH8 directory. All of these files have a ".DAT" extension so it will be easy for you to find and remove them if you like.

When you run the example programs, keep in mind that they are for demonstration purposes only. They are intended to help you understand particular algorithmic concepts and they do not spend a great deal of time validating data and trapping errors. If you enter invalid data, the programs may crash. If you have trouble figuring out what data to enter, use the program's Help menu to get instructions.

Library Source Code

The disk accompanying this book contains 45 algorithm library modules that you can add to your projects. Table I.3 lists the library modules and briefly describes what each contains.

Table I.3 Brief Contents of Library Modules

Chapter 2	
CONST.BAS	Constants used by many library modules.
DBLLINK.BAS	Doubly linked list.

GARBAGE.BAS	Unordered list with garbage collection.
LINKED.BAS	Linked list.
MANYLINK.BAS	Multiple linked lists with fixed tops. Use this if you know how many linked lists you will need.
SIM_LIST.BAS	Simple, array-based list. Use this only for small lists.

Chapter 3

ARRAY_Q.BAS	Array-based queue.
CIRCLE_Q.BAS	Circular queue. Use this if the size of the queue will not change too much.
LINKED_Q.BAS	Linked list queue. Use this if the size of the queue will vary greatly.
PRI_LIST.BAS	Linked list priority queue. Use only for small queues.
SPARSE.BAS	Sparse arrays.
TRIANG.BAS	Triangular arrays.

Chapter 5

BIN_TREE.BAS	Binary tree (fat node representation).
FSTAR.BAS	Tree of arbitrary degree (forward star representation).
LINK_SIB.BAS	Tree of arbitrary degree (linked sibling representation).
QTREE.BAS	Quadtrees.
TREESORT.BAS	Sorted binary tree.
TRIE.BAS	Tries.

Chapter 6

AVL.BAS	AVL trees.
B_PLUS.BAS	B+trees.
BTREE.BAS	B–trees.

Chapter 7

| HEUR.BAS | Searching using exhaustive search, branch and bound, and heuristics. |

Chapter 8

BUBBLE.BAS	Bubblesort.
BUCKET.BAS	Linked list and array bucketsort.
COUNTING.BAS	Countingsort.
ENCODE.BAS	String-to-number encoding and decoding.
HEAP.BAS	Heapsort.
INSERT.BAS	Insertionsort.
L_INSERT.BAS	Linked list insertionsort.
MERGE.BAS	Mergesort.
PRIORITY.BAS	Heap-based priority queue. Better than PRI_LIST for large heaps.

QUICK.BAS	Quicksort.
SELECT.BAS	Selectionsort.

Chapter 9

SEARCH.BAS	List searching using binary search and interpolation search.

Chapter 10

HASH_B.BAS	Hashing using buckets.
HASH_C.BAS	Hashing using chaining.
HASH_L.BAS	Hashing using an array with linear probing.
HASH_O.BAS	Hashing using an array with ordered linear probing.
HASH_Q.BAS	Hashing using an array with quadratic probing.
HASH_R.BAS	Hashing using an array with pseudo-random probing.
HASH_X.BAS	Hashing using an array with linear probing, removal, and rehashing.

Chapter 11

SPAN.BAS	Minimal spanning trees.
FLOW.BAS	Maximum flow.
PATH_C.BAS	Label correcting shortest paths.
PATH_S.BAS	Label setting shortest paths.

Adding Algorithms to Your Projects

You can use the algorithms presented in this book in one of three ways: exactly as they are written, as templates for making modifications, or with experimental changes.

Algorithms as Written

To use an algorithm exactly as it is written, simply use the Add File . . . command in Visual Basic's File pull-down menu to add the algorithm's code to your project. If you need to change the algorithm later, all projects that include the file will be automatically updated the next time you build them. This makes it easy for you to make enhancements to the algorithms.

Visual Basic code generally must be designed to work with data of a specific data type. A routine designed to process integers will not be able to process doubles or strings. The exception to this rule is the variant data type. A variant object can take on one of several data type values including integer, long, single, double, currency, date, and string.

The algorithms presented in this book use different data types depending on the situation. Some use variants for flexibility. Other algorithms use different data types, either because they are more appropriate or because they are necessary. The countingsort algorithm described in Chapter 8, for example, only works with numeric data.

Since variants cannot take on the values of user-defined data types (defined using the **Type** statement), any algorithm that requires user-defined data structures cannot use variants.

Algorithms as Templates

The flexibility provided by variants comes at the cost of reduced performance. Operations on more specific data types like integers are faster than operations on variants. Using variants extensively can slow your programs. In one test run, a program took 64 percent longer to sort 30,000 variants than it took to sort 30,000 longs. If you need to improve performance, you might think about converting an algorithm that uses variants into one that uses some other data type.

There are other reasons to modify an algorithm. You might want to convert an algorithm that manipulates integers into one that uses a user-defined data type or you might want to change the fundamental operations used by an algorithm. For example, you might need to sort a group of customer records based, not on a single value, but on several values such as customer name, address, city, state, and ZIP code.

In these cases you can use the standard algorithm source code as a *template* for making a new version. Begin by copying the file so you can keep an unmodified version of the original. Give the new file a name similar to the old one so you will remember what the file is.

You might also want to change the names of the algorithm's subroutines so you do not confuse them with the originals. You might add an underscore and a letter to the end of the subroutine names to indicate the data type of the new versions. If you change the QuickSort routine to handle doubles, for example, you might give the new routine the name QuickSort_D.

Next, make whatever changes are necessary in the new file. The original source code for many of the algorithms uses variants for key data. By searching for the word "Variant" you should be able to locate most of the places where you will need to make changes. You may be able to simply replace the word "Variant" with the new data type.

Before you create dozens of different files for different data types, remember that using multiple files will increase the size and complexity of your program. If your program uses different routines to sort integers, longs, singles, doubles, and strings, it will contain a lot more code than it would if it treated all of these items as variants. Before you start writing specialized code, you might build your program using variant versions of the algorithms. Then after you have had a chance to see if the program is too slow, you can consider writing separate routines for the different data types if necessary.

Algorithms with Experimental Changes

If you want to make experimental changes to an algorithm, but you do not want the changes to affect every program that uses it, copy the source code into a new file. Then add this file to your experimental project. You can modify this copied algorithm without affecting other programs. When you have finished experimenting with the algorithm, you can delete the new file if you will not need it any longer.

If you accidentally make changes to an algorithm's source code and you cannot undo the changes, use the SETUP program to reinstall the original source code. Be sure to save any changes you have made to other files if you do not want them to be replaced by the SETUP program.

All of the example programs that come on the disk use this approach of creating separate copies of algorithm source code. Some of the copies have been modified to make the example program simpler while others have been modified to emphasize different aspects of the algorithm.

The BINARY program presented in Chapter 5, for example, contains code that displays the tree's structure directly on the program's main form. This code makes displaying the tree easier but it is not really part of the binary tree algorithm. The code that displays the tree's structure is contained in the file SRC\CH5\BINARY.BAS used in the BINARY program, but it is not contained in the library source file LIB\CH5\BINARY.BAS.

Since the example programs contain their own copies of the source code, you can modify them without fear of damaging your other projects. As long as you use the library versions or your own modified versions of the algorithms in your programs, you should be safe. If you do accidentally damage a library file and you cannot repair it, you can always reinstall the original code.

1

Background

Overview

This chapter presents background material that you should understand before you begin the serious study of algorithms. The chapter begins by asking, "What are algorithms?" Before getting into programming details, it is worth spending a few moments to recall exactly what algorithms are.

The chapter then introduces *complexity theory,* the formal study of the complexity of algorithms. Using complexity theory you will be able to evaluate the theoretical performance of algorithms. This will allow you to compare different algorithms to each other and predict their performance under different circumstances. The chapter gives several examples that show how to apply complexity theory to small problems.

Some algorithms that perform well in theory may not do as well in practice, however, so this chapter discusses practical programming considerations like paging.

What Are Algorithms?

An algorithm is a list of directions for performing a particular task. When you give someone instructions to fix a lawn mower, drive a car, or bake a cake, you are creating an algorithm. Of course these sorts of everyday algorithms are described in vague intuitive terms like:

```
Make sure the car is in park.
Make sure the parking brake is set.
Turn the key.
Etc.
```

Usually you assume that the person following the instructions can handle the millions of little details like unlocking the door, opening the door, sitting down behind the wheel, fastening the seat belt, finding the parking brake, etc.

When you write an algorithm for a computer, you cannot assume the computer will understand anything you do not tell it explicitly. The computer has a very limited vocabulary (a programming language) and all of your instructions must be phrased using that vocabulary. To deal with this situation, you need to use a more formal style for writing computer algorithms.

It is an interesting exercise to try to write an algorithm for a common, everyday task in a formal style. The car driving algorithm, for example, might begin with:

```
If the door is locked then:
    Insert the key in the lock
    Turn the key
    If the door is still locked then:
        Turn key the other way
Pull up on the door handle
Etc.
```

This bit of code only gets the door open and it doesn't even check that you are opening the correct door! If the lock is sticky and hard to open (like the one on my car is), the algorithm can become extremely complicated.

Algorithms have been formalized for thousands of years. Around 300 B.C. Euclid wrote algorithms for bisecting angles, testing whether triangles were equal, and performing other geometric tasks. He started with a small vocabulary of axioms such as "parallel lines never intersect," and from those axioms built algorithms for complicated tasks.

This sort of formalized algorithm is appropriate for many scientific purposes where it is necessary to show that something is true or that some task can be accomplished, but it is less important that the instructions be efficient. For problems where someone must actually execute the instructions, like sorting a million customer records using a computer, efficiency becomes an important part of the problem. To write an algorithm for a computer, you must analyze the algorithm's performance as well as its correctness.

Analyzing Algorithms—How Fast Is Fast?

Complexity theory, as the name implies, is the study of the complexity of algorithms. There are several ways in which you can measure the complexity of an algorithm. Programmers usually focus on the speed of an algorithm but other factors are important as well. How much memory an algorithm uses and how many other resources like disk drives an algorithm requires are also common benchmarks for algorithms. A fast algorithm will not be of much use if it requires more memory than your computer has available.

Space versus Time

Many algorithms provide a tradeoff between space and time. By using more memory you can make the algorithm run faster.

A shortest path algorithm is a good example. Given a network, like the network of streets in a city, you can write an algorithm for computing the shortest distance between any two points in the network. You could precompute the shortest distances between every point and every other point, and then store the results in a table. Then when you needed to know the shortest distance between any two points, you could look the value up in the table almost instantly. On the other hand, such a table would require a huge amount of memory. The street network for a large city like Boston or Denver might contain a few hundred thousand points. The table needed to store all of the shortest distance information would have more than 10 billion entries. In this example the space versus time tradeoff is clear: by using an additional 10 gigabytes of memory you can make the program much faster.

This special relationship between time and space gives rise to the idea of *space-time complexity*. In this sort of analysis an algorithm is evaluated in terms of both time and space, and the tradeoffs between them are studied.

This book concentrates mostly on time complexity, but it points out any unusual space requirements an algorithm has. Some algorithms, like the mergesort algorithm discussed in Chapter 8, require extra "scratch space" for temporary storage. Others, like the heapsort algorithm also discussed in Chapter 8, require a fairly "natural" amount of space. Heapsort needs only enough space to store the items it is sorting.

Big O Notation

While comparing different algorithms, it is important to understand how complexity relates to the size of the problem itself. This is slightly different from looking at the time and space needed by an algorithm to solve a problem of a certain size. One algorithm may need one second to sort a thousand numbers and ten seconds to sort a million numbers. Another algorithm might need two seconds to sort a thousand numbers but only five seconds to sort a million.

While it is interesting to know the exact speeds of each algorithm, it is more important to understand the relative behaviors of the algorithms for problems of different sizes. In this example the first algorithm is faster at sorting small lists but the second algorithm is faster at sorting large lists. If you understand how the performances of the algorithms relate, you can select the best algorithm for your current needs.

You can relate the complexity and size of a problem using "Big O" notation. An algorithm has complexity $O(f(N))$, pronounced "order F of N," if the time required by the algorithm goes up at the same rate as the function $f(N)$ when the problem size N gets large. For example, consider the simple algorithm shown below which sorts N positive numbers.

```
For I = 1 To N
    ' Find the largest item in the list.
    MaxValue = 0
    For J = 1 to N
        If Value(J) > MaxValue Then
            MaxValue = Value(J)
            MaxJ = J
        End If
    Next J
```

```
    ' Print the largest item we just found.
    Print Format$(MaxJ) & ":" & Str$(MaxValue)

    ' Zero the item so we do not pick it again.
    Value(MaxJ) = 0
Next I
```

In this algorithm the variable I loops from 1 to N. Each time I changes, the variable J also loops from 1 to N. For each of the N times the outer loop is executed, the inner loop is executed N times. The total number of times the inner loop gets executed is N * N or N^2. This gives the algorithm complexity of $O(N^2)$ ("order N-squared").

If you used this algorithm to sort 100 numbers, the **If** statement within the inner loop would be executed $100^2 = 10,000$ times. If you used the algorithm to sort 200 numbers, the inner loop would be executed $200^2 = 40,000$ times.

When calculating Big O values, you should use only the fastest growing part of the run time equation. Suppose an algorithm has a run time given by $N^3 + N$. The Big O notation for that algorithm would be $O(N^3)$. Looking only at the fastest growing part of the function allows you to examine the behavior of the algorithm as the problem size N gets large.

When N is large for a function with run time $N^3 + N$, the N^3 term dominates and the entire function starts to look like N^3. When N = 100, the difference between $N^3 + N$ = 1,000,100 and N^3 = 1,000,000 is only 100, a 0.01 percent difference. Notice that this is only true for large N. When N = 2, the difference between $N^3 + N$ = 10 and N^3 = 8 is 2, a 20 percent difference.

You should also ignore constant multiples in Big O notation. An algorithm with run time $3 * N^2$ would be considered $O(N^2)$. This makes it easier to understand relative changes in the problem size. If you increase N by a factor of 2, the 2 is squared in the N^2 term so the run time would increase by a factor of about 4.

Ignoring constant multiples also gives you a little freedom in counting the steps executed by the algorithm. In the sorting example shown above, the inner loop is executed N^2 times, but how many steps should you count for each inner loop? You could count only the **If** statement because only it is executed every time through the loop. You could calculate the total number of times the statements within the **If** are executed and count those, too. Then there are the statements inside the outer loop but outside the inner loop, like the **Print** statement. Should those be counted, too?

Following these different counting methods you might decide that the algorithm had $N^2, 3 * N^2$, or $3 * N^2 + N$ complexity. With Big O notation these are all the same. They all reduce to $O(N^3)$ so it does not matter exactly which statements you count.

Looking for Complexity

Generally the most complex parts of a program will be in program loops and subroutine calls. In the sorting example shown earlier, two loops were responsible for executing most of the algorithm's statements.

When a subroutine calls another subroutine, you must think a bit about how much work that other subroutine is doing. If it is performing a constant amount of work, like printing a number, then you do not need to worry too much about that subroutine for Big O purposes. On the other hand, if it is executing $O(N)$ steps, then the function may be contributing an important part of the algorithm's run time complexity. If the subroutine call is executed within a loop, the effect may be even greater.

Suppose a program has a subroutine called Slow that has $O(N^3)$ complexity, and another subroutine Fast that has $O(N^2)$ complexity. What you can say about the complexity of the program as a whole depends on how the two subroutines are related.

If subroutine Fast calls subroutine Slow each time it runs through its loops, then the complexities of the subroutines combine. To find the combined complexity, multiply the two complexities together. In this case you would multiply $O(N^2)$ by $O(N^3)$ to get a combined complexity for the program as a whole of $O(N^3 * N^2) = O(N^5)$. The code fragment below shows this sort of behavior.

```
Sub Slow ()
Dim I As Integer
Dim J As Integer
Dim K As Integer
    For I = 1 To N
        For J = 1 To N
            For K = 1 To N
                ' Do something here.
            Next K
        Next J
    Next I
End Sub

Sub Fast ()
Dim I As Integer
Dim J As Integer

    For I = 1 To N
        For J = 1 To N
            Slow          ' Call subroutine Slow.
        Next J
    Next I
End Sub

Sub MainProgram ()
    Fast
End Sub
```

On the other hand, if the main program calls both subroutines separately, then the complexities of the subroutines add together. This gives the program a total complexity of $O(N^3) + O(N^2)$. In Big O notation you ignore the smaller $O(N^2)$ term so this is the same as $O(N^3)$. The code fragment below has this complexity.

```
Sub Slow ()
Dim I As Integer
Dim J As Integer
Dim K As Integer

    For I = 1 To N
        For J = 1 To N
            For K = 1 To N
                ' Do something here.
            Next K
        Next J
    Next I
End Sub
```

```
Sub Fast ()
Dim I As Integer
Dim J As Integer

    For I = 1 To N
        For J = 1 To N
            ' Do something here.
        Next J
    Next I
End Sub

Sub MainProgram ()
    Slow
    Fast
End Sub
```

Complexity of Recursive Algorithms

Recursive routines are routines that call themselves. They introduce complexity in a subtle way. In many recursive algorithms it is the number of times recursion occurs that determines the complexity of the algorithm. While a recursive routine may seem simple, it will contribute greatly to the complexity of the program if it calls itself many times. The code fragment below, for example, shows a subroutine that contains only two statements. When called for input N, however, this subroutine will be executed N times. That makes the complexity of this piece of code O(N).

```
Sub CountDown (N As Integer)
    If N <= 0 Then Exit Sub
    CountDown N - 1
End Sub
```

A recursive algorithm that calls itself more than once is said to be *multiply recursive*. Multiply recursive routines can be harder to analyze than singly recursive algorithms, and they can contribute much more to the algorithm's run time. The subroutine below is similar to the previous subroutine CountDown except that it calls itself twice instead of once.

```
Sub DoubleCountDown (N As Integer)
    If N <= 0 Then Exit Sub
    DoubleCountDown N - 1
    DoubleCountDown N - 1
End Sub
```

Since the routine calls itself twice, you might expect that it would have twice the run time of subroutine CountDown. That would give this routine a run time of 2 * O(N) = O(N). This is not the case, however. If you let T(N) be the number of times the routine is executed with input N, it is easy to see that T(0) = 1. When the routine is called with input 0, it simply exits.

For larger N the routine recursively calls itself twice with parameter N − 1. The number of times the routine is executed in that case is 1 + 2 * T(N − 1). Table 1.1 shows some of the values generated by the equations T(0) = 1 and T(N) = 1 + 2 * T(N − 1). If you look closely at these values, you will see that $T(N) = 2^{N+1} - 1$ giving the routine a run time

Table 1.1 Values of the Runtime Function for Subroutine DoubleCountDown

N	0	1	2	3	4	5	6
T(N)	1	3	7	15	31	63	127

of $O(2^N)$. Even though subroutines CountDown and DoubleCountDown look similar, DoubleCountDown requires many more steps to execute.

A recursive routine can also call itself indirectly by calling a second routine which then calls the first. This sort of routine is said to be *indirectly recursive*. Analyzing indirectly recursive algorithms can be even more difficult than analyzing multiply recursive algorithms. The Sierpinski curve algorithm discussed in Chapter 4 (see pages 87–90) uses four subroutines that are both multiply and indirectly recursive. Each of these routines calls itself and the other three routines up to four times. It takes a fair amount of work to show that this algorithm runs in time $O(4^N)$.

Space complexity is particularly important for some recursive algorithms. It is very easy to write a recursive subroutine that allocates a little bit of memory each time it is called. After the routine has been invoked in a long chain of recursive calls, the amount of space allocated can start to add up. For these reasons it is sometimes important to perform at least a casual space complexity analysis on recursive routines to make sure the routine does not use huge amounts of memory.

The code fragment below shows a subroutine that allocates more memory each time it is invoked. After one or two hundred recursive calls, the routine will use up all of your computer's memory and the program will stop with an "Out of memory" error.

```
Sub GobbleMemory (N As Integer)
Dim Array() As Integer

    ReDim Array (1 To 32000)
    GobbleMemory N + 1
End Sub
```

When a function or subroutine is invoked in Visual Basic, the system allocates memory from a *system stack* for bookkeeping purposes. If a recursive subroutine is invoked too many times, it can exhaust the stack even though the computer itself has memory available. If you execute the subroutine shown below, it will quickly exhaust the available stack space and halt your program with an "Out of stack space" error. You could then use the debugger to check the value of the Count variable to see how many times the subroutine called itself before the stack was exhausted.

```
Sub UseStack ()
Static Count As Integer

    Count = Count + 1
    UseStack
End Sub
```

Variables that you declare locally to a routine may also be allocated from the stack. If you modify the UseStack subroutine shown above so it allocates three variant variables each time it is called, the program will run out of stack space much sooner.

```
Sub UseStack ()
Static Count As Integer
Dim I As Variant
Dim J As Variant
Dim K As Variant

    Count = Count + 1
    UseStack
End Sub
```

In summary, the complexity of recursive subroutines is usually determined by the number of times the routine is called. Calculating the complexity of recursive routines can be difficult, especially if the routine is multiply or indirectly recursive.

If a recursive routine allocates lots of memory each time it is called, the space complexity of the routine may be as important as the run time complexity. If you are not careful, the routine will exhaust all of your computer's memory and halt your program. Even if a routine does not allocate large amounts of memory, it can exhaust the stack space if it is invoked in a long chain of recursive calls. If the routine allocates local variables, it can exhaust the stack even more quickly.

Chapter 4 has much more to say about recursive routines. The algorithms described there demonstrate many of these issues.

Average Case and Worst Case

Big O notation is used as an upper bound on the complexity of algorithms. Just because a program has a certain Big O complexity does not mean the algorithm always takes that long. Many algorithms can take far less time than analysis indicates they might. The code below shows a simple algorithm that locates an item within a list.

```
Function LocateItem (target As Integer) As Integer
    For I = 1 To N
        If Value(I) = target Then Exit For
    Next I
    LocateItem = I
End Sub
```

If the target item is at the end of the list, the algorithm will need to search all N items in the list before finding the item. That will take N steps so this is an O(N) algorithm. This is the longest the algorithm could take so it is called the *worst case analysis* of the algorithm.

On the other hand, if the target number happens to be at the very beginning of the list, the algorithm will stop almost immediately. It will execute only a couple of steps before it finds the number and stops. This makes the algorithm's *best case* run time a constant or O(1). Generally a best case like this one is not very interesting because it will be unlikely to occur in real life. It is more interesting to look at the algorithm's *average* or *expected case* behavior.

In this example, if the numbers in the list are initially mixed randomly, the target item could appear anywhere in the list. You could perform many trials where you select a random item and then locate the item in the list. Sometimes the item would be far down the list and sometimes it would be near the top. On the average you would need to examine N / 2 of the items before finding the one you wanted. This makes the average case behavior of this algorithm O(N / 2) which is the same as O(N) in Big O notation.

For some algorithms, the worst case and expected case results are different. The quicksort algorithm discussed in Chapter 8, for example, has worst case behavior $O(N^2)$ but expected case behavior $O(N * \log(N))$ which is much faster. Algorithms like these tend to go to great lengths to ensure that the worst case behavior is extremely unlikely to occur.

Common Complexity Functions

Table 1.2 lists some of the functions that commonly occur in complexity calculations. The functions are listed in increasing order of growth with the functions at the top of the list growing more slowly than the functions at the bottom. This means algorithms with run time complexities involving functions near the top of the list will be faster than those with run time complexities involving functions near the bottom of the list. It also means a complexity equation that contains more than one of these functions would reduce to the last one in the table when it came to Big O notation. For example, $O(\log(N) + N^2)$ would be the same as $O(N^2)$ in Big O notation.

Before going any further, you should review a little bit about logarithms since they play an important role in several of the algorithms presented later in the book. The logarithm of a number N in a base B is the power P that satisfies the equation $B^P = N$. For example, when you see an equation like $\log_2(8)$ you should think "2 to what power equals 8?" In this case $2^3 = 8$ so you can write $\log_2(8) = 3$.

It is easy to convert between different log bases because of the relationship $\log_B(N) = \log_C(N) / \log_C(B)$. If you wanted to convert $\log_2(N)$ into base 10, for example, you would have $\log_{10}(N) = \log_2(N) / \log_2(10)$.

The value $\log_2(10)$ is a constant that is approximately 3.32. Since you ignore constant multipliers in Big O notation, you can ignore the $\log_2(10)$ term here. In fact for any base B, the value $\log_2(B)$ will be a constant, so for purposes of Big O notation all log bases are the same. In other words, $O(\log_2(N))$ is the same as $O(\log_{10}(N))$ or $O(\log_B(N))$ for any value of B. Since all log bases are the same, it is common to omit the log base in Big O notation—you could write $O(\log(N))$ instead of $O(\log_2(N))$.

Binary representations are natural in programming so the logarithms used when analyzing run times are usually base 2. To make the notation easier, the chapters that follow will assume that $\log(N)$ means $\log_2(N)$. If a different log base is needed, the base will be written explicitly.

Whether or not an algorithm with one of the run times shown in Table 1.2 is fast enough depends on how you use the algorithm. If you need to run the algorithm once per year on a fairly small data set, $O(N^2)$ performance is probably acceptable. If you need to

Table 1.2 Common Complexity Functions

$f(N) = C$	(C is a constant)
$f(N) = \log(\log(N))$	
$f(N) = \log(N)$	
$f(N) = N^C$	(C is a constant between 0 and 1)
$f(N) = N$	
$f(N) = N * \log(N)$	
$f(N) = N^C$	(C is a constant greater than 1)
$f(N) = C^N$	(C is a constant greater than 1)
$f(N) = N!$	(i.e., $1 * 2 * \ldots * N$)

run the algorithm interactively on large data sets with a user watching, O(N) may not be fast enough.

Generally speaking, however, run times involving N * log(N) and the smaller functions are pretty fast. Run times involving N^C for small C, like N^2, are also acceptably fast if the amount of data is limited. Run times involving functions like C^N and N! are generally so long that algorithms with these complexities can be run only for very small problem sizes.

Another interesting way to think about the relative speeds of these functions is to examine the time it would take to solve problems of different sizes. Table 1.3 shows how long it would take a computer executing 1 million algorithm steps per second to execute algorithms with run times involving some of the larger complexity functions. The table shows that only very small problems can be solved when the complexity is $O(C^N)$ and only the smallest problems can be solved when the complexity is O(N!). An O(N!) problem where N = 24 would take more time to solve than the current age of the universe.

Fast versus FAST

While it is very useful to ignore smaller terms and constant multiples when studying algorithms, it is often important to consider these factors when writing programs. These numbers become particularly important when the problem size is small and the constants are large compared to the problem size.

For example, suppose you have two algorithms that can accomplish the same task. Suppose one runs in O(N) time and one runs in $O(N^2)$ time. For large problems the first algorithm will probably be the better solution.

When you look closely at the actual run time functions, however, you may find that the first is f(N) = 30 * N + 7000 and the second is f(N) = N^2. In this case the second algorithm will execute fewer steps for problems where N is under around 100. If you know that your problem size will never exceed 100, you might be better off using the second approach.

On the other hand, not all steps are equally fast on a computer. If the first algorithm uses fast memory operations and the second requires frequent slow disk accesses, the first algorithm might very well be faster in all cases.

To further confuse the issue, there are a number of other factors that have not yet been considered. The first algorithm might require a huge amount of memory which your computer may not have or which might be in use by other programs. The second algorithm may be much more complicated than the first so it might take you days longer to implement and it might become a debugging nightmare in the long run. Real-life issues like these can sometimes make any complexity analysis seem almost pointless.

Table 1.3 Times to Execute Complex Algorithms

	N = 10	*N = 20*	*N = 30*	*N = 40*	*N = 50*
N^3	.001 sec	.008 sec	.027 sec	.064 sec	.125 sec
2^N	.001 sec	1.05 sec	17.9 min	1.27 days	35.7 years
3^N	.059 sec	58.1 min	6.53 years	$3.86 * 10^5$ years	$2.28 * 10^{10}$ years
N!	3.63 sec	$7.71 * 10^4$ years	$8.41 * 10^{18}$ years	$2.59 * 10^{34}$ years	$9.64 * 10^{50}$ years

Complexity analysis is still useful for understanding the general nature of an algorithm. During the analysis you will usually figure out where the bulk of the computation is taking place and you will discover which parts of the algorithm determine the overall performance. This will tell you where improvements in the algorithm might give the greatest performance gains.

In practice the best way to determine which algorithm is better is to try all of the candidates and see which gives the best results. When you compare algorithms like this, it is very important that the data you use be as similar to the real data as possible. As you shall see later in the book, particularly in Chapter 8 on sorting, many algorithms behave quite differently when they execute on different sets of data. If you test the algorithms on unrealistic data, you may be unpleasantly surprised when you run the program in the real world.

Paging

A particularly important real-world consideration for algorithms is *paging*. Windows is a paging environment. That means the Windows operating system has reserved a certain amount of disk space that it can use for *virtual memory*. When all of your *real* memory fills up, Windows will write the contents of some of the memory onto the disk. It writes the memory in chunks called *pages* so this process is called *paging*. Windows can then use the real memory that was copied to the disk for other things. When a program needs to access the items written to disk, the system copies them back into real memory, possibly paging other memory to disk to make room.

Since accessing a disk drive is much slower than accessing real memory, paging can slow the performance of any application tremendously. If a program jumps back and forth across huge amounts of memory, the system will have to page often. All that reading and writing to the disk will slow the application.

Example program PAGER allows you to allocate bigger and bigger arrays until the system begins paging. Enter the amount of memory you want the program to allocate in megabytes and press the Page button. If you enter a small value like one or two, the program will be able to allocate the array in real memory so the program will run quickly.

If you enter a value that is close to the amount of physical memory available on your computer, the program will start to page. You will probably hear your disk drive start working overtime when this happens. You will also notice that the program suddenly takes much longer to run. A 10 percent increase in array size may result in a 100 percent increase in run time.

Program PAGER can access its memory in one of two ways. If you fill in an amount of memory to allocate and then press the Page button, PAGER walks through the memory in an orderly fashion from the beginning of the array to the end. When the program visits part of the array, the system may have to page to load that part of the array into real memory. Once a page is in real memory, the program will continue to visit that part of the array until it is finished with the entries on that page. If the program later needs more memory, it may page that part of the array to the disk. Since the program continues moving forward through the array, items that were paged to the disk need never be brought back into memory again.

Marching through the array in an orderly fashion like this reduces paging. Any given item in the array may be paged at most twice: once to move it into memory and once to move it out of memory when the memory is needed by another part of the program.

If you fill in an amount of memory to allocate and press the Thrash button, PAGER will access the memory randomly. By jumping back and forth through the allocated memory, the program greatly increases the chances that the next item it needs has been paged to the disk and must be moved back into real memory. Accessing memory randomly this way causes excessive paging which is sometimes called *thrashing*.

Figure 1.1 shows a graph of times required by program PAGER to examine various amounts of memory on a 50 megahertz 486-based PC with 8Mb of real memory. Your run times will be different and will depend on the kind of computer you have, the amount of real memory you have, the speed of your disk drives, etc.

Notice that the time needed by the tests increases about as quickly as the memory allocated does until paging begins. Then there is a sudden increase in run time. Notice also that the paging and thrashing tests have very similar behavior until paging occurs. When all of the memory allocated fits in real memory, it takes the same amount of time to access items in an orderly or random fashion. Once paging begins, however, random access to the memory is much less efficient.

While paging in general is bad, it is sometimes better than the alternatives. If your program must sort a giant list of employee records, it will page. You might try to reduce paging by rewriting the program so it stores the list on disk and loads the items from disk as they are needed. This is probably a bad idea for a couple of reasons. First, your program's loading data from the disk will be no faster than the operating system's paging to and from the disk. It will probably be slower, particularly if you are using Visual Basic, since the operating system has special purpose routines that can read and write large chunks of memory quickly.

Second, this will unnecessarily complicate your program. The whole reason paging was invented was so your program did not have to worry about how much actual memory was available in your computer. If you avoid paging in this way, you must take all the responsibility for your memory management.

There are a few things you can do to help minimize the effects of paging. Most importantly avoid wasting memory. If you can keep your memory usage down to a rea-

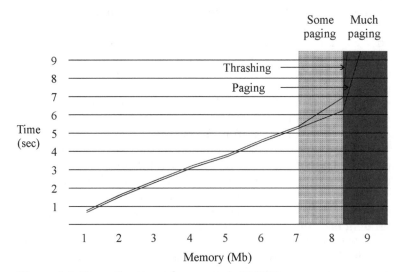

Figure 1.1 Execution times for program PAGER.

sonable level, you will never have to worry about paging. Keep in mind that other programs including Windows also use memory while your program is running, so you will not be able to use all of the physical memory on your computer. Even if you have only one or two other programs running, your program will probably page if it allocates all but one or two megabytes of your real memory. In other words, if you have 8Mb of real memory, your program will probably cause some paging if it allocates six or seven megabytes.

Sometimes you can write your program's code so it deals with memory in natural chunks before moving on to other parts of memory. When you press the PAGER program's Page button, the program accesses its array in an orderly fashion. When you press the Thrash button, the program jumps all over memory causing much more paging.

The mergesort algorithm described in Chapter 8 manipulates data in large chunks. Each of these chunks is sorted and then the chunks are merged together. The orderly way in which mergesort moves through memory minimizes paging.

The heapsort algorithm, also described in Chapter 8, jumps freely from one part of its list to another. This means that for very large lists, heapsort will cause thrashing and it will not perform as well as mergesort.

On the other hand, heapsort can arrange items in an array within that array while mergesort requires extra storage in which to merge sorted sublists. If the list is large enough, the extra storage itself may cause the program to page. This is an example of a space versus time tradeoff of the type mentioned earlier. Mergesort has good performance on huge lists but requires extra storage space. Heapsort requires no extra storage space but may cause thrashing for very large lists.

Dynamic Data Structures—Lists and Stacks

Overview

There are three main ways to allocate memory in Visual Basic: by declaring variables of the standard data types (integer, double, etc.), by declaring variables that are of user-defined data types, and by creating and redimensioning arrays. There are also a couple more unusual ways such as creating a new instance of a form or control, but these do not offer much help in creating complex data structures.

These methods alone are not flexible enough to build truly dynamic data structures—data structures that change over time. While you can easily resize an array using Visual Basic's **ReDim** statement, you cannot easily rearrange the data an array contains. To move an item from one end of an array to the other, for example, you would need to rearrange the entire array. You would need to shift every item in the array over one position to fill in the spot left by the item you moved. Then you would need to place the moved item in its new location.

Using dynamic data structures, this sort of operation is quick and easy. With only a couple of steps, you can remove an item from any position in the data structure and replace it at any other.

Languages like C and Pascal allow you to allocate arbitrary amounts of memory and keep explicit references to the addresses of that memory. Using these sorts of operations you can create flexible data structures that are useful in many sophisticated algorithms. While Visual Basic does not provide these same operations, it does provide tools you can use to build dynamic data structures.

This chapter describes fundamental methods for creating dynamic data structures in Visual Basic. These data structures are used by many algorithms throughout the rest of the book so be sure you understand how they work before you move on to later chapters.

The following section discusses lists. Different kinds of lists have different capabilities. Some are simple and provide only limited functionality. Others are more complex and support more advanced data management features. The end of this section provides a summary of basic list techniques to help you choose the best type of list to use in your programs (see pages 44–45). The sections after that examine some special list variations such as circular lists, doubly linked lists, and threaded lists.

The end of the chapter discusses *stacks*. Stacks are a special kind of list in which you add and remove items from the same end of the list. In other words you remove items from the list in last-in-first-out order. Many algorithms, including several presented in later chapters, use stacks.

Lists

In its simplest form a list is a collection of objects. It holds the objects and allows your program to examine them.

If that is all you need a list to do, you can use a simple array to store the list. You can use a variable NumInList to keep track of the number of items in the list. Whenever your program needs to examine the items in the list, it can use NumInList to determine how many items are present. It can then visit the items using a **For** loop and perform whatever actions are necessary.

If you have a program that can use this simple list storage strategy, by all means use it. This method is effective and, due to its simplicity, is easy to debug and maintain. Most programs are not this straightforward, however, and require more complicated versions of even simple objects like lists. The sections that follow discuss some of the ways in which you can build more powerful lists.

The first section describes ways to make lists that can grow and shrink over time. In some programs you may not be able to determine beforehand how large a list might need to be. You can handle this situation with a list that can resize itself as needed.

The next section discusses *unordered lists*, which allow you to remove items from any part of the list. Unordered lists give you more control over the list contents than simple lists do. They are also more dynamic since they allow the contents of the list to change freely over time.

The following sections discuss *linked lists*, which use *pointers* to create an extremely flexible data structure that allows you to add or remove items from any part of the list with very little effort. These sections also describe some linked list variations including circular linked lists, doubly linked lists, and threaded linked lists.

The final section on lists provides a summary of basic list techniques to help you choose the best type of list to use in your programs (see pages 44–45).

Simple Lists

If your program needs a list that never changes, you can build it easily using an array. It is then a simple matter to examine the items when necessary using a **For** loop.

In many programs, however, the list will grow and shrink over time. You could allocate an array big enough to handle the list at its largest, but that may not always work well. You may not know ahead of time how large the list will grow. There may also be only a small chance that the list will become huge. In that case allocating a huge array would probably be a waste of memory.

Fortunately in Visual Basic you can easily resize an array using the **ReDim** statement.

To build a simple list, declare an undimensioned array to hold the list items. Also declare a variable NumInList to keep track of the number of items in the list. Then whenever you need to add an item to the list, you can use the **ReDim** statement to make the list large enough to hold the new item. Similarly when you remove an item from the list, you can use the **ReDim** statement to shrink the array and free the memory that you no longer need.

```
Dim List () As String          ' The list of items.
Dim NumInList As Integer       ' The number of items in the list.


' Resize to make room for the new entry.
' Then add the new item to the end of the list.
Sub AddToList (value As String)
    NumInList = NumInList + 1
    ReDim Preserve List (1 To NumInList)
    List (NumInList) = value
End Sub


' Remove the last item from the list.
' Resize the array to free unused memory.
Sub RemoveFromList ()
    NumInList = NumInList - 1
    ReDim Preserve List (1 To NumInList)
End Sub
```

This simple scheme works well for small lists, but it has a couple of drawbacks. First, the array must be resized frequently. To create a list of 1,000 items, you would need to resize the array 1,000 times. Even worse, as the list gets larger, each resize operation may take longer and longer.

To reduce the number of times the array must be resized, you can add extra empty entries to the array whenever you resize it. When you enlarge the array, you can add ten entries instead of one. Then when you add new items in the future, the array will contain unused entries where you can place the new items without resizing the array. You would only need to resize the array again when it ran out of unused entries.

In a similar fashion, you can avoid resizing the array every time you remove an item from the list. You can wait until there are at least 20 unused items in the array before resizing. When you do resize the array, be sure to leave ten empty entries so you can add more items to the array without being forced to resize again.

Note that the maximum number of unused items, in this case 20, should be larger than the minimum number, in this case 10. If the two are the same, you will be forced to resize the array every time you remove an item from the list. Suppose you set both the maximum and minimum numbers of unused array entries to ten. Suppose also that you have just resized the array so it contains ten unused entries. If you remove an item from the array, the array will contain 11 unused entries which is more than the maximum number allowed, so you will need to shrink the array. When you do, you will leave ten unused entries to allow for later insertions. If you remove another item, the array will again contain 11 unused entries so you will need to shrink the array again. Every time you remove an item from the list you will need to resize the array.

With this scheme the list will usually hold some unused items, but it will not hold too many so it will not waste too much memory. The unused items give you insurance against resizing the array when you later add and remove items from the list. In fact, if you repeatedly add and remove items from the list, you might never need to resize the array. As long as the number of unused entries stays within the allowed maximum and minimum, you will not need to resize the array.

```
Dim List () As String        ' The list of items.
Dim ArraySize As Integer     ' The size of the array.
Dim NumInList As Integer     ' The number of items in use.


' If the array is full, resize the array and give it 10 unused
' entries. Then add the new item to the end of the list.
Sub AddToList (value As String)
    NumInList = NumInList + 1
    If NumInList > ArraySize Then
        ArraySize = ArraySize + 10
        ReDim Preserve List(1 To ArraySize)
    End If
    List (NumInList) = value
End Sub


' Remove the last item from the list. If there are more than
' 20 unused items in the list, resize the list to free unused
' memory.
Sub RemoveFromList ()
    NumInList = NumInList - 1
    If ArraySize - NumInList > 20 Then
        ArraySize = ArraySize - 10
        ReDim Preserve List(1 To ArraySize)
    End If
End Sub
```

For very large arrays this may still not be a good solution. If you needed a list holding 1,000 items and you typically added 100 items at a time, you would still spend a relatively large amount of time resizing the array. An obvious strategy for handling this situation is to increase the extra resize amount from 10 items to 100 or some even larger value. Then you could add items 100 at a time without causing frequent resizing.

A more flexible solution is to make the amount of extra space allocated depend on the current size of the list. When the list is small, the extra space added is small. The array would be resized more often, but it does not take too long to resize a small array. When the list is large, the amount of extra space added is larger so the array would be resized less often.

The code shown below tries to keep about 10 percent of the list array empty. When the array fills completely, the program enlarges it by 10 percent. If the amount of empty space in the array grows beyond about 20 percent of the array's size, the program resizes the array to make it smaller.

Whenever the program resizes the array, it always adds at least ten items even if 10 percent of the array size is smaller than this. This reduces the number of resizes necessary when the list is very small.

```
Const WANT_FREE_PERCENT = .1          ' Try for 10% free space.
Const MIN_FREE = 10                   ' Min free space when resizing.


Global List () As String              ' The list array.
Global ArraySize As Integer           ' Size of the list array.
Global NumItems As Integer            ' The number of items in the list.
Global ShrinkWhen As Integer          ' Shrink if NumItems < ShrinkWhen.


' If the array is full, resize it. Then add a new item to the
' end of the list.
Sub AddToList (value As String)
    NumItems = NumItems + 1
    If NumItems > ArraySize Then ResizeList
    List(NumItems) = value
End Sub


' Remove the last item from the list. Then if the array contains
' too many unused entries, resize it.
Sub RemoveFromList ()
    NumItems = NumItems - 1
    If NumItems < ShrinkWhen Then ResizeList
End Sub


' Resize the list to give it 10% empty entries.
Sub ResizeList ()
Dim want_free As Integer


    want_free = WANT_FREE_PERCENT * NumItems
    If want_free < MIN_FREE Then want_free = MIN_FREE
    ArraySize = NumItems + want_free
    ReDim Preserve List(1 To ArraySize)


    ' We will shrink the array if NumItems < ShrinkWhen.
    ShrinkWhen = NumItems - want_free
End Sub
```

Example program SIM_LIST shows this list management technique in action. If you enter an integer value in the text box and press the Add button, the program will add the item to its list, resizing the array if necessary. Whenever the list is not empty, you can press the Remove button to remove the last item from the list.

When the program resizes the list, it displays a message box telling you how large the array is, how many items in the array are unused, and the value ShrinkWhen. When the number of items in use in the array falls below the value ShrinkWhen, the program resizes the array to make it smaller. Notice that, when the array is almost empty, ShrinkWhen may become zero or negative. In that case the array will not be resized even if you remove all of the items from the list.

Program SIM_LIST adds 50 percent of the current array size as empty entries when it must resize the array, and it always keeps a minimum of one empty entry when it resizes. These values were chosen so you could easily make the program resize the array. In a real application the percentage of free memory should be smaller and the minimum number of free entries should be larger. Values more like 10 percent of the current list size and a minimum of ten unused entries would make more sense.

Unordered Lists

In some applications you may need to remove items from the middle of the list, though you can still add new items at the end of the list. This will be the case when the order of the items is not particularly important, but you may need to remove specific items from the list. This kind of list is called an *unordered list*. It is also sometimes called a *bag* or *sack*.

An unordered list should support these operations:

- Add an item to the list.
- Remove a specific item from the list.
- Determine whether a specific item is in the list.
- Perform some operation (print, display, etc.) on all of the items in the list.

You can easily modify the simple scheme presented in the previous section to handle this kind of list. When you remove an item from the middle of the list, you shift the remaining items one position to fill in the hole left behind. Figure 2.1 shows this operation graphically. Here the second item is removed from the list and the third, fourth, and fifth items are shifted to the left to fill in the hole.

Removing an item from an array in this way can take quite a bit of time, especially if the item removed is near the beginning of the list. To remove the first item in an array containing 1,000 entries you would need to move 999 of the entries one position to the left. A simple *garbage collection* scheme will allow you to remove items much more quickly.

To remove an item from the list, you do not actually delete the list entry. Instead you mark that entry as not in use. If the items in the list are simple data types like integers, you might be able to use a specific *garbage value* to mark the item. For integers you might use the value –32,767. You would assign this value to any item that was not in use. The code fragment below shows how to remove an item from this kind of list.

```
Const GARBAGE_VALUE = -32767


' Mark the item as garbage.
Sub RemoveFromList (position As Integer)
    List(position) = GARBAGE_VALUE
End Sub
```

If the items in the list are structures defined by a **Type** statement, you can add a new IsGarbage field to the structure. When you remove an item from the list, set the value of the item's IsGarbage field to true.

```
Type MyData
    Name As String         ' Data.
    IsGarbage As Integer   ' Is this entry garbage?
End Type
```

Figure 2.1 Removing an item from the middle of a simple list.

```
' Mark the item as garbage.
Sub RemoveFromList(position As Integer)
    List(position).IsGarbage = True
End Sub
```

To keep things simple, the rest of this section assumes that the data items are integers and that you can mark them with a special garbage value.

Once the list contains entries marked as garbage, you must modify other routines that use the list so they can skip the garbage values. For example, you might change a subroutine that prints the list like this:

```
' Print the items in the list.
Sub PrintItems ()
Dim I As Integer
    For I = 1 To ArraySize
        If List (I) <> GARBAGE_VALUE Then   ' If it's not garbage
            Print Str$(List(I))             '     print it.
        End If
    Next I
End Sub
```

After you use a garbage marking scheme like this for a while, the list may become full of garbage. Eventually subroutines like the one shown above will spend more time skipping garbage entries than in examining actual data.

To solve this problem you can periodically run a *garbage collection routine*. This routine moves all of the non-garbage entries to the beginning of the array. You can then add the remaining entries to the unused items at the end of the array. When you need to add more items to the list, you can reuse these entries to avoid resizing the array.

Adding the reclaimed garbage entries to the other unused entries at the end of the array may make the group of unused entries quite large. In that case you may want to resize the array to free some of the unused space.

```
' Move non-garbage items to the front of the array. Add garbage
' items to the unused entries at the end of the array. If this
' gives too many unused entries, resize the array.
Sub CollectGarbage ()
Dim I As Integer        ' Index of the item we are looking at.
Dim Good As Integer     ' Where to put the next non-garbage item.

    Good = 1             ' The first good item goes here.
    For I = 1 To LastItem
        ' If the item is not garbage, move it to its new location.
        If List(I) <> GARBAGE_VALUE Then
            List(Good) = List(I)
            Good = Good + 1
        End If
    Next I

    LastItem = Good - 1 ' This is where we put the last good item.

    ' See if we should resize the list.
    If LastItem < ShrinkWhen Then ResizeList
End Sub
```

When you perform garbage collection, you move items near the end of the list towards the beginning of the list to fill in the space occupied by garbage entries. That means the positions of the items in the list may change during garbage collection. That in turn means that other parts of the program cannot rely on the items in the list staying in their original positions. If other parts of the program must access items by their positions in the list, you will need to modify the garbage collection routine so it can update those other parts of the program. Generally this sort of thing can be confusing and can lead to big maintenance problems later.

There are several ways in which you can decide when to run the garbage collector. One way is to wait until the array reaches a certain size and there is no extra space left. In Visual Basic 3.0 an array's indexes must be integers, so an array with lower bound 1 can only expand to hold 32,767 items. When a list reaches this size, you would have to use garbage collection because you could not expand the array any further.

This method has a couple of drawbacks. First, it uses a lot of memory. If you add and remove items frequently, you will fill a lot of array entries with garbage. If you waste enough memory like this, the program might spend time paging when the list could fit completely in real memory if you rearranged it a bit.

Second, if the list starts to fill with garbage, routines that use the list will become extremely inefficient. If an array of 30,000 items contains 25,000 pieces of garbage, a subroutine like PrintItems described earlier would be terribly slow.

Finally, garbage collection for a very large array can take quite a bit of time, especially if scanning the array causes your program to page. It can be quite irritating if your program decides to perform garbage collection at the wrong time. In one story from the Artificial Intelligence Laboratory at MIT, a robot was supposed to visually track a ball through the air and catch it. The program tracked the ball, calculated the ball's flight path, and then paused for garbage collection. When garbage collection was complete, the robot reached for the ball, but by that time the ball had already hit the ground.

To help solve this problem, you can create a new variable GarbageCount to keep track of the number of garbage items in the list. When a substantial fraction of the list's memory contains garbage, you can start garbage collection.

```
Dim GarbageCount As Integer    ' Number of garbage items.
Dim MaxGarbage As Integer      ' This is set in ResizeList

' Mark the item as garbage. If there is too much garbage in
' the list, start garbage collection.
Sub RemoveFromList (position As Integer)
    List(position) = GARBAGE_VALUE
    GarbageCount = GarbageCount + 1

    ' If there's too much garbage, collect the garbage.
    If GarbageCount > MaxGarbage Then CollectGarbage
End Sub
```

Now you are ready to implement the final version of the garbage collection scheme. The complete source code for managing an unordered list is shown below.

```
Option Explicit

Const WANT_FREE_PERCENT = .10    ' Try for 10% free space.
Const MIN_FREE = 10              ' Min free space when resizing.
```

```
' This data structure holds the actual data and the
' IsGarbage field.
Type ListStruct
    Data As Variant            ' Actual data.
    IsGarbage As Integer       ' Is this item garbage?
End Type


Global List() As ListStruct    ' The list array.
Global NumItems As Integer     ' # of items (including garbage).
Global ArraySize As Integer    ' Size of the list array.
Global ShrinkWhen As Integer   ' Shrink if NumItems < ShrinkWhen.
Global GarbageCount As Integer ' # garbage entries.
Global MaxGarbage As Integer   ' Collect garbage when
                               ' GarbageCount > MaxGarbage


' Add an item to the end of the list. If the list array
' is full, resize it.


Sub AddToList (value As Variant)
    ' If the array is full, resize it.
    If NumItems >= ArraySize Then ResizeList

    NumItems = NumItems + 1
    List(NumItems).Data = value      ' Set the data value.
    List (NumItems).IsGarbage = False' This is not garbage.
End Sub



' Remove an item from the list. If this gives us more
' than MaxGarbage garbage items (this is set in
' ResizeList), call the garbage collector.
Sub RemoveFromList (position As Integer)
    List(position).IsGarbage = True
    GarbageCount = GarbageCount + 1


    ' If there's too much garbage, collect the garbage.
    If GarbageCount > MaxGarbage Then CollectGarbage
End Sub

' Move all the non-garbage entries to the front of the
' array. Then resize the array if there are too many
' unused entries.
Sub CollectGarbage ()
Dim i As Integer
Dim good As Integer
    ' Compress the good items.
    good = 1     ' This is where the first good item goes.
    For i = 1 To NumItems
        Not garbage. Compress this item.
        If Not List(i).IsGarbage Then
            List(good) = List(i)
            good = good + 1 ' This is where the next one goes.
        End If
    Next i
    NumItems = good - 1    ' Points to the last good item.
    GarbageCount = 0       ' There's no garbage in the list.
```

```
        ' Resize the array if there are too many unused entries.
        If NumItems < ShrinkWhen Then ResizeList
End Sub


' Resize the array.
Sub ResizeList ()
Dim want_free As Integer

        ' Resize the array.
        want_free = WANT_FREE_PERCENT * NumItems
        If want_free < MIN_FREE Then want_free = MIN_FREE
        ArraySize = NumItems + want_free
        ReDim Preserve List(1 To ArraySize)


        ' Perform garbage collection the next time there are
        ' more than MaxGarbage garbage items in the list.
        MaxGarbage = want_free


        ' After garbage collection, resize the list if there
        ' are more than ShrinkWhen unused items.
        ShrinkWhen = NumItems - GarbageCount - want_free
End Sub
```

Example program GARBAGE demonstrates this code. If you enter an integer and press the Add button, the program will add the new item to the end of the list. When the program displays the list, it labels garbage entries "<garbage>" and unused entries "<unused>."

If you click on an item that is in use, the program will highlight the item and enable the Remove button. If you press this button, the program will remove the item from the list and mark it as garbage.

If you fill up the list array, the program will automatically resize the list. When it does this the program will present a message box that tells you the values of the variables MaxGarbage and ShrinkWhen. If you remove enough items so more than MaxGarbage items in the list contain garbage, the program will run the garbage collector. Once the garbage collector is finished, the program will see if there are fewer than ShrinkWhen items remaining in the compacted list. If so, the program resizes the array to make it smaller and free some of the unused memory.

Notice that the garbage collector rearranges the items in the list array. This is why other parts of the program must not rely on items always remaining in the same array position.

Program GARBAGE adds 25 percent of the current list size as empty entries when it must resize the array, and it always keeps a minimum of two empty entries when it resizes. These values were chosen so you can easily make the program resize the array. In a real program the percentage of free memory should probably be smaller and the minimum number of free entries should be larger. Values more like 10 percent free and a minimum of ten entries would make more sense.

Linked Lists and Pointer Faking

Some languages, like Pascal and C, allow you to declare variables that are *pointers* to memory locations. These locations can hold other pieces of data like integers, strings, arrays of doubles, or user-defined data structures. One particularly useful way to use a pointer is to have it point to a data structure that contains another pointer. That pointer points to another data structure containing a pointer and so on.

By using data structures that contain pointers, you can create all sorts of exotic arrangements such as graphs, networks, trees, and forests of trees. Later chapters will examine some of these more complex structures. This section examines the simplest of these objects: *linked lists.*

Visual Basic does not have pointer data types. All you really need a pointer to do, however, is point to another piece of data. If you allocate a bunch of data structures in an array, you can use integers as pointers to the entries in the array. The data to which a pointer points is the array entry with the corresponding index. Throughout the rest of this book, the term "pointer" will mean an integer used as an index into an array.

There are three things you need to do to build a linked list. First, you must declare a user-defined structure to contain the data. This structure is called a *cell* in the linked list. The cell structure should contain an integer field that will be the pointer (index in the array) to the next cell in the linked list. To keep things consistent, this field is usually named "Next." The cell should also contain other fields that hold whatever data the program needs to manipulate. In a list of employee records, for example, these other fields might be employee names, Social Security numbers, job titles, etc.

```
Type EmpCell
    EmpName As String
    Next As Integer
End Type
```

Next you need to create an array of these cells. The Next fields in the cells will be indexes into this array.

```
Dim TheCells(1 To 100) As EmpCell
```

Finally you can build the linked list using the cells in the array. For example, to make cell number 3 come after cell number 1 in the linked list, you would set the Next pointer for cell number 1 to the value 3.

```
TheCells(1).Next = 3
```

Figure 2.2 shows a picture of a cell array that makes up a small linked list. The figure uses arrows to show the cell to which each Next field points. The integer variable Top holds the index of the first cell in the linked list. In this case the list begins with cell number 1, though a linked list does not need to begin with cell number 1.

Cell number 1 has a Next value of 3. That means the next cell in the linked list after cell number 1 is cell 3. Similarly, the Next field for cell number 3 has value 2 so the next cell in the list after cell 3 is cell number 2. If you continue to follow the Next pointers through the array, you will find that the complete list includes the cells in this order: 1, 3, 2, 4, 5. The Next pointer for cell 5 holds the special value –32,767. This value tells you that you have reached the end of the list. To make your code a little clearer, you can define a constant END_OF_LIST to have this value.

The code shown below follows the linked list in Figure 2.2 to print out the names of the employees in the list. The integer variable ptr is used as a pointer to the items in the list. This pointer is initialized to the value Top so it points to the beginning of the list.

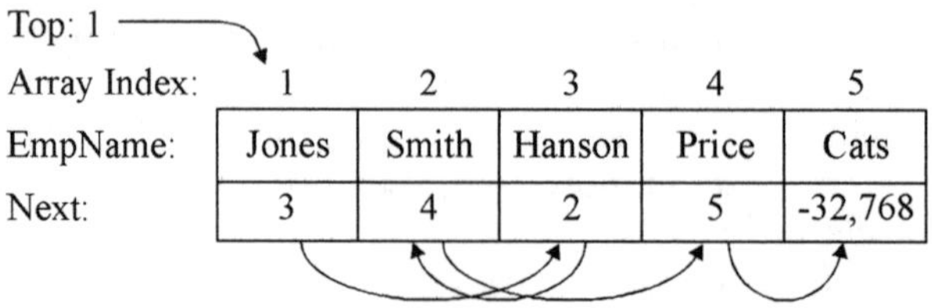

Figure 2.2 Array representation of a linked list.

The code then uses a **Do** loop to move ptr through the list. During each loop the routine prints the EmpName field for the cell pointed to by ptr. It then advances ptr so it points to the next cell in the linked list. It does this by setting ptr equal to the value of the Next field in the cell to which it currently points.

Eventually ptr reaches array entry 5. After printing the EmpName field for cell 5, the code sets ptr to the value of the Next field in cell 5. That value is −32,767, the value that indicates the end of the list, so the **Do** loop terminates.

```
' Data structure to hold cell data.
Type EmpCell
     EmpName As String        ' Data used by the program.
     Next As Integer          ' Next pointer.
End Type

' Array of cells used to build the list.
Dim TheCells(1 To 10) As EmpCell

Const END_OF_LIST = -32767    ' Pointer to indicate end of list.

Dim Top As Integer            ' Holds the top of the list.

' Print all the EmpName fields for the cells in the list.
Sub PrintNames ()
Dim ptr As Integer
     ptr = Top                     ' Start at the top of the list.
     Do While ptr <> END_OF_LIST
        ' Display this cell's EmpName field.
        Print TheCells(ptr).EmpName

        ' Advance to the next cell in the list.
        ptr = TheCells(ptr).Next
     Loop
End Sub
```

If you execute this code for the list shown in Figure 2.2, you will see a result like this:

```
Jones
Hanson
Smith
Price
Cats
```

When you work with a linked list, you generally do not care where in the cell array the list items are stored. Only the order of the items in the linked list matters. The same

Top: 3

Array Index:	1	2	3	4	5
EmpName:	Price	Cats	Jones	Hanson	Smith
Next:	2	-32,768	4	5	1

Top: 5

Array Index:	1	2	3	4	5
EmpName:	Cats	Price	Smith	Hanson	Jones
Next:	-32,768	1	2	3	4

Figure 2.3 Different arrangements of a linked list.

linked list can be stored in many different ways within an array. The arrays shown in Figure 2.3, for example, represent the same list as the one shown in Figure 2.2: Jones, Hanson, Smith, Price, Cats.

To make the structure of a linked list clearer, the following sections will draw linked lists with the cells arranged in the order that is natural for the list rather than for the array in which the list is stored. Figure 2.4 shows this sort of picture for the list shown in Figure 2.2. The little box with an "X" in it represents the special END_OF_LIST value.

Using a pointer to point to another object is called *indirection* because you use the pointer to manipulate data indirectly. Indirection can get very confusing. Even for a simple arrangement like a linked list, it is sometimes hard to remember which index points to which object. In more complicated data structures, the pointers may point to other pointers. With a couple of different pointers and several levels of indirection floating around, it is sometimes easy to get lost.

To make things a little easier, we will use pictures like the one in Figure 2.4 to help visualize the situation whenever possible. Many algorithms that use pointers are easy to describe using pictures like this.

Adding Items to a Linked List

There are several interesting things to note about the simple linked list shown in Figure 2.4. First, it is very easy to add a new cell to the beginning of the list. Start by allocating a new entry from the cell array to hold the new data. Then make the new cell's Next field point to the current value of Top. Finally set Top to point to the new cell. Figure 2.5 shows the picture corresponding to this operation.

The Visual Basic code for this operation is quite simple.

```
Sub AddToTop (new_cell As Integer)
    TheCells(new_cell).Next = Top
    Top = new_cell
End Sub
```

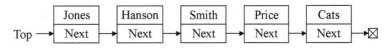

Figure 2.4 A linked list.

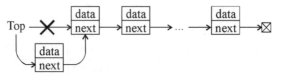

Figure 2.5 Adding an item to a linked list.

Compare this to the code which you would have needed to add a new item to the beginning of the array-based lists examined in the previous sections. In those lists you would have had to move every entry in the array one space to the right to make room for the new item. That is an O(N) operation that could take a long time if the list was large. Using a linked list you can insert a new item at the top of the list in just two steps!

It is also easy to insert a new item in the middle of a linked list. Suppose you want to insert a new item with array index K after the linked list item with array index I. Suppose also that TheCells(I).Next = J. Then to insert the new item, you first set the Next field of the new cell K so it points to the cell that will follow it in the list. That will be cell J so you set TheCells(K)=J. Next you should set the Next field in cell I so it points to the new cell: TheCells(I)=K. Figure 2.6 shows this operation graphically.

The Visual Basic code for this operation is straightforward.

```
Sub AddAfter (new_cell As Integer, after_me As Integer)
    TheCells(new_cell).Next = TheCells(after_me).Next
    TheCells(after_me).Next = new_cell
End Sub
```

Removing Items from a Linked List

It is just as easy to remove an item from the top of a linked list as it is to add one. Simply set the variable Top to point to the next cell in the list. Figure 2.7 shows the picture corresponding to this operation.

The Visual Basic source code for this operation is even simpler than the code for inserting an item.

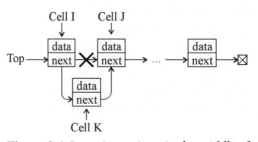

Figure 2.6 Inserting an item in the middle of a linked list.

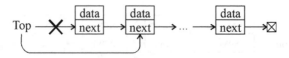

Figure 2.7 Removing an item from the top of a linked list.

```
Sub RemoveTop ()
    Top = TheCells(Top).Next
End Sub
```

Removing an item from the middle of the list is also easy. Suppose you wanted to remove the cell after cell number I. All you would need to do is set the Next field in cell I so it skips the cell you are removing. Figure 2.8 shows this operation graphically.

As is the case for other linked list operations, the Visual Basic code for removing an item is straightforward.

```
Sub RemoveAfter (after_me As Integer)
Dim remove_me As Integer

    remove_me = TheCells(after_me).Next
    TheCells(after_me).Next = TheCells(remove_me).Next
End Sub
```

You could write this operation in the single step "TheCells(I).Next = TheCells (TheCells(I).Next).Next," but that would be a bit confusing.

Again you should compare this to the code needed to perform the same operation using an array-based list. While you can quickly mark a removed item as garbage in an array-based list, this leaves garbage entries in the list. Routines that manipulate the list would need to skip over those entries. This makes the routines more complicated and it can slow them down. After you remove enough items from the list, these routines might spend more time skipping unused entries than in dealing with useful entries. Eventually you will need to run a garbage collector.

When you remove an item from a linked list, you create no gaps in the list. Routines that manipulate the list still start from the pointer Top and follow the list to its end so you do not need to modify those routines.

Sentinels

Notice that the routines for adding and removing items are different depending on whether you want to add or remove the item from the top or middle of the list. You can make both of these cases behave in the same way, and eliminate some redundant code, if you introduce a special *sentinel* item at the very top of the list. This item should never be removed and does not contain any meaningful data. It is used only to mark the top of the list.

Now instead of having to deal with the odd case of adding an entry at the very top of the list, you can add the new item after the sentinel. Similarly, you do not need to

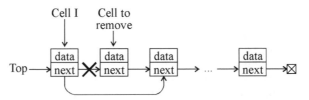
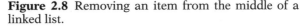

Figure 2.8 Removing an item from the middle of a linked list.

worry about the special case of removing the first item on the list—you simply remove the item after the sentinel.

For convenience you can always place the sentinel in the first position in the array. Then instead of using the AddToTop subroutine to add a new item at the top of the list, you can use the AddAfter subroutine with the parameter 1 to indicate that the new item should be added after the sentinel.

Using a sentinel makes a small difference now, but it will become much more important a little later. Sentinels play important roles in many algorithms. They generally allow your code to treat special cases, like dealing with the top of a linked list, as if they were nothing special. This means you can write and debug less code, and it makes algorithms more consistent and easier to understand.

So how does a linked list compare to the array-based lists with garbage collection presented in the previous sections? Table 2.1 compares the difficulty of performing some common operations using array-based lists with garbage collection and linked lists.

Linked lists are better overall but there is still one area where the array-based list is better: memory usage. You saw earlier that if the lists store integers or other numeric data types, and the data itself can be marked to indicate garbage items, then you can implement an array-based list with garbage collection without adding additional fields. The linked list implementation requires you to add an additional Next field to every data item. For large arrays this may take up a lot of space.

If the data items are not numeric, you must add an additional IsGarbage field to the array-based list. In this case the two systems are pretty equal in terms of memory use.

Garbage Lists

In an array-based list you can keep unused entries at the end of the array. When you need a new entry, you take it from this group of unused entries. When you are done with an entry, you mark it as garbage. You can no longer use that entry until you run a garbage collection routine that gathers the garbage entries together at the end of the array.

You can gain better control over unused list entries using linked lists. You also do not need to lose entries by marking them as garbage. To do this, create another linked list within the cell array. This list holds all of the cells in the array that are not in use. When you need to allocate a new cell, you can remove it from this garbage list. When you are finished with a cell, you can add it to the top of the garbage list so you can use it again later.

To make this a little easier, you can write a function NewCell to allocate a new cell from the garbage list. This function also checks to see if the garbage list is empty. If it is,

Table 2.1 Comparison of Array-Based Lists and Linked Lists

Operation	*Array-Based*	*Linked List*
Add item at end	Easy	Easy
Add item at top	Hard	Easy
Add item in middle	Hard	Easy
Remove item from top	Easy	Easy
Remove item in middle	Easy	Easy
List non-garbage items	Medium	Easy

it uses the **ReDim** statement to enlarge the cell array. It then places the new array entries in the garbage list so they will be easy to find later.

You can also write a subroutine FreeCell that puts a cell in the garbage list when you are done using it.

In order for these routines to work, you also need a routine that initializes the linked list and the garbage list. This routine creates the list's sentinel and sets the next cell after the sentinel to END_OF_LIST. It also sets the top of the garbage list TopGarbage to END_OF_LIST indicating that no unused cells are initially available.

```
Const END_OF_LIST = -32767


Type Cell
    Name As String
    Next As Integer
End Type

Dim TheCells() As Cell          ' The cell array.
Dim ArraySize As Integer        ' Number of cells in the array.
Dim Top As Integer              ' The top of the list of data.
Dim TopGarbage As Integer       ' The top of the garbage list.

' Create the list sentinel.
' Initialize the list and garbage list so they are empty.
Sub InitializeList ()
    ' Create the sentinel.
    ArraySize = 1
    ReDim TheCells(1 To ArraySize)

    ' Initialize lists so they are empty.
    TheCells(1).Next = END_OF_LIST  ' Nothing after the sentinel.
    TopGarbage = END_OF_LIST         ' No unused cells yet.
End Sub

' Allocate an unused cell from the garbage list.
Function NewCell ()
Dim i As Integer

    ' If the garbage list is empty, resize the array.
    If TopGarbage = END_OF_LIST Then
        ' Make the array bigger.
        new_size = ArraySize + 10
        ReDim Preserve TheCells(1 To new_size)

        ' Add the new items to the garbage list.
        TopGarbage = ArraySize + 1
        For i = TopGarbage To new_size - 1
            TheCells(i).Next = i + 1
        Next i
        TheCells(new_size).Next = END_OF_LIST

        ArraySize = new_size
    End If
    ' Allocate the first cell in the garbage list.
    NewCell = TopGarbage
    TopGarbage = TheCells(TopGarbage).Next
End Function
```

```
' Place the cell in the garbage list.
Sub FreeCell (free_me As Integer)
    TheCells(free_me).Next = TopGarbage
    TopGarbage = free_me
End Sub
```

Garbage Collection in Linked Lists

As the code above shows, it is easy to enlarge the cell array to make new unused cells when the garbage list becomes empty. When the garbage list becomes large, however, there is no easy way to shrink the cell array to reclaim the unused space. If you simply move all the cells that are in use to the beginning of the array as you can with array-based lists, the cells' Next fields will no longer point to the correct locations in the array.

One alternative is to create a temporary array, copy the items from the linked list in order into the temporary array, resize the original cell array, and then copy the items back. This sort of scheme would work like this:

```
Sub CollectGarbage ()
Dim cell As Integer
Dim new_spot As Integer
ReDim temp(1 To ArraySize) As Cell
    ' Copy the cells into the temporary array.
    new_spot = 1
    cell = 1
    Do While cell <> END_OF_LIST
        temp(new_spot) = TheCells(cell)
        cell = TheCells(cell).Next
        new_spot = new_spot + 1
    Loop

    ' Resize the list as desired.
    ArraySize = <however many cells you want in the array>
    ReDim TheCells(1 To ArraySize)

    ' Copy the cells back into the old array.
    For cell = 1 To new_spot
        TheCells(cell) = NewCells(cell)
        TheCells(cell).Next = cell + 1
    Next cell
    TheCells(new_spot).Next = END_OF_LIST

    ' Rebuild the garbage list.
    TopGarbage = new_spot + 1
    For cell = TopGarbage To ArraySize - 1
        TheCells(cell).Next = Next + 1
    Next cell
    TheCells(ArraySize).Next = END_OF_LIST
End Sub
```

While this method is easy to understand, it requires you to allocate space for a temporary array. It also requires copying the data twice: once into the temporary array and once back into the resized array. A more clever method allows you to compact the array without allocating extra memory and without moving all of the data.

First, count the cells that are in use. If you keep track of this when you add and remove items, you will already know this number so you can skip this step. Suppose your linked list contains num_used items.

If there are num_used cells in the linked list, then the rearranged list could fit within the first num_used entries in the cell array. Figure 2.9 shows a linked list with one cell that falls outside the first num_used entries in the cell array. This list contains four items so the list could fit within the first four array entries. In this case, however, the last item in the list is in array position 5 which falls outside this range. Keep in mind that the list may jump in and out of the first num_used entries several times.

Notice that for every list item that lies outside the first num_used array entries, there is one garbage list item that lies within the first num_used entries. To rearrange the linked list, you will replace each list item that is outside this range with a garbage list item that is inside the range.

Start at the sentinel. Since the sentinel is always in the first position in the array, the sentinel will always fall within the first num_used entries and you do not need to worry about moving it.

Now look through the linked list until you find an item that has index outside the first num_used entries. Once you have found such an item, look through the garbage list until you find an unused cell that has index within the first num_used entries. For every item in the list that falls outside the range, there is an item in the garbage list that falls within the range, so you know you will eventually find one.

Next replace the list item with the garbage item. Be careful to update the Next pointers in the list so the new cell is positioned correctly within the list. You must make sure the previous item's Next pointer indicates the moved item's new location and that the moved item's Next pointer indicates the next cell in the list.

When you have finished moving all of the list items, you can safely resize the array to make it smaller. Then rebuild the garbage list so it contains whatever unused entries remain at the end of the list.

The Visual Basic source code for this linked list garbage collection scheme is shown below. This version assumes that you have been keeping track of the number of garbage entries in the array. The routine uses this number to compute num_used. This number can also help you decide when you should perform garbage collection. When this number gets too large, you can run the garbage collector.

```
' Move the items in the list to the beginning of the cell array.
' Then call ResizeList to resize the list.
Sub CollectGarbage ()
Dim cell As Integer
Dim nxt As Integer
Dim new_cell As Integer
Dim num_used As Integer
```

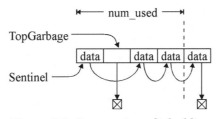

Figure 2.9 Compacting a linked list.

```
    num_used = ArraySize - GarbageCount

    ' Compact the cells that are in use.
    cell = 1                        ' The sentinel.
    nxt = TheCells(cell).Next       ' The cell after "cell."
    Do While nxt <> END_OF_LIST
        If nxt > num_used Then       ' This cell needs to move.
            ' Find an unused cell from the garbage list that
            ' is in the first part of the array.
            Do While TopGarbage > num_used
                TopGarbage = TheCells(TopGarbage).Next
            Loop
            new_cell = TopGarbage
            TopGarbage = TheCells(TopGarbage).Next

            ' Copy the cell's data and Next pointer.
            TheCells(new_cell) = TheCells(nxt)

            ' Update the previous cell's Next pointer.
            TheCells(cell).Next = new_cell

            ' Get ready to move to the next cell in the list.
            nxt = new_cell
        End If ' End moving the cell.

        ' Go on to consider the next cell in the list.
        cell = nxt
        nxt = TheCells(cell).Next
    Loop

    ' Resize the array.
    ResizeList num_used
End Sub
```

This method does not need to allocate a temporary array and is much faster than the previous method. Not only does it not need to copy each item in the list twice, but it does not need to copy many items even once. If an item already lies in the first part of the array, the routine will not need to move it. If the garbage list contains only 20 percent of the array, for example, no more than 20 percent of the items in the list can lie outside the first num_used entries. That means the routine will need to move at most 20 percent of the array entries and probably fewer since parts of the garbage list will probably lie outside the first num_used entries.

Example program LINKED implements a linked list with garbage collection. The program displays the entire cell array and uses arrows to show how the Next pointers connect the cells to form the list and the garbage list.

Click on an item to select it. Then fill in a value and press the Add After button to add a new item after the one you selected.

Click on an item and press the Remove After button to remove the item after the one you selected. You cannot remove an item after the last item in the list, nor can you remove an item from the garbage list.

As with previous example programs, LINKED presents a message box whenever it resizes the cell array. This message tells you the number of items in the cell array, the number of items in the garbage list, and the value of MaxFree. When the garbage list contains more than MaxFree items, the program will run the garbage collector to make the cell array smaller.

Coexisting Linked Lists

Many programs require more than one linked list. The most obvious way to implement multiple linked lists is to create multiple cell arrays with corresponding variables and code to manage them. This approach has a couple of disadvantages.

First, it requires duplicate code which you will have to debug and maintain. Each list will require almost identical routines for allocating new cells, putting cells in the garbage list, garbage collection, etc. In addition to causing extra maintenance work, this extra code will increase the size of your executable program.

Second, this method increases the amount of unused space allocated by the cell arrays. If your program manages the lists separately, each one will have its own garbage list. If all of the lists could be stored within a single cell array, the array would not need to keep as much unused memory in garbage lists. The size of the combined garbage list may also vary less than the size of the smaller separate lists, so the array may require resizing less often.

For example, suppose you have a program that creates ten separate lists. Each list contains about 100 items and each keeps about 10 entries in its garbage list. If you add 11 items to any of the lists, your program will need to resize that list. On the other hand, if all of the lists are kept in a single array, that array might hold the 1,000 items in the lists as well as 100 items in its garbage list. The individual lists could grow and shrink by much greater amounts without forcing the program to resize the array.

It is not hard for you to build multiple linked lists that share a common cell array and use a common garbage list. When the program needs a new cell for any of the lists, it can take one from the garbage list. When the program removes a cell from any of the lists, it returns the cell to the garbage list. Figure 2.10 shows two linked lists stored within a single cell array.

Enlarging the array to create new unused cells is still straightforward. However, garbage collection is a little trickier with multiple lists than it is when you have only one linked list.

The garbage collection routine presented in the previous section took advantage of the fact that the linked list's sentinel was in the first position in the cell array. Before resizing the cell array, the routine looped through the list moving items towards the front of the array. When all of the items were moved, the routine resized the array and made the garbage list smaller.

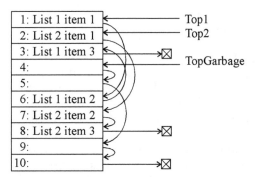

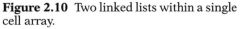

Figure 2.10 Two linked lists within a single cell array.

With more than one list present, you need to make sure that you compress each list towards the front of the array. If you know where each list begins, this is not too hard. Simply repeat the compression process for each of the linked lists.

On the other hand, if the tops of the lists are stored in another part of the program, the linked list code itself may not know where each list begins. In that case the garbage collection routine cannot rearrange all of the lists properly. There are a couple of different ways you can solve this problem.

Allow Growth Only

The simplest solution to this problem is to ignore it. If you allow the cell array to grow but never to shrink, you will never need to worry about garbage collection.

This method works well if the total number of cells in use by all of the lists does not change too much while the program runs. Many programs build several linked lists, work with the lists for a while, and then either destroy all of the lists or exit completely. In that case little memory will be wasted in the garbage list. While the growth only approach may seem inefficient, it is a fine solution for this type of program.

On the other hand, if a program builds large lists and then removes most of the items, the garbage list will contain a lot of wasted space. In that case one of the following, more complicated approaches will save memory.

Stationary List Tops

Another approach to placing multiple linked lists in the same cell array is to place the list tops in specific positions within the array. Then the garbage collection subroutine can loop through all of the lists, compacting each in turn, before it resizes the array.

A convenient place to store the list tops is at the beginning of the array or in array entries with negative indexes. To indicate that a list top is not currently in use, you can flag it by giving its Next pointer the value –1. When the program needs to start a new list, it can find an unused list top by searching for a list top cell with Next pointer –1.

Unfortunately, Visual Basic's **ReDim** statement has trouble handling the **Preserve** keyword when the lower bound of an array changes. For example, the following code causes an error.

```
Dim MyArray() As Integer

ReDim MyArray(-3 To 100)
ReDim Preserve MyArray(-2 To 100)
```

This prevents you from moving the lower bound of the array to make room for more list tops. You can avoid this problem if you know ahead of time how many lists your program might need. If you expect the program to require at most 10 linked lists, you can dimension the cell array to start at index –10 and use the first 10 entries for the list tops. If there are not too many lists, this is reasonable. If the program may need a widely varying number of lists, or if there is no way to know ahead of time how many lists the program will need, this scheme will not work.

Figure 2.11 shows graphically what this sort of strategy might look like. In this picture, room has been allocated for up to five linked list tops. Currently lists 1 and 3 are in use and the tops of these lists are stored in cell entries –1 and –3.

Example program MANYLINK demonstrates this scheme for implementing multiple linked lists in a single array. The program allocates list tops for five lists. You can easily modify the program to allocate more lists by changing the value of the constant MAX_LISTS in MANYLINK.FRM.

While the program has unused list tops available, you can press the New List button to create a new list. The program simply scans the list tops to find one that is not in use.

If you click on a list top that is in use, the program will enable the Delete List button. If you press this button, the program will delete the list you selected and place all of its cells in the garbage list.

If you enter a value and select a list top or an item in a list, the program will enable the Add After button. If you press this button, the program will insert the new item in the appropriate list after the item you selected.

Finally, if you select a list top or item that has an item after it in the list, the program will enable the Remove After button. If you press this button, the program will remove the item after the one you have selected.

As with previous example programs, MANYLINK presents a message box whenever it resizes the cell array. This message tells you the number of items in the cell array, excluding the list tops. It also tells you the number of items in the garbage list and the value of MaxFree. When the garbage list contains more than MaxFree items, the program will run the garbage collector to resize the cell array and make it smaller.

A List of Lists

If a program needs to use a widely varying number of lists, or if you cannot tell ahead of time how many lists the program might need, you can place the list tops in a list of their own and manage them separately. You can implement that list using any of the tech-

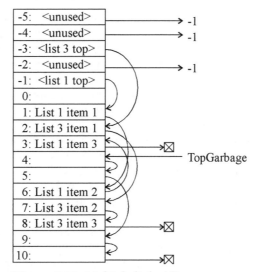

Figure 2.11 Multiple linked lists.

niques that have been described so far including array-based lists or linked lists. This approach is extremely flexible but it can also be very confusing.

Example program POLY demonstrates this method for creating multiple linked lists. The program uses an MDI interface to allow you to create any number of drawing forms. Within each of these, you can use the left mouse button to draw a polygon. Each time you click the left mouse button, the program adds a new point to the polygon. Click the right mouse button to indicate that you are done drawing the polygon.

The program allocates polygon cells in a single polygon cell array for all of the forms. Each form has its own linked list of polygons within this array. When you close a form, the program destroys all of its polygons and places them in the polygon garbage list. The polygons are represented as cells defined by:

```
Type PolygonCell
    Next As Integer

    FirstPoint As Integer
End Type
```

Each polygon in turn points to the top of a linked list of point cells. The program allocates the point cells in a single point cell array. When the program destroys a polygon, it places the polygon's points in the point garbage list. The point cells are defined by:

```
Type PointCell
    Next As Integer

    X As Single
    Y As Single
End Type
```

Each form in program POLY has a local variable FirstPolygon that points to the top of the linked list of polygons on the form. Each of those polygons points to a linked list of points that make up the polygon. If you think of the Forms collection as a list of forms, then program POLY contains a list of forms each of which contains a list of polygons each of which contains a list of points. As was mentioned earlier, when programs use many levels of indirection, things can become confusing. Figure 2.12 shows a picture of the data structure used by program POLY.

As you add new polygons and points to the drawing forms, the program's status bar shows you how many polygon cells and point cells have been allocated and how many are currently unused.

In order to keep things as simple as possible, program POLY uses a growth only strategy. When the program destroys a form, it adds the form's polygons and points to the appropriate garbage lists. No matter how large the garbage lists grow, however, the program will not resize the arrays to reclaim the unused space. This is fine for an example program that you will only run for a short time, but could be a problem for a larger application.

Program POLY also does not perform any of the many other functions that a general purpose drawing program would need. With a little work you could enhance the program to allow the user to delete or move a point in a polygon, delete a polygon from a form, make a copy of a polygon, save or load drawings from a file, etc.

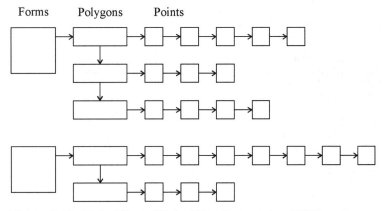

Figure 2.12 Linked lists of linked lists for program POLY.

Linked List Variations

Linked lists play a part in many algorithms and you will see them throughout the rest of this book. The following sections discuss a few specialized variations of linked lists.

Circular Linked Lists

Instead of setting the Next field of the last item in a list to an END_OF_LIST value, you could have it point back to the first item in the list. This makes a *circular list* as shown in Figure 2.13.

Circular lists can be useful when you need to loop through a set of data items indefinitely. At each step in the loop, the program moves a cell pointer to the next cell in the circular list. For example, suppose you had a circular list of items that each contained the name of a day of the week as shown in Figure 2.14. Then a program could list the days of the month like this:

```
Type DayCell
    Name As String
    Next As Integer
End Type


'       :
' Code to set up the list, etc. goes here.
'       :

' Print a calendar for the month.
'
```

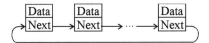

Figure 2.13 Circular linked list.

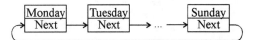

Figure 2.14 Day of the week circular linked list.

```
' FirstDay is the index of the day of the week structure for
' the first day of the month. For example, the month might
' start on a Monday.
'
' NumDays is the number of days in the month.
Sub ListMonth (FirstDay As Integer, NumDays As Integer)
Dim day As Integer
Dim i As Integer

    day = FirstDay
    For i = 1 to NumDays
        Print Format$(i) & ": " & TheDayCells(day).Name
        day = TheDayCells(day).Next
    Next i
End Sub
```

Circular lists have the interesting property of being able to reach the entire list starting from any of the elements in the list. This gives the list an appealing symmetry similar to that given by sentinels. Your program can treat all of the items in the list in pretty much the same way.

```
Sub PrintList(start_cell As Integer)
Dim cell As Integer

    cell = start_cell
    Do
        Print TheCells(cell).Data
        cell = TheCells(cell).Next
    Loop While cell <> start_cell
End Sub
```

Doubly Linked Lists

You may have noticed during the discussion of linked lists that most operations were defined in terms of doing something *after* a particular cell in the list. Given a particular cell, it is easy to add a new cell after it, delete the cell after it, or list all of the cells that come after it in the list. It is not as easy to delete the cell itself, to insert a new cell before the cell, or to list the cells that come before the cell in the list. With only a small change to the linked list, you can make these operations easy, too.

If you introduce a new pointer field that points to the *previous* cell in the list, you can create a *doubly linked list* that allows you to move both forward and backward through the items. Now you can easily delete a cell, insert before a cell, and list cells in either direction. The type declaration for this kind of cell is shown below. Figure 2.15 shows a picture of a doubly linked list that uses this kind of cell.

```
Type DblCell
    Data As String
    Prev As Integer
    Next As Integer
End Type
```

With doubly linked lists it is often useful to keep pointers to the top and bottom of the list. That makes it easy to add items at either the front or the back of the list. It is also useful to have sentinels at both the top and bottom of the list. Then as you manipulate the list, you do not need to worry about whether or not you are working on the top, middle, or bottom of the list. Figure 2.16 shows a doubly linked list with sentinels.

The code for inserting and removing items from a doubly linked list is similar to the code presented earlier for dealing with a singly linked list. The routines only need to be changed slightly to handle the Prev pointers. You can also write new routines to add an item before a given item or to delete a particular item from the list.

```
Type DblCell
    Data As String
    Prev As Integer
    Next As Integer
End Type

Dim TheCells () As DblCell

Sub RemoveItem(target As Integer)
Dim before_me As Integer
Dim after_me As Integer

    before_me = TheCells(target).Prev
    after_me = TheCells(target).Next
    TheCells(before_me).Next = after_me
    TheCells(after_me).Prev = before_me
End Sub

Sub AddAfter(new_cell As Integer, after_me As Integer)
Dim before_me As Integer

    before_me = TheCells(after_me).Next
    TheCells(after_me).Next = new_cell
    TheCells(new_cell).Next = before_me
    TheCells(before_me).Prev = new_cell
    TheCells(new_cell).Prev = after_me
End Sub

Sub AddBefore(new_cell As Integer, before_me As Integer)
Dim after_me As Integer
```

Figure 2.15 Doubly linked list.

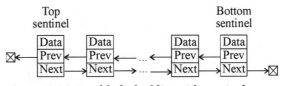

Figure 2.16 Doubly linked list with sentinels.

```
        after_me = TheCells(before_me).Prev
        TheCells(after_me).Next = new_cell
        TheCells(new_cell).Next = before_me
        TheCells(before_me).Prev = new_cell
        TheCells(new_cell).Prev = after_me
End Sub
```

Example program DBLLINK manipulates a doubly linked list. It allows you to add items before or after a selected item, and it lets you delete a selected item. With a doubly linked list, you can select the item to be removed rather than the item in front of the one you want to remove. This makes selecting an item for removal a bit more intuitive for a doubly linked list than it is for a singly linked list.

Like several of the earlier example programs in this chapter, DBLLINK presents a message box whenever it resizes the cell array to tell you how large the cell array is, how many unused items it contains, and how many items the garbage list can contain before the program will begin garbage collection.

Threads

In some applications it may be useful to traverse a linked list using more than one possible ordering. In different parts of an application you might want to list employees ordered by their last names, their salaries, their Social Security numbers, or their job classifications. Normal linked lists allow you to examine the items in one order only. By adding a new Prev pointer to a doubly linked list, you enable your program to follow the list backward. You can extend this idea further by adding more pointers to the data structure to allow you to display the list in still other orders.

The set of links that makes up one of these other orderings is called a *thread*. Linked lists can contain any number of threads, though at some point the extra work of maintaining the threads is not worth the effort. A thread listing employees ordered by their last name would make sense if your application used that ordering frequently. A thread listing employees ordered by middle initial would probably not be useful since your program would probably never use that ordering.

Some orderings do not make good threads. A thread ordering employees by sex, for example, would not be a good thread because the information it would hold is easy to reconstruct. To list the employees ordered by sex without the thread, you would simply traverse the list along any other thread while printing out the names of all the female employees. Then you would traverse the list again printing out the names of all the male employees. You would need only two passes through the list to produce this ordering.

Contrast this with the case where you want to list the employees ordered by their last names. If the list did not include a last name thread, you would have to search the list for the name that came first, then search for the name that came second, and so forth. This is an $O(N^2)$ process that is much less efficient than the $O(N)$ method for ordering employees by sex.

Generally an ordering will make a good thread if you will need to use that ordering often and the ordering would be difficult to reconstruct whenever you needed it. An ordering will make a bad thread if it is easy to recreate at any time.

Example program THREADS demonstrates a simple threaded employee list. Fill in the last name, first name, Social Security number, job class, and sex fields for a new employee. Then press the Add button to add the new employee to the list.

The program contains threads that order the list by employee last name forward and backward, by Social Security number, and by job classification forward and backward. You can use the option buttons to select the thread by which the program displays the list.

The cell structure for program THREADS is defined by:

```
Type Cell
    LastName As String
    FirstName As String
    SSN As String
    JobClass As Integer
    Sex As String * 1

    NextName As Integer         ' By name forward.
    PrevName As Integer         ' By name backward.
    NextSSN As Integer          ' By Social Security number.
    NextJobClass As Integer     ' By job classification forward.
    PrevJobClass As Integer     ' By job classification backward.
End Type
```

When you add a new entry to the employee list, the program must update all of the threads. For each thread the program must insert the new item in its proper position within the thread. To insert a record with last name "Smith," for example, the program would loop through the list using the NextName thread until it found an item with a name that should come after "Smith." The program would then insert the new entry in the NextName thread before that item. Then the last name thread would list the names in order.

Sentinels play an important role in finding where the new entry belongs in each thread. When the program initially creates the list, it also creates top and bottom sentinels. It sets the data values for the top sentinel to be small enough that any valid real data must come after it in all of the threads. Similarly it sets the data values for the bottom sentinel large enough that all valid real data must come before the bottom sentinel in all of the threads.

This program's LastName field allows you to enter only letters A-Z and a-z. The program sets the LastName entry for the top sentinel to "" (an empty string) since the empty string comes before all letters. Any valid name you enter in the LastName field will come after the value "" in the top sentinel.

Similarly the "~" character comes after all letters A-Z and a-z, so the program uses "~" for the LastName entry in the bottom sentinel. Any valid data you enter in the LastName field must come before the bottom sentinel's value "~."

By giving the sentinels the LastName values "" and "~," the program avoids the need to check for special cases where the new item should be inserted at the top or bottom of the list. All valid names will fall between the sentinels' LastName values. The code for inserting a new item in the name threads is shown below.

```
' See where the new item belongs.
after_me = 1                              ' Top sentinel.
before_me = TheCells(after_me).NextName   ' Item after after_me.
Do While TheCells(before_me).LastName < last_name Or
(TheCells(before_me).LastName = last_name And
TheCells(before_me).FirstName < first_name)
```

```
    after_me = before_me
    before_me = TheCells(before_me).NextName
Loop


' Insert the new item in the NextName thread.
TheCells(after_me).NextName = new_cell
TheCells(new_cell).NextName = before_me


' Insert the new item in the PrevName thread.
TheCells(before_me).PrevName = new_cell
TheCells(new_cell).PrevName = after_me
```

Notice that, for this to work, the program must ensure that you cannot enter values that fall outside the range bounded by the sentinels. If you managed to enter "~~" as a last name, for example, the loop would run past the bottom sentinel since "~~" comes after "~." The program would then crash when it tried to access TheCells(END_OF_LIST).

In a similar fashion, program THREADS sets the values for the sentinels' Social Security numbers and job classes so they bound the valid values you might enter. The program uses these sentinels to update the corresponding threads.

Even though the program does not maintain a sex thread, it also initializes the values of the Sex field in the sentinels. It sets the sentinel values to "A" and "Z" to bound the possible valid values "F" and "M" just as if it were building a thread. While this is not strictly necessary, it is a good practice. If the program ever displays the value "A" or "Z" in this field, you will know immediately that it is accessing a sentinel when it probably should not be. Also, if you later decide to add a sex thread, the sentinels would already be in place.

Array-Based Lists versus Linked Lists

The best algorithm for implementing a list depends on your situation. In most cases, array-based list implementations have few advantages over linked lists. The one exception is when you only need to add and remove items from one end of the list. This type of list is called a *stack*. Stacks are described in more detail later in this chapter.

The more flexible array-based methods which use garbage collection are not all that much simpler than linked lists and they do not allow as much flexibility. This means that linked lists are usually your best bet for all-purpose lists.

It is a little harder to weigh the tradeoffs between different methods for managing multiple linked lists. If you only need two or three lists, you can implement and manage each list separately with almost identical subroutines. This method is easy but it requires your program to have more code which you will have to manage and debug. It also makes your executable image larger than necessary.

If you have reason to believe that the lists in your program will not shrink much, you might be able to use a growth only strategy. In that case, multiple linked lists can allocate cells from the same cell array and replace unneeded cells in a shared garbage list.

An alternative strategy, which works well if you know ahead of time how many different lists your program may need, is to use fixed list tops as was done in program MANYLINK. When the program starts execution, it can allocate enough list tops for its later needs. Then the garbage collection routine can loop through all of the list tops when necessary.

Finally, if you do not know how many lists the program might need or if the number of lists will vary wildly, you can maintain a linked list of list tops each pointing to a linked list of items. This is the strategy followed by program POLY. While this method is the most complicated, it also gives you the greatest flexibility.

Other Linked Structures

Using pointers you can build many other useful kinds of linked structures such as trees, irregular arrays, sparse arrays, graphs, and networks. A cell can contain any number of pointers to other cells. For example, you could use a cell containing two pointers, one to a right child cell and one to a left child cell, to create a binary tree.

```
Type BinaryCell
    LeftChild As Integer
    RightChild As Integer
End Type
```

A tree built from this kind of cell is shown in Figure 2.17. Chapters 5 and 6 will have much more to say about trees.

A cell can even contain a pointer to a linked list of pointers to other cells. This allows a program to link a cell to any number of other objects. Figure 2.18 shows examples of other linked data structures. You will see structures like these throughout the rest of the book, particularly in Chapter 11 which describes network algorithms.

Stacks

A *stack* is an ordered list where items are always added and removed from the same end of the list. You can think of a *stack* as a stack of objects on the floor. You can add items to the top and remove them from the top, but you cannot add or remove an item from the middle of the pile. Because of their *"Last-In-First-Out"* behavior, stacks are sometimes called *LIFO lists* or *LIFOs*. For historical reasons, adding an item to a stack is called *pushing* an item onto the stack, and removing an item from a stack is called *popping* an item off the stack.

The first implementation of a simple list described at the beginning of this chapter is a stack. You use a counter to keep track of where the top of the list is. You then use that counter to add and remove items from the top of the list. The only minor change made here is that Pop, the routine that removes an item from the stack, saves the item in a parameter. This makes it a little easier for other subroutines to retrieve an item and

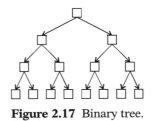

Figure 2.17 Binary tree.

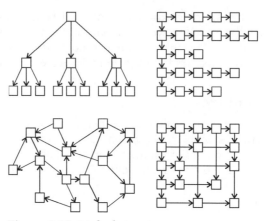

Figure 2.18 Linked structures.

remove it from the stack in one step. Other than this change, the code below is similar to the list code presented earlier.

```
Dim Stack() As Integer
Dim StackSize As Integer
Sub Push(value As Integer)
    StackSize = StackSize + 1
    ReDim Preserve Stack(1 To StackSize)
    Stack(StackSize) = value
End Sub

Sub Pop(value As Integer)
    value = Stack(StackSize)
    StackSize = StackSize - 1
    ReDim Preserve Stack(1 To StackSize)
End Sub
```

All of the previous discussion about lists also applies to this sort of stack implementation. In particular you can save time if you do not resize the array every time you push or pop an item. Example program **SIM_LIST** described earlier (see pages 16–19) demonstrates this sort of simple stack implementation.

Programs often use stacks to hold a sequence of items that the program will manipulate until the stack is empty. Operating on one item might cause others to be pushed onto the stack, but eventually they will all be removed. A simple example is an algorithm to reverse the order of the items in an array. Here each item is pushed onto the stack in order. Then each item is popped off the stack in reverse order and written back into the array.

```
' Push the items onto the stack.
For I = 1 To NumItems
    Push List (I)
Next I
' Pop the items from the stack back into the array.
For I = 1 To NumItems
    Pop List (I)
Next I
```

In this example the stack may change length many times before it is eventually emptied. If you know ahead of time how big the array might need to be, you can avoid these resizings by initially making the stack big enough to hold all of the items in the list. Then you do not need to enlarge the stack as you push items onto it. You can also skip resizing the stack when you pop items off of it. Instead you can delete the entire array in a single step when you are done reordering the list.

Even in more complicated programs you can sometimes guess how much space you will need in the stack before the program begins. In the non-recursive Hilbert curve program examined in Chapter 4, for example, you can calculate the necessary size of the stack before starting.

In other cases you may not be able to determine ahead of time how large the stack might grow. If you want to, you can still skip resizing the stack to make it smaller when you remove items. Then when the stack is completely empty, you can delete the entire array. If you need the stack for a relatively short period of time, it will contain unused entries for only a short while so you will not waste too much memory.

The code shown below allows you to preallocate a stack if you know how large it might grow. The Pop routine does not resize the array. When your program has finished using the stack, it can use the EmptyStack routine to deallocate all of the stack's memory at once.

```
Const WANT_FREE_PERCENT = .1    ' Try for 10% free space.
Const MIN_FREE = 10             ' Min unused space when resizing.

Global Stack() As Integer       ' The stack array.
Global StackSize As Integer     ' Size of the stack array.
Global LastItem As Integer      ' Last index in use.

Sub PreallocateStack(entries As Integer)
    StackSize = entries
    ReDim Stack(1 To StackSize)
End Sub

Sub EmptyStack ()
    StackSize = 0
    LastItem = 0
    Erase Stack
End Sub

Sub Push (value As Integer)
    LastItem = LastItem + 1
    If LastItem > StackSize Then ResizeStack
    Stack(LastItem) = value
End Sub

Sub Pop (value As Integer)
    value = Stack(LastItem)
    LastItem = LastItem - 1
End Sub

Sub ResizeStack ()
Dim want_free As Integer

    want_free = WANT_FREE_PERCENT * LastItem
    If want_free < MIN_FREE Then want_free = MIN_FREE
```

```
        StackSize = LastItem + want_free
        ReDim Preserve Stack(1 To StackSize)
End Sub
```

This sort of stack implementation is quite efficient in Visual Basic. The stack does not waste much memory and it does not need to be resized very often, particularly if you can guess how big the stack needs to be before starting.

Multiple Stacks

Some programs require more than one stack. As was the case for implementing multiple linked lists, there are several ways in which you can implement multiple stacks.

You can manage two stacks in the same array by placing one at the top of the array and the other at the bottom. You should keep separate Top counters for the two stacks and make the stacks grow towards each other as shown in Figure 2.19. This method allows the two stacks to grow into the same memory until they bump into each other when the array is completely full.

Unfortunately resizing these sorts of stacks is not easy. When you enlarge the array, you must shift all of the items in the upper stack to the right so you can allocate new items in the middle. When you shrink the array, you must first shift the items in the upper stack to the left before you redimension the array and reclaim the unused memory. It is also not easy to extend this method to handle more than two stacks.

A more flexible method for implementing multiple stacks is to use linked lists. To push an item onto a stack, you insert it at the top of its linked list. To pop an item off of a stack, you remove the first item from the linked list. Since all items are added and removed from the top of the list, you really do not need sentinels to implement this sort of stack.

If all of the stacks contain similar types of items, you can implement them as multiple linked lists coexisting in a single cell array. As you add and remove items from the various stacks, the cell array can perform its own memory management.

This is no different from the implementations of multiple linked lists discussed in the previous sections. In particular, all of the previous discussion about resizing multiple linked lists applies. You can allow the lists to grow only, you can allocate stationary list tops, or you can create a list of stacks. Figure 2.20 shows three stacks implemented as linked lists using stationary list tops.

The main drawback to using a linked list to implement a stack is that it requires extra memory for the cells' Next pointers. A single array-based stack containing N integers requires only 2 * N bytes of memory (2 bytes per integer). The same stack implemented as a linked list would require an additional 2 * N bytes of memory for the Next pointers, doubling the size needed to manage the stack.

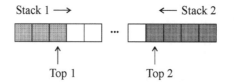

Figure 2.19 Two stacks in the same array.

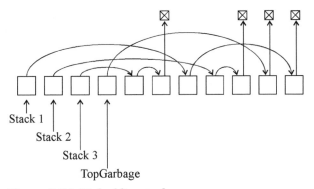

Figure 2.20 Linked list stacks.

Example program **STACKS** shows several stacks implemented as linked lists sharing a single cell array. Using the program you can push and pop items into and out of each of the lists and see how the combined cell array manages its memory. Each time the cell array is resized, the program presents a message box telling you how large the cell array is, how many unused items it contains, and how many items the garbage list can contain before the program will invoke the garbage collector.

3

Dynamic Data Structures— Queues and Arrays

Overview

This chapter continues the discussion of dynamic data structures started in Chapter 2. The first part of this chapter describes *queues*, a special kind of list where items are added at one end and removed from the other. Queues are useful in many computer applications and are used in several algorithms later in this book.

The chapter then discusses arrays. It is easy to manage simple arrays in Visual Basic. The **ReDim** statement is particularly useful for making arrays larger or smaller. There are several specialized kinds of arrays, however, that require a bit more effort to manage. These include triangular arrays, irregular arrays, and sparse arrays. Using the techniques presented in this chapter, you will be able to build flexible array structures that can greatly reduce your program's memory usage.

Queues

A *queue* is an ordered list where items are added at one end of the list and removed from the other. A group of people waiting in a store checkout line is a queue. New arrivals enter at the back of the line. When a customer reaches the front of the line, the cashier helps that customer. Due to their *"First-In-First-Out"* nature, queues are sometimes called *FIFO lists* or *FIFOs*.

You can implement queues in Visual Basic using techniques similar to the ones used to implement simple stacks. You allocate an array and keep counters that indicate where the top and bottom of the queue are. QueueFront indicates the index of the item at the front of the queue. QueueBack indicates where the next new item should be added to the queue. As items enter and leave the queue, you resize the queue array so it grows at one end and shrinks at the other.

```
Global Queue() As String       ' The queue array.
Global QueueFront As Integer   ' The next item to be removed.
Global QueueBack As Integer    ' Where the next new item goes.

Sub EnterQueue (value As String)
    ReDim Preserve Queue(QueueFront To QueueBack)
    Queue(QueueBack) = value
    QueueBack = QueueBack + 1
End Sub

Sub LeaveQueue (value As String)
    value = Queue(QueueFront)
    QueueFront = QueueFront + 1
    ReDim Preserve Queue(QueueFront To QueueBack - 1)
End Sub
```

Unfortunately Visual Basic has trouble with the **Preserve** keyword if you change the array's lower bound using a **ReDim** statement. Even if Visual Basic could perform this operation, the queue would "walk" through memory. Each time you added and removed an item from the queue, the queue array's bounds would increase. If you passed enough items through the queue, the bounds would eventually become too large to manage. In Visual Basic 3.0, for example, array bounds must be integers so they cannot exceed 32,767. After adding and removing 32,767 items from the queue, the array bounds would exceed this limit.

For these reasons, when the array must be resized you should first move the data to the beginning of the array. That may create enough unused entries near the end of the array so that you will no longer need to resize it. Otherwise you can use the **ReDim** statement to make the array larger or smaller.

While making this change, you can also apply some of the lessons learned while implementing lists. You can improve performance by adding more than one new item to the array whenever you enlarge it. You can also save time by shrinking the array only when it contains a certain minimum number of unused entries.

In a simple list or stack, you add items to one end of the array and remove them from the same end. This means that, if the list stays roughly the same size, you might not have to resize the array too often. In a queue, on the other hand, you always add items at one end and remove them from the other. Since the array entries fill up on one side and empty out at the other, you will need to rearrange the queue occasionally even if its total size stays the same.

```
Const WANT_FREE_PERCENT = .1 ' Try for 10% free space.
Const MIN_FREE = 10          ' Min free space when resizing.

Global Queue() As String     ' The queue array.
Global QueueMax As Integer   ' Largest index in the array.
```

```
Global QueueFront As Integer ' The next item to be removed.
Global QueueBack As Integer  ' Where the next new item goes.
Global ResizeWhen As Integer ' Resize if QueueFront >= this.

<During initialization the program should set QueueMax = -1 to
indicate that no memory has ever been allocated for the array.>

Sub EnterQueue (value As String)
    If QueueBack > QueueMax Then ResizeQueue
    Queue(QueueBack) = value
    QueueBack = QueueBack + 1
End Sub

Sub LeaveQueue (value As String)
    value = Queue(QueueFront)
    QueueFront = QueueFront + 1
    If QueueFront > ResizeWhen Then ResizeQueue
End Sub

Sub ResizeQueue ()
Dim want_free As Integer
Dim i As Integer

    ' Move the entries to the beginning of the array.
    For i = QueueFront To QueueBack - 1
        Queue(i - QueueFront) = Queue(i)
    Next i
    QueueBack = QueueBack - QueueFront
    QueueFront = 0

    ' Resize the array.
    want_free = WANT_FREE_PERCENT * (QueueBack - QueueFront)
    If want_free < MIN_FREE Then want_free = MIN_FREE
    Max = QueueBack + want_free - 1
    ReDim Preserve Queue(0 To Max)

' We will resize the array when QueueFront > ResizeWhen.
    ResizeWhen = want_free
End Sub
```

Example program ARRAY_Q uses this method to implement a simple queue. Enter a string and press the Enter button to add a new item to the end of the queue. Press the Leave button to remove the top item from the queue.

When the queue is resized, the program presents a message box telling you how large the queue is, how many unused items it contains, and the value ResizeWhen. When the top of the queue (the end from which items are being removed) passes this value, the program resizes the queue to reclaim unused entries.

As you run the program, notice that the queue requires resizing when you add and remove items from the queue, even if the total queue size does not change much. In fact, the queue will require resizing even if you repeatedly add and remove a single item from the queue.

Keep in mind that each time the queue is resized, the items in use are first moved to the beginning of the array. This makes resizing array-based queues more time consuming than resizing linked lists and stacks, the data structures described earlier.

Circular Queues

The queues described in the previous section require occasional rearrangement even if the total queue size does not change much. The queue will require rearrangement even if you repeatedly add and remove a single item from the queue.

If you know in advance how large a queue might need to be, you can avoid rearranging the queue by creating a *circular queue*. The idea is to treat the queue's array as if it wraps around to form a circle. You treat the last item in the array as if it comes just before the first item in the array. When you reach the end of the array, you wrap around to the beginning. Figure 3.1 shows a circular queue.

As was the case for the previous queue implementation, you can use a variable QueueFront to hold the index of the item that has been in the queue the longest. You can use a variable QueueBack to hold the index of the position in the queue array where the next item should be added to the queue.

Unlike in the previous implementation, when you update QueueFront and QueueBack you should use the **Mod** operator to make sure the indexes remain within the bounds of the queue array. When you add an item to the queue, for example, you can use code like this:

```
Queue(QueueBack) = value
QueueBack = (QueueBack + 1) Mod QueueSize
```

When QueueBack + 1 reaches the value QueueSize, the **Mod** operator sets QueueBack to 0 since QueueSize Mod QueueSize = 0. This resets QueueBack so it points to the beginning of the array. Figure 3.2 shows the process of adding a new item to a circular queue that can hold four entries. Here the item "C" is added to the queue at the

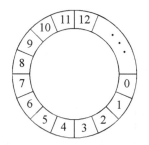

Figure 3.1 A circular queue.

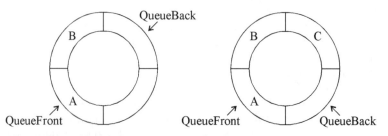

Figure 3.2 Adding an item to a circular queue.

position indicated by QueueBack. Then QueueBack is advanced to point to the next entry in the queue array.

Similarly when you remove an item from the queue, you should update QueueFront with code like this:

```
value = Queue(QueueFront)
QueueFront = (QueueFront + 1) Mod QueueSize
```

When QueueFront reaches the end of the array, the **Mod** operator resets it so it again points to the first entry in the array. Figure 3.3 shows the process of removing an item from a circular queue. The first item, in this case the item "A," is removed from the front of the list and QueueFront is updated so it indicates the next item in the array.

With circular queues it is a bit tricky to tell the difference between the queue being empty and the queue being full. In both cases QueueBottom will equal QueueTop. Figure 3.4 shows two circular queues, one empty and one full.

An easy way to solve this problem is to keep track of the number of items in the queue using a separate variable NumInQueue. This count tells you if there are any items to remove from the queue and if there is room in the queue to add new items.

Now you can write the code to manage a simple circular queue.

```
Global Queue() As String      ' The queue array.
Global QueueSize As Integer   ' Largest index in queue.
Global QueueFront As Integer  ' The next item to be removed.
Global QueueBack As Integer   ' Where the next new item goes.
Global NumInQueue As Integer  ' # items in the queue

Sub NewCircularQueue (num_items As Integer)
    QueueSize = num_items
    ReDim Queue(0 To QueueSize - 1)
End Sub
```

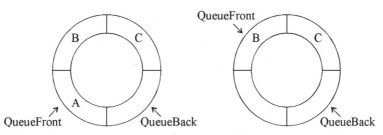

Figure 3.3 Removing an item from a circular queue.

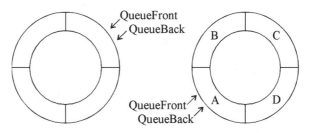

Figure 3.4 Empty and full circular queues.

```
Sub EnterQueue (value As String)
    ' If the queue is full, just exit.
    ' In a real application we would take more action.
    If NumInQueue >= QueueSize Then Exit Sub

    Queue(QueueBack) = value
    QueueBack = (QueueBack + 1) Mod QueueSize
    NumInQueue = NumInQueue + 1
End Sub

Sub LeaveQueue (value As String)
    ' If the queue is empty, just exit.
    ' In a real application we would take more action.
    If NumInQueue <= 0 Then Exit Sub

    value = Queue (QueueFront)
    QueueFront = (QueueFront + 1) Mod QueueSize
    NumInQueue = NumInQueue - 1
End Sub
```

As was the case with array-based lists, you can resize this array if the queue fills completely or if the array contains too much unused space. However, resizing a circular queue is more difficult than resizing an array-based list or stack.

When you resize the array, the list of items currently in the queue may wrap around the end of the array. Then items at the front of the queue are near the end of the array and items at the back of the queue are near the beginning of the array. If you simply enlarge the array, the newly inserted items will be at the end of the array so they will fall into the middle of the list. Figure 3.5 shows what would happen if you enlarged the array in this manner.

Similar problems occur if you just shrink the array. If the items wrap past the end of the array, you will lose the items at the end of the array which are near the front of the queue.

To avoid these difficulties, you must reorganize the array before you resize it. The easiest way to do this is using a temporary array. Copy the queue's items into the temporary array in their correct order, resize the queue array, and then copy the items from the temporary array back into the resized queue array.

```
Sub EnterQueue (value As String)
    If NumInQueue >= QueueSize Then ResizeQueue
```

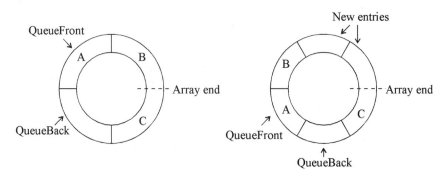

Figure 3.5 Incorrectly enlarging a circular queue.

```
            Queue(QueueBack) = value
            QueueBack = (QueueBack + 1) Mod QueueSize
            NumInQueue = NumInQueue + 1
End Sub

Sub LeaveQueue (value As String)
        If NumInQueue <= 0 Then Exit Sub

        value = Queue(QueueFront)
        QueueFront = (QueueFront + 1) Mod QueueSize

        NumInQueue = NumInQueue - 1
        If NumInQueue < ShrinkWhen Then ResizeQueue
End Sub

Sub ResizeQueue ()
Dim temp() As String
Dim want_free As Integer
Dim i As Integer

        ' Copy items into temporary array.
        ReDim temp(0 To NumInQueue - 1)
        For i = 0 To NumInQueue - 1
            temp(i) = Queue((i + QueueFront) Mod QueueSize)
        Next i

        ' Resize the array
        want_free = WANT_FREE_PERCENT * NumInQueue
        If want_free < MIN_FREE Then want_free = MIN_FREE
        QueueSize = NumInQueue + want_free

        ReDim Queue(0 To QueueSize - 1)
        For i = 0 To NumInQueue - 1
            Queue(i) = temp(i)
        Next i
        QueueFront = 0
        QueueBack = NumInQueue

        ' We will shrink the array when NumInQueue < ShrinkWhen.
        ShrinkWhen = QueueSize - 2 * want_free

        ' Don't resize tiny queues. This can get us in trouble
        ' with "ReDim temp(0 To NumInQueue - 1)" above and
        ' just plain looks silly!
        If ShrinkWhen < 3 Then ShrinkWhen = 0
End Sub
```

Example program CIRCLE_Q demonstrates this technique for implementing a circular queue. Enter a string and press the Enter button to add a new item to the queue. Press the Leave button to remove the top item from the queue.

When the program resizes the queue array, it presents a message box that tells you the size of the queue array, the number of array entries not in use, and the value of ShrinkWhen. If the number of items in use in the queue falls below ShrinkWhen, the program will resize the array to reclaim some of the unused space.

Keep in mind that each time the program resizes the queue, it first copies the items into a temporary array, resizes the queue, and then copies the items back into the queue.

The extra recopying steps make resizing circular queues more time consuming than resizing most of the previous data structures described such as linked lists and stacks. Even array-based queues, which require extra work to resize, do not take this much effort.

On the other hand, if the total number of items in the queue does not change too much, you will not need to resize a circular queue very often. If you set the resizing parameters carefully, you may never need to resize the array. Even if you need to resize the array occasionally, the reduced frequency of resizing will more than make up for the extra work required.

Linked List-Based Queues

A completely different approach to implementing queues is to use doubly linked lists. You can use sentinels to keep track of the top and bottom of the list. Add new items to the queue just *before* the bottom sentinel and remove items leaving the queue from just *after* the top sentinel. Figure 3.6 shows a doubly linked list used to implement a queue.

Like a circular queue, a queue built using a doubly linked list will not require many array resizes if the size of the queue remains fairly constant. When items are removed from the queue, their array entries are placed in a garbage list. When more items are added later, they are placed in garbage entries. Since the linked list recycles the unused entries placed in its garbage list, resizing will be necessary only when the total number of items in the list changes greatly. Like circular queues, linked list queues do not need to be resized often if the total number of items in the queue does not change too much.

This method has the advantage of being a bit more intuitive than the circular array queue. You add items at the bottom of the list and remove them from the top of the list. The routines that resize a linked list queue are also much simpler than those for resizing a circular queue. The code managing the linked list can resize the list's cell array without making the code that handles the queue itself more complicated.

This method has the drawback that it requires extra memory to hold the linked list's Next and Prev pointers. This makes linked list queues a bit less space efficient than circular queues.

A linked list queue also will not keep items in the queue adjacent to each other in the cell array. This does not matter much to the queue algorithm, but during debugging it may make more intuitive sense if the items are kept together. If the queue grows large enough, spreading the queue entries out may also cause increased paging. If the computer must jump all over the cell array to add and remove items from the queue, it may have to page memory to and from the disk more often.

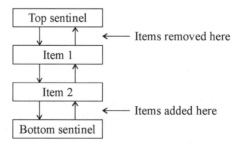

Figure 3.6 Linked list queue.

Example program LINKED_Q manages a queue using a doubly linked list. Enter a string and press the Enter button to add the new item to the bottom of the queue. Press the Leave button to remove the top item from the queue.

When the queue is resized, the program presents a message box that tells you the number of items the queue can hold, the number of items not in use, and the maximum number of unused items the queue can contain before the program will resize the queue array.

Example program QUEUES implements the three kinds of queues examined so far: an array-based queue, a circular queue, and a doubly linked list-based queue. If you fill in a string and press the Enter button, the program will add the new item to the end of all three of the queues. If you press the Leave button, the program will remove the top entry from each queue.

Whenever any of the three queues is resized, the program presents a message box that gives you information about that queue. If you add and remove many items from the queues, you will see that the array-based queue will resize more often than the circular or linked list queues.

Queue Variations

Queues have many interesting variations, two of which are examined here: *priority queues* and *multi-headed queues*.

Priority Queues

Each item in a *priority queue* has an associated priority. When the program needs to remove an item from the queue, it selects the item with the highest priority. It does not matter how the items in a priority queue are stored, as long as the program can always find the highest priority item when it is needed.

Computer operating systems often make use of priority queues for job scheduling. In the UNIX operating system, each process can have a different priority. Whenever the computer is ready to run a new process, it selects the highest priority process that is ready to run. Lower priority processes must wait until all of the higher processes have finished or are blocked, waiting for some external event like a data read on a disk drive.

Air traffic control also uses a priority queue concept. Planes that are trying to land and are running out of fuel have top priority. Other planes trying to land have second priority. Planes on the ground have third priority because they are in a safer position than planes in the air. Over time some of the priorities might change since more planes trying to land will eventually start to run low on fuel.

One simple way to build a priority queue is to keep all of the items in a list. When you need to remove an item from the queue, you can search the list to see which item has the highest priority. To add an item to the queue, you can place the new item at the top of the list. Using this method, it takes one step to add a new item to the queue. If there are N items in the queue, it takes N steps to locate and remove the highest priority item from the queue.

A slightly better scheme is to build the priority queue using a linked list and keep the items in the list sorted in priority order. The linked list cell type should contain a Priority field in addition to the usual Next field and whatever data the program needs to manipulate.

```
Type PriorityCell
    Priority As Integer    ' The item's priority.
    Next As Integer        ' The pointer to the next item.
    Value As String        ' Whatever data the program needs.
End Type
```

Figure 3.7 shows a priority queue implemented using a linked list.

When you need to add a new item to the queue, you can search down the list to see where the new item belongs and then insert the item at that position. To make it easier to find the item's correct position, you can use top and bottom sentinels.

The top sentinel allows you to treat the top of the list as you treat the rest of the list. Since you are using a singly linked list, you can only insert a new item *after* another item. You can insert an item at the top of the list by inserting it *after* the top sentinel. If you did not have a top sentinel, you would need to write special code to handle items that belonged at the top of the list.

The bottom sentinel allows you to treat the bottom of the list as you treat the rest of the list. By giving the bottom sentinel the lowest priority possible, −32,768, you know that any new item will come before the bottom sentinel in the list. When you are looking for an item's position in the list, you know that the item must come before the bottom sentinel. That means you know you will find the item's position before you reach the end of the list. If you do not use a bottom sentinel, you will need to constantly check that you have not run off the end of the list.

The code fragment below shows the heart of this search routine. Notice how the top sentinel allows you to keep the variable cell pointing to the item before the one you are examining. When you have found the new item's location, you can insert it after the item pointed to by cell. Notice also how the bottom sentinel allows you to avoid checking for the end of the list during the **Do While** loop.

```
' See where the new entry belongs in the list.
cell = 1                   ' The top sentinel.
nxt = TheCells(cell).Next
Do While TheCells(nxt).priority > priority
    cell = nxt
    nxt = TheCells(cell).Next
Loop
' Insert the item after TheCells(cell) in the list.
```

When you want to remove the highest priority item from the list, you simply remove the item after the top sentinel. Since the list is kept sorted in priority order, the top item always has the highest priority.

Adding a new item to a queue like this takes an average of N / 2 steps. Sometimes the new item will go near the top of the list and sometimes it will go near the bottom, but

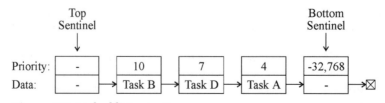

Figure 3.7 Linked list priority queue.

on the average it will fall somewhere in the middle. The previous simple list-based priority queue required O(1) step to insert a new item into the queue and O(N) steps to remove the highest priority items from the queue. The sorted linked list version requires O(N) steps to add an item to the queue and O(1) step to remove the top item. While both versions require O(N) steps for one of these operations, the sorted linked list queue needs only N / 2 steps on the average.

Example program PRI_LIST uses a sorted linked list to manage a priority queue. You can fill in priority and data values and use the Enter button to add a new item to the priority queue. Press the Leave button to remove the highest priority item from the queue.

With some extra work you can build a priority queue where insertion and deletion both take O(log(N)) steps. For very large queues the added speed is worth the extra effort. This sort of priority queue uses a *heap* which is also used by the sorting algorithm heapsort. Heaps and heap-based priority queues are discussed in more detail in Chapter 8.

Multi-Headed Queues

Another interesting type of queue is a *multi-headed queue*. Items enter the queue at the rear as usual, but the queue has more than one *front end* or *head*. The program may remove items from any of the heads.

An everyday example of a multi-headed queue is the customer service counter at a bank. All of the customers stand in a single line but they are served by more than one teller. The next teller who becomes available serves the customer at the front of the line. This sort of queue seems fair because the tellers serve customers in their order of arrival. It is also efficient since all of the tellers are kept busy as long as there are any customers waiting in the queue.

Compare this sort of queue to the multiple single-headed queues used in a typical grocery store. Here people are not necessarily serviced in their order of arrival. One person in a slow line may wait longer than someone else who arrived later but got in a faster line. The cashiers may not always be busy either since one line could empty completely while there were people waiting in other lines.

Generally multi-headed queues are more efficient than multiple single-headed queues. The reason the latter are used in grocery stores is because shopping carts take up a lot of floor space. A multi-headed queue would require customers to stand in a single line that would take up a lot of room. When a cashier became available, the customer at the front of the line would need to maneuver a bulky shopping cart across the front of the store to the available cashier. This could be difficult. In a bank, on the other hand, the customers do not have large shopping carts to push around so it is easy for them to stand in a single line.

Some airport check-in counters have a combination of both situations. Their customers have large amounts of baggage to push around, but the airline still uses a multi-headed queue. They are willing to give up the extra space needed to create a large single line for their customers.

It is not too hard to implement a multi-headed queue as a normal single-headed queue. Store the items (customers or whatever) in a normal single-headed queue. When an agent (teller, cashier, etc.) becomes available to service the queue, remove the first item from the front of the queue and assign it to the available agent.

Suppose you are in charge of designing a check-in counter for a new airline terminal and you want to compare a single multi-headed queue to multiple single-headed queues. First you would need some sort of model of customer behavior. For this example, you might make the following assumptions:

1. Each customer will require between two and five minutes at the counter.
2. When customers arrive in the multiple single-headed version, they enter the queue that has the fewest people in it.
3. Customers arrive at roughly a constant rate throughout the day.

Example program HEADED_Q runs a simulation like this one. You can modify a number of simulation parameters including:

- The number of customers that arrive per hour.
- The minimum and maximum amount of time each customer spends with a clerk.
- The number of clerks available.
- The amount of time (milliseconds) the program pauses between simulation steps.

When you run the simulation, the program shows you the elapsed simulated time, the average and maximum amounts of time customers have had to wait for service, and the percentage of time the clerks are busy.

As you experiment with different values for the input parameters, you will notice several things. First, the multi-headed queue generally gives lower average and maximum waiting times for the customers. It also keeps the clerks slightly busier than the single-headed queue.

Another interesting thing to notice about both kinds of queue is that they have a threshold beyond which customer waiting times increase dramatically. If you specify that customers will require between two and ten minutes each, then they will require six minutes each on the average. If you also specify that 60 customers per hour will enter the queue, then you will need to provide about 6 * 60 = 360 minutes of service per hour. This means you will need about six clerks.

If you run program HEADED_Q with those parameters, you will find that the queues do quite well. The multi-headed queue has an average wait time of only a couple of minutes. If you add another clerk so there are seven clerks, the average and maximum wait times decrease dramatically. On the other hand, if you decrease the number of clerks to five, the average and maximum waiting times show a large increase. The lengths of the average and maximum waits also increase over time.

Table 3.1 shows the average and maximum wait times for the two different kinds of queues. Here the program ran for three simulated hours and assumed 60 customers per hour requiring between two and ten minutes each.

Table 3.1 Waiting Times in Queues

	Multi-Headed Queue		*Single-Headed Queues*	
Clerks	*Avg Time*	*Max Time*	*Avg Time*	*Max Time*
5	11.37	20	12.62	20
6	1.58	5	3.93	13
7	0.11	2	0.54	6

Arrays

Using Visual Basic you can easily build arrays of standard data types like integers and strings, or of user-defined data types. If you initially declare an array without bounds, you can redimension it later using the **ReDim** statement.

```
Dim MyArray1() As Integer    ' Declared without bounds.
ReDim MyArray1(1 To 10)      ' MyArray1 now holds 10 items.
ReDim MyArray1(1 To 20)      ' MyArray1 now holds 20 items.
```

You can also declare and redimension multi-dimensional arrays.

```
Dim MyArray2() As Integer
ReDim MyArray2(10 To 20, 1 To 40)
```

Generally Visual Basic's arrays are pretty useful, but there are a couple of specialized kinds of arrays that are difficult to implement in Visual Basic.

Triangular Arrays

Sometimes you may need values for only half of the entries in a two-dimensional array. For example, if you had a map with 10 cities on it numbered from 0 to 9, you could use an array to make an *adjacency matrix* indicating whether or not there was a highway between any pair of cities. You would set the A(I,J) entry to true if there were a highway between city I and city J and false otherwise.

In this case half of the array would contain duplicated data because A(I,J) = A(J,I). Also A(I,I) would probably not be meaningful since you would not need to take a highway to go from city I to city I. The only entries you would really need in this array are the A(I,J) in the lower left corner where I > J. Alternatively you could use the entries in the upper right corner—either will work. Since these entries form a triangle, this sort of array is called a *triangular array*.

Figure 3.8 shows a triangular array. Entries with meaningful data are indicated by Xs. Entries that are meaningful but duplicated by other entries are left blank. The diagonal entries A(I,I) are indicated by dashes.

For a small array, the space wasted by using a normal two-dimensional array to hold this data is not too important. On the other hand, if you have a lot of cities on your map, the wasted space can be quite large. For N cities there will be N * (N – 1) / 2 duplicated entries and N entries like A(I,I) which may not be meaningful. If your map contained 100 cities, the array would contain 5,050 unused entries.

-				
X	-			
X	X	-		
X	X	X	-	
X	X	X	X	-

Figure 3.8 Triangular array.

You can avoid wasting this space by creating a one-dimensional array B and then packing the meaningful entries of array A into array B. Place the entries in array B one row at a time as shown in Figure 3.9

Notice that the array indexes are numbered starting from 0. This makes the equations that follow a little simpler.

To make this representation of a triangular array easier to use, you can write functions to translate between the indexing schemes used by arrays A and B. The equation for converting from A(I,J) to B(X) is:

```
X = I * (I - 1) / 2 + J      For I > J.
```

For example, if you plug in I = 2 and J = 1, you get X = 2 * (2 − 1) / 2 + 1 = 2. This means that A(2, 1) maps into position 2 in the B array. This agrees with Figure 3.9. Keep in mind that the arrays are numbered starting with zero.

This equation only holds when I > J. The values for the other entries in the array A are not stored in array B since they are redundant or are not meaningful. If you need to compute the value of A(I,J) where I < J, you should instead calculate the value of A(J,I) since that value is stored in array B.

The equations for converting back from B(X) to A(I,J) are:

```
I = Int((1 + Sqr(1 + 8 * X)) / 2)
J = X - I * (I - 1) / 2
```

If you plug X = 4 into these equations, you get I = Int((1 + Sqr(1 + 8 * 4)) / 2) = 3 and J = 4 − 3 * (3 − 1) / 2 = 1. This means entry B(4) maps into position A(3,1). This also agrees with Figure 3.9. Note that these equations always produce values for I and J where I > J.

Notice also that these equations are not easy to compute. They require several multiplications and divisions, and even a square root. If a program must execute these functions very frequently, it will pay a penalty in execution speed.

This is an example of a space versus time tradeoff. By packing a triangular array into a one-dimensional array, you save memory but the program runs a bit more slowly. If you store the data in a two-dimensional array, your program will be faster but the array will be more than half full of wasted space.

Using the equations above you can write Visual Basic subroutines to translate between the coordinates of the two arrays:

Array A:

A(1, 0)			
A(2, 0)	A(2, 1)		
A(3, 0)	A(3, 1)	A(3, 2)	
A(4, 0)	A(4, 1)	A(4, 2)	A(4, 3)

Array B:

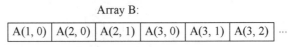

Figure 3.9 Packing a triangular array.

```
Sub AtoB (ByVal I As Integer, ByVal J As Integer, X As Integer)
Dim tmp As Integer

    If I = J Then        ' This entry is not meaningful.
        X = -1
        Exit Sub
    ElseIf I < J Then    ' Switch I and J so I > J.
        tmp = I
        I = J
        J = tmp
    End If
    X = I * (I - 1) / 2 + J
End Sub


Sub BtoA (ByVal X As Integer, I As Integer, J As Integer)
    I = Int((1 + Sqr(1 + 8 * X)) / 2)
    J = X - I * (I - 1) / 2
End Sub
```

Example program TRIANG uses these subroutines to pack a triangular array into a one-dimensional array. If you push the "A to B" button, the program puts labels in all of the entries in array A and then copies them into the corresponding entries in array B. Each label is named after the array entry it occupies so it is easy to tell how they are translated. For example, the program labels the A(2, 1) entry "A(2, 1)."

If you push the "B to A" button, the program puts labels in all of the entries in array B and then copies the labels into the corresponding entries in array A. Again the program names each label after the array entry it occupies so B(3), for example, is labeled "B(3)." Notice that more than half of the A array entries remain blank. This is because array B only stores the values for array entries A(I,J) where I > J.

Occasionally you might want to build a triangular array that includes the diagonal entries A(I,I). In this case you only need to make three changes to the index translation routines.

The translation subroutine AtoB should no longer reject cases where I = J. It should also add one to I before calculating the index in array B.

```
Sub AtoB (ByVal I As Integer, ByVal J As Integer, X As Integer)
Dim tmp As Integer

    If I < J Then ' Switch I and J so I > J.
        tmp = I
        I = J
        J = tmp
    End If
    I = I + 1
    X = I * (I - 1) / 2 + J
End Sub
```

The translation subroutine BtoA should subtract one from I just before returning.

```
Sub BtoA (ByVal X As Integer, I As Integer, J As Integer)
    I = Int((1 + Sqr(1 + 8 * X)) / 2)
    J = X - I * (I - 1) / 2
    I = I - 1
End Sub
```

Example program TRIANG2 is identical to program TRIANG except it uses these new functions to manipulate the diagonal entries in array A.

Irregular Arrays

At times you may want an array that has an irregular size and shape. You might want a two-dimensional array where the first row contains six items, the second contains three, the third contains four, and so on. One example where this would be useful is in storing a number of polygons each of which consists of a different number of points. The array should look like the picture shown in Figure 3.10.

Unfortunately in Visual Basic arrays cannot have ragged edges like this. You could create an array large enough to hold the biggest row and then put the data in this array, but that might leave many entries in the array unused. In the example shown in Figure 3.10 you would have to declare the array as in **Dim Polygons(1 To 3, 1 To 6)** and four entries would remain unused.

There are several other ways you can store irregular arrays.

Forward Star

One way you can avoid wasting extra space is by packing the data into a one-dimensional array B in a fashion similar to the way you can pack triangular arrays into one-dimensional arrays. When you are packing an irregular array, however, there are no easy formulas for computing where each row begins in array B. To handle this problem, you can create another array A that holds the offsets of each row in array B.

To make it easier to locate the points in array B that correspond to each polygon, you can add an extra sentinel entry at the end of the array A that points *just beyond* the last data item in array B. Then the points that make up polygon I would be in array B at positions A(I) through A(I + 1) − 1. To put this another way, a program could list the points that make up polygon I using the following code:

```
For J = A(I) To A(I + 1) - 1
    ' List entry B(J)
Next J
```

The sentinel tells you where the points for the last polygon end. This allows you to treat the last polygon just like all the others.

This method is called *forward star.* Figure 3.11 shows the forward star representation of the irregular array shown in Figure 3.10. In this figure the sentinel has been shaded so it is easy to see.

You can easily generalize this method to form irregular arrays of higher dimensions. You might use a three-dimensional forward star data structure to store a set of pic-

Polygon 1	(2, 5)	(3, 6)	(4, 6)	(5, 5)	(4, 4)	(4, 5)
Polygon 2	(1, 1)	(4, 1)	(2, 3)			
Polygon 3	(2, 2)	(4, 3)	(5, 4)	(1, 4)		

Figure 3.10 Irregular array.

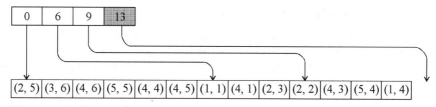

Figure 3.11 Forward star.

tures, each consisting of an arbitrary number of polygons, each of which in turn consisted of many points.

Figure 3.12 shows a schematic picture of a three-dimensional forward star data structure. In the figure the two sentinels have been shaded so they are easy to see. Both of the sentinels point one position beyond the end of the real data in the following array. Since the second sentinel occupies the position just beyond the end of the real data in the second array, the first sentinel points to the second sentinel.

These forward star representations require very little unused storage. The only "wasted" space is contained in the entries for the sentinels.

Listing the points that make up a polygon is fast and easy using a forward star data structure. Updating arrays in a forward star format is quite difficult, however. Suppose you needed to add a new point to the first polygon in Figure 3.11. First you would need to shift all of the entries to the right of the new point in array B one position to the right to make room for the new entry. Then you would need to add one to all of the entries that came after the first entry in array A to account for the new point. Finally you would insert the new item. Similar problems occur if you need to remove a point from the first polygon.

Figure 3.13 shows the forward star representation from Figure 3.11 after one point has been added to the first polygon. The entries that were updated have been shaded so they are easy to see. As you can tell, almost every item in both arrays has been updated.

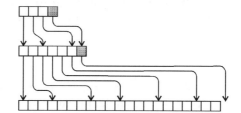

Figure 3.12 Three-dimensional forward star.

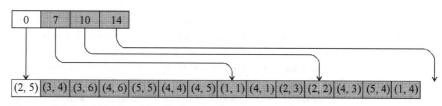

Figure 3.13 Adding a point in forward star.

Irregular Linked Lists

Another method for creating irregular arrays is to use linked lists. Each cell contains the index of the next cell at its level of the hierarchy, plus the index of the first cell in the list of cells below it in the hierarchy. A polygon cell, for example, would contain the index of the next polygon in the list of polygons, and the index of the first point cell that made up that polygon.

The code below declares the data types you would need to build a linked list of pictures, each containing a linked list of polygons. Each polygon contains a linked list of points.

```
Type PictureCell
    NextPicture As Integer
    FirstPolygon As Integer
End Type

Type PolygonCell
    NextPolygon As Integer
    FirstPoint As Integer
End Type

Type PointCell
    NextPoint As Integer
    X As Single
    Y As Single
End Type

Dim Pictures (1 To NumPictures) As PictureCell
Dim Polygons (1 To NumPolygons) As PolygonCell
Dim Points (1 To NumPoints) As PointCell
```

Using these linked techniques it is easy to add and remove pictures, polygons, or points from any position in the data structure.

Example program POLY, discussed in Chapter 2 (see page 38), uses an approach similar to this one. This program allows you to create any number of drawing forms. Within each of these you can draw any number of polygons, each consisting of many points.

Sparse Arrays

Many applications call for large arrays that contain few non-zero elements. A connectivity matrix for an airline, for example, might contain a 1 in position A(I, J) if there is a flight between city I and city J. Many airlines service hundreds of cities, but the number of flights they actually run is nowhere near the N^2 possible combinations. Figure 3.14 shows a small airline flight map, in which the airline has flights between only 11 of the 100 possible pairs of cities.

You could build the connectivity matrix for this example in a 10 by 10 array, but the array would contain mostly unused entries. You can avoid wasting this space by using pointers to build a sparse array. Each cell contains pointers to the next item in its row and column in the array. This allows the program to locate any item within the array, and to traverse the cells along any row or any column. Depending on the application, you might also find reverse pointers convenient. Figure 3.15 shows the sparse connectivity matrix that corresponds to the flight map shown in Figure 3.14.

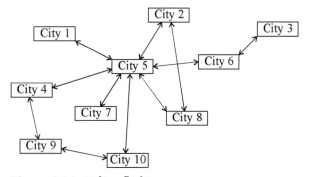

Figure 3.14 Airline flight map.

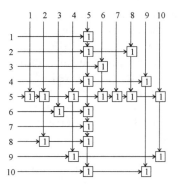

Figure 3.15 Sparse connectivity matrix.

To build a sparse array in Visual Basic, declare a user-defined structure to hold the non-blank array entries. In this case each cell represents an airline connection between two cities. To represent the connection, each cell contains the indexes of the cities it connects. These indexes essentially give the row and column numbers for the cell. If the cell represents a connection between cities I and J, it represents the A(I,J) position in the connectivity matrix A.

Each cell also contains pointers to the next cell in its row and column.

```
Type CityCell
    FromCity As Integer      ' Essentially the cell's row.
    ToCity As Integer        ' Essentially the cell's column.
    NextInRow As Integer
    NextInCol As Integer
End Type
```

The rows and columns in this array are basically linked lists. As is often the case with linked lists, it is easier to deal with the lists if they have sentinels. You can create row and column head arrays that contain the indexes of the sentinels. For example, RowHead(I) would contain the index of the sentinel for row I. To traverse row I in the array, you could use code like this:

```
Sub PrintRow (I As Integer)
Dim cell As Integer
```

```
        cell = RowHead (I)                    ' The sentinel.
        cell = TheCells (cell) .NextInRow     ' The first real entry.
        Do While cell <> END_OF_LIST
            Print Format$ (TheCells (cell) .FromCity) & " -> " & _
Format$ (TheCells(cell)).ToCity)
            cell = TheCells(cell).NextInRow
        Loop
End Sub
```

Since normal array indexing like A(I,J) will not work on this sort of structure, it is helpful to write subroutines that set and get the values of entries in the array. If the array represents a sparse matrix, it might also be handy to have subroutines to add, subtract, multiply, and perform other matrix operations on the array.

In these routines, a special constant NO_VALUE represents an empty array entry. The routine that gets array entries should return NO_VALUE when it is called upon to access the value of an entry that is not contained in the array.

Similarly, the routine that sets values should remove any entry from the array if it is being assigned the value NO_VALUE. Since entries that are not present in the array have this value by default, you will save space by removing the entry.

The particular value that NO_VALUE should have depends on the nature of your application. For an airline connectivity matrix, you might want empty entries to have the value false. Then you could set the A(I,J) value to true if there is a connection between cities I and J. If the A(I,J) entry is not in the array, the value getting routine will return false indicating that there is no connection between cities I and J.

If your array represents some other kind of sparse matrix where 0, the Visual Basic value for false, might be a valid entry, you must set NO_VALUE to something else like −32,768.

Function GetValue returns the value of the sparse array in a given row and column. The function starts at the first cell in the row and moves through the row's linked list of cells. If it finds a cell with column value equal to the target column, the function has found the required cell. Since the cells are kept in order within the row list, the subroutine can stop looking if it ever finds a cell with column value larger than target column. If it ever finds such a cell, the routine knows that it has passed the place where the cell should have been so it can stop searching.

Subroutine SetValue assigns a new value to a cell in the array. First it checks to see if the new value equals NO_VALUE. If it does, the subroutine deletes the entry from the array. Otherwise SetValue searches through the target row to find the location in the row where the new entry belongs. If the array already contains a cell for that entry, the subroutine updates the value of the cell. Otherwise it creates a new cell and adds it to the row list. It then adds the new cell at the correct position in the correct column's list of cells.

```
Const NO_VALUE = 0

Global RowHead() As Integer   ' Row headers.
Global ColHead() As Integer   ' Column headers.
Global NumRows As Integer     ' # rows allocated.
Global NumCols As Integer     ' # columns allocated.

Type Entry
    Row As Integer
    Col As Integer
```

```
        NextInRow As Integer
        NextInCol As Integer

    Data As Variant
End Type

Function GetValue (r As Integer, c As Integer) As Variant
Dim cell As Integer

    GetValue = NO_VALUE     ' Assume we will not find it.
    cell = TheCells(RowHead(r)).NextInRow     ' Skip sentinel
    Do
        If cell = END_OF_LIST Then Exit Function  ' Not found
        If TheCells(cell).Col = c Then Exit Do
        cell = TheCells(cell).NextInRow
    Loop
    GetValue = TheCells(cell).Data
End Function

Sub SetValue (r As Integer, c As Integer, value As Variant)
Dim i As Integer
Dim found_it As Integer
Dim cell As Integer
Dim nxt As Integer
Dim new_cell As Integer

    ' If value = NO_VALUE, remove the entry from the array.
    If value = NO_VALUE Then
        RemoveEntry r, c
        Exit Sub
    End If

    ' Make more rows if needed
    If r > NumRows Then
        ReDim Preserve RowHead(1 To r)
        ' Initialize a sentinel for each new row
        For i = NumRows + 1 To r
            RowHead(i) = NewCell()
            TheCells(RowHead(i)).NextInRow = END_OF_LIST
        Next i
        NumRows = r
    End If

    ' Make more columns if needed
    If c > NumCols Then
        ReDim Preserve ColHead(1 To c)
        ' Initialize a sentinel for each new row
        For i = NumCols + 1 To c
            ColHead(i) = NewCell()
            TheCells(ColHead(i)).NextInCol = END_OF_LIST
        Next i
        NumCols = c
    End If

    ' Try to locate the cell in question.
    cell = RowHead(r)
    nxt = TheCells(cell).NextInRow
    Do
```

```
            If nxt = END_OF_LIST Then Exit Do
            If TheCells(nxt).Col >= c Then Exit Do
            cell = nxt
            nxt = TheCells(cell).NextInRow
        Loop

        ' If we did not find the entry, make a new cell.
        If nxt = END_OF_LIST Then
            found_it = False
        Else
            found_it = (TheCells(nxt).Col = c)
        End If
        If Not found_it Then
            new_cell = NewCell()

            ' Place the cell in the row.
            TheCells(new_cell).NextInRow = nxt
            TheCells(cell).NextInRow = new_cell

            ' Place the cell in the column.
            cell = ColHead(c)
            nxt = TheCells(cell).NextInCol
            Do
                If nxt = END_OF_LIST Then Exit Do
                If TheCells(nxt).Col >= c Then Exit Do
                cell = nxt
                nxt = TheCells(cell).NextInRow
            Loop
            TheCells(new_cell).NextInCol = nxt
            TheCells(cell).NextInCol = new_cell

            TheCells(new_cell).Row = r
            TheCells(new_cell).Col = c

            ' We will put the value in the nxt cell.
            nxt = new_cell
        End If

    ' Set the value
    TheCells(nxt).Data = value
End Sub
```

Example program SPARSE implements a sparse array. Using the program you can set and fetch array entries. The value of NO_VALUE is zero for this program so if you set the value of an entry to zero, the program will remove the entry from the array.

Very Sparse Arrays

Some arrays contain so few non-zero entries that many rows and columns are completely empty. In that case it is better to store row and column headers in linked lists rather than arrays so the program can omit the empty rows and columns completely. The row and column headers point to the linked lists of row and column elements. Figure 3.16 shows a 100 by 100 array that contains only seven non-empty entries.

Modifying the previous code to handle this sort of array is fairly straightforward. Most of the code remains the same and you can use the same cell structure for the array entries.

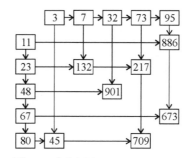

Figure 3.16 Very sparse array.

The only difference is that, instead of using arrays to store the tops of the row and column lists, you store the row and column headers in their own linked lists. Each row and column header cell holds the number of the row or column it represents, the index of the sentinel that starts the row or column, and the index of the next row or column header in the header list.

```
Type Header
    Number As Integer        ' The number of the row or column.
    Sentinel As Integer      ' The sentinel for the row or column.
    NextHeader As Integer    ' The next row or column.
End Type
```

Now when you need to access row I, for example, you first look through the linked list of row headers until you find row I. Then you can proceed down row I as before.

```
Sub PrintRow (I As Integer)
Dim row As Integer
Dim cell As Integer

    ' Find the correct row header.
    row = TopRow          ' The top of the list of row headers.
    Do While row <> END_OF_LIST
        If Headers(row).Number >= I Then Exit Do
        row = TheHeaders(row)
    Loop
    If row = END_OF_LIST Then Exit Sub    ' No such row.
    If Headers(row) <> I Then Exit Sub    ' No such row.
    ' Display the cells in the row.
    cell = Headers(row).Sentinel          ' The sentinel.
    cell = TheCells(cell).NextInRow       ' The first real entry.
    Do While cell <> END_OF_LIST
        Print Format$(TheCells(cell).FromCity) & " -> " & _
Format$(TheCells(cell).ToCity)
        cell = TheCells(cell).NextInRow
    Loop
End Sub
```

C H A P T E R

Recursion

Overview

Recursion is a powerful programming technique that is used in many algorithms. It allows you to break a problem into smaller and smaller pieces until the pieces are small enough to handle easily.

After you have gained some experience with recursion, you will find it all around you. In fact, many programmers who have recently mastered recursion get carried away and begin applying it in situations where it is not really necessary and is sometimes harmful.

The first sections of this chapter discuss factorials, Fibonacci numbers, and greatest common divisors. These provide good examples of bad uses of recursion since non-recursive versions of these programs are much more efficient. These examples are interesting and easy to understand, however, so they are worth discussing.

Next, the chapter examines some examples where recursion is more appropriate. The Hilbert and Sierpinski curves use recursion properly and efficiently.

The next sections explain why it is better to implement factorials, Fibonacci numbers, and greatest common divisors without recursion. These sections discuss the warning signs that can tell you when you should avoid recursion, and they show ways to eliminate recursion from your programs when necessary.

What Is Recursion?

Recursion occurs when a function or subroutine calls itself. A recursive routine can call itself *directly* like this:

```
Function Factorial (num As Long) As Long
    Factorial = num * Factorial(num - 1)
End Function
```

A recursive routine can also call itself *indirectly* by calling a second subroutine which later calls the first:

```
Sub Ping (num As Integer)
    Pong(num - 1)
End Sub

Sub Pong (num As Integer)
    Ping(num / 2)
End Sub
```

Recursion is useful for solving problems that naturally break into smaller instances of the same problem. You can think of the tree shown on the left in Figure 4.1, for example, as a "trunk" with two smaller trees attached. This leads to a naturally recursive procedure for drawing trees:

```
Sub DrawTree ()
    Draw a "trunk"
    Draw a smaller tree rotated -45 degrees
    Draw a smaller tree rotated 45 degrees
End Sub
```

While it can make many problems easier to understand, recursion is not a particularly intuitive way for humans to think. We tend to break tasks into small sub-tasks that can be performed one at a time in their proper order until they are all finished. To paint a fence, for instance, you might think in terms of starting at the left side of the fence and working your way to the right until you were done. You would probably not think in terms of recursively painting the left half of the fence and then recursively painting the right half.

To think recursively you need to think in terms of breaking a task into large sub-tasks, which you can then break into smaller sub-tasks, etc. At some point the sub-tasks become small enough to deal with directly. When the smallest sub-tasks are complete, the larger tasks they make up are complete. When those larger tasks are complete, the still larger tasks they make up are also complete, and so on until all of the sub-tasks are done and the original task is finished.

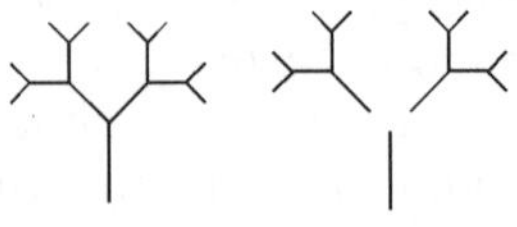

Figure 4.1 A tree made of smaller trees.

While thinking recursively is not natural for humans, nature itself is full of recursion. Trees (the kind that need water and sunlight) create a trunk, which sends out branches, which send out their own branches, which send out still more branches, until the smallest branches create leaves. Each leaf has a large vein running down the center, which sends out side veins, which send out smaller side veins, etc. The human body also contains veins which branch and branch again. The lungs, nerves, and all sorts of other biological transport systems have a recursive structure.

Recursion also arises frequently in mathematics and computer science. A common method for program design is *successive refinement.* Here you start with a large problem, initially the entire application you are trying to build. You then break the problem into smaller pieces which are typically called subsystems. Next you break the subsystems into smaller pieces. You continue breaking the pieces into smaller pieces until they reach a size that you can handle in a single subroutine. Now you write the subroutines and use them to assemble the subsystems and the complete application. This approach is naturally recursive and leads to a design methodology that can be described like this:

```
Sub DesignSolution(prob As Problem)
Dim I As Integer

    If prob is small then
        Solve prob
    Else
        Break prob into pieces
        For I = 1 To NumberOfPieces
            DesignSolution subproblem(I)
        Next I
    End If
End Sub
```

Recursive Factorial Algorithm

The factorial of a number N is written N! (pronounced "N factorial"). By convention the value of 0! is defined to be 1. Other values of the factorial are defined by:

$$N! = N*(N - 1)*(N - 2)*...*2*1$$

As was mentioned in the discussion of complexity in Chapter 1, this function grows extremely quickly. Table 4.1 shows the first ten values of the factorial function.

You can also define the factorial function recursively.

```
0! = 1
N! = N*(N - 1)! for N > 0.
```

This definition translates easily into a recursive function.

```
Function Factorial (num As Integer) As Integer
    If num <= 0 Then
        Factorial = 1
    Else
        Factorial = num * Factorial(num - 1)
    End If
End Function
```

Table 4.1 Values of the
Factorial Function

N	N!
1	1
2	2
3	6
4	24
5	120
6	720
7	5,040
8	40,320
9	362,880
10	3,628,800

This function first checks to see if the number is less than or equal to zero. The factorial function is not defined if the number is less than zero, but the function safeguards itself by checking for this condition anyway. If the function checked only to see if the number was equal to zero, it would enter an infinite recursion if the number was negative.

If the input value is less than or equal to zero, the function returns the value one. Otherwise the value of the function is the number times the factorial of the number minus one.

Two things ensure that this recursive function eventually stops. First, on each subsequent call, the value of the parameter num is smaller. Second, the value of num is bounded below by zero. When the value of num reaches zero, the function ends the recursion.

The condition, like num <= 0, which causes a recursion to end is called the *base case* or the *stopping case* of the recursion. If a recursive function has no base case, it will recursively call itself forever, or at least until it uses up all of your computer's resources and the program crashes.

Visual Basic has a chunk of memory, called the *stack*, which it uses whenever your program makes a function or subroutine call. Each time your program calls a routine, Visual Basic saves information like local variables in the stack memory. If a recursive function calls itself too many times, it will use up all of the stack space and your program will crash with an "Out of stack space" error.

The number of times a function can call itself before it uses up all of the stack space depends on how much data the program has placed on the stack. In one test a program was able to recurse 452 times before it used up all of the stack space. When the recursive function was modified to allocate ten local integer variables each time it was called, the program could only recurse 271 times before exhausting the stack.

Run Time Analysis

The factorial function takes only a single argument: the number for which it is to compute the factorial. Complexity analysis usually examines run time as a function of the *size* of the problem or the *number of inputs*. Since there is only one input in this case, that calculation could be a little strange.

For this reason algorithms that take a single parameter are usually evaluated in terms of the *number of bits required to store the input value* rather than in terms of the number of inputs. In some sense this is the size of the input since it takes that many bits to store the input value. This is not a very intuitive way to think about the problem, however. Also, while in theory a computer could store the input N in $\log_2(N)$ bits, in reality it probably stores N in some fixed number of bits. For example, if the number is an integer, the computer will store it in 16 bits.

For these reasons this chapter will analyze this sort of algorithm in terms of the input's *value* rather than its *size*. If you want to rewrite the results in terms of the size of the input, you can do so using the fact that $N = 2^M$ where M is the number of bits needed to store N. For instance, if the run time of an algorithm is $O(N^2)$ in terms of the input value N, it is $O((2^M)^2) = O(2^{2*M}) = O((2^2)^M) = O(4^M)$ in terms of the input size M.

For this particular algorithm, the factorial function is called for N, N – 1, N – 2, and so on until the input parameter reaches zero and the recursion ends. If the function is initially called with input N, the function is called a total of N + 1 times. This means the run time is O(N). In terms of the size of the input M, this would be $O(2^M)$.

O(N) functions grow pretty slowly so you might expect fairly good performance from this algorithm. In fact, that is the case. The function runs into trouble only when it exhausts the stack by executing too many recursions, or when the value of N! becomes too large to fit in an integer and your program halts with an "Overflow" error.

Since N! grows very quickly, overflow will happen first unless you are using the stack heavily for other things. Using integer data types, overflow will occur for 8! since 8! = 40,320 which is larger than the largest integer 32,767. To allow the program to compute approximate values for larger numbers, you can modify the function so it uses doubles instead of integers. Then the largest number for which the algorithm can compute N! before causing overflow is 170! which is roughly 7.257E+306.

Example program FACTO demonstrates the recursive factorial function. Enter a number and press the Go button. The program will then recursively compute the factorial of the number you entered.

Recursive Greatest Common Divisor

The *greatest common divisor* or *GCD* of two numbers is the largest integer that divides the two numbers evenly. The GCD of 12 and 9, for example, is 3 since 3 is the largest integer that divides both 12 and 9 with no remainder. Two numbers are *relatively prime* if 1 is their greatest common divisor.

The 18th century mathematician Euler discovered the interesting fact that:

```
If A divides B evenly, GCD(A,B)=A.
Otherwise GCD(A,B)=GCD(B Mod A,A).
```

You can use this fact to compute GCDs quickly. For example:

```
GCD(9,12)    =GCD(12 Mod 9,9)
             =GCD(3,9)
             =3
```

Notice that at each step the numbers being compared get smaller due to the fact that 1 <= B ModA < A if A does not divide B evenly. If the arguments continue to decrease, the argument A will eventually reach the value 1. Since 1 evenly divides any number B, the recursion must stop.

The recursion will stop before it gets to the point where A = 1 if the original numbers are not relatively prime. In that case the recursion will end when A evenly divides B. One way or another, the recursion must eventually stop.

Euler's discovery leads naturally to a simple recursive algorithm for computing GCDs.

```
Function GCD (A As Integer, B As Integer) As Integer
    If B Mod A = 0 Then       ' Does A divide B evenly?
        GCD = A               ' Yes. We're done.
    Else
        GCD = GCD(B Mod A, A) ' No.
    End If
End Function
```

It is interesting to see what this algorithm does if A > B. In this case, B Mod A will equal B. This is not 0 so the function will then compute GCD(B Mod A, A). Since B Mod A = B, this is the same as GCD(B, A). This means that, if A > B in the original call to GCD, the first thing the function does is switch the parameters around and call itself with the smaller parameter first. Since B Mod A is always less than A, the first argument will be smaller than the second during all subsequent calls to the GCD function.

Run Time Analysis

To analyze the run time of this algorithm, you must determine how quickly A decreases. Since the function must stop if A reaches the value 1, the rate at which A decreases will give an upper bound on how long the algorithm can run. It turns out that every second time the function GCD is called, the parameter A decreases by at least a factor of 1 / 2.

First, assume that A is less than B. This is true after the first call to GCD.

If B Mod A <= A / 2, the next call to GCD will have the first parameter reduced by at least a factor of 1 / 2 which is all you need to show.

Next suppose this is not the case. Suppose B Mod A > A / 2. The first recursive call to GCD will look like this:

```
GCD(B Mod A, A)
```

If you plug the values B Mod A and A into the function in place of A and B, you can see that the second recursive call will look like this:

```
GCD(A Mod (B Mod A), B Mod A)
```

But you have assumed that B Mod A > A / 2. This means that B Mod A will divide into A exactly once leaving a remainder of A – (B Mod A). Since B Mod A is greater than A / 2, the value A – (B Mod A) must be less than A / 2. This shows that the first parameter in the second recursive call to GCD is smaller than A / 2, which is what you were trying to show.

These results mean that the parameter A is reduced by a factor of at least 1 / 2 every two times the GCD function is called.

Now suppose N is the original value of the parameter A. After two calls to GCD, the value of parameter A will have been reduced to at most N / 2. After four calls the value will be no more than (N / 2) / 2 = N / 4. After six calls the value will be at most (N / 4) / 2 = N / 8.

In general, after 2 * K calls to GCD the value of parameter A will be at most $N / 2^K$. Since the algorithm must stop when the value of the parameter A reaches 1, this algorithm can only continue until $N / 2^K = 1$. This happens when $N = 2^K$ or when $K = \log_2(N)$. Since the algorithm is running for 2 * K steps, this means the algorithm must stop after at most $2 * \log_2(N)$ steps. Ignoring the constant multiplier, this means that the algorithm runs in O(log(N)) time.

This algorithm is typical of many algorithms that run in O(log(N)) time. Each time it executes a certain fixed number of steps, it halves the problem size. More generally, if an algorithm decreases the problem size by a factor of at least 1 / D after every S steps, the problem will require $S * \log_D(N)$ steps. In the GCD example, the program decreases the problem size by a factor of 1 / 2 every 2 steps so the run time is $2 * \log_2(N)$ which agrees with the previous result.

Recall from Chapter 1 that you can ignore the constant multiplier and the log base in Big O notation. Then any algorithm that runs in $S * \log_D(N)$ time is an O(log(N)) algorithm, no matter what the values of S and D are. This does not necessarily mean you can completely ignore these constants when actually implementing an algorithm. An algorithm that reduces the problem size by a factor of 1 / 10 every time it executes a step will probably be faster than an algorithm that reduces the problem size by a factor of 1 / 2 after every 5 steps. Still, they both will have run times O(log(N)).

O(log(N)) algorithms are generally very fast and the GCD algorithm is no exception. When calculating the GCD of 1,736,751,235 and 2,135,723,523 (which is 71), for example, the GCD function is called only 17 times. In fact, this algorithm can compute values for the largest possible long data type value 2,147,483,647 practically instantly. The Visual Basic **Mod** function cannot handle values larger than this, so that is the practical limit to this algorithm.

Example program GCD uses this algorithm to recursively compute greatest common divisors. Enter values for A and B and press the Go button, and the program will compute the GCD of the two numbers.

Recursive Fibonacci Numbers

You can define Fibonacci numbers recursively by the equations:

```
Fib(0) = 0
Fib(1) = 1
Fib(N) = Fib(N - 1) + Fib(N - 2)          for N > 1.
```

The third equation recursively uses the Fib function twice, once with input N – 1 and once with input N – 2. This makes it necessary to have two base cases for the recursion: Fib(0) = 1 and Fib(1) = 1. If you had only one, the recursion might be able to slip past the base case and the function would call itself recursively forever. If you knew only that Fib(0) = 0, for example, the computation of Fib(2) would look like this:

```
Fib(2) = Fib(1) + Fib(0)
       = [Fib(0) + Fib(-1)] + 0
       = 0 + [Fib(-2) + Fib(-3)]
       = [Fib(-3) + Fib(-4)] + [Fib(-4) + Fib(-5)]
       Etc.
```

You easily can translate this definition of Fibonacci numbers into a recursive function.

```
Function Fib (num As Integer) As Integer
    If num <= 1 Then
        Fib = num
    Else
        Fib = Fib(num - 1) + Fib(num - 2)
    End If
End Function
```

Run Time Analysis

The analysis of this algorithm is a little tricky. First, consider the number of times the algorithm reaches one of the base cases num <= 1. Let G(N) be the number of times the algorithm reaches a base case for input N. When N is zero or one, the function reaches the base case once and requires no recursion.

If N is greater than one, the function recursively computes Fib(N − 1) and Fib(N − 2) and then is done. In the initial call to the function, the base case is not reached—it is only reached by other, recursive calls to the function. This means that the total number of times the base case is reached for input N is the number of times it is reached for input N − 1 plus the number of times it is reached for input N − 2. You can write these three facts as:

```
G(0) = 1
G(1) = 1
G(N) = G(N - 1) + G(N - 2)        for N > 1.
```

This recursive definition is very similar to the definition of the Fibonacci numbers. Table 4.2 shows some values for G(N) and Fib(N). From the numbers you can see that G(N) = Fib(N + 1).

Next consider the number of times the algorithm reaches the recursive step. When N is zero or one, the function does not reach this step. When N is greater than one, the function reaches this step once and then recursively computes Fib(N − 1) and Fib(N − 2). Let H(N) be the number of times the algorithm reaches the recursive step for input N. Then H(N) = 1 + H(N − 1) + H(N − 2). The defining equations for H(N) are:

```
H(0) = 0
H(1) = 0
H(N) = 1 + H(N - 1) + H(N - 2)        for N > 1.
```

Table 4.3 shows some values for Fib(N) and H(N). It is easy to see from these numbers that H(N) = Fib(N + 1) − 1.

Now you can combine the results for G(N) and H(N) to see that the total run time for the algorithm is:

Table 4.2 Values of Fibonacci Numbers and G(N)

N	0	1	2	3	4	5	6	7	8
Fib(N)	0	1	1	2	3	5	8	13	21
G(N)	1	1	2	3	5	8	13	21	34

Table 4.3 Values of Fibonacci Numbers and H(N)

N	0	1	2	3	4	5	6	7	8
Fib(N)	0	1	1	2	3	5	8	13	21
H(N)	0	0	1	2	4	7	12	20	33

```
Run time    = G(N) + H(N)
            = Fib(N + 1) + Fib(N + 1) - 1
            = 2 * Fib(N + 1) - 1
```

Since Fib(N + 1) >= Fib(N) for all values of N, you know that:

```
Run time >= 2 * Fib(N) - 1
```

In Big O notation this simplifies to O(Fib(N)). It is interesting that this function is not only recursive, but that it also is used to compute its own run time!

To understand the speed at which the Fibonacci function grows compared to other functions, it helps to know that $Fib(M) > \emptyset^{M-2}$ for a certain constant $\emptyset$ which is around 1.6. This means that the run time is at least as big as the exponential function $O(\emptyset^M)$. Like other exponential functions, it will grow more quickly than polynomial functions and less quickly than factorial functions.

Since the run time function grows very quickly, this algorithm is quite slow for large inputs. In fact, this algorithm is so slow that it is not practical to compute values of Fib(N) for N larger than around 30. Table 4.4 shows the run times for this algorithm with different inputs on a 50 megahertz 486-based PC.

Example program FIBO uses this recursive algorithm to calculate Fibonacci numbers. Enter an integer and press the Go button and the program will recursively compute the corresponding Fibonacci number. Be sure to start with small numbers until you know how long your computer will take.

Recursive Hilbert Curves

Hilbert curves are one type of *self-similar* curve that is naturally defined recursively. Figure 4.2 shows Hilbert curves where the maximum depths of recursion are 1, 2, and 3.

You create a Hilbert curve, or any other self-similar curve, by breaking up a large curve into smaller pieces and then using the curve itself, properly resized and rotated, to build those pieces. You may then break those pieces into smaller pieces, and so on until the process reaches the desired depth of recursion. The depth of the curve is defined to be the greatest depth of recursion the drawing routine reaches.

To control the recursion, you pass a depth parameter to each call to the Hilbert routine. When that routine recursively calls itself to draw the pieces of its curve, it decreases

Table 4.4 Fibonacci Program Run Times

M	10	15	20	25	30
Fib(M)	55	610	6,765	75,025	832,040
Time (secs)	0.01	0.08	0.88	9.31	101.79

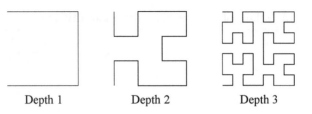

Depth 1   Depth 2   Depth 3

Figure 4.2 Hilbert curves.

the depth parameter by 1. At some point a Hilbert routine is called with depth 1. That subroutine draws the simple depth 1 curve shown in Figure 4.2 and does not call itself recursively. This is the base case for the recursion.

For example, the Hilbert curve of depth 2 is made up of four Hilbert curves of depth 1, plus three lines connecting them. Similarly, a Hilbert curve of depth 3 is made up of four Hilbert curves of depth 2, each made up of four Hilbert curves of depth 1. Figure 4.3 shows Hilbert curves of depths 2 and 3. The smaller curves that make them up are drawn using bold lines so they are easy to see.

If you use the Visual Basic **Line** method for drawing lines, you might write instructions for drawing a Hilbert curve of depth 1 like this:

```
Line -Step (Length, 0)
Line -Step (0, Length)
Line -Step (-Length, 0)
```

This code assumes that the current drawing position begins at the upper left corner of the drawing area and that Length is the desired length for each line segment.

You can sketch the method for drawing a Hilbert curve of greater depth as:

```
Hilbert(Depth)
    If Depth = 1 Then
        Draw a depth 1 Hilbert curve
    Else
        Draw and connect the four curves Hilbert(Depth - 1)
    End If
End
```

You must complicate this method slightly so the Hilbert routine can tell which direction it is heading and whether it is drawing clockwise or counter-clockwise. It needs to know this so it can tell which kinds of Hilbert curves to use when breaking a curve into smaller pieces.

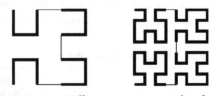

Figure 4.3 Hilbert curves made from smaller Hilbert curves.

You can give the routine this information by adding parameters Dx and Dy to indicate the direction of the first line the curve should draw. If the curve is a depth 1 Hilbert curve, then the routine should draw the first line in the curve as in **Line –Step(Dx, Dy).** If the curve has greater depth, the routine should connect the first two smaller subcurves that make up this curve using **Line –Step(Dx, Dy).** In either case, the routine can use Dx and Dy to figure out in what direction it should draw the other lines making up the curve.

In Visual Basic the code for drawing Hilbert curves is surprisingly short but a little tricky. You may need to step through the routine several times for curves of depth 1 and 2 to see exactly how Dx and Dy change to produce the different parts of the curve.

```
Sub Hilbert (depth As Integer, Dx As Single, Dy As Single)
    If depth > 1 Then Hilbert depth - 1, Dy, Dx
    HilbertPicture.Line -Step(Dx, Dy)
    If depth > 1 Then Hilbert depth - 1, Dx, Dy
    HilbertPicture.Line -Step(Dy, Dx)
    If depth > 1 Then Hilbert depth - 1, Dx, Dy
    HilbertPicture.Line -Step(-Dx, -Dy)
    If depth > 1 Then Hilbert depth - 1, -Dy, -Dx
End Sub
```

Run Time Analysis

To analyze this routine's run time, you need to determine how many times the Hilbert routine calls itself. Each time the Hilbert routine recurses, it calls itself four times. If $T(N)$ is the number of times the Hilbert routine is executed when it is called for depth N, then:

```
T(1) = 1
T(N) = 1 + 4 * T(N - 1)        for N > 1
```

If you expand the definition of $T(N)$ a bit you get:

```
T(N) = 1 + 4 * T(N - 1)
     = 1 + 4 * (1 + 4 * T(N - 2))
     = 1 + 4 + 16 * T(N - 2)
     = 1 + 4 + 16 * (1 + 4 * T(N - 3))
     = 1 + 4 + 16 + 64 * T(N - 3)
     = ...
     = 4^0 + 4^1 + 4^2 + 4^3 + ... + 4^K * T(N - K)
```

If you continue expanding this equation until you reach the base case $T(1) = 1$, you get:

```
T(N)   = 4^0 + 4^1 + 4^2 + 4^3 + ... + 4^(N - 1)
```

Now you can use the following mathematical formula to simplify this equation.

```
X^0 + X^1 + X^2 + X^3 + ... + X^M = (X^(M + 1) - 1) / (X - 1)
```

This allows you to simplify the run time equation to:

```
T(N) = (4^((N - 1) + 1) - 1) / (4 - 1)
     = (4^N - 1) / 3
```

Ignoring the constants in this equation, the Hilbert curve algorithm runs in time $O(4^N)$. Table 4.5 shows the first several values for the run time function. If you look closely at the numbers, you will see that they agree with the recursive definition:

```
T(1) = 1
T(N) = 1 + 4 * T(N - 1)        for N > 1.
```

This algorithm is typical of many algorithms that run in $O(C^N)$ time for some constant C. Each time the Hilbert subroutine is called, it increases the problem size by a factor of 4. More generally, if an algorithm increases the problem size by a factor of at least C each time it executes a certain fixed number of steps, the algorithm will have $O(C^N)$ run time.

Notice that this behavior is exactly the opposite of that shown by the GCD algorithm presented earlier. That algorithm decreased the problem size by a factor of at least $1 / 2$ every other time the GCD function was called. That gave the algorithm $O(\log(N))$ run time. The Hilbert curve algorithm increases the problem size by a factor of 4 each time the Hilbert routine is called. That gives this algorithm $O(4^N)$ run time.

The function $(4^N - 1) / 3$ is an exponential function that grows *very* quickly. In fact, this function grows so quickly that you might suspect that this is not a very efficient algorithm. While this algorithm definitely takes a lot of time, there are two reasons why this is not a bad thing.

First, any other algorithm that draws Hilbert curves cannot be much faster. Hilbert curves contain a *lot* of line segments and any algorithm that draws them all will take a long time.

Each time the Hilbert routine is called, it draws three lines. Let L(N) be the total number of lines drawn in a depth N Hilbert curve. Then $L(N) = 3 * T(N) = 4^N - 1$ so L(N) is also $O(4^N)$. Table 4.6 shows the number of lines drawn for Hilbert curves of various depths.

Since you must draw $O(4^N)$ lines to make a Hilbert curve of depth N, any algorithm that draws Hilbert curves must execute $O(4^N)$ steps. There are other algorithms for drawing Hilbert curves, but they all require about as much time as this algorithm, because they all need to draw the same number of lines.

Table 4.5 Number of Recursive Calls to the Hilbert Subroutine

N	T(N)
1	1
2	5
3	21
4	85
5	341
6	1,365
7	5,461
8	21,845
9	87,381

Table 4.6 Lines Drawn for Hilbert Curves

N	L(N)
1	3
2	15
3	63
4	255
5	1,023
6	4,095
7	16,383
8	65,535
9	262,143

The second fact which indicates that this algorithm is not too bad, is that a depth nine Hilbert curve contains so many lines that it turns most computer monitors completely black. This is not too surprising since Table 4.6 indicates that this curve contains 262,143 line segments.

This means you will probably never want to display a Hilbert curve of depth nine or greater anyway. At some depth beyond nine you would reach the limits of Visual Basic and your computer, but you reach the limits of what you might reasonably want to display first.

The conclusion is that Hilbert curves are just plain hard to draw. Drawing a quarter of a million lines is a lot of work and it will take a while no matter how clever your algorithm is.

Example program HILBERT uses this recursive algorithm to draw Hilbert curves. When you run the program, be sure to keep the depth of recursion small (under six) until you have seen how long the program takes on your computer.

Recursive Sierpinski Curves

Like Hilbert curves, Sierpinski curves are self-similar curves that are naturally defined recursively. Figure 4.4 shows Sierpinski curves with depths 1, 2, and 3.

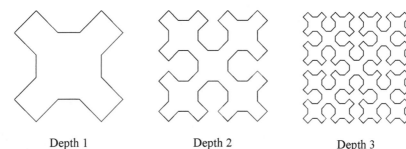

Depth 1   Depth 2   Depth 3

Figure 4.4 Sierpinski curves.

The Hilbert curve algorithm presented in the previous section uses a single subroutine to draw Hilbert curves. Sierpinski curves are easier to draw using four routines that work together. These routines are named SierpA, SierpB, SierpC, and SierpD. The routines are indirectly recursive—each routine calls the other routines which then may call the first. They draw the top, left, bottom, and right portions of a Sierpinski curve, respectively. These parts of the curve can be labeled A, B, C, and D so it is easy to see which routine draws which parts of the curve.

Figure 4.5 show how these routines are combined to form a Sierpinski curve of depth 1. The sub-curves are shown with arrows to indicate the direction in which they are drawn. Segments used to connect the four sub-curves are drawn with dashed lines.

Each of the four basic curves is composed of a diagonal line segment, followed by a vertical or horizontal line segment, followed by another diagonal line segment. When the depth of recursion is greater than 1, you must break each of these curves into smaller pieces. You can do this by breaking each of the curves' two diagonal line segments into two sub-curves.

For example, to break up a type A curve, break the first diagonal line segment into a type A curve followed by a type B curve. Then draw the horizontal line segment for the original type A curve unchanged. Finish by breaking the second diagonal line segment into a type D curve followed by a type A curve. Figure 4.6 shows how a depth 2 type A curve is built from depth 1 curves. The sub-curves are drawn with bold lines so they are easy to see.

Figure 4.7 shows how a complete depth 2 Sierpinski curve is built from four depth 1 sub-curves. Each of the sub-curves is circled with dashed lines.

If you use arrows like ↗ and ↘ to indicate the types of lines that connect the sub-curves (the thin lines in Figure 4.7), then you can list the recursive relationships among the four types of curves as shown in Figure 4.8.

The routines that draw the Sierpinski sub-curves are all very similar so only one is shown here. The relationships shown in Figure 4.8 indicate the drawing operations you should perform to draw each of the different types of curves. You can follow the relationships for a type A curve in the code below. You should also be able to use the other relationships to determine how to modify the code below to draw the other types of curves.

```
Sub SierpA (Depth As Integer, Dist As Single)
    If Depth = 1 Then
        Line -Step(-Dist, Dist)
        Line -Step(-Dist, 0)
        Line -Step(-Dist, -Dist)
    Else
        SierpA Depth - 1, Dist
        Line -Step (-Dist, Dist)
```

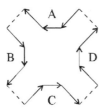

Figure 4.5 The parts of a Sierpinski curve.

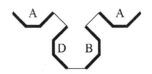

Figure 4.6 Breaking up a type A curve.

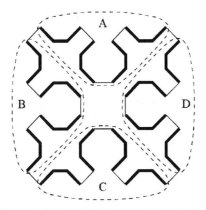

Figure 4.7 Sierpinski curve made from smaller Sierpinski curves.

A: A ↙ B ← D ↖ A
B: B ↘ C ↓ A ↙ B
C: C ↗ D → B ↘ C
D: D ↖ A ↑ C ↗ D

Figure 4.8 Recursive relationships between Sierpinski curves.

```
        SierpB Depth - 1, Dist
        Line -Step(-Dist, 0)
        SierpD Depth - 1, Dist
        Line -Step(-Dist, -Dist)
        SierpA Depth - 1, Dist
    End If
End Sub
```

In addition to routines that draw each of the four basic curves, you need a routine that uses the four of them to create the completed Sierpinski curve.

```
Sub Sierpinski (Depth As Integer, Dist As Single)
    SierpB Depth, Dist
    Line -Step(Dist, Dist)
    SierpC Depth, Dist
    Line -Step(Dist, -Dist)
    SierpD Depth, Dist
    Line -Step(-Dist, -Dist)
    SierpA Depth, Dist
    Line -Step(-Dist, Dist)
End Sub
```

Run Time Analysis

To analyze the run time of this algorithm, you must determine how many times each of the four curve drawing routines is called. Let $T(N)$ be the number of times any one of the four basic curve routines or the main Sierpinski routine is called when drawing a curve of depth N.

When the depth of the curve is one, you draw each type of curve once. Adding one for the main Sierpinski routine, you get $T(1) = 5$.

Each time one of the curve routines recurses, it calls itself or another of the routines four times. Since these routines are all pretty much the same, $T(N)$ is the same no matter which routine is called first. This makes sense because the pictures of the curves are symmetrical and contain the same number of each type of curve. Now you can write the recursive equations for T(N).

```
T(1) = 5
T(N) = 1 + 4 * T(N - 1)        for N > 1.
```

These equations are almost the same as the ones used to compute the run time for the Hilbert curve algorithm. The only difference is that, in the case of the Hilbert curve, $T(1) = 1$. Comparing a few values for these equations shows that $T_{Sierpinski}(N) = T_{Hilbert}(N + 1)$. The last section showed that $T_{Hilbert}(N) = (4^N - 1) / 3$ so $T_{Sierpinski}(N) = (4^{N+1} - 1) / 3$ which is also $O(4^N)$. As shown in Table 4.5, this exponential function grows extremely quickly.

Like the Hilbert curve algorithm, this algorithm runs in $O(4^N)$ time. As was the case for the Hilbert curve algorithm, this is not a bad thing. The Sierpinski curve also requires $O(4^N)$ lines so no algorithm will be able to draw a Sierpinski curve in less than $O(4^N)$ time.

Also like the Hilbert curve, the Sierpinski curve completely fills most computer screens for depths of nine or greater. At some depth beyond nine you would reach the limits of Visual Basic and your computer, but you reach the limits of what you might reasonably want to display first.

Example program SIERP uses this recursive algorithm to draw Sierpinski curves. When you run the program, be sure to keep the depth of recursion small (under six) until you have seen how long the program takes on your computer.

Dangers of Recursion

Recursion can be a powerful technique for decomposing large problems into smaller problems, but it has a few dangers. This section takes a look at some of these dangers and explains when recursion is appropriate and when it is not.

Infinite Recursion

The most immediate danger with recursion is infinite recursion. If you do not build your algorithm properly, the function may slip past your base case and the recursion will never stop. The easiest way to make this mistake is to simply forget the base case, as is done in the following bad version of the factorial function. Since the function does not test to see if the base case is reached, it will recursively call itself forever. When called with input 2, for example, the function will recursively call itself with input 1, 0, –1, –2, –3, etc.

```
Function BadFactorial(num As Integer) As Integer
    BadFactorial = num * BadFactorial(num - 1)
End Function
```

Another way to cause infinite recursion is to have a base case that does not stop all of the possible paths of the recursion. In the following incorrect version of the factorial function, the function will recurse forever if the input is not an integer or if it is less than zero. These values are not valid inputs for the factorial function, so you could require that the program using this function check that the inputs are valid. It would be better if the function could guarantee its own safety, however, rather than relying on the program to give it safe inputs. For this reason it is better to use a more restrictive base case, like num <= 0, that guarantees the recursion will stop even if the input value is invalid.

```
Function BadFactorial2(num As Double) As Double
    If num = 0 Then
        BadFactorial2 = 1
    Else
        BadFactorial2 = num * BadFactorial2(num-1)
    End If
End Function
```

The following version of the Fibonacci function shows a trickier example where the base case does not stop all possible recursions. Here the base case only stops some of the paths of recursion. This function also has the same problems with non-integers and values less than zero that BadFactorial2 has.

```
Function BadFib(num As Double) As Double
    If num = 0 Then
        BadFib = 0
    Else
        BadFib = BadFib(num - 1) + BadFib(num - 2)
    End If
End Function
```

If you used this function to compute BadFib(1), the function would calculate BadFib(0) and BadFib(-1). Once the function calls itself to compute BadFib(-1), it will never stop. The value of the parameter -1 is already less than the base case, num = 0. Since the parameter grows smaller in each subsequent call to BadFib, the function will never reach the base case again so it will recursively call itself forever.

```
BadFib(1) = BadFib(0) + BadFib(-1)
          = 0 + (BadFib(-2) + BadFib(-3))
          = (BadFib(-3) + BadFib(-4)) + (BadFib(-4) + BadFib(-5))
          Etc.
```

A final problem related to infinite recursion is that "infinite" really only means "until you run out of stack space." This means that even correctly written recursive routines will sometimes run out of stack space and fail. The following function, which computes the sum $N + (N - 1) + \ldots + 2 + 1$, works for values of N up to 250 or so. The exact value depends on your computer's configuration. For larger inputs it runs out of stack space before it can finish the calculation.

```
Function BigAdd (N As Double) As Double
    If N <= 1 Then
        BigAdd = 1
    Else
        BigAdd = N + BigAdd(N - 1)
    End If
End Function
```

Example program BIG_ADD demonstrates this algorithm. See how large an input you can give the program before it exhausts the stack on your computer.

Wasted Space

Wasted space is another danger of recursion. Each time your program executes a subroutine call, the computer must allocate storage space for variables local to the new procedure. If you have a complicated chain of recursive subroutine calls, as is the case in the Fibonacci algorithm, the computer will spend a considerable amount of time and memory allocating and deallocating these variables during the recursion. Even if this does not cause the program to run out of stack space, the time spent managing these variables can be large.

There are a couple of ways you can reduce the amount of space the computer must allocate during subroutine calls. First, make sure you do not have lots of unnecessary variables in the subroutine. Visual Basic will allocate space for these variables even if the subroutine does not use them. The following version of the BigAdd function will run out of stack space sooner than the previous version.

```
Function BigAdd (N As Double) As Double
Dim I1 As Integer
Dim I2 As Integer
Dim I3 As Integer
Dim I4 As Integer
Dim I5 As Integer

    If N <= 1 Then
        BigAdd = 1
    Else
        BigAdd = N + BigAdd(N - 1)
    End If
End Function
```

If you are not sure whether a variable is used in a subroutine, use the **Option Explicit** statement and comment out the variable's declaration. When you try to run the program, Visual Basic will complain if the variable is necessary.

You can further reduce the amount of stack memory used by a routine by allocating variables statically. A variable declared as **static** is shared by all instances of the subroutine so the computer does not need to allocate new copies of the variable each time the subroutine is called. Be careful when you use static variables in recursive subroutines, however. If the variable is in use by the routine while another recursive call to the routine modifies the variable's value, you may get unexpected results.

A final method for reducing memory use in recursive subroutine calls is to declare variables globally. If you declare a variable in the declarations section of a module instead of in the subroutine, the computer will not need to allocate new memory for the variable each time the subroutine is called. This method is very similar to creating static variables within the subroutine. In fact, if other subroutines do not need access to the variables, it is better to declare them statically within the subroutine instead of allocating them globally. Then other subroutines cannot accidentally change the variables' values and the declarations section of the module will not become cluttered with declarations that are only used by one subroutine.

Misuse of Recursion

A final, more subtle danger of recursion is logical misuse. Here you use recursion when it is not really the best way to get the job done. The factorial, Fibonacci, GCD, and BigAdd functions presented earlier in this chapter do not really need to be recursive. Better, non-recursive versions of these functions are described a little later in this chapter.

In the cases of the factorial and GCD functions, the unnecessary recursion is mostly harmless. Both of these functions are quite fast and they will execute for relatively large input values. Unless you have used up a lot of stack space in some other part of your program, these functions will not be limited by the size of the stack.

On the other hand, recursion destroys the Fibonacci algorithm. To compute Fib(N) the algorithm first computes Fib(N − 1) and Fib(N − 2). But to compute Fib(N − 1) it must compute Fib(N − 2) and Fib(N − 3). Here Fib(N − 2) is being computed twice. When analyzing that algorithm earlier, you saw that Fib(1) and Fib(0) are computed a total of Fib(N + 1) times during the computation of Fib(N). Fib(30) = 832,040 so to compute Fib(29) you actually compute the same values for Fib(0) and Fib(1) a total of 832,040 times! It is in computing all of these intermediate values again and again that the recursive Fibonacci algorithm spends all of its time.

The BigAdd function has a different problem. While it runs quite quickly, it enters a deep recursion and soon exhausts the stack space. The value of BigAdd(250) is only 31,375. The function could calculate values for much larger inputs if it did not exhaust the stack space first.

The factorial function has a similar problem. It, too, recurses deeply. On input N both the BigAdd and factorial functions recurse to a depth of N function calls. However, the factorial function cannot accept inputs as large as the BigAdd function can. The value of 170!, which is roughly 7.257E + 306, is the largest value that fits in a double variable, so that is the largest value the factorial function can compute. While the function is headed for deep recursion, it causes a double variable overflow before it can cause the stack to overflow.

When to Use Recursion

All of this discussion may lead you to think that recursion is always a bad thing. That is definitely not the case. Many algorithms are naturally recursive. While it is possible to rewrite any algorithm so it does not contain recursion, many are harder to understand, analyze, and maintain over time when they are written non-recursively.

The following sections present methods for removing recursion from any algorithm. Some of the resulting non-recursive algorithms are still fairly easy to understand. The non-recursive factorial, GCD, Fibonacci, and BigAdd functions are relatively straightforward.

On the other hand, the non-recursive versions of the Hilbert and Sierpinski algorithms are quite complicated. They are harder to understand, will be more difficult to maintain in the long run, and even run a bit more slowly than the recursive versions. They are presented to show you techniques you could use to remove recursion from complicated algorithms rather than because they are better than the recursive versions.

If an algorithm is naturally recursive, write it recursively. If all goes well, you will not encounter any of the problems described here. If you do run into some of these problems, you can then rewrite the algorithm without recursion using the techniques presented in the following sections. Often it is easier to rewrite an algorithm after you have written it recursively, than it is to write it non-recursively in the first place.

Tail Recursion

Recall the functions presented earlier to compute factorials and greatest common divisors. Recall also the BigAdd function which exhausts the stack for even relatively small inputs.

```
Function Factorial(num As Integer) As Integer
    If num <= 0 Then
        Factorial = 1
    Else
        Factorial = num * Factorial(num - 1)
    End If
End Function


Function GCD(A As Integer, B As Integer) As Integer
    If B Mod A = 0 Then
        GCD = A
    Else
        GCD = GCD(B Mod A, A)
    End If
End Function


Function BigAdd (N As Double) As Double
    If N <= 1 Then
        BigAdd = 1
    Else
        BigAdd = N + BigAdd(N - 1)
    End If
End Function
```

These functions have something in common: the last thing they do before returning is the recursive step. After the program returns from the recursive function call, these functions end without performing any other actions. Recursion that occurs at the end of a routine like this is called *tail recursion* or *end recursion*.

Since nothing occurs in the routine after the recursive step, there is an easy way to remove the recursion. Instead of calling the function recursively, the routine can reset its own parameters to match the ones that it normally would pass into the recursive call. It then starts over at the beginning.

Consider this general recursive subroutine:

```
Sub Recurse (A As Integer)
    ' Do stuff here, calculate B, etc.
    Recurse B
End Sub
```

You can rewrite this routine without recursion as:

```
Sub NoRecurse (A As Integer)
    Do While (not done)
        ' Do stuff here, calculate B, etc.
        A = B
    Loop
End Sub
```

This process is called *tail recursion removal* or *end recursion removal*. Notice that this process does not change the number of steps that the program executes. The recursive steps have just been replaced with passes through a **While** loop.

Tail recursion removal does eliminate subroutine calls, however, and an algorithm's speed may improve when you replace subroutine calls with iterations through a **While** loop. More importantly, this method decreases the use of the stack. Algorithms like the BigAdd function that are limited by their depths of recursion will benefit greatly.

Some compilers remove tail recursion automatically. If they identify a routine that uses tail recursion, they perform tail recursion removal when they rewrite it in machine language. Visual Basic does not do this. Otherwise the simple BigAdd function presented in the previous section would not exhaust the stack.

Using tail recursion removal, it is easy to rewrite the factorial, GCD, and BigAdd functions non-recursively.

```
Function Factorial (N As Integer) As Double
Dim value As Double

    value = 1#        ' This will be the value of the function.

    Do While N > 1
        value = value * N
        N = N - 1   ' Prepare the arguments for the "recursion."
    Loop

    Factorial = value
End Function

Function GCD (A As Double, B As Double) As Double
Dim B_Mod_A As Double

    B_Mod_A = B Mod A
    Do While B_Mod_A <> 0
        ' Prepare the arguments for the "recursion."
        B = A
        A = B_Mod_A
        B_Mod_A = B Mod A
    Loop

    GCD = A
End Function

Function BigAdd (N As Double) As Double
Dim value As Double

    value = 1#        ' This will be the value of the function.

    Do While N > 1
        value = value + N
        N = N - 1   ' Prepare the parameters for the "recursion."
    Loop

    BigAdd = value
End Function
```

For the factorial and GCD algorithms, there is little practical difference between the recursive and non-recursive versions of the algorithms. Both are fast and both can handle problems that are reasonably large without exhausting the stack.

For the BigAdd algorithm, however, there is a tremendous difference. The recursive version of this function easily exhausts the stack when the input is little bigger than 250. Since the non-recursive version does not use up the stack, it should be able to compute values for N up to around 10^{154}. Beyond that point the double data type will overflow. Of course running the algorithm for 10^{154} steps will take quite a bit of time, so you may not want to try such a large example. (Notice also that the value of this function is the same as the value of the more easily calculated function N * (N + 1)/2.)

Example programs FACTO2, GCD2, and BIG_ADD2 demonstrate these non-recursive algorithms.

Non-Recursive Fibonacci Numbers

Unfortunately the recursive algorithm for computing Fibonacci numbers does not contain only tail recursion. The algorithm uses two recursive calls to itself to calculate a value. The second call comes after the first. Since the first call does not come at the very end of the function, the first call is not tail recursion so it cannot be removed using tail recursion removal.

Perhaps this is just as well, since the recursive Fibonacci algorithm is limited by the fact that it computes too many intermediate values rather than by its depth of recursion. While tail recursion removal decreases an algorithm's depth of recursion, it does not change the number of operations performed by the algorithm. Even if you could use tail recursion removal on the Fibonacci algorithm, the function would still be extremely slow.

The trouble with the recursive Fibonacci algorithm is that it recomputes the same values many times. As was explained earlier, Fib(1) and Fib(0) are computed a total of Fib(N + 1) times when the algorithm computes Fib(N). To compute Fib(29) the algorithm computes the same values for Fib(0) and Fib(1) a total of 832,040 times.

Whenever an algorithm recomputes the same values many times, you should see if there is a way to avoid the duplicate computations. A straightforward and mechanical way to do this is to build a table of the calculated values. Then when you need an intermediate value, you can look it up in the table rather than recomputing it.

In this example you can build a table to store the values of the Fibonacci function Fib(N) for N less than 1477. For N >= 1477 the double precision variables that are used by the function overflow. The Fibonacci function with this change looks like this:

```
Const MAX_FIB = 1476 ' The largest value we will compute.
Dim FibValues(0 To MAX_FIB) As Double


Function Fib (N As Integer) As Double
    ' Compute the value if it is not in the table.
    If FibValues(N) < 0 Then
        FibValues(N) = Fib(N - 1) + Fib(N - 2)
    End If
    Fib = FibValues(N)
End Function
```

When the program begins, it should initialize each entry in the FibValues array to −1. It should then set the values of FibValues(0) to 0 and FibValues(1) to 1. When the Fibonacci function is called, it checks the array to see if it has already stored the value it needs. If it has not, it recursively computes the value as before and stores the new value in the array for later use.

Example program FIBO2 uses this method for calculating Fibonacci numbers. This program can compute values up to around Fib(297) when it is first run. For larger values of N, the program recurses too deeply and runs out of stack space.

As FIBO2 computes new values, however, the program starts to fill the FibValues array. Those values will allow the function to compute larger and larger values of the function without using deep recursion. In fact, if you ask the program to compute Fib(100), Fib(200), Fib(300), and so on, you will be able to fill the FibValues array completely and compute the largest value possible, Fib(1476). For N larger than 1476, the calculations cause an overflow error.

This process of slowly filling up the FibValues array indicates another method for computing Fibonacci numbers. While you are initializing the FibValues array, you can precompute all of the Fibonacci numbers. Once the program initializes the array, it can simply look up Fibonacci numbers in the table without ever using recursion.

```
Sub InitializeFibValues ()
Dim i As Integer

    FibValues(0) = 0
    FibValues(1) = 1
    For i = 2 To MAX_FIB
        FibValues(i) = FibValues(i - 1) + FibValues(i - 2)
    Next I
End Sub


Function Fib (N As Integer) As Double
    Fib = FibValues(N)
End Function
```

This method takes a constant amount of time to create the lookup array. If you set MAX_FIB = 1476, then it takes about 1476 steps to initialize the array. Once the array is ready, it takes only a single step to access a value in the array.

There is one more method for computing Fibonacci numbers worth mentioning at this point. The first recursive definition of the Fibonacci function worked from the top down. To get a value for Fib(N) you compute the values of Fib(N − 1) and Fib(N − 2) and add them together.

When you initialize the FibValues lookup array, on the other hand, you do so from the bottom up. You start with the values of Fib(0) and Fib(1). Then you pass through the array using smaller values to compute larger ones until the table is full.

You can use this same bottom up method to compute the value of the Fibonacci function directly each time you need a value. This way you do not need the lookup array. It takes a little longer to recompute the values each time they are needed rather than looking them up in a table, but this method saves the memory needed to store the array. This is an example of a space versus time tradeoff. By using the extra space needed to store a table of values, you avoid spending extra time computing the values when they are needed.

```
Function Fib (N As Integer) As Double
Dim Fib_i_minus_1 As Double
Dim Fib_i_minus_2 As Double
Dim fib_i As Double
Dim i As Integer

    If N <= 1 Then
        Fib = N
    Else
        Fib_i_minus_2 = 0   ' Initially Fib(0)
        Fib_i_minus_1 = 1   ' Initially Fib(1)
        For i = 2 To N
            fib_i = Fib_i_minus_1 + Fib_i_minus_2
            Fib_i_minus_2 = Fib_i_minus_1
            Fib_i_minus_1 = fib_i
        Next i
        Fib = fib_i
    End If
End Function
```

This version takes $O(N)$ steps to calculate Fib(N). This is more than the single step the previous version required, but it is much faster than the original $O(Fib(N))$ steps. On a 50 megahertz 486-based PC the original recursive algorithm took 101.79 seconds to calculate Fib(30) = 832,040. The new algorithm takes no noticeable time to determine that Fib(1476) is roughly $1.31E + 308$.

Example program FIBO3 uses this method to compute Fibonacci numbers.

Avoiding More General Recursion

The factorial, GCD, and BigAdd functions were simplified by removing tail recursion. The Fibonacci function was simplified by using a lookup table and by reformulating the problem in a bottom up rather than a top down way.

Some recursive algorithms are so complicated that these methods are difficult or impossible to use. It would be fairly hard to come up with non-recursive algorithms for drawing Hilbert and Sierpinski curves from scratch. Still other recursive algorithms are more complicated than those.

Earlier sections showed that any algorithms for drawing Hilbert and Sierpinski curves must use $O(N^4)$ steps so the original recursive implementations are pretty good. They are about as fast as they can be and their depths of recursion are not too large for practical use.

Still, you might come across other complicated algorithms that do not yield to tail recursion removal and that have too great a depth of recursion for your computer to handle. In cases like these it is still possible to convert a recursive algorithm into a non-recursive one.

The basic approach is to think about the way the computer performs recursion and then mimic the steps the computer follows. Your new algorithm will perform the "recursion" instead of making the computer do all the work.

Since the new algorithm follows pretty much the same steps the computer follows, you might wonder if there will be any increase in speed. In Visual Basic there generally is not. The computer can perform the tasks it needs for recursion more quickly than you will be able to mimic them. Handling these details yourself gives you greater control over the allocation of local variables, however, and will allow you to avoid great depths of recursion.

Normally when you make a subroutine call, the computer must do three things. First, it must save any information it needs to continue execution when the subroutine returns. Second, it must prepare for the call and transfer control to the subroutine. Third, when the called routine ends, the computer must restore the information it saved in the first step and transfer control back to the appropriate point in the program.

When you convert a recursive subroutine into a non-recursive one, you must perform these three steps yourself. Consider this generalized recursive subroutine:

```
Subr(num)
    <code block 1>
    Subr(<parameters>)
    <code block 2>
End
```

Since there is code after the recursive step, you cannot use tail recursion removal on this algorithm.

Begin by labeling the first lines in code blocks 1 and 2. You will use these labels to determine where to resume execution when a "recursion" returns. You will use the labels only to help understand what the algorithm is doing—they are not actually part of the Visual Basic code. In this example the labels would be:

```
        Subr(num)
1           <code block 1>
            Subr(<parameters>)
2           <code block 2>
        End
```

You will also use a special label 0 to indicate that a "recursion" is ending. Now you can rewrite the subroutine without recursion like this:

```
Subr(num)
Dim pc As Integer        'Tells us where to resume execution.

    pc = 1
    Do
        Select Case pc
            Case 1
                <code block 1>

                If base case has been reached Then
                    ' Skip the recursion and go to code block 2.
                    pc = 2
                Else
                    ' Save variables needed after recursion.

                    ' Save pc = 2. This is where we will resume
                    ' execution after the "recursion" returns.

                    ' Set variables needed by the recursive call.
                    ' For example, num = num - 1.
```

```
                        ' Go to code block 1 to start the recursion.
                        pc = 1
                    End If


            Case 2       ' Execute code block 2
                <code block 2>
                pc = 0


            Case 0
                If this is the last recursion Then Exit Do
                ' Otherwise restore pc and other variables saved
                ' before the recursion.
        End Select
    Loop
End
```

The variable pc (which stands for "program counter") tells you what step you should execute next. For example, when pc = 1, you should execute code block 1.

When you reach the base case, you do not recurse. Instead you change pc to 2 so you will continue execution with code block 2.

If you have not yet reached the base case, you prepare for "recursion." To do this save the value of any local variables that you will need when the "recursion" ends. Also save the value of pc for the code segment you should execute after the "recursion" returns. In this example you execute code block 2 after the "recursion" ends so you should save 2 as the next value for pc. The easiest way to save the values of the local variables and pc is using stacks like the ones described in Chapter 2.

A concrete example should make this easier to understand. Consider a slightly rewritten version of the factorial function. It is rewritten here as a subroutine that returns its value through a variable rather than as a function to make things a little easier.

```
        Sub Factorial(num As Integer, value As Integer)
        Dim partial As Integer

1           If num <= 1 Then
                value = 1
            Else
                Factorial(num - 1, partial)
2               value = num * partial
            End If
        End Sub
```

After you return from the recursion, you will need to know the original value of num so you can perform the multiplication value = num * partial. Since you will need access to the value of num after the recursion returns, you must save it before starting the recursion. The value of num and the value of pc are the only values you need to save in this example.

You can save these values in two array-based stacks. When you prepare for recursion, you should add num and pc to the ends of the stacks. When a recursion finishes, you should remove the most recently added values of num and pc from the ends of the stacks. Now you can write the non-recursive version of the factorial subroutine as:

```
Sub Factorial(num As Integer, value As Integer)
ReDim num_stack(1 to 200) As Integer
ReDim pc_stack(1 to 200) As Integer
Dim stack_top As Integer

Dim pc As Integer

    pc = 1
    Do
        Select Case pc
            Case 1
                If num <= 1 Then      ' This is the base case.
                    value = 1
                    pc = 0            ' End this recursion.
                Else                  ' Recurse.
                    ' Save num and the next pc.
                    stack_top = stack_top + 1
                    num_stack(stack_top) = num
                    pc_stack(stack_top) = 2      ' Resume at 2.

                    ' Start the recursion
                    num = num - 1
                    ' Transfer control back to the start.
                    pc = 1
                End If
            Case 2
                ' value holds the result of the recently
                ' finished recursion. Multiply it by num.
                value = value * num
                ' "Return" from a "recursion."
                pc = 0

            Case 0
                ' End a "recursion."
                ' If the stacks are empty, we are done with the
                ' original call to the subroutine.
                If stack_top <= 0 Then Exit Do

                ' Otherwise restore local variables and pc.
                num = num_stack(stack_top)
                pc = pc_stack(stack_top)
                stack_top = stack_top - 1
        End Select
    Loop
End Sub
```

Like tail recursion removal, this technique mimics the behavior of the recursive algorithm. You have replaced each recursive call with an iteration in the **While** loop. Since the steps executed are the same, you have not changed the run time of the algorithm.

Like tail recursion removal, this technique removes the need for the algorithm to recurse deeply, possibly exhausting the stack. This version also does not need to allocate the variable "partial" each time it enters a recursive subroutine. In the recursive version of the routine, Visual Basic allocated a new copy of the variable partial each time the routine was called. By rewriting the routine you avoid this and further reduce stack use.

Non-Recursive Hilbert Curves

The factorial example in the previous section turned a simple but inefficient recursive factorial function into a complicated and inefficient non-recursive subroutine. For the factorial function, there is a much better non-recursive algorithm that was presented earlier in the chapter.

For more complicated algorithms, finding a simple non-recursive version can be difficult. When the algorithm is multiply recursive or calls itself indirectly, the techniques of the previous section come in handy.

For a more interesting example of these techniques, consider again the Hilbert curve algorithm. The recursive version of this algorithm is quite good given the difficulty of the problem, so it will be hard to beat. In fact, the non-recursive version presented here is a little slower than the recursive version. It is presented only as an example showing how to convert a multiply recursive routine into a non-recursive one.

The recursive Hilbert curve algorithm is:

```
Sub Hilbert (depth As Integer, Dx As Single, Dy As Single)
    If depth > 1 Then Hilbert depth - 1, Dy, Dx
    HilbertPicture.Line -Step(Dx, Dy)
    If depth > 1 Then Hilbert depth - 1, Dx, Dy
    HilbertPicture.Line -Step(Dy, Dx)
    If depth > 1 Then Hilbert depth - 1, Dx, Dy
    HilbertPicture.Line -Step(-Dx, -Dy)
    If depth > 1 Then Hilbert depth - 1, -Dy, -Dx
End Sub
```

Following the methods of the previous section, you should number the first lines in each code block between the recursive steps. These include the first line of the routine and the other places where you might have to resume execution after a "recursion" returns.

```
        Sub Hilbert (depth As Integer, Dx As Single, Dy As Single)
1           If depth > 1 Then Hilbert depth - 1, Dy, Dx
2           HilbertPicture.Line -Step(Dx, Dy)
            If depth > 1 Then Hilbert depth - 1, Dx, Dy
3           HilbertPicture.Line -Step(Dy, Dx)
            If depth > 1 Then Hilbert depth - 1, Dx, Dy
4           HilbertPicture.Line -Step(-Dx, -Dy)
            If depth > 1 Then Hilbert depth - 1, -Dy, -Dx
        End Sub
```

Each time you begin a "recursion," you must save the values of the local variables Depth, Dx, and Dy, as well as the next value for pc. When you return from a "recursion," you must restore these values. To make these operations a little easier, you can write a pair of auxiliary routines to save and restore these values.

```
Sub SaveValues (Depth As Integer, Dx As Single, Dy As Single, pc As Integer)
    TopOfStack = TopOfStack + 1
    DepthStack(TopOfStack) = Depth
    DxStack(TopOfStack) = Dx
    DyStack(TopOfStack) = Dy
    PCStack(TopOfStack) = pc
End Sub
```

```
Sub RestoreValues (Depth As Integer, Dx As Single, Dy As Single, pc As Integer)
    Depth = DepthStack(TopOfStack)
    Dx = DxStack(TopOfStack)
    Dy = DyStack(TopOfStack)
    pc = PCStack(TopOfStack)
    TopOfStack = TopOfStack - 1
End Sub
```

Now you can use these routines to write the non-recursive version of the Hilbert subroutine like this:

```
Sub Hilbert (Depth As Integer, Dx As Single, Dy As Single)
Dim pc As Integer
Dim tmp As Single

    pc = 1
    Do
        Select Case pc
            Case 1
                If Depth > 1 Then ' Recurse.
                    ' Save the current values.
                    SaveValues Depth, Dx, Dy, 2
                    ' Prepare for the recursion.
                    Depth = Depth - 1
                    tmp = Dx
                    Dx = Dy
                    Dy = tmp
                    pc = 1 ' Go to start of recursive call.
                Else        ' Base case.
                    ' We have recursed deeply enough.
                    ' Continue with code block 2.
                    pc = 2
                End If
            Case 2
                HilbertPicture.Line -Step(Dx, Dy)
                If Depth > 1 Then ' Recurse.
                    ' Save the current values.
                    SaveValues Depth, Dx, Dy, 3
                    ' Prepare for the recursion.
                    Depth = Depth - 1
                    ' Dx and Dy remain the same.
                    pc = 1 ' Go to start of recursive call.
                Else        ' Base case.
                    ' We have recursed deeply enough.
                    ' Continue with code block 3.
                    pc = 3
                End If
            Case 3
                HilbertPicture.Line -Step(Dy, Dx)
                If Depth > 1 Then ' Recurse.
                    ' Save the current values.
                    SaveValues Depth, Dx, Dy, 4
                    ' Prepare for the recursion.
                    Depth = Depth - 1
                    ' Dx and Dy remain the same.
                    pc = 1 ' Go to start of recursive call.
                Else        ' Base case.
                    ' We have recursed deeply enough.
                    ' Continue with code block 4.
```

```
                      pc = 4
                End If
          Case 4
                HilbertPicture.Line -Step(-Dx, -Dy)
                If Depth > 1 Then        ' Recurse.
                    ' Save the current values.
                    SaveValues Depth, Dx, Dy, 0
                    ' Prepare for the recursion.
                    Depth = Depth - 1
                    tmp = Dx
                    Dx = -Dy
                    Dy = -tmp
                    pc = 1 ' Go to start of recursive call.
                Else         ' Base case.
                    ' We have recursed deeply enough.
                    ' This is the end of this recursive call.
                    pc = 0
                End If
          Case 0  ' Return from recursion.
                If TopOfStack > 0 Then
                    RestoreValues Depth, Dx, Dy, pc
                Else
                    ' The stack is empty. We are done.
                    Exit Do
                End If
          End Select
    Loop
End Sub
```

The run time for this algorithm would be quite tricky to analyze directly. Fortunately you know that the techniques for converting recursive routines into non-recursive routines do not change the algorithm's run time. That means this algorithm for drawing Hilbert curves must have the same $O(N^4)$ run time as the previous version.

This version runs a little more slowly than the recursive version, due to the fact that this code is not as good as the computer is at saving and restoring variables and transferring control to and from recursive subroutine calls.

Does this mean that this is not a good algorithm for drawing Hilbert curves? Yes, it does. The main benefit of converting a recursive algorithm into a non-recursive one is that it allows very large depths of recursion. But the Hilbert curve completely covers most computer screens when it is run with depth of recursion nine. Rewriting the algorithm non-recursively might allow greater depths of recursion, but there is no reason to run this program for depths of recursion greater than nine anyway. This, plus the fact that the non-recursive version is slightly slower and *much* more complicated, makes the recursive version the clear winner.

Example program HILBERT2 demonstrates this non-recursive algorithm for drawing Hilbert curves. Be sure to try drawing simple curves (depth under six) until you know how long the program will take on your computer.

Non-Recursive Sierpinski Curves

The Sierpinski algorithm presented earlier is not only multiply recursive, it is also indirectly recursive. Since the algorithm consists of four subroutines that call each other, you cannot number the important lines as you did with the Hilbert curve algorithm. You can deal with this problem by rewriting the algorithm a bit first.

The recursive version of this algorithm consists of four subroutines SierpA, SierpB, SierpC, and SierpD. Subroutine SierpA looks like this:

```
Sub SierpA (Depth As Integer, Dist As Single)
    If Depth = 1 Then
        Line -Step(-Dist, Dist)
        Line -Step(-Dist, 0)
        Line -Step(-Dist, -Dist)
    Else
        SierpA Depth - 1, Dist
        Line -Step(-Dist, Dist)
        SierpB Depth - 1, Dist
        Line -Step(-Dist, 0)
        SierpD Depth - 1, Dist
        Line -Step(-Dist, -Dist)
        SierpA Depth - 1, Dist
    End If
End Sub
```

The other three subroutines look pretty similar. It is not too hard to combine these four routines into a single subroutine.

```
Sub SierpAll (Depth As Integer, Dist As Single, Func As Integer)
    Select Case Func
        Case 1     ' SierpA
            <SierpA code>
        Case 2     ' SierpB
            <SierpB code>
        Case 3     ' SierpC
            <SierpC code>
        Case 4     ' SierpD
            <SierpD code>
    End Select
End Sub
```

The value of parameter Func tells the subroutine which piece of code to execute. You replace calls to the subroutines with calls to SierpAll using the appropriate value for Func. For example, you would replace a call to SierpA with a call to SierpAll with the Func parameter set to 1. Similarly you would replace calls to SierpB with calls to SierpAll with the Func parameter set to 2, and so on for SierpC and SierpD.

This new subroutine is massively recursive, calling itself directly in 16 different places. This subroutine is much larger than the Hilbert subroutine, but otherwise it has a similar structure and you can apply the same methods for making it non-recursive.

You can use the first digit of the pc labels to indicate which general piece of code to execute. Number values of pc within the SierpA code 11, 12, 13, etc. Number values of pc within the SierpB code 21, 22, 23, and so forth.

Now you can label the key lines of code within each section. For the SierpA code section the key lines are:

```
     ' SierpA code
11   If Depth = 1 Then
         Line -Step(-Dist, Dist)
         Line -Step(-Dist, 0)
         Line -Step(-Dist, -Dist)
     Else
         SierpA Depth - 1, Dist
```

```
12         Line -Step(-Dist, Dist)
           SierpB Depth - 1, Dist
13         Line -Step(-Dist, 0)
           SierpD Depth - 1, Dist
14         Line -Step(-Dist, -Dist)
           SierpA Depth - 1, Dist
       End If
```

A typical "recursion" from the SierpA code into the SierpB code would look like this:

```
SaveValues Depth, 13         ' Resume at step 13 when done.
Depth = Depth - 1
pc = 21                      ' Transfer to the start of the SierpB code.
```

As you did in the Hilbert curve algorithm, you should reserve the label 0 to indicate that you are returning from a "recursion." The Visual Basic code for the non-recursive version of SierpAll is shown below.

```
Sub SierpAll (Depth As Integer, pc As Integer)
    Do
        Select Case pc
            ' **********
            ' * SierpA *
            ' **********
            Case 11
                If Depth <= 1 Then
                    SierpPicture.Line -Step(-Dist, Dist)
                    SierpPicture.Line -Step(-Dist, 0)
                    SierpPicture.Line -Step(-Dist, -Dist)
                    pc = 0
                Else
                    SaveValues Depth, 12     ' Run SierpA
                    Depth = Depth - 1
                    pc = 11
                End If
            Case 12
                SierpPicture.Line -Step(-Dist, Dist)
                SaveValues Depth, 13         ' Run SierpB
                Depth = Depth - 1
                pc = 21
            Case 13
                SierpPicture.Line -Step(-Dist, 0)
                SaveValues Depth, 14         ' Run SierpD
                Depth = Depth - 1
                pc = 41
            Case 14
                SierpPicture.Line -Step(-Dist, -Dist)
                SaveValues Depth, 0          ' Run SierpA
                Depth = Depth - 1
                pc = 11

            ' **********
            ' * SierpB *
            ' **********
            Case 21
                If Depth <= 1 Then
                    SierpPicture.Line -Step(Dist, Dist)
```

```
                SierpPicture.Line -Step(0, Dist)
                SierpPicture.Line -Step(-Dist, Dist)
                pc = 0
            Else
                SaveValues Depth, 22     ' Run SierpB
                Depth = Depth - 1
                pc = 21
            End If
        Case 22
            SierpPicture.Line -Step(Dist, Dist)
            SaveValues Depth, 23        ' Run SierpC
            Depth = Depth - 1
            pc = 31
        Case 23
            SierpPicture.Line -Step(0, Dist)
            SaveValues Depth, 24        ' Run SierpA
            Depth = Depth - 1
            pc = 11
        Case 24
            SierpPicture.Line -Step(-Dist, Dist)
            SaveValues Depth, 0         ' Run SierpB
            Depth = Depth - 1
            pc = 21


        ' *********
        ' * SierpC *
        ' *********
        Case 31
            If Depth <= 1 Then
                SierpPicture.Line -Step(Dist, -Dist)
                SierpPicture.Line -Step(Dist, 0)
                SierpPicture.Line -Step(Dist, Dist)
                pc = 0
            Else
                SaveValues Depth, 32     ' Run SierpC
                Depth = Depth - 1
                pc = 31
            End If
        Case 32
            SierpPicture.Line -Step(Dist, -Dist)
            SaveValues Depth, 33        ' Run SierpD
            Depth = Depth - 1
            pc = 41
        Case 33
            SierpPicture.Line -Step(Dist, 0)
            SaveValues Depth, 34        ' Run SierpB
            Depth = Depth - 1
            pc = 21
        Case 34
            SierpPicture.Line -Step(Dist, Dist)
            SaveValues Depth, 0         ' Run SierpC
            Depth = Depth - 1
            pc = 31


        ' *********
        ' * SierpD *
        ' *********
        Case 41
            If Depth <= 1 Then
                SierpPicture.Line -Step(-Dist, -Dist)
```

```
                    SierpPicture.Line -Step(0, -Dist)
                    SierpPicture.Line -Step(Dist, -Dist)
                    pc = 0
                Else
                    SaveValues Depth, 42      ' Run SierpD
                    Depth = Depth - 1
                    pc = 41
                End If
            Case 42
                SierpPicture.Line -Step(-Dist, -Dist)
                SaveValues Depth, 43          ' Run SierpA
                Depth = Depth - 1
                pc = 11
            Case 43
                SierpPicture.Line -Step(0, -Dist)
                SaveValues Depth, 44          ' Run SierpC
                Depth = Depth - 1
                pc = 31
            Case 44
                SierpPicture.Line -Step(Dist, -Dist)
                SaveValues Depth, 0           ' Run SierpD
                Depth = Depth - 1
                pc = 41


            ' ****************
            ' * End recursion *
            ' ****************
            Case 0
                If StackTop <= 0 Then Exit Do
                RestoreValues Depth, pc
        End Select
    Loop
End Sub
```

As was the case with the Hilbert curve algorithm, converting the Sierpinski curve algorithm into a non-recursive format does not change the algorithm's run time. The new algorithm mimics the behavior of the recursive algorithm which you already saw runs in time $O(N^4)$. That means the non-recursive version has $O(N^4)$ run time, too. It runs a little more slowly than the recursive version and is much more complicated.

The non-recursive version would allow a much greater depth of recursion, but it is not practical to draw Sierpinski curves with depth greater than eight or nine anyway. These facts make the recursive algorithm generally the better algorithm.

Example program SIERP2 uses this non-recursive algorithm to draw Sierpinski curves. Be sure to try drawing simple curves (depth under six) until you know how long the program will take on your computer.

Summary

There are three main dangers to recursive algorithms:

- Infinite recursion—Make sure your algorithm has a solid base case that stops all recursive paths.
- Deep recursion—If the algorithm recurses too deeply, it will exhaust the stack. You can help by reducing the number of variables you allocate in the recursive

routine, by allocating the variables statically, or by allocating the variables globally. If the routine still exhausts the stack, rewrite the algorithm non-recursively using tail recursion removal if possible.

- Inappropriate recursion—Usually this results when an algorithm like the recursive Fibonacci algorithm calculates the same intermediate values many times. If your program has this problem, first try to rewrite the algorithm in a bottom up rather than top down fashion. If you cannot figure out how to do that, try to create a lookup table of intermediate values the program can use to perform its calculations.

Not all recursion is bad. Many problems are naturally described in a recursive way. In these cases, if the depth of recursion is not too large and the algorithm does not recompute too many intermediate values, recursion will be the best way to go. Your program will be easier to understand, debug, and maintain in the long run.

The Hilbert and Sierpinski curve algorithms are both examples where recursion is appropriate. Both are naturally recursive and are much easier to understand in their recursive forms. The recursive versions are even a little faster than the non-recursive ones.

If you have an algorithm that you think is naturally recursive, but you are not sure if the recursive version will cause problems, write the algorithm recursively and see. Hopefully there will be no problem. If there is, it will probably be easier for you to translate the recursive algorithm into a non-recursive one than to come up with the non-recursive version and debug it from scratch.

Trees

Overview

Chapter 2 discussed ways to create dynamic, linked data structures like those shown in Figure 5.1. These kinds of data structures are called *graphs*. Chapter 11 will discuss graph and network algorithms in some detail, but this chapter examines a special kind of graph called a *tree*.

First this chapter describes what a tree is and explains some tree terminology. Then it examines several methods for implementing trees in Visual Basic. The different methods are useful for storing different kinds of trees. The sections that follow examine tree traversal algorithms for trees stored in these different formats. The chapter finishes by discussing some specialized types of trees including sorted trees, threaded trees, tries, and quadtrees.

Definitions

You can define a tree recursively as:

- An empty structure, or
- A *node*, called the *root* of the tree, connected to zero or more *subtrees*

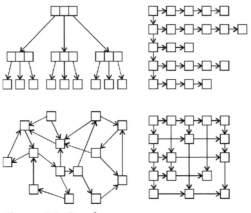

Figure 5.1 Graphs.

Figure 5.2 shows a tree. Here the root node A is connected to three subtrees starting at nodes B, C, and D. Those nodes are connected to subtrees with roots E, F, and G, and those nodes are connected in turn to the subtrees with roots H, I, and J.

Tree terminology is a hodgepodge of terms borrowed from botany and genealogy. From botany come terms like *node* to describe where a branch might occur, *branch* to describe a link connecting two nodes, and *leaf* to describe a node that has no branches leaving it.

From genealogy come terms that describe relationships. When one node is directly above another, the upper node is called the *parent* and the lower node is called the *child*. The nodes along the path from a node upward to the root are that node's *ancestors*. For example, in Figure 5.2 the nodes E, B, and A are all ancestors of node I.

The nodes below another node in the tree are that node's *descendants*. The nodes E, H, I, and J in Figure 5.2 are all descendants of node B.

Occasionally people even refer to nodes that have the same parent as *sibling* (brother or sister) nodes.

There are also a few tree terms that do not come from botany or genealogy. An *internal node* is a node that is not a leaf. In other words an internal node has one or more branches leaving it. A node's *degree* is the number of children the node has. In Figure 5.2 the degree of node D is two since node D has two children: nodes F and G.

The degree of a tree is the largest degree of all of the nodes in the tree. The degree of the tree shown in Figure 5.2 is three because the nodes with the largest degree, nodes A and E, have three children.

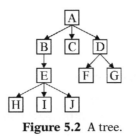

Figure 5.2 A tree.

The *depth* of a node is one plus the number of ancestors the node has in the tree. In Figure 5.2 node E has depth three. This is the same as the number of nodes you would need to visit to travel through the tree from the root to the node. To travel from the root to node E in Figure 5.2, you would visit the nodes A, B, and E.

The *depth* or *height* of a tree is the greatest depth of all of its nodes. The depth of the tree shown in Figure 5.2 is four.

A degree two tree is usually called a *binary* tree. Degree three trees are sometimes called *ternary* trees. Beyond that trees of degree N are usually called *N-ary* trees. A degree 12 tree, for example, would be called a 12-ary tree rather than a "dodecadary" tree. Some people prefer to avoid odd terminology and simply say "tree of degree 12."

Figure 5.3 illustrates some of these tree terms.

Tree Representations

Now that you know some basic tree terminology, you can think about ways to implement trees in Visual Basic. One approach would be to create different user-defined data types for each type of node in the tree. You could manage each kind of node in a separate list of user-defined data types similar to the lists described in Chapter 2. When you needed a new node, you would take it from the appropriate list. When you were done with a node, you would replace it in the appropriate garbage list so you could reuse it later.

To build the tree shown in Figure 5.3 using this method, you would need to define data structures for nodes that had zero, one, two, or three children. This would be rather inconvenient. In addition to managing four different lists of nodes, you would need to place some sort of indicators on each node so you could tell what kind of nodes its children were. Any algorithms you wrote to manipulate this sort of tree would also need to know how to deal with all of the different kinds of nodes.

Fat Nodes

A simpler solution is to define a single node type that has enough child pointers to create any of the kinds of nodes you might need. I call this the "fat node" method since some of the nodes in the tree will be larger than they really need to be.

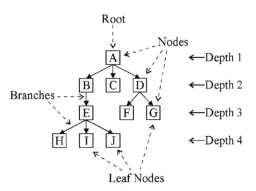

Figure 5.3 Parts of a ternary (degree 3) tree.

The tree shown in Figure 5.3 has degree three. To build this tree using the fat node method, you should define a single node type that contained pointers to three child nodes. Then you can create an array of these nodes.

```
Type MyNode
    Label As String * 1
    Child(1 To 3) As Integer
End Type

Dim Nodes(0 to 9) As MyNode
```

Now you can build a tree by using the nodes' Child entries to link the nodes together. Table 5.1 shows the entries you would use to build the tree shown in Figure 5.3. For example, array entry 0 represents the root of the tree. It has label A and its child pointers have values 1, 2, and 3. This means node 0 is connected to the nodes that occupy array positions 1, 2, and 3. Those nodes have labels B, C, and D, which agrees with Figure 5.3.

Example program BINARY uses a fat node strategy to manage a binary tree. The nodes are defined like this:

```
Type NodeRec
    LeftChild As Integer
    RightChild As Integer
End Type
```

Click on a node in the tree. The program will enable the Add Left button if the node does not already have a left child. It will also enable the Add Right button if the node does not already have a right child. The program will enable the Remove button if the node you selected is not the root node. If you select a node and press the Remove button, the program will remove that node and all of its descendants from the tree.

Since this program allows you to create nodes with 0, 1, or 2 children, it uses a fat node representation. You could easily extend this example for trees of higher degree.

Reusing Pointers

The fat node representation contains a lot of wasted space. Of the 30 array entries allocated for child pointers in Table 5.1, 21 of them are unused. Only three of the unused entries are entries for children of internal nodes. The other 18 entries are the unused child pointers of leaf nodes. Since leaf nodes never have child entries, the children of leaf nodes will always be unused. For this reason fat node representations include a lot of unused pointers.

Sometimes the kind of data stored in a leaf node will be different from the kind of data stored in an internal node. In that case you may be able to use the leaf nodes'

Table 5.1 Fat Node Tree Representation

Index	0	1	2	3	4	5	6	7	8	9
Label	A	B	C	D	E	F	G	H	I	J
Child(1)	1	4		5	7					
Child(2)	2			6	8					
Child(3)	3				9					

unused child pointers to indicate the location of the leaf node data. If you can ensure that the indexes for the leaf node children do not overlap with the indexes of the internal node children, this scheme can save some space.

For example, you can use a *parse tree* to store representations of arithmetic expressions such as ((A + C) * (A − B)) + C. The internal nodes in this tree represent operators like "+" and "*." The tree's leaf nodes represent values like "A" and "B" which cannot be divided further.

Suppose you allocate internal nodes from a list with indexes between 1 and 1000, and you allocate leaf nodes from a separate list with indexes between 1001 and 2000. Then you can easily tell the difference between internal nodes and leaf nodes. If you encounter a child pointer with value between 1 and 1000, you know that the item it points to is an internal node in the tree and you will find that item in the array of internal nodes. If you encounter a child pointer with value between 1001 and 2000, you know that the child item is a leaf node and that you can find the item in the leaf node array.

Figure 5.4 shows the parse tree for the expression ((A + C) * (A − B)) + C together with its array representation. This representation wastes no space. Each array entry either stores a pointer to a child node or it contains a pointer to leaf node data.

This sort of parse tree also leads naturally to a recursive function for evaluating the values of different parts of the tree. The value of each node is the value of the subtrees represented by its children, combined using the operation represented by the node. For example, the value of the node representing the multiplication operator "*" in the expression (A + C) * (A − B) is the value of the expression "(A + C)" multiplied by the value of the expression "(A − B)." The Visual Basic code to evaluate this sort of tree is shown below.

```
Type InternalNode
    Operation As String * 1
    LeftChild As Integer
    RightChild As Integer
End Type
```

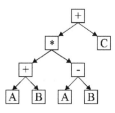

Index	1	2	3	4
Operation	+	*	+	-
LeftChild	2	3	1001	1001
RightChild	1003	4	1003	1002

Index	1001	1002	1003
Label	A	B	C
Value	127	32	1701

Figure 5.4 Parse tree for expression ((A + C) * (A − B)) + C.

```
Type LeafNode
    Label As String * 1
    Value As Double
End Type

Dim TheInternalNodes(1 To 1000) As InternalNode
Dim TheLeafNodes (1001 To 2000) As LeafNode

Function ExprValue (node As Integer) As Double
Dim Value1 As Double
Dim Value2 As Double

    If node > 1000 Then
        ' This is leaf node data.
        ExprValue = TheLeafNodes(node).Value
    Else
        ' This is an internal node.
        Value1 = ExprValue(TheInternalNodes(node).LeftChild)
        Value2 = ExprValue(TheInternalNodes(node).RightChild)
        Select Case TheInternalNodes(node).Operation
            Case "+"
                ExprValue = Value1 + Value2
            Case "-"
                ExprValue = Value1 - Value2
            Case "*"
                ExprValue = Value1 * Value2
            Case "/"
                ExprValue = Value1 / Value2
        End Select
    End If
End Function
```

This example does not handle unary operations like "–A" and "Sqr(B)." It also does not handle constant leaf node values like "7." It would be easy for you to extend the function to handle these other cases.

Linked Siblings

Sometimes the degrees of the nodes in a tree vary quite a bit and a fat node strategy would waste a lot of space. To build the tree shown in Figure 5.5 using fat nodes, you would need to give every node six child pointers even though only one node actually needed all six of them. The fat node representation of this tree would require 72 child pointers, only 11 of which would actually be used.

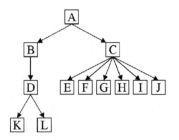

Figure 5.5 Tree with nodes of widely varying degree.

In some programs the degree of the nodes will change while the program is running. By adding and removing nodes, the program may change a node's degree so you may not be able to tell beforehand how many children a node might need. In this case the fat node strategy will not work.

You can handle both of these cases by essentially placing each node's children in a linked list. Instead of giving a node separate pointers to all of its children, you give it a pointer only to its first (leftmost) child. Then each child node contains a pointer to the next child in the parent's list of children. By following this list, you can find all of the children of a particular node. The user-defined structure that holds these nodes is shown below.

```
Type MyNode
    Label As String * 1
    FirstChild As Integer
    NextSibling As Integer
End Type
```

Figure 5.6 shows the tree from Figure 5.5 converted into a linked sibling representation.

Using a linked sibling representation, you can build trees of any degree using just one type of node. This not only simplifies list management chores, it also reduces the amount of wasted space in the data structure. To build this tree with a fat node representation would require 72 child pointers though only 11 would be used. The linked sibling representation requires only 24 first child and next sibling pointers, 11 of which are still used. Instead of wasting 61 unused child pointers, this representation leaves only 13 pointers unused.

You can analyze the space requirements for the linked sibling method more precisely. Each node except the root will be pointed to by either a FirstChild entry or a NextSibling entry. This means that, if there are N nodes in the tree, there will be N – 1 FirstChild or NextSibling entries in use and pointing to nodes.

Each node except the root will also have an unused FirstChild entry if it is a leaf node. If a node is not a leaf node, its children will have one unused NextSibling entry to mark the end of the sibling list. This means that for each node in the tree there will either be one unused FirstChild entry if it is a leaf node, or its children will have one unused

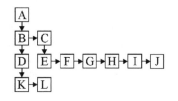

Index	0	1	2	3	4	5	6	7	8	9	10	11
Label	A	B	C	D	E	F	G	H	I	J	K	L
FirstChild	1	3	4	10								
NextSibling		2			5	6	7	8	9		11	

Figure 5.6 Linked sibling representation.

NextSibling entry. The root is a little different because it has both an unused NextSibling entry and its children have an unused NextSibling entry. This makes the total number of unused FirstChild and NextSibling array entries N + 1—one for each node plus one extra for the root.

The total number of pointer entries is the sum of the used and unused entries or (N − 1) + (N + 1). This makes the total number of pointer entries needed by the linked sibling representation 2 * N.

As was the case with the fat node method, you can use leaf child pointers to point to leaf data. If you dimension the internal node and leaf node arrays so their indexes do not overlap, you will be able to tell what kind of item you are looking at by the value of the pointer.

Similarly you could use unused sibling pointers to point to some other kind of data if you needed to associate a piece of data with each group of siblings.

Example program N_ARY uses linked siblings to allow you to create and manage a tree much as program BINARY does. In this program, however, you can add as many children as you like to each node in the tree.

To avoid making the program's user interface more complicated than necessary, the program always adds new nodes at the end of the parent's child list. If you add a child to a node that already has children, the program will place the new node to the right of the other children. You could modify the program to allow you to insert nodes in the middle of the child list, but the user interface would become fairly complicated.

Forward Star

Another compact representation of trees, and graphs and networks in general, is the *forward star* representation that was introduced in Chapter 2. In this version, an array FirstLink holds the index of the first branch leaving each node. Another array, ToNode, tells to which other node the branch points.

A sentinel entry at the end of the FirstLink array points just beyond the last entry in the ToNode array. This makes it easy to determine which branches leave each node. The branches leaving node I would be the branches numbered FirstLink(I), FirstLink(I) + 1, . . . , FirstLink(I + 1) − 1. In Visual Basic you could list the links leaving node I like this:

```
For link = FirstLink(I) To FirstLink(I + 1) - 1
    Print Format$(I) & " -> " & Format$(ToNode(link))
Next link
```

Figure 5.7 shows a tree and its forward star representation. The links out of node 3 (labeled D), for example, are the links FirstLink(3) through FirstLink(4) − 1. FirstLink(3) = 9 and FirstLink(4) = 11 so these are the links numbered 9 and 10. The ToNode entries for these links are ToNode(9) = 10 and ToNode(10) = 11 so the children of node 3 are nodes 10 and 11. These are the nodes labeled K and L. All of this indicates that the links leaving node D go to nodes K and L.

The sentinel is in the 12th position in the FirstLink array. It allows you to locate the links leaving the 11th node (labeled J). The links leaving that node are those from FirstLink(11) to FirstLink(12) − 1. FirstLink(11) is 11 and FirstLink(12) − 1 is 10 so the links are those between 11 and 10. Since 11 is greater than 10, there are no links leaving this node. If you were to use a **For** loop to iterate over this node's children, the loop would look like this:

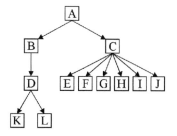

FirstLink:

Index	0	1	2	3	4	5	6	7	8	9	10	11	12
Label	A	B	C	D	E	F	G	H	I	J	K	L	
FirstLink	0	2	3	9	11	11	11	11	11	11	11	11	11

ToNode:

Index	0	1	2	3	4	5	6	7	8	9	10
ToNode	1	2	3	4	5	6	7	8	9	10	11

Figure 5.7 Forward star representation.

```
For I = FirstLink(11) To FirstLink(12) - 1
    ' Do something...
Next I
```

Since FirstLink(11) is greater than FirstLink(12) – 1, this loop would end immediately without executing the statements within the loop.

The forward star representation shown in Figure 5.7 uses 24 entries for the FirstLink and ToNode arrays. All of these entries are used, though some contain duplicated values to indicate that a node does not have any links leaving it. The linked sibling representation of this tree also required 24 first child and next sibling pointers, 11 of which were used. You can compare the space requirements of a forward star representation to those of a linked sibling representation more carefully.

Each node in the forward star representation will have one FirstLink array entry, plus there will be one extra FirstLink entry for the sentinel. If there are N nodes in the tree, this makes a total of N + 1 FirstLink entries.

For each link in the tree, there is a ToNode array entry. For any tree, every node except the root is connected to its parent by a link. That means that the number of links in a tree with N nodes is N – 1 so there must be N – 1 ToNode array entries.

The total number of FirstLink and ToNode array entries in the forward star representation is (N + 1) + (N – 1) = 2 * N. This is exactly the same amount of space that is required by the linked sibling implementation.

Given that the linked sibling and forward star representations of a tree use the same amount of space, which is better? As is so often the case, the answer depends on your circumstances. Using forward star you can quickly and easily perform operations on the links that leave a particular node. Operations like these are not much more difficult using the linked sibling representation, but they are a little more time consuming. Compare the two subroutines below.

```
Sub PrintForwardStarLinks (node As Integer)
Dim link as Integer

    For link = Nodes(node).FirstLink To Nodes(node + 1).FirstLink - 1
        Print Format$(node) & " -> " & Format$(ToNode(link))
    Next link
End Sub

Sub PrintLinkedSiblingsLinks
Dim child As Integer

    child = Nodes(node).FirstChild
    Do While child <> END_OF_LIST
        Print Format$(node) & " -> " & Format$(child)
        child = Nodes(child).NextSibling
    Loop
End Sub
```

Both of these subroutines are short and easy to understand. In Visual Basic **For** loops tend to be slightly faster than **While** loops, however, so the forward star version generally gives better performance. In one series of tests, the subroutine using a **For** loop was almost twice as fast as the version using a **While** loop.

It is partly for this reason that much of the literature about network algorithms uses a forward star representation. Many articles about shortest path calculations, for example, assume that the data is in forward star or some similar format. If you ever decide to research these algorithms in journals like *Management Science* or *Operations Research*, you will need to understand forward star.

On the other hand, the forward star format is extremely difficult to modify. If you wanted to add a new child to node A in Figure 5.7, you would have to update almost every entry in both the FirstLink and ToNode arrays. First you would need to move every entry in the ToNode array one position to the right to make room for the new node's link. Next you would insert the new ToNode entry, pointing to the new node. Finally you would run through the FirstLink array updating each entry so it pointed to the new position of the corresponding ToNode entry. Since you moved all of the ToNode entries one position to the right to make room for the new link, you would need to add one to the affected FirstLink entries. Figure 5.8 shows this tree after the new node has been added. In the forward star arrays the items that have been modified are shaded so they are easy to see.

Removing a node from the beginning of a tree's forward star representation is just as hard as adding one. If the node you are removing has children, the process becomes even more time consuming since you will need to recursively remove the children first.

In summary, the relative simplicity of linked siblings makes that representation better if you will need to modify your tree frequently. It is usually easier to understand and debug routines that modify trees using linked siblings.

On the other hand, forward star may provide better performance for some complicated tree algorithms. Forward star is also a standard data structure discussed in the literature, so you will need to be familiar with it if you want to do further research into tree and network algorithms.

Example program FSTAR uses a forward star representation to allow you to create and manage a tree with nodes of varying degree. This program is similar to program N_ARY except it uses a forward star representation instead of linked siblings.

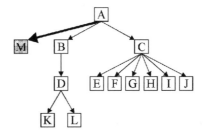

FirstLink:

Index	0	1	2	3	4	5	6	7	8	9	10	11	12	13
Label	A	B	C	D	E	F	G	H	I	J	K	L	M	
FirstLink	0	3	4	10	12	12	12	12	12	12	12	12	12	12

ToNode:

Index	0	1	2	3	4	5	6	7	8	9	10	11
ToNode	12	1	2	3	4	5	6	7	8	9	10	11

Figure 5.8 Adding a node in forward star.

If you examine the code of program FSTAR, you will see how difficult it is to add and remove nodes. The code to remove a node from a tree in forward star representation is shown below.

```
' Remove a node and its descendants.
Sub FreeNodeAndChildren (ByVal parent As Integer, ByVal link As _
Integer, ByVal node As Integer)
    ' Recursively remove the node's children
    Do While FirstLink(node) < FirstLink(node + 1)
        FreeNodeAndChildren node, FirstLink(node), _
ToNode(FirstLink(node))
    Loop

    ' Remove the link
    RemoveLink parent, link

    ' Remove the node itself
    RemoveNode node
End Sub
' Remove a link.
Sub RemoveLink (node As Integer, link As Integer)
Dim i As Integer

    ' Update FirstLink entries
    For i = node + 1 To NumNodes
        FirstLink(i) = FirstLink(i) - 1
    Next i

    ' Shift ToNode array to fill in the link's spot
    For i = link + 1 To NumLinks - 1
        ToNode(i - 1) = ToNode(i)
    Next i
```

```
        ' Remove the extra position in ToNode
        NumLinks = NumLinks - 1
        If NumLinks > 0 Then ReDim Preserve ToNode(0 To NumLinks - 1)
End Sub


' Remove a node that has no children and no parent.
Sub RemoveNode (node As Integer)
Dim i As Integer

        ' Slide FirstLink entries over to fill in the vacated spot
        For i = node + 1 To NumNodes
            FirstLink(i - 1) = FirstLink(i)
        Next i

        ' Slide NodeLabel entries over
        For i = node + 1 To NumNodes - 1
            NodeLabel(i - 1) = NodeLabel(i)
        Next i

        ' Update ToNode entries pointing to nodes after this
        For i = 0 To NumLinks - 1
            If ToNode(i) >= node Then ToNode(i) = ToNode(i) - 1
        Next i

        ' Remove the extra FirstLink entry
        NumNodes = NumNodes - 1
        ReDim Preserve FirstLink(0 To NumNodes)

        ReDim Preserve NodeLabel(0 To NumNodes - 1)
        Unload TreeForm.NodeText(NumNodes)
End Sub
```

This is much more complicated than the corresponding code used by program N_ARY to remove a node from a tree in a linked sibling representation:

```
' Put this node, its descendants, its siblings, and their
' descendants on the trash pile.
Sub TrashNode (node As Integer)
    If node = END_OF_LIST Then Exit Sub

    TrashNode Nodes(node).FirstChild
    TrashNode Nodes(node).NextSibling

    NAryForm.NodeText(node).Visible = False
    Nodes(node).NextSibling = TopGarbage
    TopGarbage = node
End Sub
```

Complete Trees

A *complete* tree has as many nodes as it can hold at each level, except it may be missing some nodes on the bottom level. Any nodes present on the bottom level are pushed to the left. Each level in a ternary tree, for example, has exactly three children, except for the leaves and possibly one node on the level above the leaves. Figure 5.9 shows a complete binary tree and a complete ternary tree.

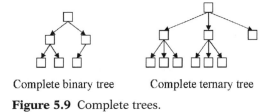

Complete binary tree   Complete ternary tree

Figure 5.9 Complete trees.

Complete trees have a number of important properties. First, they are the shortest trees that can hold a given number of nodes. The binary tree in Figure 5.9, for example, is as short as any other binary tree that can hold six nodes. There are other binary trees of height three that can hold six nodes, but there are none of height less than three.

Second, if a complete tree of degree D contains N nodes, it will have $O(\log_D(N))$ height and O(N) leaf nodes. These facts are important since many algorithms traverse trees from the top to the bottom or vice versa. An algorithm that does this once would have a run time $O(\log(N))$.

Another useful property of complete trees is that you can store them very compactly in arrays. If you number the nodes in the "natural" way, from top to bottom and left to right, you can place the tree entries in an array in this natural order. Figure 5.10 shows how you can place a complete binary tree in an array.

Begin by placing the root of the tree in array position 0. Then place the children of node I at positions 2 * I + 1 and 2 * I + 2. For example, in Figure 5.10 the children of the node at position 1 (node B) are the nodes in positions 3 and 4 (nodes D and E).

It is easy to generalize this representation for complete trees of higher degree D. Again, place the root node in array position 0. Place the children of node I at positions D * I + 1, D * I + 2, . . . , D * I + (I − 1). In a ternary tree, for instance, the children of a node at position 2 would be at positions 7, 8, and 9. Figure 5.11 shows a complete ternary tree and its array representation.

No space is wasted in these array-based representations of complete trees. In fact, while the linked sibling and forward star representations required 2 * N extra array entries for link information, this representation requires no additional space at all. This makes the array representation clearly better if you can store your data in a complete tree.

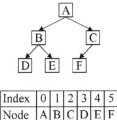

Index	0	1	2	3	4	5
Node	A	B	C	D	E	F

Figure 5.10 Placing a complete binary tree in an array.

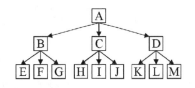

Index	0	1	2	3	4	5	6	7	8	9	10	11	12
ToNode	A	B	C	D	E	F	G	H	I	J	K	L	M

Figure 5.11 Placing a complete ternary tree in an array.

Tree Traversal

Visiting each node in a tree is called *traversing* the tree. There are several possible orders in which you might want to visit the nodes in a binary tree. The three simplest are preorder, inorder, and postorder. These each have straightforward recursive algorithms. When the algorithm is considering any given node it should:

Preorder:

1. Visit the node.
2. Recursively traverse the left subtree in preorder.
3. Recursively traverse the right subtree in preorder.

Inorder:

1. Recursively traverse the left subtree in inorder.
2. Visit the node.
3. Recursively traverse the right subtree in inorder.

Postorder:

1. Recursively traverse the left subtree in postorder.
2. Recursively traverse the right subtree in postorder.
3. Visit the node.

All three of these are *depth first* traversals. That means the traversal begins by working its way deeply into the tree until it reaches the leaves. As the recursive subroutine calls return, the algorithm works its way back up through the tree visiting paths that it passed on the way down. Depth first traversals are useful in algorithms that must visit a leaf early. The branch and bound algorithm described in Chapter 7, for example, visits a leaf node as soon as possible. It then uses the results at that leaf to reduce the size of the search it must make through the rest of the tree.

A fourth method of visiting the nodes in a tree is *breadth first* traversal. A breadth first traversal visits all of the nodes at a given level of the tree before it visits any nodes on deeper levels. Algorithms that perform an exhaustive search of a tree often use breadth first traversals. In some of these it is important that the algorithm not get too deeply into the tree until it has examined all of the upper level nodes. The label setting shortest path algorithm, described in Chapter 11, is in a sense a breadth first traversal of a shortest path tree within a network.

Figure 5.12 shows a small tree and the order in which the nodes are visited during preorder, inorder, postorder, and breadth first traversals.

For trees of degree greater than two, it still makes sense to define preorder, postorder, and breadth first traversals. There may be some ambiguity in defining an inorder traversal, however, since each node could be visited after one, two, or more of its children. In a ternary tree, for example, a node might be visited after its first child was visited or after its second child was visited.

Details of algorithms for traversing a tree will depend upon how the tree is stored. If you store the tree in a linked sibling structure, you will need to use a similar but different algorithm than the one you would use if you stored the tree in forward star format.

Complete trees stored in arrays are particularly easy to traverse. For a complete binary tree, the traversal algorithms look like this:

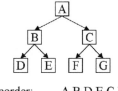

Preorder: A B D E C F G
Inorder: D B E A F C G
Postorder: D E B F G C A
Breadth first: A B C D E F G

Figure 5.12 Tree traversals.

```
Dim NodeLabel() As String      ' Stores the label of the nodes.
Dim NumNodes As Integer

' Initialize the tree somewhere.
'     ReDim NodeLabel(0 To NumNodes - 1)
'       Etc.

Sub PreorderPrint(node As Integer)
    Print NodeLabel(node)
    If node * 2 + 1 <= NumNodes Then PreorderPrint node * 2 + 1
    If node * 2 + 2 <= NumNodes Then PreorderPrint node * 2 + 2
End Sub

Sub InorderPrint(node As Integer)
    If node * 2 + 1 <= NumNodes Then InorderPrint node * 2 + 1
    Print NodeLabel(node)
    If node * 2 + 2 <= NumNodes Then InorderPrint node * 2 + 2
End Sub

Sub PostorderPrint(node As Integer)
    If node * 2 + 1 <= NumNodes Then PostorderPrint node * 2 + 1
    If node * 2 + 2 <= NumNodes Then PostorderPrint node * 2 + 2
    Print NodeLabel(node)
End Sub

Sub BreadthFirstPrint()
Dim i As Integer

    For i = 0 To NumNodes
        Print NodeLabel(i)
    Next i
End Sub
```

Example program TRAV1 demonstrates how to perform preorder, inorder, postorder, and breadth first traversals for array-based complete binary trees. If you enter the height of the tree you want to traverse and press the Create Tree button, the program will create a full binary tree of the specified height. Then you can press the Preorder, Inorder, Postorder, or Breadth First buttons to see the corresponding traversals for the tree.

The preorder and postorder traversals for trees stored in other representations are just as easy. The preorder traversal routine for a tree stored in forward star format might look like this:

```
Sub PreorderPrint(node As Integer)
Dim link As Integer

    Print NodeLabel(node)
    For link = FirstLink(node) To FirstLink(node + 1) - 1
        PreorderPrint ToNode(link)
    Next link
End Sub
```

As was mentioned earlier, it is hard to define the inorder traversal for trees of degree greater than two. If you did decide what an inorder traversal meant, however, you would not have too much trouble implementing it. If you decided that the inorder traversal for a tree should visit half of the child nodes (rounding up), then visit the node itself, and then visit the remaining child nodes, an inorder traversal algorithm for forward star might look like this:

```
Sub InorderPrint (node As Integer)
Dim mid_link As Integer
Dim link As Integer

    ' Find the middle child.
    mid_link = (FirstLink(node + 1) - 1 + FirstLink(node)) \ 2

    ' Visit the first group of children
    For link = FirstLink(node) To mid_link
        InorderPrint ToNode(link)
    Next link

    ' Visit the node
    Print NodeLabel(node)

    ' Visit the second group of children
    For link = mid_link + 1 To FirstLink(node + 1) - 1
        InorderPrint ToNode(link)
    Next link
End Sub
```

For complete trees stored in an array, the nodes just happen to be stored in breadth first order. This makes a breadth first traversal easy for this kind of tree. If the tree is not a complete tree stored in an array, performing a breadth first traversal is not as simple.

To traverse other kinds of trees, you can use a queue to store the nodes that you have not yet visited. Start by placing the root node in the queue. To visit a node, remove it from the front of the queue and add its children to the back. Repeat this process until the queue is empty. Since you add all of a node's children to the end of the queue at the same time, you will later visit the children one after another before you visit any of their children. For a tree represented in forward star, the breadth first traversal routine might look like this:

```
Sub BreadthFirstPrint ()
Dim node As Integer
Dim link As Integer

    ' Start with the root in the queue.
    EnterQueue 0
```

```
    ' Repeatedly process the top item in the queue until
    ' the queue is empty.
    Do While QueueBack - QueueFront > 0
        node = LeaveQueue()

        ' Visit the node
        Print NodeLabel(node)

        ' Add the node's children to the queue.
        For link = FirstLink(node) To FirstLink(node + 1) - 1
            EnterQueue ToNode(link)
        Next link
    Loop
End Sub
```

Example program TRAV2 demonstrates tree traversal for a tree stored in forward star format. The program is basically a combination of program FSTAR, which lets you create and manage a tree in forward star format, and program TRAV1, which demonstrates traversals for complete trees. Click on a node and then press the Add Child button to add a new child to that node. Click on a node and press the Remove Child button to remove that node and its descendants from the tree. Press the Preorder, Inorder, Postorder, or Breadth First buttons to see the corresponding traversals for the tree.

Sorted Trees

Binary trees are often a natural way to store and manipulate information in computer programs. Since many computer operations are binary, they map naturally onto binary trees. As was shown earlier in this chapter, the arithmetic operators +, –, *, and / are all binary and you can use them to manipulate arithmetic expressions as binary parse trees (see pages 115–116).

Like binary operations, binary relationships map well onto binary trees. The "less than" relationship is a good example. If you use nodes to mean "the left child is less than the right child," you can use a binary tree to build and store a sorted list. Figure 5.13 shows a binary tree holding a sorted list containing the numbers 1, 2, 4, 6, 7, 9.

The algorithm for inserting a new item into this kind of tree is simple. Begin at the root node. As you examine each node, compare that node's value to the value of the new item. If the new item's value is less than or equal to the value at the node, continue down the left branch of the tree. If the new item's value is greater than the value at the node, continue down the right branch. When you reach a leaf node, insert the item at that position.

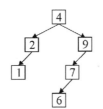

Figure 5.13 The sorted list: 1, 2, 4, 6, 7, 9.

To insert the value 8 in the tree shown in Figure 5.13, you would begin at the root which has value 4. Since 8 is greater than 4, you would follow the right branch in the tree to the node with value 9. Then, since 8 is less than 9, you would follow the left branch to the node with value 7. Since 8 is greater than 7, you would next try to follow the right branch again, but this node has no right child. This is where you insert the new item giving the tree shown in Figure 5.14.

In Visual Basic you can write this algorithm as:

```
' Add a new item to the tree.
Sub InsertItem (node As Integer, node_data As Integer)
    If node = END_OF_LIST Then
        ' We have reached a leaf. Insert the item.
        node = NewNode(node_data)
    ElseIf node_data <= Nodes(node).NodeData Then
        ' Branch left
        InsertItem Nodes(node).LeftChild, node_data
    Else
        ' Branch right
        InsertItem Nodes(node).RightChild, node_data
    End If
End Sub
```

When this routine reaches the bottom of the tree, something fairly subtle occurs. In Visual Basic when you pass a parameter to a subroutine, that parameter is *passed by reference* unless you use the **ByVal** keyword. This means that the subroutine works with the same copy of the parameter that the calling routine uses. If the subroutine changes the value of the parameter, the value is changed for the calling routine as well.

The reason this is important in this example is that, when it recursively calls itself, subroutine InsertItem passes itself a pointer to a child in the tree. For example:

```
InsertItem Nodes(node).RightChild, node_data
```

This right child pointer is passed as the node parameter in the subroutine call. If the called routine changes the value of the node parameter, the child pointer will be automatically updated in the calling routine as well.

In this algorithm when a call to InsertItem finally reaches the bottom of the tree, it creates a new node to hold the new item. It also sets the value of the node parameter to point to this new node. Since the node parameter was passed into InsertItem by the calling routine, this automatically sets the value of the proper child pointer in the calling routine and the node is automatically added to the tree. In the example above, Nodes(node).RightChild is automatically set to point to the new node.

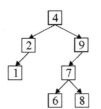

Figure 5.14 The sorted list: 1, 2, 4, 6, 7, 8, 9.

Removing an item from this kind of tree is a bit trickier than inserting one. Whenever you remove an item, you may need to rearrange the other nodes so the "less than" relationship still holds throughout the tree. There are several cases to consider.

First, if the item being removed has no children, you can just remove it from the tree. Since it has no children, the ordering of the nodes remaining in the tree will not be changed when you remove this item.

Second, if the item has one child, you can replace the item with its child. The ordering of the descendants of the node will stay the same since they are also descendants of the child. The fact that the node being removed had only one child makes it possible for the child to take the place of its parent. Figure 5.15 shows a tree where the node 4, which has only one child, is being removed.

The final case to consider is when the node being removed has two children. In this case you cannot necessarily replace the node with one of its children. If the child you wanted to move also has two children, there will not be room for all of the children at the removed node's location. Since the node you are removing has one extra child, and the child node you are moving has two children, you would need to assign three children to the node in the new location.

To solve this problem, you can replace the removed node with the rightmost node to the left of it in the tree. In other words, move down the left branch out of the node being removed. Then move down right branches from there until you encounter a node with no right branch. That is the rightmost node to the left of the node you are removing.

In the tree on the left in Figure 5.16, node 3 is the rightmost node to the left of node 4. You can replace node 4 with node 3 and preserve the tree's ordering.

One last detail remains if the replacement node has a left child. In that case, you can move this child into the position vacated by the replacement node and the tree will again be in proper order. You know that the rightmost node does not have a right child, otherwise it would not have been the rightmost node. That means you do not need to worry about the replacement node having two children.

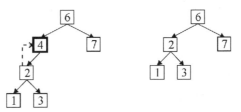

Figure 5.15 Removing a node with one child.

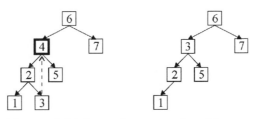

Figure 5.16 Removing a node with two children.

Figure 5.17 shows this complicated situation. In this example, the node 8 is being removed from the tree. The rightmost node to the left of node 8 is node 7. Node 7 also has a child—node 5. To remove node 8 while preserving the tree's ordering, replace node 8 with node 7, and node 7 with node 5. Notice that node 7 gets completely new children while node 5 keeps its single child.

In Visual Basic the algorithm for removing a node from a binary tree using a fat node representation looks like this:

```
' Remove an item from the tree.
Sub DeleteItem (node As Integer, Value As Integer)
Dim target As Integer

    ' If we did not find the item, say so
    If node = END_OF_LIST Then
        Beep
        MsgBox "Item " & Format$(Value) & " is not in the tree."
        Exit Sub
    End If


    If Value < Nodes(node).NodeData Then
        ' Continue down left subtree
        DeleteItem Nodes(node).LeftChild, Value
    ElseIf Value > Nodes(node).NodeData Then
        ' Continue down right subtree
        DeleteItem Nodes(node).RightChild, Value
    Else
        ' This is the target
        target = node
        If Nodes(target).LeftChild = END_OF_LIST Then
            node = Nodes(node).RightChild
        ElseIf Nodes(target).RightChild = END_OF_LIST Then
            node = Nodes(node).LeftChild
        Else
            ReplaceRightmost node, Nodes(node).LeftChild
        End If
        FreeNode target
    End If
End Sub


' Look for the replacement node.
Sub ReplaceRightmost (target As Integer, repl As Integer)
Dim old_repl As Integer
```

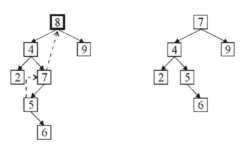

Figure 5.17 Removing a node when the replacement node has a child.

```
    If Nodes(repl).RightChild <> END_OF_LIST Then
        ReplaceRightmost target, Nodes(repl).RightChild
    Else
        ' Remember what node repl is.
        old_repl = repl

        ' Replace repl with its left child.
        repl = Nodes(repl).LeftChild
        ' Replace target with repl.
        Nodes(old_repl).LeftChild = Nodes(target).LeftChild
        Nodes(old_repl).RightChild = Nodes(target).RightChild
        target = old_repl
    End If
End Sub
```

This algorithm uses the trick of passing parameters by reference into recursive subroutines in two places. First, subroutine DeleteItem uses this trick to make the target node's parent point to the replacement node. The subroutine is invoked as:

```
DeleteItem Nodes(node).RightChild, Value
```

When the routine finally finds the target node (node 8 in Figure 5.17), it receives the parent node's pointer to the target in the node parameter. In the example above, this pointer is Nodes(node).RightChild. By setting this parameter to the index of the replacement node (node 7), DeleteItem sets the parent's child so it points to the new node. Nodes(Node).RightChild is assigned the value 7.

Similarly, subroutine ReplaceRightmost calls itself as in:

```
ReplaceRightmost target, Nodes(repl).RightChild
```

When this routine finds the rightmost node to the left of the node being removed (node 7 in Figure 5.17), the Repl parameter holds the pointer from the parent to the rightmost node. When the routine sets the value of Repl to Nodes(Repl).LeftChild, it automatically connects the rightmost node's parent to the rightmost node's left child (node 5). In this example, ReplaceRightmost sets Nodes(Repl).RightChild to point to the left child.

Example program TREESORT uses these routines to create and manage a sorted binary tree. Enter an integer and press the Add button to add an item in its proper position in the tree. Enter an integer and press the Remove button to remove that item from the tree. When you remove a node, the tree will automatically rearrange itself as described above to preserve the "less than" ordering.

A useful fact about this kind of tree is that the inorder traversal visits the nodes in their sorted order. The inorder traversal of the tree shown in Figure 5.18, for instance, visits the nodes in the order 2-4-5-6-7-8-9 which is the sorted ordering of the tree's items. The fact that inorder traversals of sorted trees visit the items in sorted order leads to a simple sorting algorithm:

1. Add the items to a sorted tree.
2. Print the items using an inorder traversal.

This algorithm usually works quite well. If you add items to a tree in certain orders, however, the tree may become tall and thin. Figure 5.19 shows the sorted tree you get if

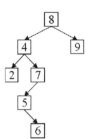

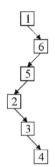

Figure 5.18 Inorder traversal of a sorted tree: 2, 4, 5, 6, 7, 8, 9.

Figure 5.19 Tree obtained by adding items in the order 1, 6, 5, 2, 3, 4.

you add items to it in the order 1, 6, 5, 2, 3, 4. You can obtain similar tall thin trees by adding the items in one of many other orders. Unfortunately if you add the items in sorted or reverse sorted orders, you also get a tall thin tree. This can be a problem since many programs store items in sorted order.

The taller a sorted tree becomes, the longer it takes to add new items at the bottom of the tree. In the worst case, after you add N items, the tree will have height O(N). The total time to insert all of the items into the tree will have been O(N²). Since it takes O(N) time to traverse the tree, the total time needed to sort the numbers using the tree would be O(N²) + O(N) = O(N²).

If the tree remains fairly short, it will have height O(log(N)). In that case it will take only O(log(N)) steps to insert an item in the tree. To insert all N items in the tree would require O(N * log(N)) steps. Then to sort the items using the tree would take time O(N * log(N)) + O(N) = O(N * log(N)).

This O(N * log(N)) time is much better than O(N²). To build a tall thin tree containing 1,000 items, for example, would take about 1 million steps. To create a short tree of height O(log(N)) would take only around 10,000 steps.

If the items are initially randomly arranged, the tree's shape will probably be somewhere between these two extremes. While it may have height slightly larger than log(N), it will not be too tall and thin so the sorting algorithm will perform well.

Chapter 6 describes ways in which you can rebalance trees so they do not grow tall and thin no matter what order you add the items in. Those methods are rather complicated, however, and they are really not worth applying to this tree-based sorting algorithm. Many of the sorting algorithms described in Chapter 8 provide better performance than this algorithm and they are easier to implement.

Threaded Trees

Chapter 2 described how you could add threads to a linked list to make it easier to list the items in different orders (see pages 42–44). You can use the same idea to make it easier to visit the nodes in a tree in more than one order. By placing threads in the unused child pointers contained in a binary tree, you can make it easier to list the tree's nodes in the order of the tree's inorder and reversed inorder traversals. If the tree is a sorted tree, these are the nodes' sorted and reversed sorted orders.

To create the threads, store the indexes of the nodes' inorder predecessors and successors in the unused child pointers. If a node has an unused left child pointer, store a thread in that position indicating the node's predecessor in the inorder traversal. If a node has an unused right child pointer, store a thread in that position indicating the node's successor in the inorder traversal. Since the threads are symmetric, with left child threads pointing to predecessors and right child threads pointing to successors, this kind of tree is called a *symmetrically threaded tree*. Figure 5.20 shows a symmetrically threaded tree with the threads drawn in dashed lines.

Since the threads occupy the positions of child pointers in the tree, you need a way to tell the difference between thread pointers and normal child pointers. The easiest way to do this is to dimension the array of nodes starting with index one. Then assign to each thread the negative of the index of the node to which it points. If a thread should point to node number 12, give it the value –12. Then if you encounter a pointer with value greater than zero, you know you are dealing with a pointer to a child node. When you find a pointer with value less than zero that is not a special value like END_OF_LIST, you are dealing with a thread.

To use the threads to find the predecessor of a node, examine the node's left child pointer. If the pointer is a thread, the thread indicates the node's predecessor. If the pointer is the value END_OF_LIST, this node is the first node in the inorder traversal of the tree and has no predecessor. Otherwise follow the pointer to the node's left child. Then follow the descendants' right child pointers until you reach a node that has a thread instead of a right child. That node (not the one indicated by the thread) is the predecessor of the original node. This node is the rightmost node to the left of the original node in the tree.

The Visual Basic code for this algorithm is:

```
Function Predecessor (node As Integer) As Integer
Dim child As Integer

    If Nodes(node).LeftChild = END_OF_LIST Then
        ' This is the first node in the inorder traversal.
        Predecessor = END_OF_LIST
    Else If Nodes(node).LeftChild < 0 Then
        ' The thread points to the predecessor.
        Predecessor = -Nodes(node).LeftChild
    Else
        ' Else find the rightmost node to the left.
        child = Nodes(node).LeftChild
        Do While Nodes(child).RightChild > 0
            child = Nodes(child).RightChild
```

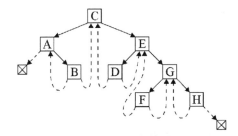

Figure 5.20 A symmetrically threaded tree.

```
        Loop
        Predecessor = child
    End If
End Function
```

Using the threads to locate the successor of a node is similar. Start by examining the node's right child pointer. If the pointer is a thread, the thread indicates the node's successor. If the pointer is the value END_OF_LIST, this node is the last node in the inorder traversal of the tree and has no successor. Otherwise follow the pointer to the node's right child. Then follow the descendants' left child pointers until you reach a node that has a thread for a left child pointer. That node is the successor of the original node. This node is the leftmost node to the right of the original node in the tree.

```
Function Successor (node As Integer) As Integer
Dim child As Integer

    If Nodes(node).RightChild = END_OF_LIST Then
        ' This is the last node in the inorder traversal.
        Successor = END_OF_LIST
    Else If Nodes(node).RightChild < 0 Then
        ' The thread points to the successor.
        Successor = -Nodes(node).RightChild
    Else
        ' Else find the leftmost node to the right.
        child = Nodes(node).RightChild
        Do While Nodes(child).LeftChild > 0
            child = Nodes(child).LeftChild
        Loop
        Successor = child
    End If
End Function
```

It is also convenient to have functions that locate the first and last nodes in the tree. To find the first node, simply follow the left child pointers down from the root until you reach a node that has a left child pointer with value END_OF_LIST. To find the last node, follow the right child pointers down from the root until you reach a node that has a right child pointer with value END_OF_LIST.

```
Function FirstNode ()
Dim node As Integer

    node = Root
    Do While Nodes(node).LeftChild <> END_OF_LIST
        node = Nodes(node).LeftChild
    Loop
    FirstNode = node
End Function


Function LastNode ()
Dim node As Integer

    node = Root
    Do While Nodes(node).RightChild <> END_OF_LIST
        node = Nodes(node).RightChild
```

```
    Loop
    FirstNode = node
End Function
```

Using these functions you can easily write routines that display the nodes in the tree in their forward and backward orders.

```
Sub PrintInorder
Dim node As Integer

    ' Find the first node.
    node = FindFirstNode(Root)

    ' Traverse the list.
    Do While node <> END_OF_LIST
        Print node
        node = Successor(node)
    Loop
End Sub

Sub PrintReverseInorder
Dim node As Integer

    ' Find the last node.
    node = FindLastNode(Root)

    ' Traverse the list.
    Do While node <> END_OF_LIST
        Print node
        node = Predecessor(node)
    Loop
End Sub
```

The inorder printing routine presented earlier in the chapter (see pages 124–127) used recursion. These new routines use neither recursion nor the stack you might use to remove recursion. The memory that would be needed by a stack is contained in the threads. The threads occupy the positions of child pointers which would have been unused anyway. Threads allow you to traverse the tree without using any extra memory or recursion.

Every child pointer in the tree contains either a link to a child or a thread to a predecessor or successor. Since each node has two child pointers, if there are N nodes in the tree there must be 2 * N links and threads. During these traversal algorithms each link and each thread in the tree is traversed once so the algorithms require $O(2 * N) = O(N)$ steps.

You can make these subroutines a bit faster if you keep track of the indexes of the first and last nodes in the tree in addition to the index of the root node. Then you will not need to search for the first or last node whenever you want to list the nodes in order. Since the algorithms must visit each node in any case, and since there are N nodes in the tree, the run time for the algorithms will still be $O(N)$, but they will be a little faster in practice.

In order to maintain a threaded tree, you must be able to add and remove nodes from the tree while keeping it properly threaded.

Suppose you want to add a new node to the tree as the left child of node A. Since you are inserting the node in this position, the left child of node A must currently be unused as a child pointer and therefore it contains a thread. That thread points to the predecessor of node A. Since the new node will be the left child of node A, it will now become node A's predecessor. Node A will be the new node's successor. Finally, the node that was the predecessor of node A now becomes the predecessor of the new node.

If you are keeping track of the index of the first and last nodes in the tree, you should check at this point whether the new node is the new first node in the tree. If the predecessor thread of the new node has the value END_OF_LIST, then this is the new first node in the tree.

Figure 5.21 shows the tree in Figure 5.20 after the new node X has been added as the left child of node H.

Using all of these facts, it is easy to write a routine to insert a new left child for a node. Inserting a right child is similar.

```
Sub AddLeftChild(parent As Integer, child As Integer)
    ' The parent's predecessor becomes the new node's predecessor.
    Nodes(child).LeftChild = Nodes(parent).LeftChild

    ' Insert the node.
    Nodes(parent).LeftChild = child

    ' The parent is the new node's successor.
    Nodes(child).RightChild = -parent

    ' See if the new node is the first node in the tree.
    If Nodes(child).LeftChild = END_OF_LIST Then FirstNode = child
End Sub

Sub AddRightChild(parent As Integer, child As Integer)
    ' The parent's successor becomes the new node's successor.
    Nodes(child).RightChild = Nodes(parent).RightChild

    ' Insert the node.
    Nodes(parent).RightChild = child

    ' The parent is the new node's predecessor.
    Nodes(child).LeftChild = -parent

    ' See if the new node is the last node in the tree.
    If Nodes(child).RightChild = END_OF_LIST Then LastNode = child
End Sub
```

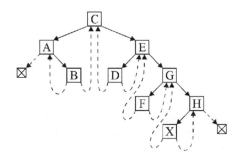

Figure 5.21 Threaded tree with node X added.

Before removing a node from the tree, remove its descendants. Once the node has no children, it is easy to remove.

Suppose the node being removed is the left child of its parent. The child's left pointer is a thread indicating the child's predecessor in the tree. When the child is removed, that predecessor becomes the predecessor of the parent node. To remove the child, simply set the parent node's left child pointer to the same value as the child's left child pointer.

The child's right child pointer is a thread indicating its successor in the tree. Since the child is the left child of its parent, that thread will indicate the parent node and it can be discarded when the child is removed. Figure 5.22 shows the tree in Figure 5.21 after the node F has been removed.

The method for removing a right child is similar.

```
Sub RemoveLeftChild(parent As Integer)
Dim child As Integer

    child = Nodes(parent).LeftChild
    Nodes(parent).LeftChild = Nodes(child).LeftChild
End Sub

Sub RemoveRightChild(parent As Integer)
Dim child As Integer

    child = Nodes(parent).RightChild
    Nodes(parent).RightChild = Nodes(child).RightChild
End Sub
```

Tries

Many applications manipulate long strings of characters like names, addresses, or inventory codes. If you store this sort of information in a sorted tree like the ones described in the previous sections, the time you spend comparing items in the tree can become quite large. If the strings are 40 or 50 characters long, comparing strings as you search down the tree can take quite a bit of time.

A *trie* is a special kind of tree that compares strings one character at a time to reduce the time needed to locate an item within a tree. While the term "trie" comes

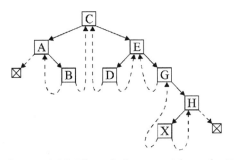

Figure 5.22 Threaded tree with node F removed.

from the word "*retrie*val," trie is usually pronounced "try" to avoid confusing it with the word "tree."

In a trie every node represents a single character of a string. Every node has a branch corresponding to each letter that appears in the words contained in the tree.

To locate an item within a trie, begin at the root node. Examine the first character in the string and follow the appropriate branch. If the character is an "A," follow the "A" branch.

When you reach the next node in the trie, examine the second letter in the string and follow the appropriate branch. Continue this way through the trie until you reach a leaf node. The leaf either represents the string you are trying to find, or the string is not in the trie. Figure 5.23 shows a trie that contains the names of six colors.

The easiest way to build a trie in Visual Basic is to use nodes that contain an array of 27 child pointers. The child pointers correspond to the letters in the alphabet plus one extra entry to indicate the end of a word. To determine which pointer corresponds to a particular character, you can use the character's ASCII value as the index into this array of child pointers.

```
Const ASC_A = 65      ' ASCII code for "A".
Const ASC_END = 91    ' ASCII code for "Z" plus 1 for end of word.


Type TrieNode
    Child(ASC_A To ASC_END) As Integer
End Type
```

You can store leaf nodes, which contain the values of the strings stored in the tree, in a separate array. To tell the difference between internal and leaf nodes in the trie, you must ensure that the indexes of the internal nodes do not overlap the indexes of the leaf nodes. If you dimension the TrieNode array starting at 1, and the array of leaf node information starting at 10,001, you can have up to 10,000 internal nodes in the trie before the indexes of these two arrays overlap.

Subroutine AddToTrie shown below locates or adds an item to a trie. At each node it checks three cases. First, if the node is an empty leaf node, the routine creates a new leaf and inserts the item there. Second, if the node is a leaf node that is already occupied, the routine calls SplitNode to extend the tree downwards and insert the new item. Finally, if the node is an internal node, the routine continues down the appropriate branch in the trie searching for the target item.

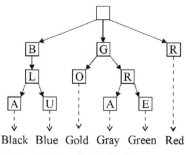

Figure 5.23 Trie of color names.

```
' Add a string to the trie.
Sub AddToTrie (node As Integer, depth As Integer, value As String)
Dim child_num As Integer

    If node = END_OF_LIST Then
        ' This is an empty leaf. Insert the item here.
        node = NewLeaf(value)
    ElseIf node >= FIRST_LEAF Then
        ' This is an occupied leaf. Add the item if needed.
        If Leaves(node) = value Then
            ' The item is already in the tree.
            MsgBox "Item " & value & " is already in the trie."
            Exit Sub
        End If


        ' Add the new item to the tree.
        SplitNode node, depth, value
    Else
        ' Continue down the tree.
        If Len(value) < depth Then
            child_num = ASC_END
        Else
            child_num = Asc(Mid$(value, depth, 1))
        End If
        AddToTrie Nodes(node).Child(child_num), depth + 1, value
    End If
End Sub
```

Subroutine AddToTrie calls SplitNode when it encounters a leaf node that is already in use. SplitNode replaces the occupied leaf node with a new internal node and makes the old leaf a child of the new node. If the new item and the current value of the node differ in the next character, the routine adds the new string in a new leaf below the new internal node. If the two strings have the same next character, SplitNode recursively calls itself again to split the new internal node further.

```
' Split the indicated leaf node and add the new item.
Sub SplitNode (node As Integer, depth As Integer, value As String)
Dim new_node As Integer
Dim old_leaf As Integer
Dim new_leaf As Integer
Dim old_num As Integer
Dim new_num As Integer

    old_leaf = node
    node = NewNode(Mid$(value, depth - 1, 1))

    ' See down which branches the entries belong.
    If Len(Leaves(old_leaf)) < depth Then
        old_num = ASC_END
    Else
        old_num = Asc(Mid$(Leaves(old_leaf), depth, 1))
    End If
    If Len(value) < depth Then
        new_num = ASC_END
    Else
        new_num = Asc(Mid$(value, depth, 1))
    End If
```

```
' Insert the old leaf below the new internal node.
Nodes(node).Child(old_num) = old_leaf

If new_num <> old_num Then
    ' Insert the new leaf and we're done.
    new_leaf = NewLeaf(value)
    Nodes(node).Child(new_num) = new_leaf
Else
    ' They belong down the same branch. Split again.
    SplitNode Nodes(node).Child(old_num), depth + 1, value
End If
End Sub
```

Example program TRIE allows you to build a trie. Enter a string value and press the Add button to add an item to the trie.

If the items within a trie are evenly distributed, the trie will remain fairly short. In that case it will take only a few comparisons to locate a given item within the trie. If the items are perfectly evenly distributed, a trie containing N items would only reach height roughly $log_{27}(N)$. If this were the case, a trie only four levels deep could store more than 450,000 words. A trie such as this could locate a four character string in a list of 450,000 entries using only four comparisons. A binary sorted tree like the ones described earlier would require a minimum of $log_2(450,000)$ or about 19 comparisons to locate the same string.

The reason a trie can locate items using fewer comparisons is that it uses the ASCII code of the characters in the string to determine which of 27 branches it should follow out of each node in the trie. By using the ASCII code, the trie can decide which branch to follow in a single step. Using comparisons alone you would need to examine several values to determine which of the 27 branches to follow.

Unfortunately the letters in words are not evenly distributed. In English the letter E appears more often than other letters. Similarly the letters Q, X, and Z appear less frequently. This means that if you add a huge number of items to a trie, the trie will not be as evenly balanced as possible.

On the other hand, the trie will probably not be all that tall, either. The trie can only be as tall as the longest string that it contains. If your data consists of strings up to 20 characters long, the trie can grow to a height of at most 20. Unless the data items share long prefixes, like "adversarial" and "adversary" do, the trie will probably be much shorter.

Quadtrees

A *quadtree* describes the spatial relationships between items within a physical area. For example, the area might be a map and the items might be the locations of houses or businesses on the map.

Each node in a quadtree represents a part of the total area represented by the quadtree. Each node can have four children that represent the northwest, northeast, southeast, and southwest quadrants of the area represented by the node.

To build a quadtree, start with a root node that represents the entire area being considered. Initially the root node contains all of the data items. Then examine the root node to see if it is large enough for you to consider subdividing it.

As you consider each node, you can check whether it contains more than a certain desired number of items. If it does, create four children for the node. Then distribute the items among the four children and recursively examine the children to see if they should be divided further. Continue dividing the nodes until each node contains no more than the desired number of items. Figure 5.24 shows a picture of several data items arranged in a quadtree. Here each region has been subdivided until it contains no more than two items.

Quadtrees are useful for locating objects near specific locations. Suppose you had a program that drew a map with several locations on it. When the user clicked on the map, you would like your program to find the location nearest to the point where the user clicked. One way to do this is to search through the entire list of locations and check each one to see how close it is to the target point. If there are N possible locations, this is an O(N) algorithm.

A quadtree can make this operation much faster. Begin at the root node. Each time you examine a node, see which of the node's quadrants contains the point where the user clicked. Then move down the tree to the corresponding child node. If the user clicked in the upper right corner of the node's area, for instance, you would descend into the northeast child. Continue down the tree until you locate the leaf node that contains the point where the user clicked.

Then examine the locations within that quadtree leaf node to see which location is closest to the point. This will usually be the location that really is closest to the user's point. If the point is close to the boundary between two leaf nodes, however, a location in a nearby leaf node might be closer.

Suppose D_{min} is the distance from the user's selected point to the closest location you have found so far. If D_{min} is less than the distance from the user's point to the edge of the leaf node, you are done. The location is too far from the edge of the leaf for there to be a closer location in another leaf.

Otherwise start back at the root node again and move down the tree examining any quadtree nodes that are within distance D_{min} of the user's point. If you find any points that are closer, revise D_{min} and continue searching with the new value. When you have finished checking all of the leaf nodes that are close to the user's point, you will have found the closest location.

```
' Quadtree nodes.
'
' If this is a leaf node, SWChild = END_OF_LIST and
' NWChild stores the index of the first item in the
' item linked list.
Type QtreeNode
```

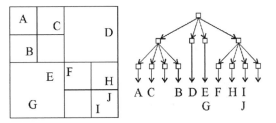

Figure 5.24 A quadtree.

```
        NWChild As Integer
        NEChild As Integer
        SEChild As Integer
        SWChild As Integer
        NumItems As Integer
End Type


' Linked list of items within each leaf node.
Type QtreeItem
    x As Single
    y As Single
    NextItem As Integer
End Type


Function FindPoint (x As Single, y As Single, comparisons As Long) _
As Integer
Dim leaf As Integer
Dim item As Integer
Dim dist As Single

    ' See what leaf the point is in.
    leaf = LocateLeaf(x, y)

    ' Find the closest point within the leaf.
    NearPointInLeaf leaf, x, y, item, dist, comparisons

    ' Check nearby leaves.
    CheckNearbyLeaves 1, leaf, x, y, item, dist, comparisons, _
Gxmin, Gxmax, Gymin, Gymax


    FindPoint = item
End Function


Function LocateLeaf (x As Single, y As Single) As Integer
Dim xmin As Single
Dim xmid As Single
Dim xmax As Single
Dim ymin As Single
Dim ymid As Single
Dim ymax As Single
Dim node As Integer
)
    xmin = Gxmin
    xmax = Gxmax
    ymin = Gymin
    ymax = Gymax
    node = 1 ' Start at the root.
    ' Loop until we hit a leaf.
    Do While QtreeNodes(node).SWChild <> END_OF_LIST
        xmid = (xmax + xmin) / 2
        ymid = (ymax + ymin) / 2
        If x <= xmid Then
            If y <= ymid Then
                node = QtreeNodes(node).NWChild
                ymax = ymid
            Else
                node = QtreeNodes(node).SWChild
                ymin = ymid
            End If
```

```
                    xmax = xmid
                Else
                    If y <= ymid Then
                        node = QtreeNodes(node).NEChild
                        ymax = ymid
                    Else
                        node = QtreeNodes(node).SEChild
                        ymin = ymid
                    End If
                    xmin = xmid
                End If
        Loop
        LocateLeaf = node
End Function

Sub NearPointInLeaf (leaf As Integer, x As Single, y As Single, _
best_item As Integer, best_dist As Single, comparisons As Long)
Dim item As Integer
Dim Dx As Single
Dim Dy As Single
Dim new_dist As Single

        best_item = QtreeNodes(leaf).NWChild

        ' If there are no items in the leaf, stop now.
        If best_item = END_OF_LIST Then
            best_dist = 10000000
            Exit Sub
        End If


        comparisons = comparisons + 1
        Dx = Items(best_item).x - x
        Dy = Items(best_item).y - y
        best_dist = Dx * Dx + Dy * Dy
        item = Items(best_item).NextItem
        Do While item <> END_OF_LIST
            comparisons = comparisons + 1
            Dx = Items(item).x - x
            Dy = Items(item).y - y
            new_dist = Dx * Dx + Dy * Dy
            If best_dist > new_dist Then
                best_dist = new_dist
                best_item = item
            End If
            item = Items(item).NextItem
        Loop
End Sub

Sub CheckNearbyLeaves (node As Integer, exclude As Integer, x As _
Single, y As Single, best_item As Integer, best_dist As Single, _
comparisons As Long, xmin As Single, xmax As Single, ymin As _
Single, ymax As Single)
Dim xmid As Single
Dim ymid As Single
Dim new_dist As Single
Dim new_item As Integer

        ' If this is the leaf we are to exclude, stop now.
        If node = exclude Then Exit Sub
```

```
        ' If this is a leaf node, check it out.
        If QtreeNodes(node).SWChild = END_OF_LIST Then
            NearPointInLeaf node, x, y, new_item, new_dist, comparisons
            If best_dist > new_dist Then
                best_dist = new_dist
                best_item = new_item
            End If
            Exit Sub
        End If


        ' See which children fall within best_dist of the point.
        xmid = (xmax + xmin) / 2
        ymid = (ymax + ymin) / 2
        If x - Sqr(best_dist) <= xmid Then
            ' The West children are eligible.
            If y - Sqr(best_dist) <= ymid Then
                ' Check the NorthWest child.
                CheckNearbyLeaves QtreeNodes(node).NWChild, exclude, _
x, y, best_item, best_dist, comparisons, xmin, xmid, ymin, ymid
            End If
            If y + Sqr(best_dist) > ymid Then
                ' Check the SouthWest child.
                CheckNearbyLeaves QtreeNodes(node).SWChild, exclude, _
x, y, best_item, best_dist, comparisons, xmin, xmid, ymid, ymax
            End If
        End If
        If x + Sqr(best_dist) > xmid Then
            ' The East children are eligible.
            If y - Sqr(best_dist) <= ymid Then
                ' Check the NorthEast child.
                CheckNearbyLeaves QtreeNodes(node).NEChild, exclude, _
x, y, best_item, best_dist, comparisons, xmid, xmax, ymin, ymid
            End If
            If y + Sqr(best_dist) > ymid Then
                ' Check the SouthEast child.
                CheckNearbyLeaves QtreeNodes(node).SEChild, exclude, _
x, y, best_item, best_dist, comparisons, xmid, xmax, ymid, ymax
            End If
        End If
End Sub
```

Example program QTREE demonstrates the use of a quadtree. When the program begins, it asks you how many data items it should create. It then creates that many items and draws them as points on a form. You should start with a small number of items (1000 or so) until you know how long it will take your computer to create and manage the items.

Quadtrees are most interesting when the data items are not evenly distributed, so the program selects the points using a *strange attractor* function from *chaos theory*. It selects the data points in a way that seems random, yet contains clusters that make the data more interesting.

If you click anywhere on the form, the program will locate the data point closest to the spot where you clicked. It will also display the number of items it examined while finding the item in the lower left corner of the form.

You can use the Options menu to tell the program whether it should use the quadtree or not. If you check the Use Quadtree option, the program will display the quadtree and use it to locate items. If you do not check this option, the program will not display the quadtree and will not use it when searching for items. Instead it will exhaustively search through all of the data items.

As you run the program you will see that the quadtree examines far fewer items than the exhaustive search in every case. Unless you have a very fast computer, you will also notice that the exhaustive search takes noticeably longer. If your computer is so fast that you do not notice this effect, try running the program with 30,000 items. Even on a 90 megahertz Pentium processor this produces a noticeable difference.

Another interesting experiment to perform with the program is to modify the value of CUTOFF defined in the declarations section of QTREE.BAS. This is the maximum number of items that will fit within a quadtree node before that node must be subdivided. The program initially uses the value CUTOFF = 100. If you make this number small, like 10, each leaf node will contain fewer data items so the program will need to examine fewer items to locate the one closest to the spot you click. This means it will take less time to locate items. On the other hand, the program will create far more quadtree nodes and that will take up a lot of memory.

Conversely if you increase CUTOFF to 1,000, the program will create fewer quadtree nodes. While it will take a bit longer to locate data items, it will create a smaller quadtree that requires less memory.

This is an example of a time versus space tradeoff. If you use more quadtree nodes, you use more memory and can locate items more quickly. If you use fewer quadtree nodes, you save memory but it takes longer to locate items. In this example a value for CUTOFF around 100 seems to give a reasonable balance between speed and the amount of memory used.

Octtrees

An *octtree* is similar to a quadtree except it divides a three-dimensional area. While each quadtree node may contain four children, an octtree node can contain eight children. These represent the eight octants that make up a three-dimensional area. These octants are the northwest top, northwest bottom, northeast top, northeast bottom, etc.

Octtrees are useful for managing objects spatially in three dimensions. A robot, for example, might use an octtree to keep track of nearby objects.

Balanced Trees

As a program works with a tree, adding and removing nodes over time, the tree may become unbalanced. When that happens, algorithms that manipulate the tree become less efficient. If the tree becomes sufficiently unbalanced, it becomes little more than a complicated form of list and the programs using the tree may give very poor performance.

This chapter discusses techniques you can use to keep a tree balanced even when many items are added and removed from the tree. By keeping a tree balanced, you keep it efficient.

The chapter begins by describing what it means for a tree to be unbalanced and explaining how an unbalanced tree can ruin performance. Then it discusses AVL trees. In an AVL tree the heights of the left and right subtrees at any node always differ by at most one. By maintaining this property, you can keep the tree from growing unbalanced.

Next the chapter discusses B–trees and B+trees. These trees use nodes with a variable number of branches to ensure that all of the leaf nodes have the same depth. By keeping all of the leaves at the same depth, and by making sure that the number of branches in each node is within certain limits, these trees keep themselves balanced. B–trees and B+trees are commonly used in database programming and the final example program in this chapter uses a B+tree to implement a simple yet powerful database.

Overview

As was mentioned in Chapter 5, the shape of a tree depends on the order in which you add items to it. Figure 6.1 shows two different trees created by adding the same items to the trees in different orders.

There are many ways in which you can add items to a tree that will make it tall and thin like the one on the left in Figure 6.1. In fact, if you add the items in sorted or reverse sorted order, the tree will be tall and thin. This sort of tall, thin tree is called *unbalanced*.

An unbalanced tree like the one on the left in Figure 6.1 can have up to O(N) depth. This means inserting or locating an item in the tree could take O(N) steps. Even if new items are placed randomly within the tree, on the average they will wind up at depth N/2 which is still O(N).

For example, suppose you build a tree containing 1,000 nodes. If the tree is balanced, the height of the tree will be around $\log_2(1,000)$ or about 10. Adding a new item to the tree will take only 10 steps. If the tree is tall and thin, it could have height 1,000. In this case adding a new item at the bottom of the tree will take 1,000 steps.

Now suppose you wanted to add 1,000 more nodes to the tree. If the tree remains balanced, all 1,000 nodes will fit on the next couple of levels of the tree and it will only take about 10 * 1,000 = 10,000 steps to add the new items. If the tree continues to grow in an unbalanced fashion, however, each new item will make the tree grow taller. In that case you will need around 1000 + 1001 + . . . + 2000 = 1.5 million steps to add the new items to the tree.

Generally you cannot guarantee that items will enter and leave a tree in a particular order. However, you can use techniques to keep a tree more or less balanced no matter how items are added or removed. When the tree starts to become unbalanced, you can rearrange the items in the tree to make it balanced again.

AVL Trees

AVL trees (named after the Russian mathematicians Adelson-Velskii and Landis who invented them) are trees where, at every node in the tree, the heights of the left and right subtrees differ by at most one. Figure 6.2 shows several AVL trees.

While an AVL tree may not be as short as a complete tree containing the same number of nodes, it still has depth O(log(N)). This means you can locate nodes within an AVL

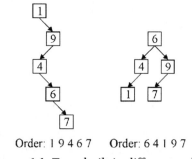

Order: 1 9 4 6 7   Order: 6 4 1 9 7

Figure 6.1 Trees built in different orders.

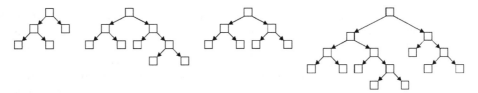

Figure 6.2 AVL trees.

tree in time O(log(N)) which is relatively fast. It is not as obvious, but it is also possible to add or remove items from an AVL tree in O(log(N)) time.

Adding Nodes to an AVL Tree

Each time you add a node to an AVL tree, you must check to see if the AVL property is still satisfied. After adding a node, you can follow the node's ancestors back up towards the root verifying that the subtrees at each ancestor have heights differing by at most one. If you find a spot where this is not true, you can shuffle some of the nodes around to rebalance the subtrees while still keeping the tree properly ordered.

The routine that adds a new node to the tree recursively descends into the tree searching for the item's correct location. After inserting the new item, the recursive calls to the routine return and backtrack up the tree. As each call returns, the routine checks to see if the AVL property still holds at the higher level in the tree. This sort of backwards recursion, where the routine performs an important action on the way out of a chain of recursive calls, is often called *bottom-up* recursion.

As the routine returns up the tree, it also checks to see if the height of the subtree it is examining has changed. If the routine ever reaches a point where the height of the subtree has not changed, the heights of any subtrees farther up the tree cannot have changed either. In that case the tree must once again be balanced so the routine can stop checking. A concrete example should make this a little more clear.

The tree on the left in Figure 6.3 is a properly balanced AVL tree. If you add a new item E to the tree, you get the tree shown in the middle. You then begin searching upwards through the tree from the new node E. The tree is balanced at node E because the two subtrees at this node are both empty and have the same height: zero.

The tree is also balanced at node D. The left subtree at node D is empty so it has height zero. The right subtree contains the single node E so it has height one. Since the heights of these subtrees differ by only one, the tree is balanced at node D.

The tree is not balanced at node C. The left subtree at node C has height zero while the right subtree has height two.

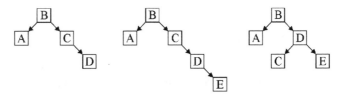

Figure 6.3 Adding a node to an AVL tree.

You can rebalance the subtrees at this node as shown on the right in Figure 6.3. Here node D has replaced node C. The subtree rooted at node D now contains nodes C, D, and E and has height two. Notice that the original subtree located at this position, which was rooted at node C, also had height two before the new node was added to the tree. Since the height of this subtree has not changed, you know that the tree is now balanced at all the nodes above this one in the tree. In this case the only node above this one is node B.

The height of the left subtree below node B was one before the new node was added to the tree and that height did not change. The height of the right subtree below node B was two before the new node was added. After rearranging nodes C, D, and E, the height of that subtree is again two. Since the heights of both subtrees beneath node B remained unchanged, the tree must still be balanced at node B.

When you add a node to an AVL tree, there are four possible ways the tree can become unbalanced depending on where in the tree the node was added. Each of these requires a different rebalancing of the tree. The rebalancing techniques are called right rotation, left rotation, left-right rotation, and right-left rotation. These are abbreviated R, L, LR, and RL respectively.

Suppose you add a new node to an AVL tree and the tree is now unbalanced at node X. Figure 6.4 shows such an AVL tree. The node X and its two children are shown explicitly. The other parts of the tree are indicated by triangles since you will not need to look closely at those parts of the tree.

The new node may have been placed in any of the four subtrees drawn as triangles below node X. When you place the new node in one of these triangles, you must use the corresponding rotation to rebalance the tree. Keep in mind that the new node may not unbalance the tree, so sometimes no rebalancing will be necessary.

Right Rotation

First, suppose that you have added a new node to the R subtree shown in Figure 6.4. In that case you do not need to worry about the right two subtrees below node X, so you can group them together in a single triangle as shown in Figure 6.5. The new node has been added to tree T_1 causing the subtree T_A rooted at node A to be at least two levels taller than subtree T_3.

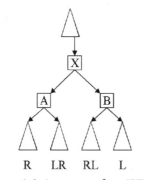

R   LR   RL   L

Figure 6.4 Anatomy of an AVL tree.

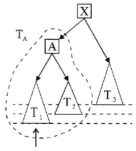

Node added here

Figure 6.5 Adding a new node to the R subtree.

In fact, because the tree was an AVL tree before you added the new node, you know that T_A used to be at *most* one level taller than subtree T_3. You added only one node to the tree so T_A has grown only one level taller. That means that T_A must now be exactly two levels taller than subtree T_3.

You also know subtree T_1 is not more than one level taller than subtree T_2. Otherwise node X would not have been the lowest node in the tree that had unbalanced subtrees. If T_1 were two levels taller than T_2, the tree would have been unbalanced at node A and node A would have been the lowest node with unbalanced subtrees.

Now you can rearrange the nodes using a right rotation as shown in Figure 6.6. This rearrangement is called a right rotation because the nodes A and X seem to have been rotated one position to the right.

Notice that this rotation preserves the "less than" ordering of the tree. An inorder traversal of either of these trees would visit the subtrees and nodes in the order: T_1, A, T_2, X, T_3. Since the inorder traversals of both trees are the same, the orderings of the items within the trees are the same.

It is also important to note that the height of the subtree you are working with has remained the same. Before you added the new node, the height of the subtree was two plus the height of subtree T_2. After adding the node and applying the right rotation, the height of the subtree is still two plus the height of subtree T_2. This means that any parts of the tree that lie above node X must now be balanced, so you do not need to worry about rebalancing the rest of the tree.

Left Rotation

A left rotation is similar to a right rotation. You use a left rotation to rebalance a tree when you add a new node to the L subtree shown in Figure 6.4. The AVL tree is shown before and after a left rotation in Figure 6.7.

As was the case with right rotation, left rotation does not change the height of the subtree. The height is two plus the height of subtree T_2 before you add the new node. It is again two plus the height of subtree T_2 after you add the new node and rebalance the tree. This means the rest of the tree will be balanced after the rotation.

A left rotation also does not change the order of the items within the tree. The inorder traversal of the tree both before and after the rotation would visit the subtrees and nodes in the order: T_1, X, T_2, B, T_3. Since the inorder traversals before and after the rotation are the same, the ordering of the items within the tree has not changed.

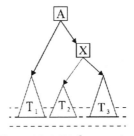

Figure 6.6 Right rotation.

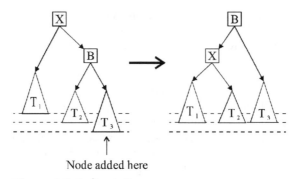

Figure 6.7 Left rotation.

Left-Right Rotation

If you add a new node in the LR subtree shown in Figure 6.4, you must look one level deeper into the LR subtree. Figure 6.8 shows the tree assuming that the new node has been added on the left side T_2 of the LR subtree. It could just as easily have been added to the right subtree T_3. In either case the T_A and T_C subtrees still have the AVL property but the T_X subtree does not.

Since the tree was an AVL tree before you added the new node, you know that T_A used to be at most one level taller than subtree T_4. You added only one node to the tree, so T_A has grown only one level taller. That means that T_A must now be exactly two levels taller than subtree T_4.

You also know that subtree T_2 must have height at most one greater than the height of subtree T_3. Otherwise T_C would not be balanced, and node X would not be the lowest node in the tree with unbalanced subtrees.

Also subtree T_1 must reach the same depth as subtree T_3. If it were shorter, T_A would be unbalanced, again contradicting the assumption that node X is the lowest node in the tree that has unbalanced subtrees. If T_1 reached a greater depth than T_3, then subtree T_1 would reach a depth 2 greater than the depth reached by subtree T_4. In that case the tree would have been unbalanced before you added the new node.

All of this means that the bottoms of the trees are exactly as shown in Figure 6.8. T_2 reaches the greatest depth, T_1 and T_3 reach a depth one level above that, and T_4 reaches one level above T_1 and T_3.

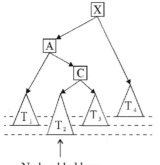

Figure 6.8 Adding a new node to the LR subtree.

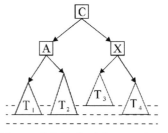

Figure 6.9 Left-right rotation.

Using these facts you can rebalance the tree as shown in Figure 6.9. This is called a left-right rotation because it looks as if nodes A and C have been rotated one position to the left, and then nodes C and X have been rotated one position to the right.

Like the other rotations, this rotation does not change the order of the items within the tree. The inorder traversal of the tree before and after the rotation visits the subtrees and nodes in the order: T_1, A, T_2, C, T_3, X, T_4. Since the inorder traversal of the tree remains unchanged, the ordering of the items within the tree is unchanged.

As was the case with the right and left rotations, the height of the subtree being rebalanced has not changed. Before you added the new node, the height of the subtree was two plus the height of subtree T_1. After the tree is rebalanced, the height of the subtree is again two plus the height of subtree T_1. This means the rest of the tree must now be balanced, so you do not need to continue rebalancing other parts of the tree.

Right-Left Rotation

A right-left rotation is similar to a left-right rotation. You can use a right-left rotation to rebalance a tree after you add a new node to the RL subtree shown in Figure 6.4. The AVL tree is shown before and after the right-left rotation in Figure 6.10.

As was the case with the other rotations, this rotation preserves the ordering of the items within the tree. The inorder traversal of the tree before and after rebalancing visits the subtrees and nodes in the order: T_1, X, T_2, D, T_3, B, T_4. Since the inorder traversal of the tree remains the same, the ordering of the items within the tree remains the same.

As was also the case with the other rotations, the height of the subtree being rebalanced has not changed. Before you added the new node, the height of the subtree was two plus the height of subtree T_4. After the tree is rebalanced, the height of the subtree is again two plus the height of subtree T_4, so the rest of the tree must now be balanced.

Summary of Rotations

Figure 6.11 shows all of the rotations you need to rebalance an AVL tree. Each of these rotations preserves the tree's inorder traversal so in all four cases the ordering of the items in the tree remains unchanged. The height of the tree is also unchanged by each of the rotations so, after adding a new item and applying the appropriate rotation, the tree will again be balanced.

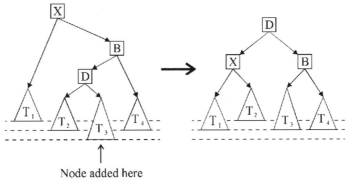

Node added here

Figure 6.10 Right-left rotation.

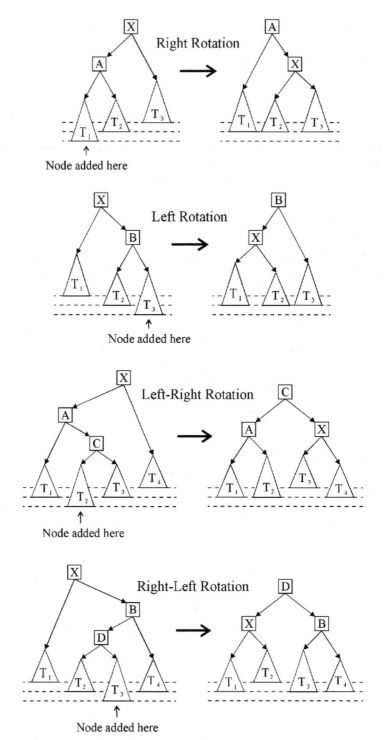

Figure 6.11 Summary of AVL tree rotations.

Adding Nodes in Visual Basic

Before moving on to consider how to remove a node from an AVL tree, this section discusses some of the details of adding a node to an AVL tree in Visual Basic.

First you must define the node structure used by the program. In addition to the usual LeftChild and RightChild fields, this structure should contain a Balance field. This field indicates which subtree at the node is taller. You will give the field the value –1 if the left subtree is taller, 1 if the right subtree is taller, and 0 if the two subtrees have the same height. To make the program easier to read, you can use constants LEFT_HEAVY, RIGHT_HEAVY, and BALANCED to represent these values.

```
Const LEFT_HEAVY = -1
Const BALANCED = 0
Const RIGHT_HEAVY = 1

Type NodeRec
    LeftChild As Integer
    RightChild As Integer
    Balance As Integer        ' Tells which subtree is taller.
End Type
```

Subroutine InsertItem, shown below, recursively descends through the tree looking for the new item's location. When it reaches a node, it checks to see if the new item belongs to the left or right of that node and it continues down the tree along the corresponding branch. When InsertItem finally reaches the bottom of the tree, it creates the new node and adds the new item to the tree.

Subroutine InsertItem then uses bottom-up recursion to rebalance the tree. As the recursive calls to InsertItem return, the subroutine recursively travels back up the tree. Each time the subroutine returns, it sets the parameter has_grown to be true if the subtree it is leaving has grown taller. In the instance of InsertItem that made the recursive call, the routine uses this parameter to determine whether the subtree it is currently examining is out of balance. If it is, the routine applies the correct rotation to rebalance the subtree.

For example, suppose the subroutine is currently examining node X. Suppose it has just returned from visiting the right subtree beneath node X and that the parameter has_grown has been set to true indicating that the right subtree just grew taller. If the subtrees below node X previously had the same height, then the right subtree is now taller than the left. The subtree rooted at node X has also grown since its right subtree grew taller.

If the left subtree below node X was previously taller than the right, then the left and right subtrees are now the same height. The height of the subtree rooted at node X has not changed—it is still one plus the height of the left subtree. In this case InsertItem would reset variable has_grown to false indicating that the tree is balanced.

Finally, if the right subtree below node X was previously taller than the left, the growth of the right subtree makes the tree unbalanced at node X. In this case InsertItem invokes subroutine RebalanceRightGrew to rebalance the tree. Subroutine RebalanceRightGrew performs either a left or right-left rotation depending on the exact situation.

Subroutine InsertItem follows a similar procedure if the new item was inserted into the left subtree.

```
' Insert a new item into the tree.
Sub InsertItem (parent As Integer, txt As String, has_grown As _
Integer)
Dim child As Integer
Dim grandchild As Integer

    ' If this is the bottom of the tree, create the new
    ' node and leave the parent pointing to it.
    If parent = END_OF_LIST Then
        parent = NewNode(txt)
        Nodes(parent).Balance = BALANCED
        TreeForm.NodeText(parent).Caption = txt
        has_grown = True
        Exit Sub
    End If


    ' Continue down the left or right subtree.
    If txt <= Nodes(parent).Value Then
        ' Insert the child in the left subtree
        InsertItem Nodes(parent).LeftChild, txt, has_grown


        ' See if rebalancing is necessary. It will not be
        ' if the addition never unbalanced the tree or if
        ' we rebalanced the tree at a deeper level of
        ' recursion. In either case has_grown will be False.
        If Not has_grown Then Exit Sub


        If Nodes(parent).Balance = RIGHT_HEAVY Then
            ' Was right heavy, now balanced. This subtree
            ' did not grow so the tree is balanced.
            Nodes(parent).Balance = BALANCED
            has_grown = False
        ElseIf Nodes(parent).Balance = BALANCED Then
            ' Was balanced, now left heavy. This node is
            ' still balanced but it grew so we need to
            ' continue checking up the tree.
            Nodes(parent).Balance = LEFT_HEAVY
        Else
            ' Was left heavy, now left unbalanced. Perform
            ' a rotation to rebalance at this node.
            RebalanceLeftGrew parent
            has_grown = False
        End If ' End checking this node's balance.
    Else
        ' Insert the child in the right subtree
        InsertItem Nodes(parent).RightChild, txt, has_grown


        ' See if rebalancing is necessary. It will not be
        ' if the addition never unbalanced the tree or if
        ' we rebalanced the tree at a deeper level of
        ' recursion. In either case has_grown will be False.
        If Not has_grown Then Exit Sub
        If Nodes(parent).Balance = LEFT_HEAVY Then
            ' Was left heavy, now balanced. This subtree
            ' did not grow so the tree is balanced.
            Nodes(parent).Balance = BALANCED
            has_grown = False
        ElseIf Nodes(parent).Balance = BALANCED Then
            ' Was balanced, now right heavy. This node is
```

```
                           ' still balanced but it grew so we need to
                           ' continue checking up the tree.
                           Nodes(parent).Balance = RIGHT_HEAVY
                   Else
                           ' Was right heavy, now right unbalanced.
                           ' Perform a rotation to rebalance at this node.
                           RebalanceRightGrew parent
                           has_grown = False
                   End If ' End checking this node's balance.
           End If ' End if (down left) ... else (down right)
End Sub


' Perform a left or right-left rotation to rebalance
' this node.
Sub RebalanceRightGrew (parent As Integer)
Dim child As Integer
Dim grandchild As Integer


       child = Nodes(parent).RightChild


       If Nodes(child).Balance = RIGHT_HEAVY Then
               ' Perform a left rotation.
               Nodes(parent).RightChild = Nodes(child).LeftChild
               Nodes(child).LeftChild = parent
               Nodes(parent).Balance = BALANCED
               parent = child
       Else
               ' Perform a right-left rotation.
               grandchild = Nodes(child).LeftChild
               Nodes(child).LeftChild = Nodes(grandchild).RightChild
               Nodes(grandchild).RightChild = child
               Nodes(parent).RightChild = Nodes(grandchild).LeftChild
               Nodes(grandchild).LeftChild = parent
               If Nodes(grandchild).Balance = RIGHT_HEAVY Then
                   Nodes(parent).Balance = LEFT_HEAVY
               Else
                   Nodes(parent).Balance = BALANCED
               End If
               If Nodes(grandchild).Balance = LEFT_HEAVY Then
                   Nodes(child).Balance = RIGHT_HEAVY
               Else
                   Nodes(child).Balance = BALANCED
               End If
               parent = grandchild
       End If ' End if (right rotation)... else (double right rotation)
       Nodes(parent).Balance = BALANCED
End Sub


' Perform a right or left-right rotation to rebalance
' this node.
Sub RebalanceLeftGrew (parent As Integer)
Dim child As Integer
Dim grandchild As Integer


       child = Nodes(parent).LeftChild


       If Nodes(child).Balance = LEFT_HEAVY Then
               ' Perform a right rotation.
```

```
            Nodes(parent).LeftChild = Nodes(child).RightChild
            Nodes(child).RightChild = parent
            Nodes(parent).Balance = BALANCED
            parent = child
    Else
        ' Perform a left-right rotation.
        grandchild = Nodes(child).RightChild
        Nodes(child).RightChild = Nodes(grandchild).LeftChild
        Nodes(grandchild).LeftChild = child
        Nodes(parent).LeftChild = Nodes(grandchild).RightChild
        Nodes(grandchild).RightChild = parent
        If Nodes(grandchild).Balance = LEFT_HEAVY Then
            Nodes(parent).Balance = RIGHT_HEAVY
        Else
            Nodes(parent).Balance = BALANCED
        End If
        If Nodes(grandchild).Balance = RIGHT_HEAVY Then
            Nodes(child).Balance = LEFT_HEAVY
        Else
            Nodes(child).Balance = BALANCED
        End If
        parent = grandchild
    End If ' End if (right rotation)... else (left-right rotation)
    Nodes(parent).Balance = BALANCED
End Sub
```

Removing Nodes from an AVL Tree

In Chapter 5 you saw that it is harder to remove an item from a sorted tree than it is to insert one. If the removed node has no children, it is easy to remove it from the tree. If the node has one child, you can replace it with that child and still preserve the tree's ordering. If the removed node has two children, you must replace it with the rightmost node to the left in the tree. If that rightmost node has a left child, you must also replace the rightmost node with its left child.

Since AVL trees are a special type of sorted tree, you still need to perform these same steps. After you have finished, however, you must then travel back up the tree from the point where you removed a node to make sure that the tree still has the AVL property.

When you find a node where the AVL property does not hold, you can perform left, right, left-right, and right-left rotations to rebalance the tree. The rotations are the same ones used earlier for inserting a new node in the tree. The cases you must look for are similar but not identical to those described before.

Left Rotation

Suppose first that you are removing a node from the left subtree under node X. Suppose also that the right subtree is either evenly balanced or its right half has height one greater than its left half. Then a left rotation will rebalance the tree at node X. Figure 6.12 shows this rotation.

The bottom level of subtree T_2 in Figure 6.12 is shaded to indicate that the subtree T_B is either evenly balanced (T_2 and T_3 have the same height) or its right half is taller (T_3 is taller than T_2). In other words the shaded part may or may not be part of subtree T_2.

If T_2 and T_3 have the same height, then the subtree T_X rooted at node X does not change in height when you remove the node. The height of T_X was and remains two plus

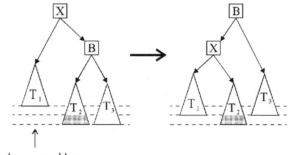

Node removed here

Figure 6.12 Left rotation when removing a node.

the height of subtree T_2. Since the height of this subtree does not change, the tree above this node must be balanced.

If T_3 is taller than T_2, then subtree T_X grows shorter by one. In that case the tree above node X may not be balanced so you must continue up the tree checking to see if the AVL property still holds for the ancestors of node X.

Right-Left Rotation

Now suppose that the node removed is taken from the left subtree under node X but the left half of the right subtree is taller than the right half. Then you need to use a right-left rotation to rebalance the tree. Figure 6.13 shows this rotation.

Whether subtree T_2 or T_3 is taller, the right-left rotation will rebalance the subtree T_X. The rotation will also reduce the height of T_X by 1. This means the tree above node X may not be balanced so you must continue up the tree checking to see if the AVL property still holds for all of the ancestors of node X.

Other Rotations

The other rotations are similar to these. In these cases the node being removed is in the right subtree below node X. All four of these rotations are the same as the rotations used to balance the tree after adding a node, with one exception.

When you add a new node to the tree, the first rotation you perform rebalances the subtree T_X without changing its height. That means the tree above T_X must still be bal-

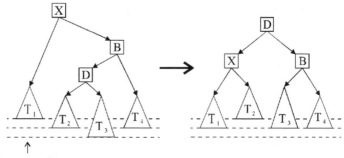

Node removed here

Figure 6.13 Right-left rotation when removing a node.

anced. When you use the rotations after removing a node from the tree, the rotation might reduce the height of the subtree T_X by one. In that case you cannot be sure that the tree above node X is still balanced. You must continue up the tree making sure that the AVL property holds at each node.

Removing Nodes in Visual Basic

Subroutine DeleteItem handles the removal of items from the tree. It recursively descends through the tree looking for the item to be deleted. When it finds the target node, it removes the node. If the target node has no children, the routine is done. If the node has a single child, it replaces the node with its child.

If the node has two children, it calls routine ReplaceRightmost to replace the target node with the rightmost node to the target's left. ReplaceRightmost performs its duty much as it did in Chapter 5 where it was used to remove items from a normal (not balanced) sorted tree. The main difference occurs when the routine returns and recursively moves back up the tree. As it does so, ReplaceRightmost uses bottom-up recursion to make sure the tree is balanced at each node.

Each time a call returns, the calling instance of ReplaceRightmost invokes RebalanceRightShrunk to ensure that the tree is balanced at that point. Since Replace-Rightmost descended through the right branches, it always uses RebalanceRightShrunk rather than RebalanceLeftShrunk to perform the rebalancing.

DeleteItem invoked the first call to ReplaceRightmost by sending it down the left branch below the node being removed. When the first call to ReplaceRightmost returns, DeleteItem uses RebalanceLeftShrunk to ensure the tree is balanced at that point.

After this, the recursive calls to DeleteItem return one at a time and work their way back up the tree. Like ReplaceRightmost, subroutine DeleteItem uses bottom-up recursion to make sure that the tree is balanced. As each call to DeleteItem returns, the calling routine invokes RebalanceRightShrunk or RebalanceLeftShrunk, depending on which path it followed down into the tree, to make sure the tree is balanced at that node.

```
' Remove the indicated item from the tree.
Sub DeleteItem (node As Integer, txt As String, shrunk As Integer)
Dim target As Integer

    If node = END_OF_LIST Then
        Beep
        MsgBox "Item " & txt & " is not in the tree."
        shrunk = False
        Exit Sub
    End If


    If txt < Nodes(node).Value Then
        DeleteItem Nodes(node).LeftChild, txt, shrunk
        If shrunk Then RebalanceLeftShrunk node, shrunk
    ElseIf txt > Nodes(node).Value Then
        DeleteItem Nodes(node).RightChild, txt, shrunk
        If shrunk Then RebalanceRightShrunk node, shrunk
    Else
        target = node
        If Nodes(target).RightChild = END_OF_LIST Then
            ' No children or left child only
            node = Nodes(target).LeftChild
```

```
                    shrunk = True
            ElseIf Nodes(target).LeftChild = END_OF_LIST Then
                ' Right child only
                node = Nodes(target).RightChild
                shrunk = True
            Else
                ' Two children
                ReplaceRightmost Nodes(target).LeftChild, shrunk, node
                If shrunk Then RebalanceLeftShrunk node, shrunk
            End If
            FreeNode target
        End If
End Sub


' Replace the target node with the rightmost node to the
' left of it.
Sub ReplaceRightmost (repl As Integer, shrunk As Integer, target _
As Integer)
Dim old_repl As Integer

    If Nodes(repl).RightChild <> END_OF_LIST Then
        ReplaceRightmost Nodes(repl).RightChild, shrunk, target
        If shrunk Then RebalanceRightShrunk repl, shrunk
    Else
        ' Remember what ndoe repl is.
        old_repl = repl

        ' Replace repl with its left child.
        repl = Nodes(repl).LeftChild

        ' Replace target with repl.
        Nodes(old_repl).LeftChild = Nodes(target).LeftChild
        Nodes(old_repl).RightChild = Nodes(target).RightChild
        Nodes(old_repl).Balance = Nodes(target).Balance
        target = old_repl

        shrunk = True
    End If
End Sub


' Rebalance for the case where the Right branch has shrunk.
Sub RebalanceRightShrunk (node As Integer, shrunk As Integer)
Dim child As Integer
Dim child_bal As Integer
Dim grandchild As Integer
Dim grandchild_bal As Integer

    If Nodes(node).Balance = RIGHT_HEAVY Then
        ' Was Right heavy, now it is balanced.
        Nodes(node).Balance = BALANCED
    ElseIf Nodes(node).Balance = BALANCED Then
        ' Was balanced, now it is Left heavy.
        Nodes(node).Balance = LEFT_HEAVY
        shrunk = False
    Else
        ' Was Left heavy, now unbalanced.
        child = Nodes(node).LeftChild
        child_bal = Nodes(child).Balance
        If child_bal <= 0 Then
```

```
                ' Right rotation.
                Nodes(node).LeftChild = Nodes(child).RightChild
                Nodes(child).RightChild = node
                If child_bal = BALANCED Then
                    Nodes(node).Balance = LEFT_HEAVY
                    Nodes(child).Balance = RIGHT_HEAVY
                    shrunk = False
                Else
                    Nodes(node).Balance = BALANCED
                    Nodes(child).Balance = BALANCED
                End If
                node = child
            Else
                ' Left-right rotation.
                grandchild = Nodes(child).RightChild
                grandchild_bal = Nodes(grandchild).Balance
                Nodes(child).RightChild = Nodes(grandchild).LeftChild
                Nodes(grandchild).LeftChild = child
                Nodes(node).LeftChild = Nodes(grandchild).RightChild
                Nodes(grandchild).RightChild = node
                If grandchild_bal = LEFT_HEAVY Then
                    Nodes(node).Balance = RIGHT_HEAVY
                Else
                    Nodes(node).Balance = BALANCED
                End If
                If grandchild_bal = RIGHT_HEAVY Then
                    Nodes(child).Balance = LEFT_HEAVY
                Else
                    Nodes(child).Balance = BALANCED
                End If
                node = grandchild
                Nodes(grandchild).Balance = BALANCED
            End If
        End If
    End If
End Sub


' Perform left or right-left rotations to rebalance the
' tree after a left branch has shrunk.
Sub RebalanceLeftShrunk (node As Integer, shrunk As Integer)
Dim child As Integer
Dim child_bal As Integer
Dim grandchild As Integer
Dim grandchild_bal As Integer

    If Nodes(node).Balance = LEFT_HEAVY Then
        ' Was left heavy, now it is balanced.
        Nodes(node).Balance = BALANCED
    ElseIf Nodes(node).Balance = BALANCED Then
        ' Was balanced, now it is right heavy.
        Nodes(node).Balance = RIGHT_HEAVY
        shrunk = False
    Else
        ' Was right heavy, now unbalanced.
        child = Nodes(node).RightChild
        child_bal = Nodes(child).Balance
        If child_bal >= 0 Then
            ' Left rotation.
            Nodes(node).RightChild = Nodes(child).LeftChild
            Nodes(child).LeftChild = node
            If child_bal = BALANCED Then
```

```
                    Nodes(node).Balance = RIGHT_HEAVY
                    Nodes(child).Balance = LEFT_HEAVY
                    shrunk = False
                Else
                    Nodes(node).Balance = BALANCED
                    Nodes(child).Balance = BALANCED
                End If
                node = child
            Else
                ' Right-left rotation.
                grandchild = Nodes(child).LeftChild
                grandchild_bal = Nodes(grandchild).Balance
                Nodes(child).LeftChild = Nodes(grandchild).RightChild
                Nodes(grandchild).RightChild = child
                Nodes(node).RightChild = Nodes(grandchild).LeftChild
                Nodes(grandchild).LeftChild = node
                If grandchild_bal = RIGHT_HEAVY Then
                    Nodes(node).Balance = LEFT_HEAVY
                Else
                    Nodes(node).Balance = BALANCED
                End If
                If grandchild_bal = LEFT_HEAVY Then
                    Nodes(child).Balance = RIGHT_HEAVY
                Else
                    Nodes(child).Balance = BALANCED
                End If
                node = grandchild
                Nodes(grandchild).Balance = BALANCED
            End If
        End If
    End If
End Sub
```

Example program AVL allows you to manipulate an AVL tree. Enter a text value and press the Add button to add the new item to the tree. Enter the value of an item in the tree and press the Remove button to remove that item from the tree. As you add and remove items, the program automatically rebalances the tree when necessary.

B-trees

B-trees (pronounced "bee trees") are a different form of balanced tree that you may find a bit more intuitive than AVL trees. Each node in a B-tree can hold several data keys and several pointers to child nodes. Since each node holds several data items, the nodes are often called *buckets*.

Between each pair of adjacent child pointers in a node is a key that you can use to determine which branch to take when you are inserting or looking for an item. For example, in the tree shown in Figure 6.14, the root node contains two keys: G and R. To locate an item with value that comes before G, you would look down the first branch out of the root node. To find a value that comes between G and R, you would look down the second branch. To locate an item that comes after R, you would look down the third branch.

To find the item L in the B-tree in Figure 6.14, you would start at the root node and compare "L" to the keys there. Since L comes after G but before R, you would branch down the second child pointer. At the next node you would find the value L and you would be done.

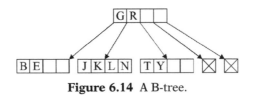

Figure 6.14 A B-tree.

More precisely a B-tree of *order* K must have these properties:

1. Each node holds at most 2 * K keys.
2. Each node, except possibly the root, holds at least K keys.
3. An internal node containing M keys has M + 1 children.
4. All leaves are at the same level in the tree.

The B-tree in Figure 6.14 has order 2. Each node can hold up to 4 keys. Each node, except possibly the root, must hold at least 2 keys. For convenience B-tree nodes generally hold an even number of keys so the order can be a whole number.

Requiring that each node in a B-tree of order K contain between K and 2 * K keys keeps the tree balanced. Since each node must hold at least K keys, it must have at least K + 1 children so it cannot grow too tall and thin. A B-tree containing N nodes can have height at most $O(\log_{K+1}(N))$. This means searching the tree will be an $O(\log(N))$ operation. While it is less obvious, inserting and removing items from a B-tree are also $O(\log(N))$ operations.

B-tree Performance

B-trees are particularly useful in large database applications. If the order of the B-tree is reasonably large, you will be able to locate any item in the tree after examining only a few nodes. For example, a B-tree of order 10 containing 1 million records can be at most $\log_{11}(1,000,000)$ or about six levels tall. That means you would need to examine at most six nodes in the tree before finding the one you wanted.

In practice, performance will be slightly better since most nodes will contain more than 10 items. If every node held 15 items, for example, you would need to examine at most $\log_{16}(1,000,000)$ or about five nodes before finding the target item.

A balanced binary tree containing the same 1 million items would have height $\log_2(1,000,000)$ or about 20. These nodes would be smaller than B-tree nodes, however. While examining a single B-tree node, you might need to compare the target item to as many as 20 keys. To locate an item in a B-tree you might examine 5 nodes and 100 keys. To find the item in a binary tree you would examine 20 nodes but only 20 keys.

The B-tree will be faster if it is relatively easy to examine keys but relatively difficult to examine nodes. This will be true if the database is stored on a hard disk or other slow storage device. Reading data from the disk will be slow, but once that data is loaded into memory, examining it will be quite fast.

Disk drives read data in large chunks and it takes no longer to read an entire chunk of data than it takes to read a single byte. If a B-tree's nodes are not too large, it will take no longer to read a B-tree node from a disk than it takes to read a node in a binary tree. In that case searching five nodes in a B-tree will require five slow disk accesses plus up to 100 fast memory accesses. Searching 20 nodes in a binary tree will require 20 slow disk accesses plus 20 fast memory accesses. The binary search will be slower because the time spent on the 15 extra slow disk accesses will be much greater than the amount of time saved by avoiding 80 fast memory accesses. Disk access issues are discussed further on pages 172–174 later in this chapter.

Inserting Items in a B-tree

To insert a new item into a B-tree, locate the leaf node in which the new item should be placed. If that node contains fewer than 2 * K keys, there is room to add the new item to that node. In that case add the new item in the correct position so the items in the node are still in their proper order. Then create the corresponding new child pointer, setting it to END_OF_LIST.

If the node already contains 2 * K items, there is no room for the new item. To make room, break the node into two new nodes. Counting the new item, there are 2 * K + 1 items to distribute between the two new nodes. Place K items in each node, keeping them in their proper order, and move the middlemost item up to the nodes' parent.

For example, suppose you want to insert the item "Q" into the B-tree shown in Figure 6.14. This new item belongs in the second leaf node which already contains the items J, K, N, and P. Since this node is full, you will need to split it into two new nodes. Then you can divide the items J, K, N, P, and Q between the two new nodes. Place the first two items, J and K, in the left node. Place the last two items, P and Q, in the right node. Then move the middle item, N, up to the nodes' parent. Figure 6.15 shows the new tree after the new item Q has been added. Notice how the keys and pointers have been rearranged so the tree's ordering is preserved.

Breaking a node into two nodes like this is called a *bucket split*. When there is a bucket split, the parent node gets a new key and a new pointer. If the parent is already full, adding the new key and pointer will cause the parent to split. That in turn will require a new entry in the original node's grandparent, which may cause another bucket split, and so on up the tree. In the worst case, inserting an item can cause a chain reaction that rises up the tree until the root node splits.

When a root split occurs, the B-tree grows taller. That is the only way a B-tree grows taller. This gives B-trees the strange property of always growing from the leaves towards the root rather than at the bottom of the tree.

Removing Items from a B-tree

In theory removing an item from a B-tree is as simple as adding an item. In practice the details are pretty complicated.

If the item being removed is not in a leaf node, you must replace it with another item so the tree maintains a proper ordering of the items. This is much like the case of removing an item from a sorted tree or from an AVL tree and you can handle it in a similar way. Replace the item with the rightmost item to its left in the tree. This rightmost

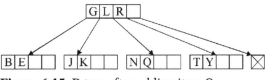

Figure 6.15 B-tree after adding item Q.

item will always be in a leaf node. After you have replaced the removed item with the rightmost item to its left, you can treat the removal as if you had removed the item in the leaf node.

To remove an item from a leaf node, first slide the other items to the left if necessary to fill in the hole left by removing the item. If you are removing the rightmost item, as is the case when you have swapped it to a higher part of the tree, you do not need to rearrange the other items.

Remember that each node in a B-tree of order K must hold between K and 2 * K items, otherwise the tree could become unbalanced. After you remove an item from a leaf node, the leaf may contain only K – 1 items.

In this case you can try to borrow some items from one of the leaf's sibling nodes. You can then redistribute the items in the two nodes so they each have at least K items. In Figure 6.16 an item has been removed from the leftmost leaf in the tree leaving that node only one remaining item. Redistributing items between that node and its right sibling gives both nodes at least two keys. Notice how the middlemost item J was moved up into the parent node.

When you try to rebalance the nodes in this way, you may find that the sibling node contains only K items. Then between the node being removed and its sibling, there are only 2 * K – 1 items, so there are not enough for the two nodes to share. In that case all of the items in both nodes can fit within a single node, so you can merge them. Remove the key that separates the two nodes in their parent. Add that item to the 2 * K – 1 items already contained in the two nodes. Place all 2 * K of the items in a new node. This process of merging two nodes is called a *bucket merge* or *bucket join*. Figure 6.17 shows how to merge two nodes.

When you merge two nodes, you remove a key from the nodes' parent and place it in the combined node. After the parent loses a key, it may contain only K – 1 items. In that case you will need to rebalance or merge it with one of its siblings. That in turn may cause the grandparent node to contain K – 1 items and the whole process will start over again. In the worst case the deletion will cause a chain reaction of bucket merges that will reach all the way to the root.

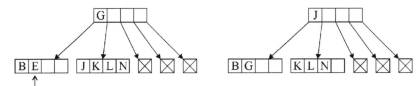

Figure 6.16 Rebalancing after removing an item.

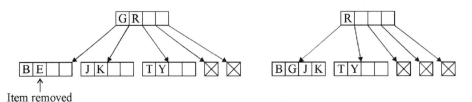

Figure 6.17 Merging after removing an item.

If you remove the last item from the root node, merge the two remaining children of the root into a new root and shorten the tree by one level. The only way a B-tree grows shorter is when the children of the root node merge to form a new root.

Example program BTREE allows you to manipulate a B-tree. Enter a text value and press the Add button to add a new item to the tree. Enter the value of an item that is in the tree and press the Remove button to remove the item from the tree. As you add and remove items, the program will automatically rebalance the tree when necessary.

B-tree Variations

There are several variations on B-trees, only a few of which are described here. The first, top-down B-trees, is another way to manage the B-tree structure already described. By splitting full nodes whenever they are encountered, this variation is able to perform a more intuitive top-down recursion rather than a bottom-up recursion when adding items. It also reduces the chances of having long cascades of bucket splits later.

The second variation is a B+tree (pronounced "bee plus tree"). B+trees store only data keys in internal nodes and store data records as leaf node data. This allows them to store more items in each bucket, so it reduces the amount of data the program must move when rearranging nodes.

Top-Down B-trees

The subroutine described earlier that adds a new item to a B-tree first searches recursively down through the tree to find the bucket where the item belongs. When it tries to insert the new item, the routine may find that the bucket is already full. In that case it splits the bucket and moves one of the items up to the leaf's parent.

As the routine returns from its recursive calls, the calling routine checks to see if the parent node must also split. If so, an item is passed up to its parent. Each time the routine returns from a recursive call, the calling routine must see if it should split the next ancestor node. Since these bucket splits occur as the routine is leaving its recursive subroutine calls, this is bottom-up recursion. B-trees managed in this way are sometimes called *bottom-up B-trees*.

An alternative strategy is to split any full nodes encountered on the way down. As the routine searches for a bucket to hold the new item, it splits any node it encounters that is already completely full. Each time it splits a node, it passes an item up to the parent. Since the routine has split every full node it encountered on the way down, there will always be room for the new item in the parent node. If there were no room in the parent, the routine would have already split the parent.

When the routine reaches the bucket where the new item belongs, you know that the parent node is not full. Then if the leaf node that will hold the new item must be split, there will always be room to pass the middlemost item up to the parent. That means the routine will not need to perform bottom-up recursion to make sure there is room in the parent for the middlemost item. B-trees managed in this way are called *top-down B-trees*.

This method causes bucket splits to occur sooner than they are absolutely necessary. A top-down B-tree will split a full node even if its child nodes contain lots of unused space. In that case the split is not really needed at that time, though it may become necessary later when all of the children are full. By splitting nodes early, the top-down method will cause the tree to hold more empty space at any given time than a bottom-up B-tree.

On the other hand, by performing node splits early, this method reduces the chances of creating a long cascade of splits all at the same time. Consider a root node split, for example. With a bottom-up B-tree, a root node split happens only when you add a new node at the bottom of the tree and the split cascades all the way up to the root. Every node along the path from the bottom of the tree to the top splits when you add the new item. In fact, the only way a bottom-up B-tree grows taller is when a root node split occurs. That only happens when there is a long cascade of splits that travels all the way from the bottom of the tree to the top.

If the root node becomes full in a top-down B-tree, the root will split the next time any item is inserted into the tree. This makes the B-tree one level taller. When a top-down B-tree grows taller, it is possible that only the root node will split. While it is also possible that one of the root's children will split, too, it is extremely unlikely that every node from the root to the bottom of the tree will split at the same time. Adding a new node to a top-down B-tree is more likely to cause a single bucket split than adding a node to a bottom-up B-tree, but it is less likely to cause a long cascade of bucket splits.

Unfortunately there is no top-down version for node merging. As the node removal routine descends down the tree, it cannot merge nodes that are half empty as it encounters them. It cannot know at that time whether two children of a node will be merged and an item removed from their parent. Since it cannot know if the parent will lose an item, it cannot tell if the parent should be merged with one of its siblings. The routine could perform some sort of rebalancing between a node and one of its siblings, but that would be very time consuming and would probably produce little benefit.

B+trees

B-trees are often used to store large records. A typical B-tree might hold employee records, each occupying several kilobytes of memory. The B-tree would arrange the records according to some key field such as employee name or ID number.

In this case rearranging data items could be extremely slow. If you needed to merge two buckets, you would have to move many records, each of which was quite large. Similarly, to split a bucket you would need to move many large records. If the merge or split cascaded up the tree, you would have to move even more data and this would take longer still.

You can avoid moving large amounts of data by storing only the records' keys in the B-tree nodes. Along with the keys, you store a pointer to the actual data records that are stored elsewhere. Now when you need to rearrange buckets, you only need to move the record keys and pointers, not the entire records themselves. This type of B-tree is called a B+tree.

By keeping the items in the B+tree nodes small, you also make it possible to store more keys in each node. This is particularly important if the database is large and the nodes are stored on a disk drive or other slow device. As was mentioned earlier, disk drives read data in large chunks and it takes no longer to read an entire chunk of data than it takes to read a single byte. If a B+tree's nodes hold many keys, you will be able to read more information in a single disk access.

For example, suppose you have an order two B-tree that stores between two and four large data records in each node. Then each node would have between three and five children. To hold a database of 1 million records, this tree would need to have height between $\log_5(1,000,000)$ and $\log_3(1,000,000)$ or between 9 and 13. To locate an item in this tree you might need to perform as many as 13 disk accesses.

Now suppose you store the same 1 million records in a B+tree using nodes of roughly the same size in bytes. Since a B+tree stores only keys in its nodes, this tree may be able to hold the keys for up to 20 records in each node. In that case the tree would have between 11 and 21 children per node so the tree would need to have height between $\log_{21}(1,000,000)$ and $\log_{11}(1,000,000)$ or between five and six. To locate an item in this B+tree, you would only need to perform at most six disk accesses to find the item's key, and then one additional disk access to retrieve the item itself. Disk access issues are discussed more fully on pages 172–174.

You can make the B+tree even more efficient by storing pointers to item data only in the leaf nodes. As they are designed so far, the leaf node pointers of a B-tree or B+tree all contain the value END_OF_LIST. Chapter 5 showed how you could use leaf child pointers to store pointers to leaf data. As long as the indexes of the internal nodes and the leaf nodes do not overlap, you can use the value of a child pointer to determine whether it points to an internal node or leaf data.

With a B-tree or B+tree, it is even easier to tell if a child pointer indicates a node in the tree or leaf node data. Since all the leaf nodes in a B-tree or B+tree are at the same level, you can tell whether a pointer holds the index to a node or leaf data by checking its depth in the tree. As a routine recursively moves down through the tree, it can keep track of its current depth. When the depth count is the same as the height of the tree, the routine has reached a leaf node. Using this technique, a routine can determine when it has reached a leaf node even if the indexes of the tree's nodes and the leaf data overlap.

In this type of B+tree, each data item comes immediately after the corresponding key in an in order traversal of the B+tree. Figure 6.18 shows a small B+tree. Leaf node pointers to the data records are drawn with dashed arrows. Most of the data records come immediately after their corresponding key in a leaf node. The "K data" record, for example, comes immediately after the key K in the second leaf node.

The inorder traversal for this tree is: END_OF_LIST, B key, B data, E key, E data, G key, G data, J key, J data, etc. Even though the key G does not appear in a leaf node, the "G data" record comes immediately after key G in the tree's inorder traversal.

To maintain this property the previous routines for managing B-trees must be modified slightly. Before, when you removed an item from a B-tree that was not in a leaf node, you replaced that item with the rightmost item to its left in the tree. In this kind of

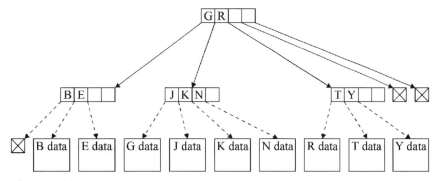

Figure 6.18 A B+tree.

B+tree, all of the data items in a B+tree are located below the leaf nodes. Since all of the data is contained below leaf nodes, you no longer need to worry about removing items from non-leaf nodes. You can simply remove the item from its leaf node and move the other items in that node over to fill in the gap.

If the item you have removed is the first item in the leaf node, however, the key corresponding to that item is not stored in the leaf node. The key will be in one of the node's ancestors farther up the tree. In that case you must also update the ancestor that contains the key. In Figure 6.18, for example, the item "G data" is the first item in the second leaf node in the B+tree. The corresponding key G is in this node's parent. If you remove the "G data" item from the tree, you must update the parent as well, giving the B+tree shown in Figure 6.19. In taller trees the key might be higher up in the tree so the routine must examine all of the leaf's ancestors as it returns from the recursion.

Improving B-trees

This section discusses two techniques for improving the performance of B-trees and B+trees. The first technique allows you to rearrange items within a node and its siblings to avoid splitting a bucket. The second allows you to load or reload your data to add unused entries to the tree. This reduces the chances of bucket splits occurring later.

Rebalancing to Avoid Bucket Splits

When you need to add an item to a bucket that is full, you normally split the bucket. You can avoid the bucket split if you rebalance the node with one of its siblings. For example, adding a new item Q to the B-tree shown on the left in Figure 6.20 normally causes a bucket split. You can avoid this by rebalancing the node containing J, K, N, and P with its left sibling containing B and E. This results in the tree shown on the right in Figure 6.20.

This sort of rebalancing has a couple of advantages. By rebalancing the nodes you have increased the usage of the buckets. There are now fewer unused tree entries so you have decreased the amount of "wasted" memory. If you had performed a bucket split, you would have added several more unused entries to the tree and increased the amount of "wasted" space.

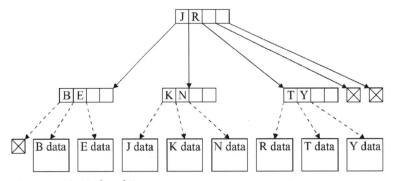

Figure 6.19 Updated B+tree.

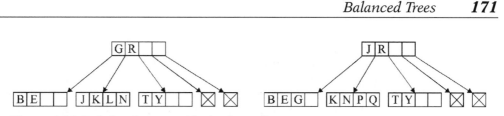

Figure 6.20 Rebalancing to avoid a bucket split.

Even more importantly, if you do not split the bucket you do not need to move an item up to the bucket's parent node. If you did move an item up to the parent and the parent was already full, the parent would split. This would send another item up to its parent, possibly causing a cascade of bucket splits that could reach all the way to the root. By rebalancing instead of splitting the original bucket, you avoid causing this sort of cascade.

On the other hand, while reducing the number of unused entries in the tree decreases the amount of "wasted" space, it also increases the chances of bucket splits in the future. Since there is less empty space in the tree, the nodes are more likely to be full.

While rebalancing the tree makes future bucket splits a bit more likely, their increased probability is more than offset by the bucket splits you have avoided in the meantime. Remember that the tree can only grow during a bucket split. If you have a large tree with lots of unused entries, you must have had many bucket splits in the past. On the other hand, if you have a smaller tree with fewer unused entries, you must have had fewer bucket splits in the past.

Initial Loading

Suppose you had a small customer database that contained ten customer records. You could load the records into a B-tree so they filled each bucket completely. The resulting tree would contain little wasted space as shown in Figure 6.21. When you wanted to add a new item to this tree, however, you would immediately need to perform a bucket split. If your database was larger and you still loaded the records into the tree so they filled each node completely, almost every node in the tree would be full. In that case any bucket split would cascade up the tree, probably all the way to the root.

Figure 6.22 shows another way you could load the tree. Here some empty entries have been added to each node in the tree. While this makes the tree a bit larger and results in more unused entries, it allows you to add new items to the tree without immediately causing long chains of bucket splits.

Most B-trees in real applications have larger orders than the trees shown here. In that case initially loading the tree with a small amount of empty space can greatly reduce

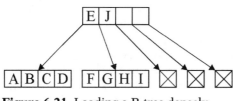

Figure 6.21 Loading a B-tree densely.

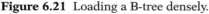

Figure 6.22 Loading a B-tree loosely.

the number of times you must rebalance nodes or split buckets. A B-tree of order ten, for example, could hold up to 20 keys in each node. If you initially loaded the tree so it contained 10 percent empty space, each node would have room for two new items. After adding two items to a bucket, you could still avoid splitting the bucket by rebalancing it with one of its siblings. Even after you were forced to split the bucket, the parent would have two empty entries so the split would not cascade up the tree. You could work with this tree for quite a while before you caused any long chains of bucket splits.

This is an example of a space versus time tradeoff. By adding empty space to the tree, you make the tree larger but you reduce the chances of causing bucket splits, making it faster to add new items to the tree.

Loading items into a tree in this way is not necessarily easy. To do this you must know pretty much where each item belongs in the tree. Otherwise you will spend a lot of time rearranging the tree and you will have gained nothing.

Once the items have been added to a tree, however, a simple inorder traversal of the tree will give you the complete ordering of the items. Then you could easily build a new tree with exactly the amount of empty space you wanted. After you had used the tree for a while, the amount of free space might decrease to the point where bucket splits were likely. Then you could rebuild the tree to again give it the amount of empty space you wanted it to have.

Disk Access Issues

B-trees and B+trees are particularly well suited for large database applications. A typical B+tree might hold hundreds of thousands or even millions of records. In that case only a small fraction of the tree would fit in memory at any one time. Each time you accessed a node in the tree, you would need to retrieve the node from a hard disk or other relatively slow storage device. This section describes two issues that are particularly important when the data is stored on a hard disk: bucket size and root caching.

Selecting a Bucket Size

In general, the more items you can fit into the nodes of a B-tree, the shorter the tree will be and the fewer nodes you will need to examine to locate an item.

A B-tree of order two always has between two and four items and between three and five children at each node. This tree could store 1,024 items with depth at most seven. A B-tree of order ten, on the other hand, would have between 10 and 20 items and between 11 and 21 children at each node. This tree could store 1,024 items with depth at most three.

You can increase the number of items stored in each node by using a B+tree. Since a B+tree only stores small keys in each bucket instead of large data records, you will be able to fit more entries in buckets of the same size. If you can fit twice as many small keys into a bucket as you can fit large records, you will need fewer nodes to store all of the records' keys. While each bucket can be as much as half empty in either case, the tree will contain fewer buckets so you will save space.

A final consideration when selecting a bucket size is the fact that disk drives read data in natural chunks. Most disk drives read data in blocks of 512 or 1,024 bytes, or some other number of bytes which is a power of 2. It takes the disk drive no more time to read one of these blocks of data than it takes it to read a single byte.

To take advantage of this fact, you should try to build your buckets so they are some multiple of the size your disk naturally reads. Then you should pack as many records or keys as possible into that size. For example, you might decide to make your buckets roughly 2,048 bytes in size. If you were building a B+tree with 80 byte keys, you would be able to pack up to 24 keys plus their 25 pointers (assuming 2 byte integer pointers) plus the integer Num Keys into each bucket. You could then create an order 12 B+tree with buckets declared as:

```
Global Const ORDER = 12
Global Const KEYS_PER_NODE = 2 * ORDER

Type NodeRec
    NumKeys As Integer                      ' # keys in use.
    Key (1 to KEYS_PER_NODE) As String * 80 ' Data key.
    Child (0 To KEYS_PER_NODE) As Integer   ' Child pointers.
End Type
```

In order to make Visual Basic read as much data as possible as quickly as possible, be sure to use the **Get** statement to read data one complete node at a time. If you use a **For** loop to read the key and child data for a node one item at a time, Visual Basic will need to access the disk separately for each item. This will be much slower than allowing Visual Basic to read the entire node's data all at once. In one test with a user-defined type that contained an array of 1,000 items, it took almost 27 times as long to read the items one at a time as it took to read them all at once. The code below shows the good and bad ways to read the data for a node.

```
Dim i As Integer
Dim node As NodeRec

    ' Get the data the slow way.
    Get #filenum, , node.NumKeys
    For i = 1 To KEYS_PER_NODE
        Get #filenum, , node.Key(i)
    Next i
    For i = 0 To KEYS_PER_NODE
        Get #filenum, , node.Child(i)
    Next i

    ' Get the data the fast way.
    Get #filenum, , node
```

Node Caching

Every search through a B-tree starts at the root node. You can make searching a little faster if you always keep the root node in memory. Then each time you search for an item, you perform one less disk access. Keep in mind that you will still need to write the root node to disk any time it changes. Otherwise if your program crashes the B-tree will not be up to date.

You might also try to cache other B-tree nodes in memory. If you can keep all of the children of the root node in memory, you will not need to read them from disk either. Remember that, for a B-tree of order K, the root node is the only node in the tree that can contain fewer than K keys. The root node will have between 1 and 2 * K keys and therefore will have between 2 and 2 * K + 1 children. That means you will have to cache between 2 and 2 * K + 1 nodes.

If the order of the B-tree is large and the nodes themselves are large, caching the second level nodes will take up quite a bit of memory. For example, suppose you have a B-tree of order 10 and the nodes each occupy 2K of memory. Then caching the second level nodes will take up to 42K of memory. That is a fair amount of memory to save one disk access. If you will be searching the B-tree very frequently, however, the time you save may be worth the extra price in memory.

Another time when you might cache nodes is when you perform a traversal of the B-tree. In a preorder traversal, for example, you visit a node and then recursively visit its children. You descend into one child and, when you return, you descend into the next. Each time you return from visiting one of the children, you need to look at the parent node again to see what child to visit next.

If you do not keep the parent node in memory, you will have to read it from disk again. If the B-tree has order K, you would have to read each internal node between K + 1 and 2 * K + 1 times. If you cache each node when you first visit it and then release it when you are done visiting its children, you only need to read each node from the disk once.

Using this method you do not need to keep many nodes in memory at the same time. If the B-tree has height H, you will need to cache at most H nodes at a time. If the B-tree is fairly short, this will not require too much memory even if the order of the tree is fairly large.

Using recursion you can also keep the nodes in memory without using a complicated caching scheme. Each call to the recursive traversal algorithm can declare a local variable to hold the node while it is needed. When the recursive call returns, Visual Basic will automatically free this variable and release the memory the node occupied. The code below shows how you might implement this traversal algorithm in Visual Basic.

```
Sub PreorderPrint (node_index As Integer)
Dim i As Integer
Dim node As NodeRec

    GetBucket node, node_index          ' Cache the node.
    Print node_index                    ' Visit this node.
    For i = 0 To node.NumKeys
        PreorderPrint node.Child(i)     ' Visit the child.
    Next i
End Sub

Sub GetBucket (rec As Bucket, recnum As Long)
    Get #IdxFile, recnum, rec
End Sub
```

A B+tree Database

Example program B_PLUS manages a B+tree database using the two data files CUSTS.DAT and CUSTS.IDX.

The customer data records are stored in CUSTS.DAT.

The first record in CUSTS.IDX holds header information such as the index of the root node, the indexes of the first garbage bucket and data records, etc. The remaining records in CUSTS.IDX hold the B+tree buckets.

Enter data in the Customer Record area and press the Add button to add a new item to the database. Enter a first name and a last name in the top part of the form and press the Find button to locate the corresponding record in the database.

When you have added a new record or found an old one, the program selects that record. If you then press the Remove button, the program will remove the selected record from the database.

If you select the Internal Nodes command from the Display pull-down menu, the program will present a message that shows the structure of the tree. It will display the keys at each node indented to show the tree's internal structure.

If you select the Complete Tree command from the Display pull-down menu, the program will present a message showing the complete structure of the tree. Node keys will be indented to show the tree's structure and customer data will be shown within pointed brackets.

In addition to fields like name and address which you would expect to find in a customer record, these records also contain a NextGarbage field. The program uses this field to create a linked list of the unused records. Since this field is only used when a customer record is not in use, you could use a different field in the record to hold the NextGarbage value. You might store the index of the next unused record in the LastName field, for example. It is simpler to give the record a separate NextGarbage field, however, and the program is complicated enough as it is. The type declaration for the customer records looks like this:

```
Type CustRecord                   ' Size (bytes)
    LastName As String * 20       ' 20
    FirstName As String * 20      ' 20
    Address As String * 40        ' 40
    City As String * 20           ' 20
    State As String * 2           ' 2
    Zip As String * 10            ' 10
    Phone As String * 12          ' 12
    NextGarbage As Long           ' 4
End Type                ' Total size: 128
Const CUST_ SIZE = 128  ' Size of the customer record.
```

The program stores customer data records in CUSTS.DAT and accesses them by record number using the Visual Basic **Get** and **Put** statements.

The internal B+tree nodes contain keys used to locate customer data records. The key for a record will be the customer's last name padded with blanks to 20 characters, followed by a comma, followed by the customer's first name padded with blanks to 20 characters. For example, "Washington   ,George   ". This gives each key a total length of 41 characters.

Each internal node also stores pointers to child nodes in the tree. To allow for a huge tree, the program uses long integers for these pointers. Since these pointers are used to indicate the locations of the customer data records in CUSTS.DAT, using long integers will also allow the database to hold a huge number of records.

To decide how many items should go in each bucket, you must first pick a desired bucket size. This program will read and write data in blocks of roughly 1,024 bytes. If you assume that you will have at most K keys per bucket, then each bucket will hold K keys of length 41 characters, K + 1 child pointers of length 4 bytes, and the 2 byte integer Num Keys. You want to make the buckets as large as possible while still fitting within

1,024 bytes. Solving the equation 41 * K + 4 * (K + 1) + 2 <= 1,024 for K, you get K <= 22.62 which you can round down to 22. The B+tree should have order 11 so it contains 22 keys per bucket. Each bucket will occupy 41 * 22 + 4 * (22 + 1) + 2 = 996 bytes. If the disk drive reads in blocks of 1,024 bytes, it will be able to read one bucket per disk access.

The buckets can now be defined like this:

```
Const KEY_SIZE = 41
Const ORDER = 11
Global Const KEYS_PER_NODE = 2 * ORDER

Type Bucket
    NumKeys As Integer
    Key (1 To KEYS_PER_NODE) As String * KEY_SIZE
    Child (0 To KEYS_PER_NODE) As Long
End Type
Const BUCKET_SIZE = KEYS_PER_NODE * KEY_SIZE + 4 * (KEYS_PER_NODE + 1) + 2
```

Program B_PLUS stores the B+tree buckets in file CUSTS.IDX and accesses them by record number using the Visual Basic **Get** and **Put** functions. The first record in CUSTS.IDX contains header information that describes the current state of the B+tree. This information includes the index of the root node, the current height of the tree, the index of the first garbage bucket in CUSTS.IDX, and the index of the first garbage data record in CUSTS.DAT.

To make reading and writing the header information easier, you can define another structure that has exactly the same size as a B+tree bucket but which contains the header information fields. The last field in the declaration is a string that pads this structure out so it has exactly the same size as the Bucket structure.

```
Const PAD = BUCKET_SIZE - 30
Type HeaderRecord                    ' Size (bytes)
    NumBuckets As Long               ' 4
    NumRecords As Long               ' 4
    Height As Integer                ' 2
    Root As Long                     ' 4
    NextTreeRecord As Long           ' 4
    NextCustRecord As Long           ' 4
    FirstTreeGarbage As Long         ' 4
    FirstCustGarbage As Long         ' 4
    Padding As String * PAD ' Makes the total BUCKET_SIZE.
End Type
```

When the program begins, it opens the B+tree data files CUSTS.DAT and CUSTS.IDX. If these files do not exist, it creates them and initializes the header information for an empty tree. Otherwise the program reads the tree's header information from CUSTS.IDX. It then reads the root node and caches it in memory.

When the program is inserting or deleting an item from the tree, it recursively descends into the tree to see where the item belongs. As it descends through the tree, the program caches the nodes it visits. As it recursively returns back up the tree, it may need to use these nodes again if there has been a bucket split, merge, or other node rearrangement. Since the program caches the nodes on the way down, they will be available if they are needed again on the way back up.

B+trees are particularly well suited for large database applications because they provide quick access to any record in the database with few disk accesses. In this example the B+tree's order is 11. That means each node will contain between 11 and 22 keys and will have between 12 and 23 children. If the tree contains N data records, it can grow to height at most $\log_{12}(N)$ and the program can require at most $\log_{12}(N)$ disk accesses to locate any given item. If the database contained 10 million records, for example, the program could locate any record in at most $\log_{12}(10,000,000)$ or about 7 disk accesses.

If your disk drive can load more than 1,024 bytes each time it accesses the disk, you can make the B+tree's nodes even larger. The nodes will then hold more keys each so you will be able to locate records with even fewer disk accesses. If you used 2,048 byte buckets, you could build a B+tree of degree 22. Then you could locate any given record in a 10 million record database in at most $\log_{23}(10,000,000)$ or about 5 disk accesses.

This efficiency makes it hard to test program B_PLUS thoroughly. To make the B+tree grow to height 2, you would have to add 23 items to the database. To make it grow to height 3, you would need to add more than 250 additional items.

To make it a little easier to test the program, you might want to change the B+tree's order to two. In file B_PLUS.BAS, comment out the line that sets the order to 11 and uncomment the line that sets the order to 2.

```
'Const ORDER = 11
Const ORDER = 2
```

The program's Create Data command in the Data pull-down menu allows you to create many data records quickly. Enter the number of records you want to create and the number the program should use to build the first item. The program will then create the records and insert them into the B+tree. For example, if you tell the program to create 100 records starting from value 200, the program will create entries for 200, 201, 202, . . . , 299 similar to this one:

```
FirstName:  First 0000200
LastName:   Last 0000200
Address:    Addr 0000200
City:       City 0000200
```

7

Decision Trees

Many difficult real-world problems can be modeled using *decision trees*. Each node in the tree represents a partial solution to the problem. Each branch in the tree represents a decision that leads to a more complete solution. Leaf nodes represent a complete solution. The goal is to find the "best" path through the tree from the root to a leaf while satisfying certain constraints. Exactly what the constraints are and what the "best" path means depends on the problem.

This sort of tree is usually extremely large. The decision tree for selecting the best move in tic-tac-toe, for example, contains more than half a million nodes. Tic-tac-toe is a fairly simple game and many problems are much more complicated. The corresponding decision trees may contain more nodes than there are stars in the universe.

This chapter examines some techniques you can use to search these huge trees. First it will examine *game trees*. Using tic-tac-toe as an example, it will discuss ways to search game trees to find the best possible move.

Next the chapter examines ways to search more general decision trees. For the smallest trees, you can use *exhaustive searching* to examine every node in the tree. For slightly larger trees you can use *branch and bound* techniques. Branch and bound allows you to avoid searching much of the tree while still guaranteeing that you will find the best possible solution.

The following sections describe a few *heuristic* methods for searching a tree. Using these methods you can search practically any tree. The solution you find may not be the absolute best possible solution, but hopefully it will be close enough to be useful.

Finally this chapter discusses several very difficult problems that you can try to solve using branch and bound and heuristic techniques. Many of these problems have important applications and finding good solutions is critical.

Searching Game Trees

A strategy board game like chess, checkers, or tic-tac-toe can be modeled using a *game tree*. Each branch out of a node corresponds to a different move by one of the players. If a player has 30 possible moves at some point in the game, that node in the game tree will have 30 branches.

For example, in tic-tac-toe the root node corresponds to the initial, empty board position. The first player to move can place an X in any of the nine squares on the board. Corresponding to each of those nine moves is a branch in the game tree leaving the root node. The nine nodes below these branches correspond to the nine different board positions where player X has chosen a square.

Once X has taken the first square, O can select any of the remaining eight squares. Corresponding to each of these eight possible moves is a branch leading out of whichever node represents the current board position. That branch leads to a node that represents the resulting board position where X has taken one square and O has taken another. Figure 7.1 shows a small part of the tic-tac-toe game tree.

As you can see from Figure 7.1, the tic-tac-toe game tree grows extremely quickly. If the tree continued to grow like this, with each node in the tree having one fewer branches than its parent, the complete tree would have 9 * 8 * 7 * 6 * 5 * 4 * 3 * 2 * 1 = 362,880 leaves. To think of it another way, there would be 362,880 paths through the tree corresponding to 362,880 possible tic-tac-toe games.

In fact, many of the 362,880 possible nodes are missing from the tic-tac-toe game tree because they are forbidden by the rules of the game. In the first three moves, if the X player selects the upper left, upper center, and upper right squares, X wins and the game ends. The node representing this board position has no children because the game has ended. This game is shown in Figure 7.2. X has moved three times and O two times so the game tree stops at this point, only five levels from the root.

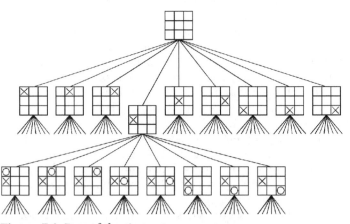

Figure 7.1 Part of the tic-tac-toe game tree.

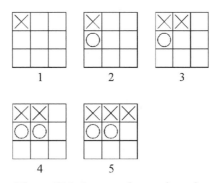

Figure 7.2 A game that ends early.

There are many other ways in which X or O can win before the board is completely full. These combinations cut off other potential paths through the game tree so it does not contain all of the 362,880 possible leaf nodes. If you write a program to examine every possible move, you will find that there are only about a quarter million leaf nodes and a total of around a half million nodes in the complete game tree.

This is still a pretty big tree and searching it exhaustively could take quite a while. For more complicated games like checkers, chess, or go, the game trees are enormous. If each player could move in only 16 ways during each move in a chess game, the game tree would have more than 1 trillion nodes after each player had moved only five times! Some of the later sections in this chapter talk a little more about searching these enormous game trees. The next section sticks to the relatively simple example of tic-tac-toe.

Minimax Searching

To begin searching a game tree, you will need to be able to determine the *value* of a board position. In tic-tac-toe X would place a high value on a board position with three Xs in a row because in that position player X wins. At the same time the O player would place a very low value on that board position since player O would lose.

For each player you can assign one of four values to a particular board position. The value 4 means the board position will result in a win for this player. A value of 3 means it is not clear from the current board position who will eventually win. The value 2 means the board position will result in a draw ("cat's game") with neither player winning. The value 1 means the board position will result in a win for the other player.

To search the game tree exhaustively, you can use a *minimax* strategy. Here you try to *minimize* the *maximum* value your opponent can get from the current board position. You can do this by determining the maximum value the opponent can achieve for each of your possible moves. You then take the move which gives your opponent the smallest board value.

The subroutine BoardValue computes the value of a board position. This routine examines each of the possible moves in turn. For every possible move it recursively calls itself to see what the opponent's value for the new board position would be. It then uses a minimax strategy and selects the move that gives the opponent the smallest of those values.

To determine the value of a board position, BoardValue recursively calls itself until one of three things happens.

First, BoardValue might find a board position in which one player or the other has won. In that case it sets the value of that board position to 4 indicating that the player who has just moved has won the game.

Second, the routine might find a board position in which no player can move. In that case the game is a draw so the program sets the value of the board position to 2 indicating that the game ended in a tie.

Finally, BoardValue might reach a predetermined maximum depth of recursion. If the BoardValue subroutine exceeds the allowed depth of recursion, it assigns the board position a value 3 indicating that it cannot tell which player will win.

You can use the maximum depth of recursion to prevent the program from taking too long while searching the game tree. This is particularly important with more complicated games like chess where the program could search the game tree practically forever. You can also use the maximum depth of recursion to set the skill level of the program. The deeper into the decision tree the program is allowed to look, the better will be the moves it finds.

Figure 7.3 shows a tic-tac-toe game tree near the end of a game. It is X's turn and X has three possible moves. To select the best move for player X, the BoardValue subroutine recursively examines each of the three possible moves X can make. It will find that the first and third moves (the left and right branches in the tree) result in wins for player O. That gives those board positions the value 4 for player O. The second possible move results in a draw which has value 2 for player O. In this case the BoardValue subroutine will pick the second move because it gives player O the smallest board value. That move will result in a tie instead of a win for player O.

The Visual Basic code for subroutine BoardValue is shown below.

```
Global Const VALUE_HIGH = 5          ' Higher than possible.
Global Const VALUE_WIN = 4           ' We will win.
Global Const VALUE_UNKNOWN = 3       ' We cannot tell who will win.
Global Const VALUE_DRAW = 2          ' We will draw.
Global Const VALUE_LOSE = 1          ' We will lose.
Global Const VALUE_LOW = 0           ' Lower than possible.
```

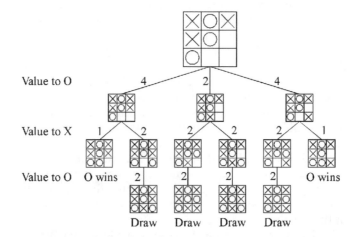

Figure 7.3 The bottom of a game tree.

```
Global Const PLAYER_NONE = -1      ' No one owns the square.
Global Const PLAYER_DRAW = 0       ' The game is a draw.
Global Const PLAYER_X = 1          ' Player X owns the square.
Global Const PLAYER_O = 2          ' Player Y owns the square.


Type Board
    Owner(NUM_SQUARES) As Integer  ' Each entry holds the player
End Type                           ' who owns the square.


' Find the value of this board. Return the best move and
' the best value for the board through best_move and
' best_value.
'
' p11 is the player about to move. p12 is the other
' player. Depth is the current depth of recursion. We use
' this to stop looking at a certain depth.
Sub BoardValue (best_move As Integer, best_value As Integer, p11 _
As Integer, p12 As Integer, depth As Integer)
Dim p1 As Integer
Dim i As Integer
Dim good_i As Integer
Dim good_value As Integer
Dim enemy_i As Integer
Dim enemy_value As Integer

    ' If we are in too deep, we know nothing.
    If depth >= SkillLevel Then
        best_value = VALUE_UNKNOWN
        Exit Sub
    End If


    ' If this board is finished, we know how we would do.
    p1 = Winner()
    If p1 <> PLAYER_NONE Then
        ' Convert the value for the winner p1 into the
        ' value for player p11.
        If p1 = p11 Then
            best_value = VALUE_WIN
        ElseIf p1 = p12 Then
            best_value = VALUE_LOSE
        Else
            best_value = VALUE_DRAW
        End If
        Exit Sub
    End If


    ' Try all the legal moves.
    good_i = -1
    good_value = VALUE_HIGH
    For i = 1 To NUM_SQUARES
        ' If the move is legal, try it.
        If Board(i) = PLAYER_NONE Then
            ' See what value this would give the opponent.
            Board(i) = p11              ' Make the move.
            BoardValue enemy_i, enemy_value, p12, p11, depth + 1
            Board(i) = PLAYER_NONE ' Unmake the move.

            ' See if this is lower than the previous best.
            If enemy_value < good_value Then
```

```
                    good_i = i
                    good_value = enemy_value
                    ' If we will win, things can get no better
                    ' so take the move.
                    If good_value <= VALUE_LOSE Then Exit For
                End If
            End If ' End if Board(i) = PLAYER_NONE ...
        Next i


        ' Translate the opponent's value into ours.
        If good_value = VALUE_WIN Then
            ' Opponent wins, we lose.
            best_value = VALUE_LOSE
        ElseIf enemy_value = VALUE_LOSE Then
            ' Opponent loses, we win.
            best_value = VALUE_WIN
        Else
            ' DRAW and UNKNOWN are the same for both players.
            best_value = good_value
        End If
        best_move = good_i
    End Sub
```

Example program TICTAC uses subroutine BoardValue to run a tic-tac-toe program. The bulk of the program manages interaction with the user. It draws the board, allows the user to select squares, allows the user to set options like the skill level, etc.

When you run the program you will notice that performance is much better if you do not activate the "Show Test Moves" option in the Options menu. When this option is activated, the program displays each move as it is being considered. This constant updating of the display can take much longer than the actual search for the best move.

Other commands in the Options menu allow you to play either X or O, and to set the skill level of the program. The skill level is the maximum depth of recursion allowed for the BoardValue subroutine. You will notice that the first moves take much longer if the skill level is high than they do if the skill level is low.

Giving Up

This method for computing board values has an interesting side effect. If the program has more than one equally good move, it will take the first one it finds. Usually this is not much of a problem. The program will never use certain moves but the moves it does use are just as good as the ones it doesn't. This may reduce the variety of the game a little, but the moves will generally be reasonable.

There are times, however, when this behavior can seem quite strange. If the program is looking far enough down the game tree that it can tell you will win no matter what move it makes, it will select the first move it examines. Sometimes that move will not make much sense to a human being. It may seem as if the computer has given up and is making a move at random. In a way that is exactly what the computer is doing.

To see an example, run the TICTAC program using skill level three (the default). Number the squares as shown in Figure 7.4. Begin by taking square 6. The program will respond by taking square 1. Next take square 3 and the program will answer by taking square 9. Now when you take square 5 you threaten to win by taking either square 4 or square 7.

1	2	3
4	5	6
7	8	9

Figure 7.4 Tic-tac-toe board numbering.

When the computer makes its next move, it can search the game tree far enough to see that you will win no matter what move it makes. In this situation a human opponent would probably either move to block one of your possible wins, or move to create two O's in a row and threaten a win for O. In a more complicated game, a human opponent might try one of these strategies hoping that you do not yet see a way to force a win.

The program, however, assumes that you know as much as it does and that you know you will win in the next few moves. Since it does not matter what move it makes, the program will pick the first move it examines, in this case square 2. This move seems strange since it does not block either of your possible wins, nor does it set the computer up for a win. It seems as if the computer has given up. This game is shown in Figure 7.5.

This sort of behavior can seem even stranger in more complicated games like chess. If the computer realizes that it will lose many moves in advance, it may start making seemingly random moves long before the end of the game is near. It may even start making these moves before the human opponent notices that the computer will lose.

One way to prevent this behavior is to provide more distinctions between different board values. In the TICTAC program, all losing board positions have the same value. You could modify the program so a position that loses the game in two moves has a higher value than one that loses in one move. Then the program would select moves that would make the game continue as long as possible.

In this case that change would have no effect since you are in a position to win in one move no matter what square the computer takes. You could give a board position that gives the opponent two possible winning moves a lower value than a board position that gives the opponent only one winning move. In this case the computer would move to block one of your possible wins.

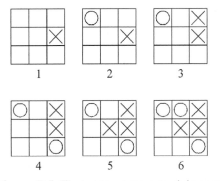

Figure 7.5 Tic-tac-toe program giving up.

Improving Game Tree Searching

If the only tool you had for searching game trees was minimax, it would be pretty hard to search large trees. A game like chess is so complicated that a program could not hope to search more than a couple of levels of the tree. Fortunately there are several tricks you can use to make searching large game trees a little easier.

Precomputed Initial Moves and Replies

First, the program can store some initial moves chosen by game experts. You might decide that the tic-tac-toe program should always take the center square whenever it moved first. This essentially picks the first branch in the game tree so the program can ignore all of the paths that do not take this first branch.

Better still, the program will not have to search the game tree until its opponent has also made a move. At that point both the computer and its opponent have selected branches in the tree so the tree remaining to be searched is much smaller. The tree below the second level contains fewer than 7! = 5,040 paths. By precomputing only one move, you can reduce the size of the game tree from around a quarter million paths to no more than 5,040.

Similarly you can save some replies to initial moves in case the computer's opponent moves first. In this case the opponent has nine choices for a first move so you would need to store nine responses. If you used these stored moves to make the computer's first move, the program would not have to start searching the game tree until the opponent had moved twice and the computer had moved once. By that time the game tree could have no more than 6! = 720 paths remaining. By storing nine moves you will have reduced the size of the game tree tremendously. This is an example of a space versus time tradeoff. By using extra memory to store replies to moves, you can greatly reduce the time needed to search the game tree.

Example program TICTAC2 uses ten precomputed moves to make the initial move if it goes first and to reply to your initial move if you go first. To see the effects of the pre-computed moves, run the program using skill level nine. Then run program TICTAC using skill level nine. You will see an enormous difference in speed.

You could continue this strategy by saving responses to more and more moves, but at some point the time saved is not worth the memory required. By storing only ten responses, you can reduce the number of possible paths through the tic-tac-toe game tree to a few thousand. That makes the program so fast that storing more responses is not worth the additional effort. The game trees of more complicated games like chess grow so quickly that storing any but a few of the first moves is impractical.

Commercial chess programs usually begin by using stored moves. There are only a few initial moves which are generally used by chess experts and a chess program will usually pick one of them. Many chess programs also store responses to these standard openings. When you play against a chess program, you will notice how quickly the program can make its first couple of moves. Once the game has progressed beyond the range of its stored responses, the program will start to take more time to make each move.

Recognizing Important Patterns

Another way to improve game tree searches is to look for important board patterns. When the program identifies one of these patterns, it can take specific action or it can alter the way in which it searches the tree.

During a chess game the players will often arrange the pieces to guard each other. Then if the opponent captures a piece, the player will be able to capture one of the opponent's pieces. Often that capture will allow the opponent to capture another piece and so forth. Sometimes a series of exchanges like this can involve quite a few pieces.

Many chess programs look for possible sequences of trades. If the program recognizes a trade, it will temporarily break its limits on how far down the tree it can search, and it will examine the sequence of trades to its end. This allows the computer to decide whether or not the exchange will be profitable. If the exchange takes place, the number of pieces remaining will also be reduced so the game tree will be easier to search in the future.

Some chess programs also look for patterns such as possible castling moves, moves that threaten more than one of the opponent's pieces at the same time, moves that threaten the opponent's king or queen, etc.

Heuristics

At some point you have to admit that you will be unable to search the entire game tree. In games more complicated than tic-tac-toe, it is almost never possible to search even a tiny fraction of the tree. In these cases you must resort to some sort of *heuristic* (pronounced "you-riss-tik"). A heuristic is an algorithm or rule of thumb that is likely, but not guaranteed, to produce a good result.

A common heuristic in chess is, "When ahead, trade mercilessly." That means that if your opponent has lost more valuable pieces than you have, and all else is equal, you should exchange pieces whenever possible as long as you do not lose on the deal. For example, if you can capture a knight but you will lose a knight in exchange, you should do so. By reducing the number of pieces remaining, you make the decision tree smaller and you make your relative strength advantage greater. While this strategy does not guarantee that you will win the game, it improves your chances.

Another heuristic which is valid in many strategy games is to assign different values to different parts of the board. In chess the squares nearest the center of the board are considered most valuable because pieces in those positions can attack a large part of the rest of the board. When the BoardValue subroutine calculates the value of a particular board position, it can give greater weight to pieces that hold these key squares or to pieces that can attack those squares.

Searching Other Decision Trees

Branch and Bound

Branch and bound is a technique for *pruning* a decision tree so you do not need to consider all of the tree's branches. The general strategy is to keep track of bounds on the solutions you have discovered so far and on the solutions that are possible below each point in the decision tree. If you ever reach a point where the solutions found so far are better than the best possible solution available below a node in the tree, you can ignore all of the paths below that node.

For example, suppose you have $100 million to spend and you have several business investments from which to choose. Each has a different cost and each will provide you with a different expected return. Your problem is to decide how to spend your money to get the greatest possible profit.

This sort of problem is called a *knapsack* problem. The idea is that you have several items (investments) that you want to fit into a knapsack with a fixed size ($100 million). Each of the items has some cost (money) and a value (also money). You want to find a selection of items that fits in the knapsack and gives you the greatest possible profit.

This problem can be modeled as a decision tree. Each node in the tree represents a combination of items placed in the knapsack. Each branch represents the decision to put an item in the knapsack or to leave an item out. For the investment example, the left branch at the first node would correspond to spending money on the first investment. The right branch would correspond to not spending money on the first investment.

Figure 7.6 shows a decision tree for four possible investments. The leftmost leaf in the tree corresponds to spending money on all four investments. The next leaf corresponds to investing in choices A, B, and C. The third to investing in A, B, and D, and so on.

The decision tree for this problem is a complete binary tree of depth equal to the number of investments you are considering. Each leaf node corresponds to a complete selection of items that should and should not be part of the investment package.

Since the depth of the tree depends on the number of items you are considering, the size of the tree grows quickly. If you are considering ten investment opportunities, there will be $2^{10} = 1{,}024$ leaf nodes in the tree and 1,024 possible combinations of investments. If you are considering 20 investments, there will be more than 1 million possible combinations. Searching a tree with 1 million leaves is possible, but you do not have to add too many more investment choices to make the search unreasonably large.

To use branch and bound, you use an array to keep track of the items in the best solution you have found so far. You begin by initializing this array so it does not contain any items. You also use a variable to keep track of the value of that solution. Initially you set this to some value smaller than the value any real solution might have. That way the first real solution you find will be better than the empty solution so the new solution will be chosen instead.

While you search the decision tree, if you ever reach a point where the solution you are examining has no chance of improving to the point where it is better than the current best solution, you can stop searching down that path in the tree. Also if you ever reach a point where the selections cost more than the $100 million spending allowance, you can stop searching down that path.

As a concrete example, suppose you can make any of the investments shown in Table 7.1. Figure 7.6 shows the decision tree that corresponds to these investments.

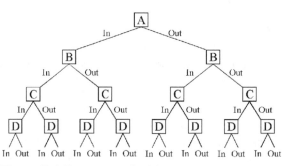

Figure 7.6 Investment decision tree.

Table 7.1 Possible Investments

Investment	Cost (millions)	Return (millions)	Profit (millions)
A	45	55	10
B	52	65	13
C	46	54	8
D	35	39	4

Some of these investment packages violate the problem's constraints. The leftmost path, for example, would require you to invest in all four opportunities at a total cost of $178 million, which is more money than you have available to spend. You can improve the tree searching technique if you place an upper bound on the branches you follow and abandon any branches that are too expensive. If a branch becomes too expensive, stop following it. While this seems like a small change, it can dramatically reduce the number of nodes you must visit in the tree.

In a similar fashion you can create a lower bound on the value of the branches you follow. If you keep track of how much profit could be generated by the items that you have not yet considered, you can determine the maximum amount by which a path can improve. If you find a branch that cannot improve enough to become more valuable than the best value found so far, you do not need to continue searching down that branch.

For example, suppose you have started searching the tree shown in Figure 7.6. You have found that you could invest in options A and B at a cost of $97 million for a profit of $23 million. This package corresponds to the fourth leaf node from the left in Figure 7.6.

Now as you continue searching the tree, you will soon come to the second node labeled C in Figure 7.6. This node corresponds to investment packages that include option A, do not include option B, and may or may not include options C and D. At this point the package already costs $45 million for option A and produces a profit of $10 million.

The only remaining options to consider are C and D. These can produce profits of $8 million and $4 million respectively. Together they can improve the current path by at most $12 million. The current path has a value of $10 million so the best possible path below this node can have a value of no more than $22 million. Since this is smaller than the $23 million solution you have already found, you do not need to continue down this path. By not continuing down this path, you can avoid examining four nodes in the tree. While it may seem as if you have not saved much time, this technique will eliminate many more nodes in a larger tree.

As the program moves through the tree, it does not need to continuously check to see if the partial solution it has found is better than the best solution so far. If a partial solution is an improvement, the rightmost leaf node below that partial solution will also be an improvement. That leaf will represent the same combination of items as the partial solution and any items that have not yet been considered by the partial solution are excluded. This means the program only needs to check to see if it has found an improved solution when it reaches a leaf node.

In fact, any leaf node the program reaches will *always* be an improvement over the best solution found so far. If it were not, then it would have been trimmed from the tree when the program considered the node's parent. At that point moving to the leaf would have reduced the total value of the unassigned items to zero. If the value of the solution were not already larger than the best solution so far, the lower bound test would stop the program from continuing to the leaf. Using this fact, the program can update the best solution it has found so far any time it reaches a leaf node.

Putting the upper and lower bound tests together you can write the branch and bound algorithm in Visual Basic.

```
Type Item
    Cost As Integer
    Profit As Integer
End Type

Global Items(0 To MAX_ITEM) As Item
Global MaxItem As Integer       ' Index of the last item in use.

Global ToSpend As Integer        ' The amount can spend.
Global best_profit As Integer   ' The best profit so far.

' best_solution is an array of "used" flags corresponding
' to the best solution so far.
Dim best_solution(0 To MAX_ITEM) As Integer

' The solution we are testing.
Dim test_solution(0 To MAX_ITEM) As Integer
Dim test_cost As Integer
Dim test_profit As Integer

' Initialize variables and begin the search.
Sub Search (search_type As Integer)
Dim i As Integer

    ' Initialize as if we are investing in nothing.
    best_profit = 0
    unassigned_profit = 0
    For i = 0 To MaxItem
        best_solution(i) = False
        test_solution(i) = False
        unassigned_profit = unassigned_profit + Items(i).Profit
    Next i
    test_profit = 0
    test_cost = 0

    ' Start the search with the first item.
    BranchAndBound 0
End Sub

' Perform a branch and bound search starting with
' this item.
Sub BranchAndBound (item As Integer)
Dim i As Integer

    NodesVisited = NodesVisited + 1

    ' If this is a leaf node, it must be a better solution
    ' than we have so far or it would have been cut off
    ' earlier in the search.
    If item > MaxItem Then
        For i = 0 To MaxItem
```

```
                best_solution(i) = test_solution(i)
                best_profit = test_profit
                best_cost = test_cost
        Next i
        Exit Sub
    End If
    ' Otherwise descend down the child branches.

        ' First try including this item. Make sure it fits
        ' within the cost bound.
        If test_cost + Items(item).Cost <= ToSpend Then
            test_solution(item) = True
            test_cost = test_cost + Items(item).Cost
            test_profit = test_profit + Items(item).Profit
            unassigned_profit = unassigned_profit - Items(item).Profit

            BranchAndBound item + 1

            test_solution(item) = False
            test_cost = test_cost - Items(item).Cost
            test_profit = test_profit - Items(item).Profit
            unassigned_profit = unassigned_profit + Items(item).Profit
        End If

        ' Now try excluding the item. See if the remaining
        ' items have enough profit to make a path down this
        ' branch reach our lower bound.
        unassigned_profit = unassigned_profit - Items(item).Profit
        If test_profit + unassigned_profit > best_profit Then _
    BranchAndBound item + 1
        unassigned_profit = unassigned_profit + Items(item).Profit
    End Sub
```

Example program BANDB demonstrates the exhaustive search and branch and bound techniques for the knapsack problem. You can enter item costs and values yourself, or have the computer generate them randomly. To have the computer generate values, enter the maximum and minimum costs and values you want assigned to the items and the number of items you want created. Then press the Randomize button and the computer will generate the items.

Next use the option buttons at the bottom of the form to select either exhaustive search or branch and bound. When you press the Go button, the program will use the method you selected to find the best solution to the knapsack problem. The program will display the best solution along with the number of nodes in the complete decision tree, the number of nodes the program actually visited, and the elapsed time.

Be sure to try small examples before you let the program run an exhaustive search on 20 items. A 50 megahertz 486-based PC can take one and a half minutes or more to exhaustively search for a solution to the 20 item knapsack problem (0.08 seconds using branch and bound). Do not run such a large problem on a 386-based PC unless you are willing to wait for a long time. Table 7.2 compares run times for exhaustive searches and searches using branch and bound techniques on a 50 megahertz 486-based PC.

Notice that the branch and bound search visits far fewer decision tree nodes than the exhaustive search. The decision tree for a 20 item knapsack problem contains 2,097,151 nodes. An exhaustive search will visit them all while a branch and bound search may visit only 1,500 or so.

Table 7.2 Exhaustive and Branch and Bound Search Times

# Items	Exhaustive Search	Branch and Bound
10	0.10	0.01
11	0.18	0.01
12	0.37	0.02
13	0.73	0.03
14	1.47	0.04
15	3.02	0.04
16	5.88	0.05
17	12.05	0.05
18	23.84	0.06
19	47.44	0.08
20	94.59	0.09

The number of nodes that branch and bound can trim from the tree depends on the nature of the problem. If the costs of the items are large, only a few items at a time will fit into a valid solution. Once a few items have been placed in the test solution, the remaining items will be too expensive to consider so much of the tree will be trimmed away.

On the other hand, if the items have relatively small costs, many of them will be able to fit into a valid solution. In that case there will be many valid combinations that the algorithm will need to explore. Table 7.3 shows the number of nodes program BANDB visited in a series of tests with different values for the items' costs. In each case the program randomly generated 20 items and the total allowed cost of the solution was 100.

While the number of nodes visited using the branch and bound algorithm changed depending on the nature of the data, the number of nodes visited by exhaustive search stayed the same. In all cases, however, the branch and bound search was much faster than the exhaustive search.

Heuristics

Sometimes even branch and bound algorithms will have trouble searching decision trees. The decision tree for a knapsack problem involving 100 items contains more than 2×10^{30} nodes. Even if a branch and bound algorithm visited only a tiny fraction of those nodes, your computer might be unable to solve the problem within your lifetime.

In cases where even the best algorithms are not fast enough, you can use a heuristic. Many problems that are hard to solve exactly can be solved approximately using

Table 7.3 Nodes Visited by Exhaustive and Branch and Bound Searches

Average Item Cost	Exhaustive Search	Branch and Bound
60	2,097,151	203
50	2,097,151	520
40	2,097,151	1,322
30	2,097,151	4,269
20	2,097,151	13,286
10	2,097,151	40,589

heuristics. If the quality of the solution is not critical, the answer given by a heuristic may be close enough to be useful.

In some cases you may not know the input data with perfect accuracy. Then a good heuristic solution may be as valid as the theoretically "best" solution. In the knapsack example of the preceding sections, you used branch and bound to pick the best choices from a list of investment opportunities. Investments are risky, however, and the exact results of an investment are often not known ahead of time. You may not know the exact profit or even cost of some or all of the investments. In that case a good heuristic solution may be just as likely to produce good results as the best solution you could calculate exactly.

This section discusses some heuristics which you can use to locate good solutions for many difficult problems. In cases like uncertain investments, these solutions may be just as valid as the best solutions that can be produced by exhaustive searching or branch and bound.

Example program HEUR demonstrates each of the heuristics. It also allows you to compare the results produced by the heuristics with those given by exhaustive search and branch and bound. Enter information in the Parameters area to tell the program how to generate the test data. Then use the check boxes to select the algorithms you want to test and press the Go button. The program will display the total cost and total profit of the best solution found by each of the methods you have selected. It will also display the time required by each method. Be sure to use branch and bound on relatively small problems and exhaustive search only on the smallest problems.

Hill Climbing

A *hill climbing* heuristic tries to make changes to the current solution that will take it as close as possible to the goal. The process is called hill climbing because it is like a lost hiker at night searching for the top of a mountain. Even if it is too dark to see very far, the hiker can try to reach the mountain top by always moving uphill.

Of course there is a chance that the hiker will become stuck on a smaller hill and not make it all the way to the peak. This sort of problem can also occur when using a hill climbing strategy for examining a decision tree. The algorithm can find a solution which locally looks like a good one, but which is not the best solution possible.

In the knapsack problem the goal is to select a collection of items with total cost no more than an allowed limit and with a large total value. A hill climbing technique for this problem would select the item that gives the largest profit at each step. At each step you would move closer to the goal of maximizing the total profit.

You would start by adding the item with the largest profit to the solution. Then you would add the item with the next largest profit that still fit within the total cost allowance and continue adding the item with the next largest profit that fit within the allowance until no more items could fit within the solution.

For the investments shown in Table 7.4, you would start by adding option A to the solution since this option has the largest profit at $9 million. Next you would add option C to the solution since it has the next largest profit at $8 million. At this point you would have used up $93 million of the $100 million allowance and no more items would fit in the solution.

The solution produced by the hill climbing heuristic includes items A and C, has a total cost of $93 million, and gives a total profit of $17 million.

The hill climbing heuristic will fill the knapsack quickly. If the items are initially sorted in order of decreasing profit, this is an O(N) algorithm. You simply move through the list adding each item if there is room. Even if the list is not sorted, this is only an $O(N^2)$ algorithm. That is much better than the $O(2^N)$ steps required for an exhaustive search of every node in the tree. For 20 items, this heuristic would require around 20 steps, compared to a couple thousand for branch and bound, and more than 2 million for an exhaustive search.

The HEUR program uses an array test_solution to indicate which items are in the solution. The value of test_solution(I) is true if investment opportunity number I is part of the solution.

The hill climbing subroutine repeatedly passes through the list of investment opportunities looking for the largest that is not already in the solution and which will fit within the cost allowance. Since the subroutine may have to search the list O(N) times, this is an $O(N^2)$ process.

```
Sub HillClimbing ()
Dim i As Integer
Dim j As Integer
Dim big_value As Integer
Dim big_j As Integer
    ' Repeatedly pass through the list looking for the
    ' remaining item with the largest profit that will fit
    ' within the cost bounds.
    For i = 1 To NumItems
        big_value = 0
        big_j = -1
        For j = 1 To NumItems
            ' Make sure it is not already in the solution.
            If (Not test_solution(j)) And (test_cost + _
Items(j).Cost <= ToSpend) And (big_value < Items(j).Profit) Then
                big_value = Items(j).Profit
                big_j = j
            End If
        Next j

        ' Stop when we cannot find another item that fits.
        If big_j < 0 Then Exit For

        test_cost = test_cost + Items(big_j).Cost
        test_solution(big_j) = True
        test_profit = test_profit + Items(big_j).Profit
    Next i
End Sub
```

Table 7.4 Possible Investments

Investment	Cost	Return	Profit
A	63	72	9
B	35	42	7
C	30	38	8
D	27	34	7
E	23	26	3

Least-Cost

A strategy which in some sense is the opposite of hill climbing is *least-cost*. Instead of moving the solution as far as possible towards the goal at each step, you move the *cost* of the solution as little as possible towards the constraint. In the knapsack example, you would add the item that has the lowest cost to the solution at each step.

Using this strategy you will fit as many items as possible into the solution. If the items all have roughly the same profits, this will produce a good solution. If a very expensive option has a relatively large profit, the least-cost strategy will miss that option and not produce the best result possible.

For the investments shown in Table 7.4, a least-cost strategy would start by adding option E to the solution at a cost of $23 million. It would then add option D at $27 million, and then option C at $30 million. At this point the algorithm would have spent $80 million of the $100 million allowance and it would not be able to fit any more items into the solution.

The solution produced by the least-cost heuristic includes items C, D, and E, has a total cost of $80 million, and gives a total profit of $18 million. This is $1 million better than the solution produced by the hill climbing heuristic. It is not always true, however, that the least-cost heuristic produces a better solution than the hill climbing method. Which is the better solution depends on the exact values of the data.

In structure the least-cost heuristic is almost identical to the hill climbing heuristic. The only difference is in selecting the next item to add to the test solution. The least-cost heuristic chooses the item that has the lowest cost while the hill climbing method picks the item with the largest profit. Since the two methods are so similar, they have the same run time. If the items are initially sorted properly, they can each run in time O(N). Even with the items arranged randomly, it is easy to write these algorithms so they run in $O(N^2)$ time.

Since the Visual Basic code for the two heuristics is so similar, only the lines where the new item is selected are shown here.

```
        If (Not test_solution(j)) And (test_cost + _
Items(j).Cost <= ToSpend) And (small_cost > Items(j).Cost) Then
    small_cost = Items(j).Cost
    small_j = j
        End If
```

Balanced Profit

The basic hill climbing strategy does not take into account the cost of the items being added to the solution. At each step it selects the most profitable item even if that item has a very large cost. On the other hand, the least-cost strategy does not take into account the profit returned by an item. At each step it adds the item with the lowest cost to the solution even if the item has a very low profit.

In a *balanced profit* heuristic you compare the profit and cost of the items while deciding which item to add to the solution. Instead of looking only at profit or cost, you look at the ratio of profit to cost. At each step you add the next item in the list that has the highest profit/cost ratio.

Table 7.5 shows the same data as Table 7.4 with an additional profit/cost column. Using this data, a balanced profit strategy would first pick option C since at 0.27 it has the highest profit/cost ratio. Next it would add option D to the solution since it has the next highest ratio at 0.26. The algorithm would then add option B to the solution with its ratio of 0.20. At this point the heuristic would have spent $92 million of the $100 million allowance and it could not add any more items to the solution.

The solution produced by the balanced profit heuristic includes items B, C, and D, has a total cost of $92 million, and gives a total profit of $22 million. This is $4 million better than the solution produced by the least-cost heuristic and $5 million better than the solution produced by hill climbing. In this example this is also the best possible solution and would be found by either an exhaustive search or a branch and bound search. The balanced profit method is still a heuristic, however, and it does not always find the best possible solution. While it often does better than the hill climbing and least-cost heuristics, it is not guaranteed to do so.

In structure the balanced profit heuristic is almost identical to the hill climbing and least cost heuristics. The only difference is in the way the heuristic selects the next item to add to the solution. Since the Visual Basic code for these heuristics is so similar, only the lines where the new item is selected are shown here.

```
            If (Not test_solution(j)) And (test_cost + _
Items(j).Cost <= ToSpend) And (good_ratio < Items(j).Profit / _
CDbl (Items(j).Cost)) Then
                good_ratio = Items(j).Profit / CDbl (Items(j).Cost)
                good_j = j
            End If
```

Random Searching

A *random search* is pretty much what you might guess. At each step the algorithm adds a randomly chosen item that will fit within the cost bounds. This kind of search is also called a *Monte Carlo search* or a *Monte Carlo simulation*.

Since a randomly selected solution is unlikely to give the best possible solution, you generally need to repeat the random search many times to get a reasonable result. Even if you repeat the process $O(N)$ or $O(N^2)$ times, the decision tree has $O(2^N)$ leaf nodes so it is extremely unlikely that you will find the absolute best solution.

While it may seem the odds are stacked against you, this method can sometimes produce surprisingly good results. Depending on the values of the data, a random solution is often better than the solutions produced by a hill climbing or least-cost strategy. Random solutions are also occasionally better than solutions produced by the balanced profit method.

This heuristic also has the advantage of being easy to understand. With different problems it is sometimes hard to decide how to select items to produce a hill climbing,

Table 7.5 Possible Investments with Profit/Cost Ratio

Investment	Cost	Return	Profit	Profit/Cost
A	63	72	9	0.14
B	35	42	7	0.20
C	30	38	8	0.27
D	27	34	7	0.26
E	23	26	3	0.13

least-cost, or balanced profit heuristic. It is always easy to pick items at random. Even if your problem is quite complicated, you will be able to use a random search to provide some sort of solution.

The random search subroutine in program HEUR uses function AddToSolution to add a random item to the solution. This function returns the value true if it can find an item that fits within the cost allowance and false otherwise. To create a random solution, the random search heuristic calls function AddToSolution until no more items will fit within the cost allowance.

```
Sub RandomSearch ()
Dim num_trials As Integer
Dim trial As Integer
Dim i As Integer

    ' Make several trials and keep the best.
    num_trials = NumItems ' Use N trials.
    For trial = 1 To num_trials
        ' Make random selections until no more items fit.
        Do While AddToSolution()
            ' All the work is done by AddToSolution.
        Loop
        ' See if this solution is an improvement.
        If test_profit > best_profit Then
            best_profit = test_profit
            best_cost = test_cost
            For i = 1 To NumItems
                best_solution(i) = test_solution(i)
            Next i
        End If

        ' Reset the test solution for the next trial.
        test_profit = 0
        test_cost = 0
        For i = 1 To NumItems
            test_solution(i) = False
        Next i
    Next trial
End Sub


Function AddToSolution () As Integer
Dim num_left As Integer
Dim j As Integer
Dim selection As Integer

    ' See how many items remain that will fit within
    ' the cost bound.
    num_left = 0
    For j = 1 To NumItems
        If (Not test_solution(j)) And (test_cost + Items(j).Cost _
<= ToSpend) Then num_left = num_left + 1
    Next j

    ' Stop when we cannot find another item that fits.
    If num_left < 1 Then
        AddToSolution = False
        Exit Function
    End If
```

```
    ' Pick one at random.
    selection = Int((num_left) * Rnd + 1)

    ' Find the randomly chosen item.
    For j = 1 To NumItems
        If (Not test_solution(j)) And (test_cost + Items(j).Cost _
<= ToSpend) Then
            selection = selection - 1
            If selection < 1 Then Exit For
        End If
    Next j

    test_profit = test_profit + Items(j).Profit
    test_cost = test_cost + Items(j).Cost
    test_solution(j) = True

    AddToSolution = True
End Function
```

Incremental Improvement

You can also use random selections to make *incremental improvements* to a solution. Starting with a randomly generated solution, you test random changes to the solution and see if there is an improvement. If there is, you make the change permanent and you continue to make other random changes.

It is particularly easy to generate random changes for the knapsack problem. Given a test solution, you simply pick an item in the solution at random and remove it from the current solution. Then you randomly add items back into the solution until no more items will fit. If the item you removed from the solution has a very large cost, you may be able to add more than one new item to the solution.

Once you have finished making the change, you see if there has been an improvement. If not, you reset the solution to the way it was before you made the random change. Otherwise you keep the new solution and continue testing random changes.

Like a random search, this heuristic is easy to understand. While it may be hard to design hill climbing, least-cost, and balanced profit heuristics for a difficult problem, it is usually easy to write an incremental improvement heuristic.

When to Stop

Once you start making random changes, you must decide when to stop. There are a couple of good ways to make this decision. First, you can perform a fixed number of changes. For an N item problem, you might make N random changes and then stop.

In program HEUR the MakeChangesFixed subroutine uses this approach. It makes a certain number of random changes to a number of different trial solutions. The subroutine takes as parameters the number of items it should randomly replace in the trial solutions, the number of trials it should run, and the number of times it should make random changes to each trial solution.

```
Sub MakeChangesFixed (K As Integer, num_trials As Integer, _
num_changes As Integer)
Dim trial As Integer
Dim change As Integer
Dim i As Integer
Dim removal As Integer
```

```
For trial = 1 To num_trials
    ' Find a random test solution to use as a
    ' starting point.
    Do While AddToSolution()
        ' All the work is done by AddToSolution.
    Loop

    ' Start with this as the trial solution.
    trial_profit = test_profit
    trial_cost = test_cost
    For i = 1 To NumItems
        trial_solution(i) = test_solution(i)
    Next i

    For change = 1 To num_changes
        ' Remove K random items.
        For removal = 1 To K
            RemoveFromSolution
        Next removal

        ' Add back as many random items as will fit.
        Do While AddToSolution()
            ' All the work is done by AddToSolution.
        Loop

        ' If this improves the trial, save it.
        ' Otherwise reset the trial to the previous
        ' value.
        If test_profit > trial_profit Then
            ' Save the improvement.
            trial_profit = test_profit
            trial_cost = test_cost
            For i = 1 To NumItems
                trial_solution(i) = test_solution(i)
            Next i
        Else
            ' Reset the trial.
            test_profit = trial_profit
            test_cost = trial_cost
            For i = 1 To NumItems
                test_solution(i) = trial_solution(i)
            Next i
        End If
    Next change

    ' If this trial is better than the best solution
    ' so far, save it.
    If trial_profit > best_profit Then
        best_profit = trial_profit
        best_cost = trial_cost
        For i = 1 To NumItems
            best_solution(i) = trial_solution(i)
        Next i
    End If

    ' Reset the test solution for the next trial.
    test_profit = 0
    test_cost = 0
    For i = 1 To NumItems
```

```
                    test_solution(i) = False
            Next i
        Next trial
End Sub
```

An alternative strategy is to make changes until you get no more improvements for several test changes. For an N item problem you might continue making changes until you saw no improvement for N changes in a row.

In program HEUR the MakeChangesNoChange subroutine follows this strategy. It runs trials until a certain number of trials in a row show no improvement over the best solution it has found so far. For each trial it makes random changes to the trial solution until it finds no improvement in a certain number of random changes in a row. The subroutine takes as parameters the number of items it should randomly replace in the trial solutions, the number of trials without improvement it should run, and the number of changes without improvement it should run for each trial.

```
Sub MakeChangesNoChange (K As Integer, max_bad_trials As Integer, _
max_non_changes As Integer)
Dim i As Integer
Dim removal As Integer
Dim bad_trials As Integer    ' # consecutive ineffective trials.
Dim non_changes As Integer   ' # consecutive ineffective-changes.

    ' Repeat trials until we have max_bad_trials runs
    ' in a row without an improvement.
    bad_trials = 0
    Do
        ' Find a random test solution to use as a
        ' starting point.
        Do While AddToSolution()
            ' All the work is done by AddToSolution.
        Loop

        ' Start with this as the trial solution.
        trial_profit = test_profit
        trial_cost = test_cost
        For i = 1 To NumItems
            trial_solution(i) = test_solution(i)
        Next i

        ' Repeat until we try max_non_changes in a row
        ' without an improvement.
        non_changes = 0
        Do While non_changes < max_non_changes
            ' Remove K random items.
            For removal = 1 To K
                RemoveFromSolution
            Next removal

            ' Add back as many random items as will fit.
            Do While AddToSolution()
                ' All the work is done by AddToSolution.
            Loop

            ' If this improves the trial, save it.
            ' Otherwise reset the trial to the previous
            ' value.
            If test_profit > trial_profit Then
```

```
                  ' Save the improvement.
                  trial_profit = test_profit
                  trial_cost = test_cost
                  For i = 1 To NumItems
                      trial_solution(i) = test_solution(i)
                  Next i
                  non_changes = 0 ' This was a good change.
              Else
                  ' Reset the trial.
                  test_profit = trial_profit
                  test_cost = trial_cost
                  For i = 1 To NumItems
                      test_solution(i) = trial_solution(i)
                  Next i
                  non_changes = non_changes + 1 ' Bad change.
              End If
          Loop      ' Continue trying random changes.

          ' If this trial is better than the best solution
          ' so far, save it.
          If trial_profit > best_profit Then
              best_profit = trial_profit
              best_cost = trial_cost
              For i = 1 To NumItems
                  best_solution(i) = trial_solution(i)
              Next i
              bad_trials = 0         ' This was a good trial.
          Else
              bad_trials = bad_trials + 1     ' Bad trial.
          End If

          ' Reset the test solution for the next trial.
          test_profit = 0
          test_cost = 0
          For i = 1 To NumItems
              test_solution(i) = False
          Next i
      Loop While bad_trials < max_bad_trials
  End Sub
```

Local Solutions

If you randomly replace only a single item in a test solution, you may find a solution that you cannot improve but which is also not the best possible solution. For example, consider the investment options shown in Table 7.6.

Suppose the algorithm randomly selects items A and B for its initial solution. This solution has a total cost of $90 million and a total profit of $17 million.

If you remove either item A or B from the solution, the solution will still have a cost large enough that you could add only one new item to the solution. Since items A and B

Table 7.6 Possible Investments

Investment	Cost	Return	Profit
A	47	56	9
B	43	51	8
C	35	40	5
D	32	39	7
E	31	37	6

have the largest profits, replacing one of them with one of the other items will decrease the total profit of the solution. In this case the improvement strategy will remove either item A or B from the solution and then add it right back into the solution. Randomly removing one item from the solution will never result in an improvement.

The best solution, however, contains items C, D, and E. That solution has a total cost of $98 million and a total profit of $18 million. To find this solution the algorithm would need to remove both items A and B from the solution at the same time and then add new items.

This kind of solution where small changes cannot improve the solution is called a *local optimum*. There are two ways you can try to prevent the program from getting stuck in a local optimum so it can search for the *global optimum*.

First, you can modify the program so it removes more than one item when it makes its random changes. If the program removes two random items and then replaces them with new items, it will find the correct solution to this example. For larger problems, however, removing two items may not be enough. You may need to remove three, four, or even more items from the initial solution.

An easier alternative is to run several trials starting with different initial solutions each time. The different starting solutions may lead to different final solutions. Some of those solutions may be dead ends, but hopefully one will be the global optimum.

Example program HEUR demonstrates four incremental improvement strategies. Method "Fixed 1" makes N trials. During each trial it selects a random solution and then tries to improve the solution 2 * N times by randomly removing a single item.

Method "Fixed 2" makes only one trial. It selects a random solution and then tries to improve the solution 10 * N times by randomly removing two items.

Heuristic "No Changes 1" runs trials until it finds no improvements in N successive trials. During each trial the program selects a random solution and then tries to improve it by randomly removing one item until it finds no improvement during N successive changes.

Heuristic "No Changes 2" runs a single trial. It selects a random solution and then tries to improve it by randomly removing two items until it finds no improvement during N successive changes.

The names and descriptions of the heuristics are summarized in Table 7.7.

Simulated Annealing

The method of *simulated annealing* was inspired by thermodynamics. When a metal is annealed, it is heated to a high temperature. While the metal is hot, the molecules in the

Table 7.7 Incremental Improvement Strategies

Name	*# Trials*	*# Changes*	*Items Removed per Change*
Fixed 1	N	2 * N	1
Fixed 2	1	10 * N	2
No Changes 1	No change in N trials	No change in N changes	1
No Changes 2	1	No change in N changes	2

metal move rapidly in relation to each other. If the metal is cooled slowly, the molecules start to line up with each other to form crystals. These crystals are the minimum energy arrangements of the molecules they contain.

As the metal is slowly cooled, different crystals that are adjacent to each other will merge. The molecules in one crystal will temporarily leave their minimum energy arrangement and line up with the molecules in the other crystal. At that point the new, larger crystal will have a lower energy state than the two smaller crystals did together. If the metal is cooled slowly enough, the crystals will become huge. The final arrangement of molecules will be in a very low energy state and the metal will be quite hard.

The reason this process is mentioned here is that, starting from a high energy state, the molecules in the metal eventually reach a low energy state. On the way to the final solution, they pass through many local minimums in energy. Every combination of crystals represents a local minimum in energy. Only by temporarily raising the energy of the system can the crystals combine so the molecules fall into an even lower energy state.

The method of simulated annealing uses an analogous method to find the best solution to a problem. As the program works its way towards a solution, it may become stuck in a local optimum. To prevent this from happening, the program occasionally makes a random change to the solution even though the change does not immediately improve the result. This may allow the program to break free of a local optimum and find a better solution later. If the change does not lead to a better solution, the program will probably undo the change in a short time anyway.

To prevent the program from making these random modifications forever, the algorithm changes the probability of making the backwards modifications over time. The probability of making one of these changes is given by $P = 1/Exp(E/(k * T))$. Here E is the amount of "energy" being added to the system, k is a constant chosen to fit the problem, and T is a "temperature" variable.

Initially T should be fairly large so $P = 1/Exp(E/(k * T))$ is reasonably large. Otherwise random changes would never occur. Over time the value of T is slowly reduced so the probability of random changes grows smaller. Once the simulation has reached the point where it cannot find any more changes that give an improvement, and T is small enough that random changes are rare, the algorithm can stop.

For a knapsack problem, the "energy" E is the amount by which the profit of the solution is decreased by the change. For instance, if you remove an item that has profit $10 million and replace it with an item having profit $7 million, E will be 3.

Notice that if E is large, the probability $P = 1/Exp(E/(k * T))$ is small. This makes the chances of a large random change occurring smaller than the chances of a small random change occurring.

The simulated annealing algorithm in example program HEUR sets the constant k to the difference between the largest and smallest profits of the possible investment choices. It initially sets T to 0.75. Each time the program introduces a certain number of random changes, it multiplies T by 0.95 to make it smaller. Eventually T becomes small enough that the program does not generate further random changes.

```
Sub AnnealTrial (K As Integer, max_non_changes As Integer, _
max_back_slips As Integer)
Const TFACTOR = .95

Dim i As Integer
Dim removal As Integer
Dim non_changes As Integer
```

```
Dim T As Double
Dim max_profit As Integer
Dim min_profit As Integer
Dim do_it As Integer
Dim back_slips As Integer

    ' See what items have the largest and smallest profits.
    max_profit = Items(1).Profit
    min_profit = max_profit
    For i = 2 To NumItems
        If max_profit < Items(i).Profit Then max_profit = _
Items(i).Profit
        If min_profit > Items(i).Profit Then min_profit = _
Items(i).Profit
    Next i

    T = .75 * (max_profit - min_profit)
    back_slips = 0

    ' Find a random test solution to use as a
    ' starting point.
    Do While AddToSolution()
        ' All the work is done by AddToSolution.
    Loop

    ' Start with this as the trial solution.
    best_profit = test_profit
    best_cost = test_cost
    For i = 1 To NumItems
        best_solution(i) = test_solution(i)
    Next i

    ' Repeat until we try max_non_changes in a row
    ' without an improvement.
    non_changes = 0
    Do While non_changes < max_non_changes
        ' Remove a random item.
        For i = 1 To K
            RemoveFromSolution
        Next i

        ' Add back as many random items as will fit.
        Do While AddToSolution()
            ' All the work is done by AddToSolution.
        Loop

        ' If this improves the trial, save it.
        ' Otherwise reset the trial to the previous
        ' value.
        If test_profit > best_profit Then
            do_it = True
        ElseIf test_profit < best_profit Then
            do_it = (Rnd < Exp((test_profit - best_profit) / T))
            back_slips = back_slips + 1
            If back_slips > max_back_slips Then
                back_slips = 0
                T = T * TFACTOR
            End If
        Else
```

```
            do_it = False
        End If
        If do_it Then
            ' Save the improvement.
            best_profit = test_profit
            best_cost = test_cost
            For i = 1 To NumItems
                best_solution(i) = test_solution(i)
            Next i
            non_changes = 0 ' This was a good change.
        Else
            ' Reset the trial.
            test_profit = best_profit
            test_cost = best_cost
            For i = 1 To NumItems
                test_solution(i) = best_solution(i)
            Next i
            non_changes = non_changes + 1    ' Bad change.
        End If
    Loop    ' Continue trying random changes.
End Sub
```

Comparing Heuristics

Different heuristics behave differently for different problems. For the knapsack problems discussed so far, the balanced profit heuristic does quite well considering how simple it is. The different incremental improvement strategies usually do as well and sometimes better, but they take much longer for large problems. For problems other than the knapsack problem, the best heuristic may be one of the others or it may even be a completely different heuristic not discussed here.

Heuristics are much faster than branch and bound searching. Some, like hill climbing, least-cost, and balanced profit, are extremely fast since they only consider one possible solution. Since these algorithms are fast, it makes sense to run them all and take the best solution found by any of them. While this still does not guarantee that you will find the best solution possible, you will have some confidence that your solution is fairly good.

Other Hard Problems

There are many other problems like the knapsack problem that are extremely difficult to solve. Many have no known polynomial time solutions. In other words there are no algorithms for solving these problems that run in $O(N^C)$ time for any constant C, not even $O(N^{1,000})$.

The following sections briefly describe a few of these problems. They also explain in general terms why each problem is difficult and how large the most straightforward decision tree might be. You may want to test the branch and bound and heuristic techniques on a few of them.

Satisfiability (SAT)

Given a logical statement like "(A And Not B) Or C," is there an assignment of true and false values to the variables A, B, C, etc. that makes the statement true? In the example above, it is easy to see that the statement will be true if you assign A = true, B = false, and C = false. For more complicated statements it is not always easy to tell whether or not there is a way to make the statement true.

Using a method similar to the one used to solve the knapsack problem, you can build a satisfiability decision tree. Each branch in the tree represents a decision to set a variable to either true or false. The left branch leaving the root, for example, would correspond to setting the first variable's value to true.

If there are N variables in the logical statement, the decision tree will be a binary tree of height N + 1. This tree will have 2^N leaf nodes, each representing a different assignment of the values true and false to the variables.

In the knapsack problem you can use branch and bound to avoid searching much of the tree. As you examine the tree, you can generate intermediate solutions and use the values of those solutions to trim down the tree's size. If you find a path that exceeds the cost allowance, you can stop searching that path. If you find a path that cannot improve enough to beat the best solution found so far, you can abandon that path, too.

An assignment of values in the satisfiability problem, however, either makes the statement true or false. It does not provide you with a partial solution that you can use to trim other paths out of the tree.

You still may be able to remove some of the branches in the tree, however. If you can determine from a partial assignment of values that you cannot make the statement true, you do not need to continue down that branch of the tree. For example, suppose you are testing the statement "(Not A) And (B Or Not C)." Once you have given variable A the value true, the entire statement must be false no matter what values you give B and C. In this case you do not need to continue assigning values to variables B and C.

You cannot use heuristics as you can with the knapsack problem to find approximate solutions for the satisfiability problem. Whatever assignments of values a heuristic produces, those assignments will make the statement either true or false. There is no such thing as an approximate solution in logic. While a heuristic or random assignment of values may produce a correct solution, it is pretty unlikely. If there are no assignments of values that make the logical statement true, a heuristic will not find such an assignment, but you will never be sure that there is none.

With weakened branch and bound techniques and no useful heuristics, the satisfiability problem is generally quite difficult to solve. You can only solve satisfiability problems that are relatively small.

The Partition Problem

Given a collection of items with values $X_1, X_2, \ldots, X_N$, is there a way to divide the items into two groups so the total value of the items in each group is the same? For example, if the items have values 3, 4, 5, and 6, you can divide them into the groups {3,6} and {4,5}, both of which have total value 9.

To model this problem as a tree, let the branches correspond to placing an item in one of the two groups you are creating. The left branch out of the root node would correspond to placing the first item in the first group. The right branch out of the root node would correspond to placing the first item in the second group.

If there are N items to consider, the decision tree will be a binary tree of height N + 1. This means it will contain 2^N leaf nodes and 2^{N+1} nodes altogether. Each leaf node will correspond to a complete assignment of the items into the two groups.

As was the case with satisfiability, you can use a form of branch and bound to skip parts of the decision tree. As you examine partial solutions in the tree, you can keep track of the amount by which the two groups of items differ. If you ever reach a branch where placing all of the remaining items in the smaller group cannot make that group at least as big as the larger, you do not need to continue down that branch of the tree.

For the example above, with items 3, 4, 5, and 6, suppose you have placed items 5 and 6 in the first group and no items in the second. Even if you added all of the remaining items to the second group, you could not make it as large as the first. That means there is no way to continue assigning items to the groups so they will finish with the same total values.

As is the case for the satisfiability problem, you cannot generate approximate solutions for the partition problem. An assignment of items will create two groups that either do or do not have the same total values. This means that heuristics like the ones used for the knapsack problem will not help you find an even partition.

The partition problem can be generalized to: Given a collection of items with values $X_1, X_2, \ldots, X_N$, in what way should they be divided into two groups so the total values of the groups are as close in size as possible?

This problem is more difficult than the partition problem to solve exactly. After all, if there were an easy way to solve this problem, you could use that method to solve the partition problem. You would simply find the groups that are closest in size, and see if their sizes were equal.

You can use a branch and bound technique similar to the one used in the partition problem to avoid searching the entire tree. You can also use heuristics to provide approximate solutions. One method would be to examine the items in decreasing order of value, placing the next item in the smaller of the two groups. It would also be easy to use a random search, incremental improvement, or simulated annealing heuristic to find approximate solutions.

The Hamiltonian Path Problem (HAM)

Given a network, a *Hamiltonian path* is a path that visits every node in the network exactly once and then returns to its starting point. Figure 7.7 shows a small network with a Hamiltonian path drawn with bold lines.

The Hamiltonian path problem is: Given a network, does the network contain a Hamiltonian path?

Since every node in the network will be present in a Hamiltonian path, you do not need to decide which nodes to visit. You only need to determine the order in which they should be visited to produce a Hamiltonian path.

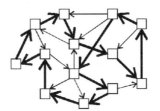

Figure 7.7 A Hamiltonian path.

To model this problem as a tree, let branches correspond to selecting which node to visit next in the path. The root node would have N branches corresponding to starting the path at each of the N nodes. The nodes beneath the root would each have N − 1 branches, one for each of the remaining N − 1 nodes that you could visit next. Nodes in the next level of the tree would have N − 2 branches, and so forth. At the bottom of the tree there would be N! leaf nodes corresponding to the N! possible orderings of the nodes. The tree as a whole would contain O(N!) nodes.

As is the case for the satisfiability and partition problems, you cannot generate partial or approximate solutions for Hamiltonian paths. A path is either a valid Hamiltonian path or it is not. This means that branch and bound techniques and heuristics will not help you locate a Hamiltonian path. To make matters worse, the Hamiltonian path decision tree contains O(N!) nodes. This is far more than the $O(2^N)$ nodes contained in the satisfiability and partition decision trees. For example, 2^{20} is roughly 1×10^6 while 20! is about 2.4×10^{18}. Since this tree is so large, you will be able to solve only the smallest Hamiltonian path problems.

The Traveling Salesman Problem (TSP)

The traveling salesman problem is closely related to the Hamiltonian path problem. The traveling salesman problem is: What is the shortest Hamiltonian path through a network?

This problem has a similar relationship to the Hamiltonian path problem as the generalized partitioning problem has to the partitioning problem. The first problem asks if a solution exists. The second asks what the best approximate solution is. If there were an easy solution to the second problem, you could use it to find a solution to the first problem.

Typically the traveling salesman problem only arises for networks that contain many Hamiltonian paths. In a common example a salesman must visit several customer locations and he wants to find the shortest path that will visit them all. In a normal street network, there are always paths between any two points in the network. That means that any ordering of the customer locations gives a valid Hamiltonian path. The problem is only to find the ordering of the customer locations that gives the shortest path.

Like the Hamiltonian path problem, the decision tree for this problem contains O(N!) nodes. Like the generalized partition problem, you can use branch and bound techniques to trim the tree and make finding a solution possible for problems of moderate size.

There are also several good incremental improvement heuristics for the traveling salesman problem. In the 2-opt improvement strategy, you examine pairs of links within the path. You check whether there would be an improvement if you removed those links and replaced them with two new links that would keep the path connected. Figure 7.8 shows how the path would change if links X_1 and X_2 were replaced with links Y_1 and Y_2. Similar improvement strategies consider replacing three or even more links at one time.

Typically you would repeat this sort of improvement many times or until you had tried all of the possible pairs of links in the path. Once you had improved the path as much as you could, you would save the results and start all over again with a different initial path. By trying many different initial paths, you would have a reasonably good chance of finding an improved path that was not too far from the best path possible.

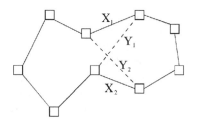

Figure 7.8 Improving a Hamiltonian path using 2-opt.

The Firehouse Problem

Given a network, a number F, and a distance D, is there a way to place F firehouses on nodes in the network in such a way that no node in the network is more than distance D away from the nearest firehouse?

You can model this problem with a decision tree where each branch determines where in the network a particular firehouse will be located. The root node will have N branches corresponding to placing the first firehouse at each of the network's N nodes. Nodes at the next level of the tree will have N – 1 branches corresponding to placing the second firehouse at each of the remaining N – 1 nodes. If there are F firehouses, this tree will have height F and will contain $O(N^F)$ nodes. It will have N * (N – 1) * . . . * (N – F) leaf nodes corresponding to the possible locations where you could place the firehouses.

Like the satisfiability, partitioning, and Hamiltonian path problems, this problem asks a yes or no question. That means you cannot use partial or approximate solutions while examining the decision tree.

You may be able to use some sort of branch and bound technique if you can decide early on that certain firehouse placements will not lead to good solutions. For example, you gain nothing by placing a new firehouse between two other closely spaced firehouses. If all of the nodes within distance D of the new firehouse are already within distance D of another firehouse, you should place the new firehouse somewhere else. Making this sort of calculation is quite time consuming, however, so the firehouse problem is still very difficult to solve.

Just as the partitioning and Hamiltonian path problems have generalizations, so does the firehouse problem. The generalized question is: Given a network and a number F, at what nodes should you place F firehouses so the greatest distance between any node and a firehouse is minimized?

As was the case in the other generalized problems, you can use branch and bound techniques and heuristics to find partial and approximate solutions to this problem. That makes examining the decision tree a bit easier. While the decision tree is still enormous, you can at least find approximate solutions, even if they are not the absolute best solutions possible.

Summary of Hard Problems

While reading the previous sections you may have noticed that many of these problems come in pairs. The first version of a problem asks, "Is there a solution of a certain quality to this problem?" The second, more general question asks, "What is the best solution to this problem?" For example, the Hamiltonian path problem asks, "Given a network, is there a path through the network that visits every node exactly once?" The corresponding more general question is the traveling salesman problem which asks, "What is the shortest Hamiltonian path through the network?"

Both of the related problems use the same decision trees. In the first problem, you examine the decision tree until you find any solution. Then you know that the problem has a solution and you can stop searching. Since these problems do not have partial or approximate solutions, you generally cannot use branch and bound or heuristics to greatly reduce your work.

While solving the second, more generalized version of the problem, you can often use partial solutions to apply branch and bound techniques to the decision tree. This does not make it easier to find a solution to the problem, so it will not help in solving the more specialized problem. For example, it is harder to find the *shortest* Hamiltonian path through a network than it is to find *any* Hamiltonian path through the same network.

On the other hand, you usually do not ask these related questions about the same data. You generally ask if a network has a Hamiltonian path when the network is very sparse and it is hard to tell if there is such a path. You would usually ask for the shortest Hamiltonian path when the network was dense and there were many such paths to choose from. In that case it will be easy to find partial solutions and branch and bound techniques may simplify the problem greatly.

C H A P T E R

Sorting

Sorting is one of the most heavily studied topics in computer algorithms. There are several reasons for this.

First, sorting is a very common task in many computer applications. Almost any list of data is more meaningful if it is sorted in some way. Frequently the same data must be analyzed by sorting it in several different ways.

Second, the many different sorting algorithms make interesting examples. They demonstrate important techniques such as partial ordering, recursion, merging of lists, and storing binary trees in an array.

Each of the sorting algorithms has different advantages and disadvantages over the others. The performance of different algorithms can depend on the number, data types, initial arrangement, size, and values of the items being sorted. It is important to understand many of the algorithms available so you can pick the one that best fits your particular needs.

Finally, sorting is one of the few problems with exact theoretical performance bounds. It is a bit beyond this book, but it can be shown that any sorting algorithm that uses comparisons must take at least O(N * log(N)) time. There are several algorithms, like mergesort and heapsort, that actually achieve this time so you know they are optimal in the sense of Big O notation. There are even a few algorithms, like countingsort, which do not use comparisons and which have times faster than O(N * log(N)).

General Considerations

The following sections describe many different sorting algorithms. They each behave differently under different circumstances. For example, bubblesort is faster than quicksort when the items to be sorted are already mostly in sorted order, but it is slower if the items are initially arranged randomly.

The peculiarities of each algorithm are described in the section that describes the algorithm. Before discussing the specific algorithms, the chapter begins by taking a look at a couple of issues that generally affect all of the sorting algorithms.

Array Bounds in Visual Basic 3.0

This section describes ways in which you can work around Visual Basic 3.0 array bounds limitations. If you are using Visual Basic 4.0, you can safely skip this section.

In Visual Basic 3.0, array bounds must be between –32,768 and 32,767. Many of the sorting algorithms presented in the following sections can easily handle lists of much greater size. Countingsort, for example, can sort 32,000 items in about two seconds on a 50 megahertz 486-based PC. If it were not for the array bound limitations, this algorithm could sort lists containing a few hundred thousand items in a reasonable amount of time.

To handle larger lists in Visual Basic 3.0, you can try a couple of things. First, you can keep the list in a multi-dimensional array. For instance, you could store 327,680 items in an array dimensioned by **Dim A(0 To 9, 0 To 32767).** You could then modify the sorting algorithms to use modular arithmetic to locate items to manipulate. For example, item number 100,000 would be in array entry A(100000\32768, 100000 Mod 32768).

Using this technique I have written programs that have sorted lists containing more than 1 million integers. While this method is fairly simple and requires only small changes to your algorithms, performing a division and **Mod** operation every time you need to access an item does slow the algorithms down a bit.

Another option is to sort sublists of the items separately and then merge the sorted sublists using techniques like those used in the mergesort algorithm discussed later in this chapter. This method may be faster than the previous method, but it is more complicated.

A third technique for handling a large list is to divide the list into buckets. Each item in bucket I belongs after all of the items in bucket I – 1 and before all of the items in bucket I + 1. First, create the buckets. You can create the buckets as linked lists or as columns in a 2-dimensional array. Next make a single pass through the list moving items into their appropriate buckets. Sort the buckets and then merge them back into the original array.

For example, suppose you needed to sort 100,000 employee records by last name. You could divide the records into 26 buckets. The first bucket would contain records with last name starting with "A," the next bucket would hold records with last name starting with "B," and so forth. If there were at most 10,000 last names starting with the same letter, you could create the buckets with a statement like **ReDim Bucket(0 To 25, 1 To 10000).** Next you would move the records into the appropriate buckets. You would then sort the buckets and move the records back into the original list.

This method is quick and easy to understand, but it requires that you allocate a lot of space for the buckets. In the example above you would have allocated an array of 260,000 strings to hold the buckets.

You must also be sure that the buckets divide the larger list in a fairly even way. When you divide records by last name, for example, sublist 16 (Q) may be fairly empty while the sublist 18 (S) may not fit within the −32,768 to 32,767 array bounds limits.

Index Tables

As your program sorts the data items, it arranges them within some sort of data structure. Depending on what the items being sorted are, this can be fast or slow. Moving an integer to a new position in an array is fast. Moving a user-defined data structure to a new position in an array might be much slower. The data structure might be an employee record and might contain hundreds or thousands of bytes of data. In that case copying one data item to another may take quite some time.

One trick for improving performance while sorting large objects is to place the key data fields that you will use for sorting in an *index table*. This table contains the keys for the records plus indexes into another array that stores the complete data records themselves. Then you can sort the index table without ever moving the large data records. For example, suppose you wanted to sort employee records defined like this:

```
Type Employee
    ID As Integer
    SSN As String
    LastName As String
    FirstName As String
    Title As String
    Bio As String
    <lots more stuff>
End Type
```

If you wanted to sort the employee records by their ID fields, you could create an index table that contained only the ID field values and an index. An entry's index would indicate which record in the EmployeeData array held the complete data record.

```
Type IdIndex
    ID As Integer
    Index As Integer
End Type

Type Employee
    ID As Integer
    SSN As String
    LastName As String
    FirstName As String
    Title As String
    Bio As String
    <lots more stuff>
End Type

Dim EmployeeData(1 To 10000)
Dim IdIndexData(1 To 10000)
```

You would initialize the index table so the first entry's index pointed to the first data record, the second pointed to the second data record, etc.

```
For I = 1 To 10000
    IdIndexData(I).ID = EmployeeData(I).ID
    IdIndexData(I).Index = I
Next I
```

Next you would sort the index table using the entries' ID values. When you were finished, the Index field in each index record would point to the corresponding data record. For example, the first data record in the sorted list would be EmployeeData-(IdIndexData(1).Index). Figure 8.1 shows the relationship between the index table and the data records before and after the list has been sorted.

If you need to display the data in more than one order, you can create several different index tables and manage them separately. By accessing the data through the appropriate index table, you can list the data in one of several orders. In this example you might keep a separate index table that ordered employees by their last names. This is similar to the way in which you can use threads to order linked lists in more than one way as described in Chapter 2 (see pages 42–44). When you add or remove a record from the data, you must update each of the index tables separately.

Keep in mind that index tables take up extra memory. If you create an index table for every field in the data structure, you will more than double the amount of memory you use.

Key Combination and Compression

Sometimes it is possible to store and operate on a list's keys in a combined or compressed form.

If you wanted to sort a list of employees by their first and last names, you could *combine* the two name fields by concatenating them into one key. This would make comparisons simpler and faster. Notice the differences between the following two code fragments that compare two employee records.

```
' Using separate keys:
If emp1.LastName > emp2.LastName Or (emp1.LastName = emp2.LastName _
And emp1.FirstName > emp2.FirststName) Then

    Etc.
```

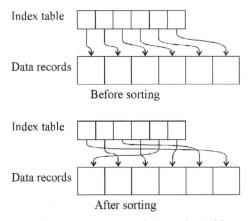

Figure 8.1 Sorting with an index table.

```
' Using a combined key:
If emp1.CombinedName > emp2.CombinedName Then

Etc.
```

You can also sometimes *compress* keys. Compressed keys take up less space, making index tables smaller. This will allow you to sort larger lists without running out of memory, will make it faster to move items around within the list, and will probably make comparing the items faster as well.

One method for compressing strings is to encode them as integers or some other numeric data type. Numeric data types take up less space than strings and the computer can compare two numeric values much more quickly than it can compare two strings. Of course normal string operations will not work on numeric encodings of strings.

For example, suppose you wanted to encode strings consisting of upper case letters into integers. You can think of each character in the string as a base 27 digit. You need to use base 27 because you need to represent 26 letters plus one extra digit that represents the end of a word. Without an end of word marker, the encoding of "AA" would come after the encoding of "B" since "AA" has two digits but "B" has only one.

The base 27 encoding of a three character string would be 27 * 27 * (1st letter – "A" + 1) + 27 * (2nd letter – "A" + 1) + (3rd letter – "A" + 1). If the string has fewer than three characters, you would use 0 instead of (the letter – "A" + 1).

For example, the encoding of "FOX" is:

$$27 * 27 * (\text{"F"} - \text{"A"} + 1) + 27 * (\text{"O"} - \text{"A"} + 1) + (\text{"X"} - \text{"A"} + 1) =$$
$$27 * 27 * 6 + 27 * 15 + 24 =$$
$$4,803$$

The encoding of "NO" is:

$$27 * 27 * (\text{"N"} - \text{"A"} + 1) + 27 * (\text{"O"} - \text{"A"} + 1) + (0) =$$
$$27 * 27 * 14 + 27 * 15 + 0 =$$
$$10,611$$

Notice that 10,611 is greater than 4,803. This makes sense because "NO" > "FOX."

You can use similar techniques to encode strings of six uppercase letters in a long integer and strings with up to ten uppercase letters in a double. The following two subroutines convert strings into doubles and back:

```
Const STRING_BASE = 27
Const ASC_A = 65          ' ASCII code for "A"


' Convert a string into a double encoding.
'
' full_len is the full length the string should have.
' We need it if the string is short (e.g. "AX" as a
' three character string).
Function StringToDbl (txt As String, full_len As Integer) As Double
Dim strlen As Integer
Dim i As Integer
Dim value As Double
Dim ch As String * 1
```

```
    strlen = Len(txt)
    If strlen > full_len Then strlen = full_len

    value = 0#
    For i = 1 To strlen
        ch = Mid$(txt, i, 1)
        value = value * STRING_BASE + Asc(ch) - ASC_A + 1
    Next i

    For i = strlen + 1 To full_len
        value = value * STRING_BASE
    Next i

    StringToDbl = value
End Function

' Turn a double string encoding back into a string.
Function DblToString (ByVal value As Double) As String
Dim strlen As Integer
Dim i As Integer
Dim txt As String
Dim power As Integer
Dim ch As Integer
Dim new_value As Double

    txt = ""
    Do While value > 0
        new_value = Int(value / STRING_BASE)
        ch = value - new_value * STRING_BASE
        If ch <> 0 Then txt = Chr$(ch + ASC_A - 1) + txt
        value = new_value
    Loop
    DblToString = txt
End Function
```

Example program ENCODE allows you to create a list of random strings and sort them using numeric encodings. The program uses all of the encodings possible so you can compare the results. If you tell the program to create strings of length ten, for instance, the program will sort the list as both strings and as double encodings. If you request strings of length six, the program will sort the list as strings, double encodings, and long encodings.

Table 8.1 shows the times required by program ENCODE to sort 1,000 strings of different lengths on a 50 megahertz 486-based PC. Notice that the results are constant for each encoding. It takes about the same amount of time to sort 1,000 doubles whether they represent 3 letter strings or 10 letter strings.

You can also encode strings containing characters other than capital letters. You could encode a string allowing uppercase letters and digits using a string base of 37 instead

Table 8.1 Times to Sort 1,000 Strings Using Different Encodings

String length	3	6	10	11
String	7.19	7.20	7.30	7.36
Double	4.83	4.83	4.83	
Long	3.79	3.79		
Integer	3.57			

of 27. "A" would map to 1, "B" to 2, . . . , "Z" to 26, "0" to 27, . . . , and "9" to 36. The three character string "AH7" would be encoded as 37 * 37 * (1) + 37 * (8) + (35) = 1,700.

Of course with a larger string base, the longest string you could encode in an integer, long, or double data type would be shorter. With a base of 37 you could fit two character strings into an integer, five character strings into a long, and you could still fit ten character strings into a double.

Paging

Chapter 1 discussed paging (see pages 11–13). When your computer runs out of physical memory, it copies some of the memory to disk. It then reuses the physical memory to continue calculations. When the computer needs the memory written to disk again, it reads it back into physical memory. The process of copying memory into and out of memory is called paging.

Since reading from a disk drive is much slower than reading physical memory, paging makes any program slower. Paging can be a particular problem when you are running sorting algorithms. Many of the algorithms jump all over the list of items and if paging occurs, this can cause memory thrashing. Once paging begins, the program will have to page very frequently and this will slow your program down tremendously.

When paging begins you may hear your disk drive running like crazy. You may also notice a sharp increase in program run time. A sorting program may take 10 seconds to sort 25,000 items, 11 seconds to sort 26,000 items, 12 seconds to sort 27,000 items, and 3 minutes to sort 28,000 items. By adding only a few extra items, you have increased the program's run time dramatically.

There are a few things you can do to decrease the possibility and effects of paging. First, keep your use of data small. If you sort only small lists, you will not use up all of your physical memory and the program will not page.

Second, structure your program so it moves through memory from one end of the list to the other. The quicksort and mergesort programs described later in this chapter access memory in this way. Many of the other sorting algorithms, like heapsort and countingsort, jump all over the list array and may cause excessive paging.

Finally, use index tables and key compression to reduce the amount of data your program needs to move around. While your program may eventually need to page to retrieve large data records, it will not need to page if you are sorting only small keys. You may even want to keep the data records in a file on your hard disk and then load records only when you need them. That way you may be able to load all of the keys into memory without paging.

Example Programs

To make it easier for you to compare the performance of different sorting algorithms, most of them have been placed in the single example program SORT. This program allows you to specify the number of items to be sorted, the maximum value of the items, and whether the original list should begin sorted, sorted backwards, or randomly arranged. This program creates a list of random longs, and sorts it using the sorting algorithm you select. Be sure you run the program with small lists before you try sorting long lists, especially when you use insertionsort, link insertionsort, selectionsort, or bubblesort, which are particularly slow.

Insertionsort

Insertionsort is a fairly simple sorting algorithm. The idea is to build a new, sorted list from the original list by considering each item in the original list in turn. As the algorithm considers each item, it looks through the growing sorted list to see where the new item belongs. It then moves the items in the new list that come after this position to the right to make room for the new item. Finally it inserts the new item in the sorted list. When it has inserted all of the items in the new list, the algorithm is done.

```
Sub InsertionSort (list() As Long, min As Integer, max As Integer)
Dim i As Integer
Dim j As Integer
Dim k As Integer
Dim num_sorted As Integer
Dim next_num As Long

    num_sorted = 0
    For i = min To max
        ' This is the number we are inserting
        next_num = list(i)

        ' See where it belongs in the list
        For j = 1 To num_sorted
            If list(j) >= next_num Then Exit For
        Next j
        ' Bump the bigger sorted numbers down to make
        ' room for the new number
        For k = num_sorted To j Step -1
            list(k + 1) = list(k)
        Next k

        ' Insert the new number
        list(j) = next_num

        ' Increment the count of the sorted items
        num_sorted = num_sorted + 1
    Next i
End Sub
```

For each item in the original list, the algorithm might have to examine all of the items in the sorted list. This will happen, for example, if the items were in sorted order in the original list. In that case the algorithm places each new item at the end of the growing sorted list.

An even worse case is if the original list is in reversed sorted order. Then the algorithm must place the new item at the beginning of the sorted list. To do that it must move every other item over one position to the right to make room for the new item.

In any case, each time the algorithm adds a new item to the sorted list it must examine or move every item in the sorted list. That means the total number of steps executed will be $1 + 2 + 3 + \ldots + (N - 1)$ which is $O(N^2)$. This is not very efficient compared to the theoretical $O(N * \log(N))$ possible for algorithms that sort by comparisons. In fact, it turns out that this algorithm is not even as fast as other $O(N^2)$ algorithms like selectionsort.

Insertion with Linked Lists

You can make insertionsort much quicker in some cases if the items to be sorted are kept in linked lists rather than in an array. Once the algorithm determines where each new item belongs in the sorted linked list, it can quickly insert the item into the list without needing to move the other items over one position to make room.

```
Sub LinkInsertionSort (list() As Long, NextInList() As Integer, _
first As Integer)
Dim top As Integer
Dim item As Integer
Dim nxt As Integer
Dim spot As Integer
Dim item_value As Long

    If NextInList(first) = END_OF_LIST Then Exit Sub

    top = first
    first = NextInList(first)
    NextInList(top) = END_OF_LIST

    Do While first <> END_OF_LIST
        item = first
        first = NextInList(first)
        item_value = list(item)
        If item_value <= list(top) Then
            nxt = NextInList(item)
            NextInList(item) = top
            top = item
        Else
            spot = top
            Do
                nxt = NextInList(spot)
                If nxt = END_OF_LIST Then Exit Do
                If item_value <= list(nxt) Then Exit Do
                spot = nxt
            Loop
            NextInList(spot) = item
            NextInList(item) = nxt
        End If
    Loop
    first = top
End Sub
```

As the algorithm considers each item in the original list, it might have to compare the item to every item on the sorted list. This will happen if the original list starts already sorted so each new item must be added at the end of the sorted list. This makes the algorithm $O(N^2)$ in this worst case.

The best case for this algorithm occurs when the original list starts sorted in reverse order. Then each new item considered is smaller than the one before so the algorithm will place it at the beginning of the sorted list. The algorithm will only need to compare the item to one other item, making the best case run time for the algorithm $O(N)$.

In the average case the algorithm will have to search about half way through the sorted list before it finds the correct location for the new item. This means the algorithm will execute roughly $1 + 1 + 2 + 2 + \ldots + N/2$ or $O(N^2)$ steps to sort the entire list.

Table 8.2 shows the times required on a 50 megahertz 486-based PC for insertion-sort and insertion with linked lists to sort 1,000 long integers. Insertion with linked lists is faster for the random and backwards sorted cases because it is much better at inserting the new item at the beginning or in the middle of the sorted list. It is slower when the data is initially sorted because it takes longer to traverse a linked list than an array. Still, insertion with linked lists is faster in the random case so it will generally be a better choice.

Insertion with linked lists also has the advantage of moving only linked list pointers rather than complete data records. If the items being sorted are large user-defined types, it will be quicker to move pointers rather than to recopy whole records whenever an item must be moved.

Selectionsort

Selectionsort is another $O(N^2)$ algorithm. The idea here is to search the list for the smallest item. Then swap that item with the one at the top of the list. Next find the second smallest item and swap it with the second item in the list. Continue swapping items until every item in the list has been swapped into its final sorted position.

```
Sub SelectionSort (list() As Long, min As Integer, max As Integer)
Dim i As Integer
Dim j As Integer
Dim best_value As Long
Dim best_j As Integer

    For i = min To max - 1
        best_value = list(i)
        best_j = i
        For j = i + 1 To max
            If list(j) < best_value Then
                best_value = list(j)
                best_j = j
            End If
        Next j
        list (best_j) = list(i)
        list(i) = best_value
    Next i
End Sub
```

While looking for the Ith smallest item, the algorithm must examine each of the N – I items that have not yet been placed in their final positions. This means the algorithm takes time $N + (N - 1) + (N - 2) + \ldots + 1$ or $O(N^2)$ time. This is theoretically no better than the $O(N^2)$ run times for the previous algorithms.

Table 8.2 Times to Sort 1,000 Items

	Random	*Sorted*	*Sorted Backwards*
Insertionsort	4.32	3.74	4.73
Insertion with Linked Lists	3.57	7.02	0.06

Once the algorithm has found the smallest item, however, it swaps that item with whatever item occupies its final position. It does this in only a couple of steps rather than in the O(N) steps needed to insert an item in the sorted list using insertionsort. Table 8.3 shows the times required by insertionsort, insertion with linked lists, and selectionsort to arrange 1,000 long integers.

Selectionsort performs quite well on random and sorted lists. When the list starts sorted backwards, selectionsort does not do as well. While it is looking for the smallest item in the list, selectionsort executes these lines of code:

```
If list(j) < best_value Then
    best_value = list(j)
    best_j = j
End If
```

If the list begins in reverse sorted order, the condition **list(j) < best_value** will be true much of the time. During the first pass through the list, for example, it will be true for every item since each item is smaller than the one before. That means the algorithm will have to execute the lines of code within the **If** statement many times and that slows the algorithm down a bit.

The three sorting algorithms discussed so far all have $O(N^2)$ performance. Because of this you might wonder why you should bother with them at all since some of the following algorithms have $O(N * \log(N))$ performance.

The main reason is that these three algorithms are extremely simple. Not only does that make them easy to implement and debug, but it also makes them very fast for small problems. Most of the other algorithms presented in this chapter are so complicated that they actually run slower than these three when the list of items is small.

Table 8.4 shows the time required by a 50 megahertz 486-based PC to sort 10 long integers 1,000 times using some of the algorithms presented in this chapter. As you can see, the more elaborate algorithms do not perform as well as the simple $O(N^2)$ algorithms. For this reason many of the more complicated algorithms stop processing when there are only a few items left to sort. They then use selectionsort to finish the job quickly.

Bubblesort

Bubblesort is an algorithm designed to sort lists that are already in mostly sorted order. If the list begins completely sorted, the algorithm runs in O(N) time and is extremely fast. If some of the items are out of order, the algorithm runs more slowly. When all of the items start in random order, the algorithm runs in $O(N^2)$ time. For that reason it is extremely important for you to be certain that the items will be mostly in sorted order before you decide to use bubblesort.

Table 8.3 Times to Sort 1,000 Items

	Random	*Sorted*	*Sorted Backwards*
Insertionsort	4.32	3.74	4.73
Insertion with Linked Lists	3.57	7.02	0.06
Selectionsort	3.74	3.74	5.16

Table 8.4 Times to Sort 10 Items 1,000 Times

Algorithm	Time
Bubblesort	0.25
Selectionsort	0.68
Insertionsort	0.68
Insertion with Linked Lists	0.96
Quicksort	1.32
Heapsort	1.48
Mergesort	1.98
Bucketsort	5.55
Countingsort	18.10

The idea behind bubblesort is to scan through the list of items until you find two adjacent items that are out of order. The algorithm then switches them and continues. The algorithm repeats this process until no more items are out of order.

During bubblesort passes, if you follow an item that begins below its final position in the array, like the item 3 in Figure 8.2, the item seems to "bubble" towards the top of the array. During each pass the item moves one position closer to its final correct position. This "bubbling" effect is what gives bubblesort its name.

In the example shown in Figure 8.2, the algorithm first finds that items 6 and 3 are out of order so it switches them. During the next pass through the array, the algorithm notices that items 5 and 3 are out of order so it switches them. In the next pass it switches items 4 and 3. After one more pass through the array, the algorithm finds that there are no more items out of order so it stops.

There are several refinements you can make to this algorithm, by examining its behavior. First, if you watch an item that begins above rather than below its correct position in the array, you see a very different picture than the one shown in Figure 8.2. In Figure 8.3 the algorithm first notices that item 6 and item 3 are out of order so it switches them. The algorithm then continues its pass down through the array and notices that items 6 and 4 are now out of order so it switches them, too. The algorithm next switches items 6 and 5, and item 6 will be in its final correct position.

During downward passes through the array, items that need to move up can only move up one position. Items that need to move down can move many positions. You can

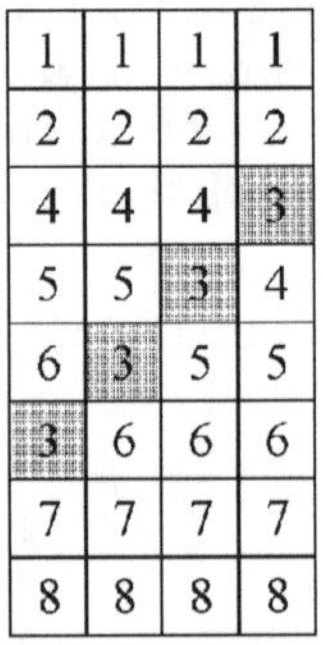

Figure 8.2 Bubbling an item up

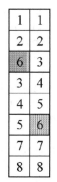

Figure 8.3 Bubbling an item down.

use this fact to make the first refinement to the bubblesort algorithm. If you alternate downward and upward passes through the array, items will be able to move quickly both upward and downward.

During downward passes the largest item that is out of order will be moved into its final position. During upward passes the smallest item that is out of order will be moved into its final position. If there are M items out of order in the list, the algorithm will need at most M passes upward and downward through the array to put all of the items in order. If there are N items in the list, the algorithm will need N steps per pass through the list. That makes the total run time for this algorithm O(M * N).

If the list is initially randomly arranged, a large fraction of the items will be out of order. In that case the number of items out of order M will be close to the total number of items N so the run time O(M * N) becomes O(N^2).

After introducing upward and downward passes, the next refinement you can make is to hold items in a temporary variable while they undergo multiple swaps. In the example shown in Figure 8.3, the item 6 is swapped three times in a row. The steps to perform these swaps could have been executed in this order:

```
tmp = List(3)          ' Swap 6 and 3.
List(3) = List(4)
List(4) = tmp
tmp = List(4)          ' Swap 6 and 4.
List(4) = List(5)
List(5) = tmp
tmp = List(5)          ' Swap 6 and 5.
List(5) = List(6)
List(6) = tmp
```

If you hold item 6 in a temporary variable while you consider the other items, you can rewrite the steps above like this:

```
tmp = List(3)          ' Hold 6.
List(3) = List(4)      ' Move 3.
List(4) = List(5)      ' Move 4.
List(5) = List(6)      ' Move 5.
List(6) = tmp          ' Move 6.
```

This can save the algorithm many steps when items are being moved long distances through the array.

One last refinement you can make is in bounding the passes through the array. After a pass through the array, the last items swapped mark the last part of the array which could be out of order. In a downward pass, for example, the largest item that is out of order will be moved to its final position. No items larger than that item will need to be moved later. That means the algorithm can start its next upward pass through the list at this position. It can also end downward passes through the array when it reaches this position.

Similarly when the algorithm makes an upward pass through the list, it can adjust the position in the list where it starts the next downward pass and ends future upward passes.

The Visual Basic implementation of bubblesort uses variables min and max to indicate the first and last items in the list which might be out of order. As the algorithm makes passes through the list, it updates these variables to indicate where the last swaps took place.

With all of these refinements, alternating upward and downward passes, holding the bubbling item in a temporary variable, and adjusting min and max, the bubblesort algorithm can be written like this:

```
Sub BubbleSort (list() As Long, ByVal min As Integer, ByVal max As _
Integer)
Dim last_swap As Integer
Dim i As Integer
Dim j As Integer
Dim tmp As Long

    ' Repeat until we are done.
    Do While min < max
        ' Bubble up.
        last_swap = min - 1
        ' For i = min + 1 To max
        i = min + 1
        Do While i <= max
            ' Find a bubble.
            If list(i - 1) > list(i) Then
                ' See where to drop the bubble.
                tmp = list(i - 1)
                j = i
                Do
                    list(j - 1) = list(j)
                    j = j + 1
                    If j > max Then Exit Do
                Loop While list(j) < tmp
                list(j - 1) = tmp
                last_swap = j - 1
                i = j + 1
            Else
                i = i + 1
            End If
        Loop
        ' Update max.
        max = last_swap - 1

        ' Bubble down.
        last_swap = max + 1
        ' For i = max - 1 To min Step -1
        i = max - 1
        Do While i >= min
            ' Find a bubble.
```

```
            If list(i + 1) < list(i) Then
                ' See where to drop the bubble.
                tmp = list(i + 1)
                j = i
                Do
                    list(j + 1) = list(j)
                    j = j - 1
                    If j < min Then Exit Do
                Loop While list(j) > tmp
                list(j + 1) = tmp
                last_swap = j + 1
                i = j - 1
            Else
                i = i - 1
            End If
        Loop
        ' Update min.
        min = last_swap + 1
    Loop
End Sub
```

You can test the bubblesort algorithm using example program SORT. To properly test bubblesort, check the Sorted box in the Initial Ordering area. Then enter a number of items in the # Unsorted field. When you press the Go button, the program will create a list, sort it, and then switch some pairs of items around to give the list the proper number of unsorted items. For example, if you enter 10 in the # Unsorted field, the program will switch five randomly selected pairs of numbers so there will be ten items out of order.

If you specify only a few unsorted items, bubblesort will be much faster than the other algorithms. If you specify many unsorted items, most of the other algorithms will be faster than bubblesort. When only 10 percent of the list is out of order, all of the algorithms except the other $O(N^2)$ algorithms (insertionsort, insertion with linked list, and selectionsort) will be faster. For this reason, you must be careful when you use bubblesort. If your list of items is not already mostly sorted, you will be better off using a different algorithm.

Table 8.5 shows the times required by a 50 megahertz 486-based PC to bubblesort 2,000 items where the original list was sorted in varying degrees.

From the table you can see that bubblesort performs well only when the list begins in mostly sorted order. The quicksort algorithm described later in this chapter can sort the same list of 2,000 items in about 0.50 seconds no matter how the list is initially ordered. Bubblesort can beat this time only when the list is initially around 99 percent correctly sorted.

Despite the fact that bubblesort is generally slower than many of the algorithms described in this chapter, it still has its uses. Bubblesort is often faster than these other algorithms if the list being sorted begins in almost sorted order. If your program manages a list that is initially sorted and is then modified a little bit at a time, bubblesort may be the best choice for you.

Quicksort

Quicksort is a recursive algorithm that uses a divide-and-conquer technique. While the list of items to be sorted is at least a certain minimum size, quicksort divides it into two sublists and recursively calls itself to sort the two sublists.

Table 8.5 Times to Bubblesort 2,000 Items

% Sorted	Time
0	16.20
10	14.99
20	13.18
30	12.42
40	11.20
50	8.95
60	8.24
70	6.15
80	4.45
90	2.52
95	1.04
96	0.77
97	0.71
98	0.55
99	0.33
99.5	0.15

The initial version of quicksort discussed here is quite simple. If the algorithm is called with a sublist containing zero or one items, the sublist is already sorted so the subroutine ends.

Otherwise the subroutine picks an item in the list to use as a dividing point to break the list into two smaller sublists. All of the items that fall before the dividing point are placed in the first sublist and all of the other items are placed in the second sublist. The subroutine then recursively calls itself to sort the new, smaller sublists.

```
Sub QuickSort (list() As Long, ByVal min As Integer, ByVal max As _
Integer)
Dim med_value As Long
Dim hi As Integer
Dim lo As Integer

    ' If there is 1 (or 0) element, this sublist is done.
    If min >= max Then Exit Sub

    ' Pick a value to be the dividing value.
    med_value = list(min)

    lo = min
    hi = max
    Do
        ' Look down from hi for a value < med_value.
        Do While list(hi) >= med_value
            hi = hi - 1
            If hi <= lo Then Exit Do
        Loop
        If hi <= lo Then
            list(lo) = med_value
```

```
            Exit Do
        End If


        ' Swap the lo and hi values.
        list(lo) = list(hi)


        ' Look up from lo for a value >= med_value.
        lo = lo + 1
        Do While list(lo) < med_value
            lo = lo + 1
            If lo >= hi Then Exit Do
        Loop
        If lo >= hi Then
            lo = hi
            list(hi) = med_value
            Exit Do
        End If


        ' Swap the lo and hi values
        list(hi) = list(lo)
    Loop
    ' Recursively sort the two sublists.
    QuickSort list(), min, lo - 1
    QuickSort list(), lo + 1, max
End Sub
```

There are a couple of important features worth mentioning about this version of the algorithm. First, the dividing item med_value is not included in either of the sublists. This means the two sublists together contain one less item than the list from which they were made. Since the lists are getting smaller, the algorithm must eventually finish no matter how the items are divided between the two sublists.

Another important feature is that this algorithm uses the first item in its list as the dividing value to break the list into sublists. Ideally this value will belong somewhere in the middle of the list so the two sublists will be of about equal size. If the list is initially in sorted order, however, the item will be the smallest item in the list. Then the algorithm would divide the items by placing no items in the first sublist and all of the other items in the second sublist. The algorithm would take a path of execution like the one shown in Figure 8.4.

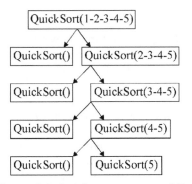

Figure 8.4 Quicksort on a sorted list.

In this case each call to the subroutine will require O(N) steps while the algorithm moves all of the items into the second sublist. Then the algorithm will have to recursively call itself a total of N – 1 times. This makes the run time O(N²) which is no improvement on the algorithms already examined.

Even worse is the fact that the recursion is N – 1 levels deep. Visual Basic cannot handle many levels of recursion before it exhausts its stack and the program crashes. In one test this version of quicksort could arrange only 294 items without using up all of the stack space.

One way to avoid exhausting the stack would be to rewrite the algorithm to remove recursion using the techniques described in Chapter 4. There is a better solution, however, which also addresses the problem of the O(N²) run time. That solution is to select a different item as the dividing point when breaking the list into two sublists.

There are a number of ways in which you can select the dividing item. You could use the item that currently occupies the middle position in the list. Chances are this item would do a reasonable job of making the sublists about the same size. Still, you might get unlucky and this item might be near the largest or smallest item in the list. That would make one sublist much larger than the other and, if you were unlucky with other choices, would give O(N²) performance and deep recursion.

Another strategy would be to look through the list, compute the actual median of the list, and use that as the dividing value. This would probably work well but it is a lot of effort. While an O(N) pass through the list will not change the total theoretical run time (you need to do an O(N) pass through the list to create the sublists anyway), it would probably hurt the overall performance.

A third strategy used by some is to look at the first, last, and middle item in the list and pick whichever item is between the other two. This method has the advantage of being quick, since you only need to look at three items. The item selected is guaranteed not to be the absolute largest or smallest item in the list, and probably will be somewhere near the middle.

A final strategy, and the one actually used in the implementation given here, is to randomly select an item in the list and use that as the dividing point. Chances are the item selected will be a good choice. Even if it is not, odds are the next time the algorithm divides the list it will make a better choice. The chances of the algorithm making a bad choice every time and causing O(N²) performance are extremely small.

An interesting fact about this method is that it turns "a small chance of bad run time always" into "always a small chance of bad run time." This rather confusing statement is explained below.

With the earlier methods of selecting a dividing point, there was a small chance that the list would be arranged in a way that would produce O(N²) run time. While the odds of the list starting in such a bad arrangement are small, if you did encounter such an arrangement you would definitely experience O(N²) run time no matter what.

By selecting the dividing point randomly, the initial arrangement of the items makes no difference to the performance of the algorithm. While there is a small chance that the algorithm will select a bad item to use as a dividing point, the odds of it selecting a bad item every time are extremely small. That is what is meant by "always a small chance of bad run time." No matter what list you start with, there will be a very small chance that the algorithm will give O(N²) performance.

There is still one case when all of these methods have trouble. If there are very few *distinct* values in the list, the algorithm will place a large number of identical values in the same sublist each time it is called. If every item in the list had the value "1," for instance, the algorithm would follow the sequence of execution shown in Figure 8.5. This sequence again causes $O(N^2)$ performance and deep recursion.

The same sort of behavior will occur if there are a large number of duplicates of more than one value. If a list of 10,000 items contained only values between 1 and 10, the algorithm would quickly divide the list into sublists that contained only one value. Then the problem would quickly begin to show itself.

The easiest way to handle this problem is to ignore it. If you know that your data does not have such an unusual distribution, this will not be a problem. If you do know that your data will cover only a small number of values, you might want to consider another sorting algorithm. Countingsort, described later in this chapter, is extremely fast at sorting lists where the range of the data values is small.

Countingsort does not deal well with a small number of widely separated values, however. If you had a list of 10,000 items that included only 10 distinct values between 1 and 30,000, bucketsort would give better performance.

If you are completely in doubt about the arrangement of your data, heapsort and mergesort will both provide fast sorting that is completely independent of the initial ordering and value distribution of your data.

You can make one final improvement to quicksort. As was noted in the earlier section describing selectionsort, most of the more complicated algorithms do not perform well for very small lists. Due to its simplicity, selectionsort is faster if there are only a dozen or so items in the list.

You can improve the performance of quicksort if you stop the recursion while there are still some items left in the list and use selectionsort to finish the sorting. Table 8.6 shows times required by a 50 megahertz 486-based PC to quicksort 20,000 items, stopping the recursion after the size of the list reaches a certain cutoff value. In this test the best cutoff value was somewhere around 15 items.

```
Sub QuickSort (list() As Long, ByVal min As Integer, ByVal max As _
Integer)
Const CutOff = 15

Dim med_value As Long
Dim hi As Integer
Dim lo As Integer
Dim i As Integer
```

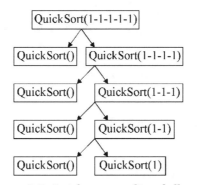

Figure 8.5 Quicksort on a list of all ones.

Table 8.6 Times to Quicksort 20,000 Items

Cutoff	Time
1	7.03
5	6.15
10	6.04
15	5.88
20	6.09
25	6.21
30	6.37

```
' If the list has no more than CutOff elements,
' finish it off with SelectionSort.
If max - min < CutOff Then
    SelectionSort list(), min, max
    Exit Sub
End If


' Pick the dividing value.
i = Int((max - min + 1) * Rnd + min)
med_value = list(i)


' Swap it to the front.
list(i) = list(min)


lo = min
hi = max
Do
    ' Look down from hi for a value < med_value.
    Do While list(hi) >= med_value
        hi = hi - 1
        If hi <= lo Then Exit Do
    Loop
    If hi <= lo Then
        list(lo) = med_value
        Exit Do
    End If


    ' Swap the lo and hi values.
    list(lo) = list(hi)
    ' Look up from lo for a value >= med_value.
    lo = lo + 1
    Do While list(lo) < med_value
        lo = lo + 1
        If lo >= hi Then Exit Do
    Loop
    If lo >= hi Then
        lo = hi
        list(hi) = med_value
        Exit Do
    End If


    ' Swap the lo and hi values.
    list(hi) = list(lo)
Loop
```

```
    ' Sort the two sublists.
    QuickSort list(), min, lo - 1
    QuickSort list(), lo + 1, max
End Sub
```

Mergesort

Like quicksort, mergesort is a recursive algorithm. Also like quicksort, it divides the list to be sorted into two sublists and recursively sorts the sublists.

Quicksort divides its list by selecting a dividing item and placing all items less than the dividing item in one list and the items greater than the dividing item in the other. Mergesort divides its list in the middle to form two sublists of equal size. It then recursively sorts the sublists. The algorithm then merges the two sorted sublists to form the completely sorted list.

While the merging step is easy to understand, it is also the most interesting part of the mergesort algorithm. First the sublists are merged into a scratch array, and then the merged list is copied back into the original list. The fact that you must create a scratch array can be a drawback, particularly if the list of items is very large. If the scratch array is too large, it may cause the algorithm to page, slowing performance greatly. Using a scratch array also forces you to spend a good deal of time copying items back and forth between the arrays and that slows the algorithm down.

Begin the merge step by initializing counters i1 and i2 to point to the beginning of the two sublists, and counter i3 to point to the beginning of the scratch array. Then compare list(i1) and list(i2). Move the smaller of the two items into the scratch array and increment the corresponding counter and the i3 counter. Continue in this way until one of the sublists is empty. Then finish by copying the remaining items from the other list into the scratch array.

As was the case with quicksort, you can speed mergesort up by stopping the recursion after the list being sorted reaches a certain minimum size. After the list reaches this size, the algorithm can use selectionsort to finish the job.

```
Sub MergeSort (list() As Long, scratch() As Long, ByVal min As _
Integer, ByVal max As Integer)
Const CutOff = 15

Dim middle As Integer
Dim i1 As Integer
Dim i2 As Integer
Dim i3 As Integer
    ' If the list has no more than CutOff elements,
    ' finish it off with SelectionSort.
    If max - min < CutOff Then
        SelectionSort list(), min, max
        Exit Sub
    End If

    ' Recursively sort the sublists.
    middle = max \ 2 + min \ 2
    MergeSort list(), scratch(), min, middle
    MergeSort list(), scratch(), middle + 1, max

    ' Merge the sorted lists.
    i1 = min          ' Index in list 1
```

```
        i2 = middle + 1 ' Index in list 2
        i3 = min         ' Index in merged list
        Do While i1 <= middle And i2 <= max
            If list(i1) <= list(i2) Then
                scratch(i3) = list(i1)
                i1 = i1 + 1
            Else
                scratch(i3) = list(i2)
                i2 = i2 + 1
            End If
            i3 = i3 + 1
        Loop

        ' Empty out whichever list is not already empty.
        Do While i1 <= middle
            scratch(i3) = list(i1)
            i1 = i1 + 1
            i3 = i3 + 1
        Loop
        Do While i2 <= max
            scratch(i3) = list(i2)
            i2 = i2 + 1
            i3 = i3 + 1
        Loop

        ' Move the merged list back into list.
        For i3 = min To max
            list(i3) = scratch(i3)
        Next i3
    End Sub
```

Mergesort is generally a little slower than quicksort. In one test on a 50 megahertz 486-based PC, mergesort required 18.46 seconds to sort 30,000 items while quicksort needed only 11.26 seconds.

Mergesort does have the advantage that its times remain the same no matter what the distribution or initial arrangement of the data is. As was mentioned in the previous section, quicksort gives $O(N^2)$ performance and enters deep recursion if there are many duplicated item values in the list. If the list being sorted is large, quicksort may exhaust the stack and crash.

Since mergesort always divides the list into equal parts, it does not have trouble with deep recursion. If there are N items in the list, mergesort can reach only $\log(N)$ depth of recursion so it can sort much larger lists.

In one test using 30,000 items with values between 1 and 100, mergesort took 18.62 seconds to sort the list while quicksort needed 56.41 seconds. With a list of 30,000 items with values between 1 and 50, mergesort still took 18.62 seconds while quicksort exhausted the stack and crashed the program.

Merging Lists

Merging lists is useful in situations other than mergesort. Very large databases are often managed using *transaction processing*. Here a list of transactions is kept for some time before they are merged with a master data file to produce a new version of the master file.

Telephone billing systems, for example, use a customer master file that includes all of the important information about the customers: name, phone number, service start date, type of service, account balance, payment history, etc. As you make payments and phone calls, the credits and debits to your account are stored in transaction files. When it is time to produce your monthly bill, these transaction files are merged with the customer master file to update your information and produce a new bill.

Large databases like this often merge more than two files at one time. Your phone bill might include charges from more than one long distance carrier, basic services charges, and local calling charges. Each of these may be stored in separate files.

If these files are stored on separate disks with separate disk controllers, it may be possible to merge them all at the same time fairly efficiently. Since each disk operates independently, they can access different points in their respective files at the same time. As the program merges the files, each disk can be updated to move through its file without interfering with the others.

This is even more important when some or all of the files are stored on slower media like magnetic tape. In that case it is very important that the files be stored on separate tapes and that each tape drive can operate independently because searching back and forth across a tape is extremely slow.

Heapsort

Heapsort uses a special data structure called a *heap* to store the items in a list. Heaps are also interesting in their own right and are useful for implementing priority queues.

This section begins by describing heaps and explaining how you can implement a heap in Visual Basic. It then shows how you can use a heap to build an efficient priority queue. Then with the tools developed to manage heaps and priority queues, it is easy to implement heapsort.

Heaps

It will be easiest to understand heaps if you think of them as complete binary trees where each node in the tree is at least as large as the two nodes below it. This does not say anything about the relationship between the two child nodes. While both must be smaller than their parent, either one may be larger than the other. Figure 8.6 shows a small heap.

Since each node is at least as large as the two nodes below, the root node will always be the largest node in the entire heap. This makes heaps a good data structure for implementing priority queues. Whenever you need to find the highest priority item in the queue, it will always be sitting at the top of the heap.

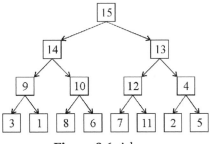

Figure 8.6 A heap.

Since a heap is a complete binary tree, you can use techniques like those covered in Chapter 5 for storing a complete tree in an array (see pages 122–123). Place the root node at array position 0. Place the children of node I in positions 2 * I and 2 * I + 1. Figure 8.7 shows the heap in Figure 8.6 stored in an array.

To see how to build a heap, notice that a heap is made up of smaller subheaps. The subtree starting at any given node in a heap also forms a heap. For example, in the heap shown in Figure 8.8 the subtree rooted at the node labeled 13 is also a heap.

Using this fact you can build a heap from the bottom up. First, place the list of items in a tree as shown in Figure 8.9. Then make heaps out of the little three node trees at the bottom of the complete tree. Since there are only three nodes in these trees, this is fairly simple. Just compare the top node in the little tree with each of its child nodes. If either of the children is larger than the top, swap it with the node on top. If both children are larger than the parent, swap the parent with the larger child.

When considering the rightmost three node tree in Figure 8.9, for instance, you would swap the 4 and 5 nodes to make that subtree a heap. Repeat this step until all of the three node subtrees at the bottom of the tree are heaps. This gives the tree shown in Figure 8.10.

Once you have made the three node heaps, begin joining little heaps to form larger heaps. In Figure 8.10 the small heaps with tops 15 and 5 plus the item 7 are joined to form a larger heap. To join the two smaller heaps, compare the new top item 7 with each of its children. If one of the children is bigger than this item, swap the item with the larger child. In this case 15 is larger than 7 and 4 so you should swap node 15 with node 7.

Since you have not modified the right subtree starting with node 4, that subtree is still a heap. You have made a change to the left subtree, however. To determine whether the left subtree is still a heap, compare its new top, node 7, to the child nodes 13 and 12. Since 13 is larger than 7 and 12, you should swap the 7 and 13 nodes.

If the subtree you were examining was taller, you would continue pushing the 7 node down into the subtree. Eventually you would hit the bottom of the tree or you would reach a point where the 7 node was larger than both of its child nodes. Figure 8.11 shows the tree after this subtree has been turned into a heap.

Index	1	2	3	4	5	6	7	8	9	10	11	12	13	14	15
Value	15	14	13	9	10	12	4	3	1	8	6	7	11	2	5

Figure 8.7 Array representation of a heap.

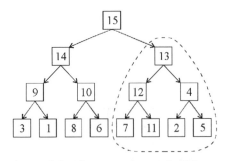

Figure 8.8 A heap made up of subheaps.

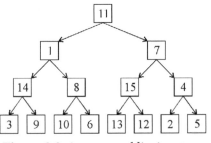

Figure 8.9 An unsorted list in a tree.

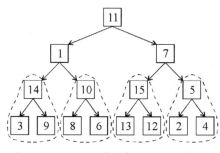

Figure 8.10 Two-level trees are heaps.

Figure 8.11 Combining heaps into larger heaps.

Continue this process of joining heaps to form larger heaps until you have combined all of the items in the array into one large heap like the one shown in Figure 8.6.

The algorithm for pushing an item down through a heap is shown below.

```
Sub HeapPushDown (list() As Long, ByVal min As Integer, ByVal max _
As Integer)
Dim tmp As Long
Dim j As Integer

    tmp = list(min)
    Do
        j = 2 * min
        If j <= max Then
            ' Make j point to the larger of the children.
            If j < max Then
                If list (j + 1) > list(j) Then j = j + 1
            End If

            If list(j) > tmp Then
                list(min) = list(j)
                min = j
            Else
                Exit Do
            End If
        Else
            Exit Do
        End If
    Loop
    list(min) = tmp
End Sub
```

The complete algorithm for using HeapPushDown to create a heap out of a list of items is shown here.

```
Sub BuildHeap()
Dim i As Integer

    For i = (max + min) \ 2 To min Step -1
        HeapPushDown list(), i, max
    Next i
End Sub
```

Priority Queues

Using the BuildHeap and HeapPushDown subroutines, it is easy to manage a priority queue using a heap. In a priority queue, each item in the queue is assigned a priority. When you remove an item from a priority queue, you remove the item that has the highest priority.

If you use a heap as a priority queue, the item with the highest priority will always be at the top of the heap. That will make it easy to remove the highest priority item from the queue. When you remove this item, however, you are left with a rootless tree that is certainly not a heap.

To turn the rootless tree back into a heap, take the last item in the heap (the rightmost item on the bottom level) and place it at the top of the heap. Also update the number of items in the tree so you remember that the tree holds one less item.

Then use the HeapPushDown routine discussed in the previous section to push the new root node item down into the tree until the tree is once again a heap. At this point the priority queue is ready to output the next highest priority item.

The source code for this operation is shown below.

```
Sub LeavePQueue (value As Long)
    If NumInPQueue < 1 Then Exit Sub
    value = PQueue(1)
    PQueue(1) = PQueue (NumInPQueue)
    NumInPQueue = NumInPQueue - 1


    HeapPushDown PQueue(), 1, NumInPQueue
End Sub
```

To add a new item to the priority queue, first enlarge the heap to make room for the new item. Then place the new item in the empty position at the end of the array. The resulting tree may no longer be a heap.

To make the tree a heap again, compare the new item with its parent. If the new item is bigger than its parent, swap the two. You already know that the parent's other child is smaller than the parent, so you do not need to compare the new item to the other child. If the new item is larger than the parent, it will also be larger than this other child so the heap property for the node will be maintained.

Continue comparing the new item to its parent, moving it up through the tree, until you find a parent that is already larger than the new item. At that point the tree is once again a heap and the priority queue is ready for business.

The code for pushing an item up through the heap is similar to the code for pushing an item down through the heap.

```
Sub HeapPushUp (list() As Long, ByVal max As Integer)
Dim tmp As Long
Dim j As Integer

    tmp = list(max)
    Do
        j = max \ 2
        If j < 1 Then Exit Do
        If list(j) < tmp Then
            list(max) = list(j)
            max = j
```

```
        Else
            Exit Do
        End If
    Loop
    list(max) = tmp
End Sub
```

The code that adds items to the priority queue uses subroutine HeapPushUp as shown below.

```
Sub EnterPQueue (value As Long)
    NumInPQueue = NumInPQueue + 1
    If NumInPQueue > PQueueSize Then ResizePQueue

    PQueue(NumInPQueue) = value
    HeapPushUp PQueue(), NumInPQueue
End Sub
```

Heap Analysis

When you first turn the list of items into a heap, you do so by building a lot of smaller heaps. For every internal node in the tree, you build a smaller heap rooted at that node. If the tree contains N items, there are O(N) internal nodes in the tree so you end up building O(N) heaps.

As you build each heap, you might need to push the top item down the heap, possibly until it reaches a leaf node. The tallest heaps you build have height O(log(N)). Since you build O(N) heaps and the tallest requires at most O(log(N)) steps to build, you can build all of the heaps in O(N * log(N)) time.

In fact, it does not take even that much time to build the heaps. Only a few of the heaps have height O(log(N)). Most are much shorter. Only one heap actually has height equal to log(N) while half of them have height only 2. It turns out that, if you add up all of the steps needed to build all of the heaps, you will require at most O(N) steps.

To see why this is true, suppose the tree contains N nodes. Let H be the height of the tree. Since this is a complete binary tree, H = log(N).

Now suppose you are building larger and larger heaps within the tree. You will build a heap of height I for each internal node in the tree that is H − I levels from the root of the tree. There are 2^{H-I} such nodes in the tree so in total you will build 2^{H-I} heaps of height I.

When you build these heaps, you might have to push the top item down until it reaches a leaf. In that case you will spend I steps pushing the item down through a heap of height I. If you build 2^{H-I} heaps in at most I steps each, the total number of steps you spend building heaps of height I is $I * 2^{H-I}$.

Adding together all of the steps you spend building heaps of different sizes, you get $1 * 2^{H-1} + 2 * 2^{H-2} + 3 * 2^{H-3} + \ldots + (H-1) * 2^1$. If you then divide out a factor of 2^H, you get $2^H * (1/2 + 2/2^2 + 3/2^3 + \ldots + (H-1)/2^{H-1})$.

It can be shown that the sum $(1/2 + 2/2^2 + 3/2^3 + \ldots + (H-1)/2^{H-1})$ is less than 2. In that case the number of steps you spend building all of the heaps is less than $2^H * 2$. But H is the height of the tree and equals log(N) so the total number of steps is less than $2^{\log(N)} * 2 = N * 2$. That means it takes only O(N) steps to initially build a heap.

When you remove an item from a priority queue, you move the last item to the top of the tree. You then push the item down through the tree until it reaches its final position and the tree is again a heap. Since the tree has height log(N), this process can take at most log(N) steps. This means you can remove an item from a heap-based priority queue in O(log(N)) steps.

When you add a new item to the heap, you start it at the bottom of the tree and push it towards the top until it comes to rest. Since the tree has height log(N), this operation can take at most log(N) steps. That means you can add a new item to a heap-based priority queue in O(log(N)) steps.

Another way to manage a priority queue would be to keep the list of items completely sorted at all times. You could use quicksort to build the initial queue in O(N * log(N)) expected time. When you removed an item from the queue, the list would be mostly sorted so you could use bubblesort to put the list back in order in O(N) time. Similarly when you added an item to the queue you could use bubblesort to reorder the list in O(N) time.

These times are fast but not as fast as the times you can achieve using a heap. A queue holding 1,024 items, for example, would require about 1,024 steps to insert a new item using a sorted list and bubblesort. It would require only ten steps using a heap. In a queue holding about a million items, insertion using a sorted list would take about a million steps while insertion using a heap would take only 20 steps.

Example program PRIORITY uses a heap to manage a priority queue. Enter a number and press the Add button to add the new item to the queue. Press the Leave button to remove the highest priority item from the queue.

The Heapsort Algorithm

With the algorithms already described for manipulating heaps, the actual heapsort algorithm is straightforward. The idea is to build a priority queue and then remove each item from the queue one at a time. Each item removed from the queue will be the largest item left in the queue. If you remove every item, you will have pulled them out in largest to smallest order.

As you remove each item, swap it with the last item in the heap. This places the largest item in its proper final position at the end of the array. Then reduce the size of the list by one so you do not consider the last position in the array to be part of the heap again. That way the largest item will remain in its correct position.

After you have removed the largest item from the heap and swapped it with the last item, the array will no longer be a heap since the new top item may be smaller than its new children. To turn the array back into a heap, you can use the HeapPushDown routine to push the new item down to its proper position.

Continue swapping items, shrinking the array, and rebuilding the heap until there are no items left. At that point the list will be sorted. The complete heapsort algorithm is shown below.

```
Sub HeapSort (list() As Long, ByVal min As Integer, ByVal max As _
Integer)
Dim i As Integer
Dim tmp As Long

    ' Make a heap (except for the root node).
    For i = (max + min) \ 2 To min + 1 Step -1
        HeapPushDown list(), i, max
    Next i
```

```
' Repeatedly:
' 1. HeapPushDown.
' 2. Output the root.
For i = max To min + 1 Step -1
    ' HeapPushDown.
    HeapPushDown list(), min, i
    ' Output the root.
    tmp = list(min)
    list(min) = list(i)
    list(i) = tmp
Next i
End Sub
```

While discussing priority queues, you saw that it takes O(N) steps to build the initial heap. After that it takes O(log(N)) steps to rebuild the heap when you remove an item from the queue. Heapsort does this N times to sort the list so it needs a total of O(N) * O(log(N)) = O(N * log(N)) steps to pull the sorted list out of the heap. That makes the total run time for heapsort O(N) + O(N * log(N)) = O(N * log(N)).

This is the same as the run time for mergesort and the average run time for quicksort. Like mergesort, heapsort does not depend on the values or distribution of the items being sorted. While quicksort can have trouble with lists that have many duplicated values, mergesort and heapsort have no trouble at all.

Furthermore, while heapsort is usually a little slower than mergesort, it does not require the temporary scratch space that mergesort does. You can build the initial heap and pull the sorted items out of the heap all within the array that initially contains the unsorted list.

Countingsort

Countingsort is a specialized algorithm that works extremely well if the data items are integers within a fairly small range. The algorithm will work very well, for example, if the values of all of the data items are between 1 and 1,000.

As long as your list meets these conditions, countingsort is amazingly fast. In one test on a 50 megahertz 486-based PC, countingsort was able to sort 30,000 items with values between 1 and 30,000 in 2.16 seconds. To sort the same items, quicksort required 10.72 seconds—almost 5 times as long.

The reason countingsort is so fast is that it does not use comparisons to sort the items. As was mentioned earlier, any algorithm that uses comparisons to sort items must take at least O(N * log(N)) steps. By not using comparisons countingsort is able to sort items in O(N) time.

To use countingsort, start by creating an array to count the items that have each data value. If the data items range in value from min_value to max_value, create a Counts array with lower bound min_value and upper bound max_value. If you resize a previously used Count array or create a new one from scratch, Visual Basic automatically initializes all of the array entries to zero. If you reuse a Count array that was used in a previous run of countingsort, you will need to reinitialize the array entries to zero yourself. If M is the size of the Count array, this will take O(M) time.

Next count the occurrences of each data value in the list. Examine each item in the list and increment the value of the Counts array corresponding to that item's value. If an item's value is 37, increase the Counts(37) entry by one. When you are finished, Counts(37) should contain the number of entries in the list that have value 37. During this counting process you examine each item in the list once, so this step takes O(N) time. The code that calculates the counts is quite simple.

```
For i = min To max
    counts(list(i)) = counts(list(i)) + 1
Next i
```

Then run through the Counts array converting the counts into offsets. The offsets will indicate where in the sorted list the items with a certain value belong. For example, suppose the smallest value in the list has value one. Then the offset for value one should be one since items with value one will begin in the first position in the sorted list.

If there are 10 items with value one, those items will occupy positions 1 through 10 in the sorted array. In that case items with value two must begin at position 11 so the offset for value two is 11. If there are 5 items with value two, those items will occupy positions 11 through 15. Then the offset for items with value three should be 16.

Continue in this manner to convert each Counts array entry from an item count into a value offset. During this phase you update each entry in the Counts array once so this phase requires O(M) steps. The code that converts the item counts into array offsets is also straightforward.

```
next_spot = 1
For i = min_value To max_value
    this_count = counts(i)
    counts (i) = next_spot
    next_spot = next_spot + this_count
Next i
```

Now you are ready to place the items in their final sorted positions. Examine each item in turn and look in the Counts array to determine where the item belongs. Place the item in the correct location and increment the offset so the next item with the same value goes into the next position. Since this phase requires you to examine each item in the list again, this phase takes O(N) steps.

```
' Place the values
For i = min To max
    new_index = counts(list(i))
    counts(list(i)) = counts(list(i)) + 1
    sorted_list(new_index) = list(i)
Next i
```

The complete algorithm takes $O(M) + O(N) + O(M) + O(N) = O(M + N)$ steps. If M is relatively small compared to N, this will be very fast indeed. If M < N, for example, $O(M + N) = O(N)$ which is quite a bit faster than the best $O(N * \log(N))$ algorithms examined so far. As was mentioned above, in one test countingsort was able to arrange 30,000 items with values between 1 and 30,000 in 2.16 seconds while quicksort took 10.72 seconds to sort the same items.

On the other hand, if M is larger than $O(N * \log(N))$, then $O(M + N)$ will be larger than $O(N * \log(N))$. In another test countingsort needed 0.60 seconds to sort 1,000 items with values between 1 and 30,000 while quicksort took only 0.28 seconds.

Countingsort relies on the fact that the data values are integers, so the algorithm cannot sort noninteger data. In Visual Basic you cannot create an array with bounds "AAA" to "ZZZ".

As was mentioned earlier in this Chapter (see pages 214–217), you can sometimes encode non-integer data using integers and then you can still use countingsort. You can convert a three letter uppercase string into an integer, for example, by setting the value of the integer to 27 * 27 * (1st letter – "A" + 1) + 27 * (2nd letter – "A" + 1) + (3rd letter – "A" + 1). For example, "FOX" becomes:

$$27 * 27 * ("F" - "A" + 1) + 27 * ("O" - "A" + 1) + ("X" - "A" + 1) =$$
$$27 * 27 * 6 + 27 * 15 + 24 =$$
$$4,803$$

Longer strings may not fit into an integer, however. If you cannot encode your data as integers, you will have to use a different sorting algorithm.

Bucketsort

Like countingsort, bucketsort does not use comparisons to sort items. It uses the values of the data to divide the data into buckets, and then it sorts the buckets recursively. Once the buckets have reached a sufficiently small size, the algorithm can stop and use a simpler algorithm like selectionsort to finish sorting the items.

In a sense this algorithm is a bit like quicksort. Quicksort divides the items into two sublists and recursively sorts the sublists. Bucketsort does pretty much the same thing except it divides the list into many buckets instead of just two sublists.

To divide the list into buckets, the algorithm assumes that the data values are fairly evenly distributed. It then divides the items evenly among the buckets. For example, suppose the data items have values ranging from 1 to 100 and the algorithm is using 10 buckets. Then the algorithm will place items with values 1–10 in the first bucket, items with values 11–20 in the second bucket, and so forth. Figure 8.12 shows a list of 10 items with values between 1 and 100 which have been placed in 10 buckets.

If the data items are evenly distributed, each bucket will receive about the same number of items. If there are N items in the list and you use N buckets, each bucket will receive only one or two items. You can then sort the one or two items in a constant number of steps so the total run time for the algorithm will be O(N).

In practice the data will usually not be perfectly evenly distributed. Some buckets will receive more items and some will receive fewer. If the distribution is at all close to even, however, each bucket will receive only a small number of items. Even if there is a clump in the data and one bucket receives many items, the items within the bucket will probably be fairly evenly distributed. When the algorithm recursively sorts this large

Unsorted list	1	74	38	72	63	100	89	57	7	31

Bucket number	1	2	3	4	5	6	7	8	9	10
Bucket	1		38		57	63	74	89		100
	7		31				72			

Figure 8.12 Placing items in buckets.

bucket, the items will be divided pretty evenly among the new buckets, and the broken up clump will be handled easily in the second round of the algorithm.

It is possible to concoct a strange data set that behaves badly even after several recursive calls to bucketsort. To make the data as bad as possible, the data should be arranged so the algorithm places almost all of the items in the same bucket. Then each time bucketsort recursively sorts the large bucket, it should divide the items in the same uneven way.

If you define a recursive function F where F(N) is the value of the Nth item in the hard-to-sort list, you can define such a list by:

```
F(1) = 1
F(N) = N * F(N-1)
```

This definition is exactly the same as the recursive definition of the factorial function described in Chapter 4 (see pages 77–79).

With a list of size N, the bucketsort algorithm would use N buckets. Since F(N) = N! is larger than all of the other items in the list, the range of data values will be 1 to N!. Then the first bucket in the list will contain items with data values between 1 and N! / N. But N! / N is the same as (N – 1)! which is F(N – 1) and F(N – 1) is the second largest item in the list. That means the item with value N! will go in the last bucket and all of the other items will go in the first.

As bucketsort recursively tries to sort the first bucket, it will again place one item in the last bucket and all of the others in the first bucket. Eventually this will cause $O(N^2)$ performance and deep recursion.

This is a rather bizarre list of items, however. Not only will you probably not have a data distribution like this, but if you did the list could not be very long anyway. The factorial function grows so quickly that you cannot store many values of the function in your computer. In Visual Basic the largest value for the factorial function that a double variable can hold is 170! which is around 7.257E + 306. This means that, for practical purposes, a list arranged in this kind of weird distribution could only contain about 170 items.

A much less bizarre case that can cause trouble occurs when there are relatively few distinct values in the list. If every item has the same value, for example, bucketsort would put them all in the same bucket. If it did not detect this, the algorithm would recursively put them all in the same bucket again and again, causing runaway recursion which would quickly use up all of the stack space.

You can implement bucketsort in Visual Basic in a couple of ways. First, you can make the buckets linked lists. This makes it easy to move items from one bucket to another as the algorithm progresses.

This method has the disadvantage that you must move all of the items from the original array into a linked list and back into the array when you are done sorting. It also requires extra memory for the linked list's Next pointers.

The Visual Basic code for a linked list bucket sort is shown below.

```
Sub LinkBucketSort (list() As Long, NextInList() As Integer, first _
As Integer)
Dim count As Integer
Dim min_value As Long
Dim max_value As Long
```

```
Dim item As Integer
Dim bucket() As Integer
Dim value_scale As Double
Dim bucket_num As Integer
Dim i As Integer
Dim nxt As Integer


    ' Count the items and find the min and max values.
    count = 1
    min_value = list(first)
    max_value = list(first)
    item = NextInList(first)
    Do While item <> END_OF_LIST
        count = count + 1
        If min_value > list(item) Then min_value = list(item)
        If max_value < list(item) Then max_value = list(item)
        item = NextInList(item)
    Loop


    ' If min_value = max_value, there is only one item
    ' value so the list is sorted.
    If min_value = max_value Then Exit Sub


    ' If the list has no more than CutOff elements,
    ' finish it off with LinkInsertionSort.
    If count <= CutOff Then
        LinkInsertionSort list(), NextInList(), first
        Exit Sub
    End If


    ' Create and initialize the empty buckets.
    ReDim bucket (1 To count)
    For i = 1 To count
        bucket(i) = END_OF_LIST
    Next i


    value_scale = CDb1 (count - 1) / CDb1(max_value - min_value)


    ' Drop the items into the buckets.
    Do While first <> END_OF_LIST
        item = first
        first = NextInList (first)
        If list(item) = max_value Then
            bucket_num = count
        Else
            bucket_num = Int((list(item) - min_value) * value_scale) + 1
        End If
        NextInList (item) = bucket(bucket_num)
        bucket(bucket_num) = item
    Loop


    ' Recursively sort the buckets with more than one item.
    For i = 1 To count
        nxt = bucket(i)
        If nxt <> END_OF_LIST Then nxt = NextInList (nxt)
        If nxt <> END_OF_LIST Then LinkBucketSort list(), NextInList(), bucket (i)
    Next i
```

```
    ' Merge the sorted lists.
    first = bucket(count)
    For i = count - 1 To 1 Step -1
        item = bucket(i)
        If item <> END_OF_LIST Then
            nxt = NextInList(item)
            Do While NextInList(item) ;ls> END_OF_LIST
                item = nxt
                nxt = NextInList(item)
            Loop
            NextInList(item) = first
            first = bucket(i)
        End If
    Next i
End Sub
```

You can also implement bucketsort in an array using concepts similar to those used in countingsort. Each time the algorithm is invoked, it first counts the items that it will place in each bucket. It next uses the counts to compute offsets in a temporary scratch array much as countingsort did. The algorithm then uses the offsets to place the items in those positions in the scratch array. Finally it recursively sorts the buckets and moves the sorted data back into the original array.

This version of bucketsort has the advantage that it does not require linked lists. It has the disadvantage that it requires a large scratch array.

The Visual Basic code for this version of bucketsort is shown below.

```
Sub ArrayBucketSort (list() As Long, scratch() As Long, min As _
Integer, max As Integer, NumBuckets As Integer)
Dim counts() As Integer
Dim offsets() As Integer

Dim i As Integer
Dim min_value As Long
Dim max_value As Long
Dim value_scale As Double
Dim bucket_num As Integer
Dim next_spot As Integer
Dim num_in_bucket As Integer

    ' If the list has no more than CutOff elements,
    ' finish it off with SelectionSort.
    If max - min + 1 < CutOff Then
        SelectionSort list(), min, max
        Exit Sub
    End If

    ' Find the min and max values.
    min_value = list(min)
    max_value = list(min)
    For i = min + 1 To max
        If min_value > list(i) Then min_value = list(i)
        If max_value < list(i) Then max_value = list(i)
    Next i

    ' If min_value = max_value, there is only one
    ' value so the list is sorted.
    If min_value = max_value Then Exit Sub
```

```
    ' Create and initialize the empty buckets.
    ReDim counts(1 To NumBuckets)
    For i = 1 To NumBuckets
        counts(i) = 0
    Next i


    value_scale = CDb1 (NumBuckets - 1) / CDb1(max_value - min_value)


    ' Create bucket counts.
    For i = min To max
        If list(i) = max_value Then
            bucket_num = NumBuckets
        Else
            bucket_num = Int((list(i) - min_value) * value_scale) + 1
        End If
        counts(bucket_num) = counts(bucket_num) + 1
    Next i


    ' Turn the counts into offsets.
    ReDim offset(1 To NumBuckets)
    next_spot = min
    For i = 1 To NumBuckets
        offsets(i) = next_spot
        next_spot = next_spot + counts(i)
    Next i


    ' Place the values in their buckets.
    For i = min To max
        If list(i) = max_value Then
            bucket_num = NumBuckets
        Else
            bucket_num = Int((list(i) - min_value) * value_scale) + 1
        End If
        scratch(offsets(bucket_num)) = list(i)
        offsets(bucket_num) = offsets(bucket_num) + 1
    Next i


    ' Recursively sort the buckets with more than one item.
    next_spot = min
    For i = 1 To NumBuckets
        If counts(i) > 1 Then ArrayBucketSort scratch(), list(), _
next_spot, next_spot + counts(i) - 1, counts(i)
        next_spot = next_spot + counts(i)
    Next i
    For i = min To max
        list(i) = scratch(i)
    Next i
End Sub
```

Both of these versions of bucketsort have roughly the same performance. In the example program SORT, the linked list version does slightly better. This is mostly because, in the linked list version, the items are placed in a linked list before the algorithm begins so the extra time needed to create the linked list is not counted. The array-based version must create its scratch space as it runs and this takes a little extra time.

Both versions of bucketsort can stop when there are fewer than a certain minimum number of items in the buckets and then use a simpler algorithm to finish sorting. The array-based version can use selectionsort to finish sorting and the linked list version can use a linked list insertionsort.

Since the run times of these two versions of bucketsort are so close, you should use the version that fits in best with the rest of your program. If you are already storing the data in a linked list, use the linked list version. If you are storing the data in an array, use the array-based version.

Countingsort is an O(M + N) algorithm where N is the number of items in the list and M is the range covered by the item values. Bucketsort is an O(N) algorithm. This means that when M is large compared to N, bucketsort will perform better than countingsort.

Since countingsort builds a count array with one entry for each data value in the list, it has difficulty if the data values vary too widely. If the values range from 1 to 30,000, it will have to create a very large array to count them all. Countingsort also cannot handle non-integer data types like doubles and strings. Bucketsort can easily handle widely varying data values and non-integer data types.

Table 8.7 shows the times required to sort several different lists of items using countingsort and bucketsort on a 50 megahertz 486-based PC.

Summary of Sorting Routines

Table 8.8 shows the advantages and disadvantages of the sorting algorithms discussed in this chapter. Taking these into account, which sorting routine should you use for your situation? Here are some suggestions.

- If your list is more than 99 percent sorted already, use bubblesort.
- If you have a very small list (under 100 items or so), use selectionsort.
- If the items in your list range over a small number of integer values (up to several thousand), use countingsort.
- If the values vary over a wide range or are not integers, use linked list or array-based bucketsort.
- If you cannot spare the extra memory required by bucketsort, use Quicksort.

Table 8.7 Times to Sort Various Lists

List Size	Data Range	Countingsort	Linked List Bucketsort	Array-Based Bucketsort
100	1–30,000	0.55	0.03	0.05
1,000	1–30,000	0.55	0.32	0.44
30,000	1–1,000	1.61	3.96	4.57
30,000	1–30,000	2.20	4.12	4.74

Table 8.8 Advantages and Disadvantages of Sorting Algorithms

Algorithm	Advantages	Disadvantages
Insertionsort	• Very simple • Easy to understand • Fast for small lists	• Very slow for large lists
Insertion With Linked Lists	• Simple • Fast for small lists • Moves pointers, not data	• Slow for large lists
Selectionsort	• Very simple • Easy to understand • Very fast for small lists	• Slow for large lists
Bubblesort	• Very fast for lists that are almost sorted	• Very slow sorting all other lists
Quicksort	• Very fast for large lists	• Trouble if there are lots of duplicate data values
Mergesort	• Fast for large lists • Good paging performance • Fast for any initial data arrangement and distribution	• Requires scratch space • Not as fast as quicksort
Heapsort	• Fast for large lists • No scratch space required • Fast for any initial data arrangement and distribution	• Not as fast as mergesort
Countingsort	• Extremely fast when the data is distributed over a small range (e.g., between 1 and 1,000)	• Slower when data range $> \log(N)$ • Requires extra memory • Only works with integer data
Bucketsort	• Extremely fast when the data is evenly distributed • Handles data spread over wide ranges • Handles non-integer data	• Generally slower than countingsort

C H A P T E R 9

Searching Lists

Once you have sorted a list of items using one of the techniques presented in Chapter 8, you might want to locate a particular item within the list. This chapter describes several algorithms for locating items within sorted lists.

The chapter begins by briefly discussing exhaustive searching. While not as fast as the other algorithms discussed, exhaustive searching is very simple. That makes it easy to program, debug, and maintain over time. Its simplicity also makes exhaustive searching faster than other algorithms for very small lists.

Next the chapter describes binary searching. A binary search repeatedly subdivides the list to locate an item and is much faster than exhaustive searching for larger lists. While the idea behind binary searching is simple, the implementation is a little tricky.

The chapter then discusses interpolation searching. Like a binary search, an interpolation search repeatedly subdivides the list to locate an item. Unlike binary search, this method uses interpolation to perform the subdivision in a way similar to the way in which bucketsort places items in buckets. This makes interpolation search much faster than binary search if the data is evenly distributed.

Finally the chapter discusses hunt and search methods. If you need to locate many items within a list and you suspect that each consecutive item will be near the previous item, a hunt and search technique can make your search faster.

Example Programs

Example program SEARCH demonstrates all of the algorithms described in this chapter. Enter the number of items you want the list to contain and a target value for the program to locate. Use the check boxes to select the algorithms the program should use.

When you press the Search button, the program will create a list of the indicated size if it has not done so already. The value of each item in the list will be between 0 and 4 larger than the previous item. In other words List(i) <= List(i + 1) <= List(i) + 4. The program will display the value of the largest item in the list so you know what range the values include. Since the items are not all consecutive, you may need to search for several different values before you find a value that is in the list.

Once a list has been created, the program will continue to use that list unless you change the number of items in the list. You can enter new target values and press Search to make the program locate the new values in the same list using the algorithms you have selected.

The program also allows you to specify the number of times it should repeat each search. For even large lists the binary and interpolation search algorithms are very fast, so you may need to use many repetitions if you want to compare the speeds of the algorithms. Be sure to keep the number of repetitions small until you get an idea of how long your computer will take for each algorithm.

Exhaustive Search

To perform an *exhaustive* or *linear* search, simply start at the beginning of the list and examine every item in turn looking for the target item. If the list is stored as an array, for example, the search routine might look like this:

```
Function LinearSearch(target As Long) As Integer
Dim i As Integer

    For i = 1 To NumItems
        If list(i) = target Then Exit For
    Next i
    If i > NumItems Then
        Search = 0
    Else
        Search = i
    End If
End Function
```

Since it examines each item in order, this algorithm will locate items near the front of the list more quickly than items near the end of the list. The worst case for this algorithm is when the item is near the end of the list or is not present at all. In these cases the algorithm will have to search all of the items in the list so the method has O(N) worst case behavior.

If the item does appear in the list, the algorithm will have to examine N / 2 entries on the average before it finds the target item. This gives the algorithm an average behavior of O(N).

Even though this O(N) behavior is not particularly fast, the algorithm is simple enough that it is quite fast in practice. For lists up to around 15 items in size, the simplicity of this algorithm makes it faster than the more complicated algorithms discussed later in the chapter.

Searching Sorted Lists

Exhaustive searching as described above does not take into account the fact that the list is sorted. If the list is sorted, you can modify the algorithm to get slightly better performance.

As the algorithm searches the list, if it ever finds an item that has value greater than the target item, the algorithm can stop. Since it has passed the position where the target item would belong if it were in the list, the item must not appear in the list. For example, suppose you are searching for the value 12 and you come to the value 17. You have passed the position where 12 would have been so you know the value 12 is not in the list. The Visual Basic code for this version of the exhaustive search algorithm is shown below.

```
Function LinearSearch (target As Long) As Integer
Dim i As Integer

    For i = 1 To NumItems
        If List(i) >= target Then Exit For
    Next i
    If i > NumItems Then
        LinearSearch = 0
    ElseIf List(i) <> target Then
        LinearSearch = 0
    Else
        LinearSearch = i
    End If
End Function
```

This modification makes the algorithm faster when the target item is not in the list. The previous version of this function needed to search all the way to the end of the list if the target item was not present. The new version will stop as soon as it finds an item greater than the target item. If the target item is randomly chosen between the smallest and largest items in the list, the algorithm will require an average of N / 2 steps to determine that the item is not there. Example program SEARCH uses this version of the algorithm.

Searching Linked Lists

Exhaustive searching is the only way to search a linked list. Since you have access to items only through their Next pointers, you must start at the beginning of the list and step through the items one at a time until you find the one you seek.

As is the case with exhaustive search in an array, if the list is sorted, you can stop searching when you find an item that has value greater than the target item's value. Once you have passed the position where the target item would be if it were in the list, you know that the item is not there.

```
Function LLListSearch (target As Long) As Integer
Dim cell As Integer

    cell = TopCell
    Do While cell <> END_OF_LIST
        If Cells(cell).Value >= target Then Exit Do
```

```
            cell = Cells(cell).Next
    Loop
    If cell = END_OF_LIST Then
        LListSearch = END_OF_LIST
    ElseIf Cells(cell).Value <> target Then
        LListSearch = END_OF_LIST
    Else
        LListSearch = cell
    End If
End Function
```

Example program SEARCH uses this algorithm to locate items within a linked list. When you run the program, you will notice that this algorithm is slower than the previous exhaustive search algorithm, even though both lists hold the same number of items. This is caused by the fact that Visual Basic does a better job optimizing **For** loops than it does optimizing **While** loops. In general, examining the items in a linked list is a little slower than examining the items in an array.

You can make one more change to the linked list search algorithm to make it a little faster. If you keep track of the bottom of the list, you can add a new cell to the end of the list that contains the target value. This item is called a sentinel and serves a purpose similar to the sentinels used in the lists built in Chapter 2. It allows the program to treat a special case as if it were not special.

In this instance, by adding the sentinel to the end of the list, you ensure that you will eventually find the item when you look for it. This means you will not run off the end of the list so you do not need to check that **cell <> END_OF_LIST** each time the **While** loop executes. The Visual Basic code for this version of the linked list search is shown below.

```
Sub SentinelSearch (target As Long)
Dim cell As Integer
Dim sentinel As Integer

    ' Create the sentinel.
    sentinel = NewCell()
    Cells(sentinel).Value = target
    Cells(BottomCell).Next = sentinel

    ' Find the target.
    cell = TopCell
    Do While Cells(cell).Value < target
        cell = Cells(cell).Next
    Loop

    ' See if we found it.
    If cell = sentinel Or Cells(cell).Value <> target Then
        SentinelSearch = END_OF_LIST
    Else
        ListSearch = cell
    End If
    ' Remove the sentinel.
    Cells(BottomCell).Next = END_OF_LIST
    FreeCell sentinel
End Sub
```

While this may seem like a small change, the **cell <> END_OF_LIST** test being removed is contained within a frequently executed loop. For large lists this loop is executed many times and the savings add up. In Visual Basic this linked list search runs about 20 percent faster than the previous version.

Example program SEARCH demonstrates this version in addition to the previous linked list search algorithm so you can compare the performance of the two.

Binary Search

As was mentioned in the previous sections, an exhaustive search is very fast for small lists. For larger lists you can do much better using a binary search. To perform a binary search, first pick an item in the center of the list and compare that item to the target item. If the target item is smaller than the center item, continue searching the first half of the list. If the target item is larger than the center item, continue searching the second half of the list. Figure 9.1 shows this process graphically.

While this algorithm is naturally recursive, it is fairly easy to write without recursion. Since the algorithm is easy to understand either way, it is written non-recursively here to save the expense of making a lot of function calls.

While the general idea behind the algorithm is simple, the details are a little tricky. You need to keep careful track of the variables that bound the portion of the array that might contain the target item. Otherwise the algorithm may miss the target.

The algorithm uses two variables, Min and Max, to keep track of the minimum and maximum indexes of the array entries that could contain the target item. While the algorithm runs, the target will always have an index between Min and Max. In other words Min <= target index <= Max.

During each pass of the algorithm, let Middle = (Min + Max)/2 and then examine the item with index Middle. If the middle item has the same value as the target item, you have found the target and you are done.

If the target item is smaller than this middle item, set Max to Middle – 1 and continue searching. Since the range of indexes that might contain the target item is now Min to Middle – 1, you will only be searching the first half of the list.

If the target item is larger than the middle item, set Min to Middle + 1 and continue searching. Since the range of indexes that might hold the target item is now Middle + 1 to Max, you will only be searching the second half of the list.

Eventually you will either find the item, or Min will be raised and Max lowered until Min is greater than Max. When you move Min and Max, you do so in a way that guarantees that the index of the target item is always between them. Since there are no more indexes between Min and Max at this point, you know the item is not in the list.

The Visual Basic code for this algorithm is shown below.

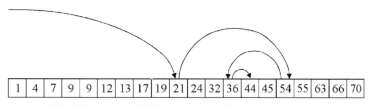

| 1 | 4 | 7 | 9 | 9 | 12 | 13 | 17 | 19 | 21 | 24 | 32 | 36 | 44 | 45 | 54 | 55 | 63 | 66 | 70 |

Figure 9.1 Binary search for the value 44.

```
Function BinarySearch (target As Long) As Integer
Dim Min As Long
Dim Max As Long
Dim Middle As Long

    ' During the search the target's index will be
    ' between Min and Max: Min <= target index <= Max
    Min = 1
    Max = NumItems
    Do While Min <= Max
        Middle = (Max + Min) / 2
        If target = List(Middle) Then      ' We have found it!
            BinarySearch = Middle
            Exit Function
        ElseIf target < List(Middle) Then ' Search the left half.
            Max = Middle - 1
        Else                              ' Search the right half.
            Min = Middle + 1
        End If
    Loop
    ' If we get here the target is not in the list.
    BinarySearch = 0
End Function
```

At each step this algorithm cuts the list of items that still might contain the target item in half. For a list of size N, the algorithm will need at most O(log(N)) steps to locate any given item or to decide that it is not contained in the list. This makes a binary search much faster than an exhaustive search. To exhaustively search a list of 1 million items would take an average of 500,000 steps. The binary search algorithm would need at most log(1,000,000) or 20 steps.

While exhaustive searching is slow in general, its simplicity makes it faster than other algorithms for very small lists. If you use the SEARCH program to compare the speeds of the exhaustive and binary searches, you will find that the exhaustive search is faster for lists containing about 15 or fewer items. For larger lists binary search is much faster.

Interpolation Search

Binary searching is a great improvement over exhaustive searching because it eliminates large portions of the list without actually examining all of the eliminated values. If you know that the values are fairly evenly distributed in the list, you can use interpolation to eliminate even more values at each step. Interpolation is the process of using known values to guess where an unknown value lies. In this case you use the indexes of known values in the list to guess what index the target value should have.

For example, suppose you had the same list of values shown in Figure 9.1. This list contains 20 items with values distributed between 1 and 70. Now suppose you wanted to locate the item in this list with value "44." If you assume the values of the items are evenly distributed, then, since 44 is about 64 percent of the way between the values 1 and 70, you would expect the target item to be about 64 percent of the way through the list or at index 13.

If the position chosen by the interpolation is incorrect, the search compares the target value to the value at the chosen position. If the target value is smaller, the search continues to locate the target in the first part of the list. If the target value is larger, the search continues to locate the target in the second part of the list. Figure 9.2 shows an interpolation search graphically.

During a binary search you subdivide the list by examining the middle item in the list. During an interpolation search you subdivide the list by examining an item that should be close to the target item in the list. You pick this dividing point by interpolation using the statement:

```
Middle = Min + (target - List(Min)) * ((Max - Min) / (List(Max) - List(Min)))
```

This statement places Middle between Min and Max in a way that reflects where the target value lies between List(Min) and List(Max). If the target is close to List(Min), the "Target – List(Min)" term is close to zero. Then the complete statement is close to Middle = Min + 0 so the value of Middle is near Min. This makes sense. You would expect the item to have an index near Min if its value is close to List(Min).

Similarly if the target is close to List(Max), the "Target – List(Min)" term is about the same as the "List(Max) – List(Min)" term. Then these two terms cancel out and the statement is close to Middle = Min + (Max – Min). This simplifies to Middle = Max and also makes sense. You would expect the item to have an index near Max if its value is close to List(Max).

Once you have computed Middle, compare the item at that position to the target item much as you would during a binary search. If the item matches the target, you have found the item and you are done. If the target is smaller than this middle item, set Max to Middle – 1 and continue searching the smaller items in the list. If the target is larger than the middle item, set Min to Middle + 1 and continue searching the larger items in the list.

Notice that the statement which calculates the new value for Middle divides by (List(Max) – List(Min)). If List(Min) and List(Max) have the same value, this statement tries to divide by zero and the program crashes. This can happen if the list has two identical values in it. Since this algorithm keeps Min <= target index <= Max, this problem can also occur if Min is raised and Max is lowered until Min = Max.

To handle this problem, check whether List(Min) and List(Max) are the same before performing the division. If they are the same, there is only a single distinct value left in the list that you must consider. All you need to do is check whether or not you have found a match and you are done searching for the item.

One other detail you must handle is that the value calculated for Middle is sometimes not between Min and Max. The simplest case where this occurs is when the target

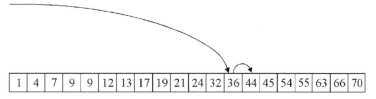

Figure 9.2 Interpolation search for the value 44.

is outside the range of values in the list. Suppose you are looking for the value 300 in the list 100, 150, 200. The first time you calculate Middle you have Min = 1 and Max = 3. This gives Middle = 1 + (300 − List(1)) * (3 - 1)/(List(3) − List(1)) = 1 + (300 − 100) * 2/(200 − 100) = 5. The index 5 is not only outside the range Min <= target index <= Max, but it is also outside the array bounds. If you try to access List(5), the program will crash with a "Subscript out of range" error.

A similar problem can occur if the values between Min and Max are very unevenly distributed. Suppose you want to locate the value 100 in the list 0, 1, 2, 199, 200. The first time you calculate Middle you will get Middle = 1 + (100 − 0) * (5 − 1)/(200 − 0) = 3. You will then compare List(3) to the target 100. Since List(3) = 2, which is less than 100, you will set Min = Middle + 1 so Min = 4.

When you next calculate Middle you will get Middle = 4 + (100 − 199) * (5 − 4)/(200 − 199) = −98. The value −98 is outside the range Min <= target index <= Max and is also far outside the array bounds.

If you look closely at the calculation of Middle, you will see that there are two ways in which the new value for Middle can be smaller than Min or larger than Max. First, suppose Middle is less than Min.

```
Min + (target - List(Min)) * ((Max - Min) / (List(Max) - List(Min)) < Min
```

Subtracting Min from both sides you get:

```
(target - List(Min)) * ((Max - Min) / (List(Max) - List(Min)) < 0
```

Since Max >= Min, the (Max − Min) term must be greater than zero. Since List(Max) >= List(Min), the (List(Max) − List(Min) term must also be greater than zero. Then the only way the entire value can be less than zero is if the (target − List(Min)) term is less than zero. That means the target value is less than List(Min). In that case the target item cannot be in the list since you have eliminated all of the list entries smaller than List(Min).

Now suppose Middle is larger than Max.

```
Min + (target - List(Min)) * ((Max - Min) / (List(Max) - List(Min)) > Max
```

Subtracting Min from both sides you get:

```
(target - List(Min)) * (Max - Min) / (List(Max) - List(Min)) > Max - Min
```

Multiplying both sides by (List(Max) − List(Min))/(Max − Min), this becomes:

```
target - List(Min) > List(Max) - List(Min)
```

Finally by adding List(Min) to both sides you get:

```
target > List(Max)
```

That means the target value is greater than List(Max). In that case the target item cannot be in the list since you have already eliminated all of the list entries larger than List(Max).

Putting these results together, the only way the new value for Middle can be outside the range Min to Max is if the target value is outside the range List(Min) to List(Max). You should use this fact whenever you calculate a new value for Middle. First check to see if the new value is between Min and Max. If it is not, you can conclude that the target item is not in the list and you are done.

The Visual Basic code for the interpolation search algorithm is shown below.

```
Function InterpSearch (target As Long) As Integer
Dim Min As Long
Dim Max As Long
Dim Middle As Long

    Min = 1
    Max = NumItems
    Do While Min <= Max
        ' Prevent division by zero.
        If List(Min) = List(Max) Then
            ' This must be the item (if it's in the list).
            If List(Min) = target Then
                InterpSearch = Min
            Else
                InterpSearch = 0
            End If
            Exit Function
        End If

        ' Compute the dividing point.
        Middle = Min + (target - List(Min)) * ((Max - Min) / (List(Max) - List(Min)))

        ' Make sure we stay in bounds.
        If Middle < Min Or Middle > Max Then
            InterpSearch = 0
            Exit Function
        End If

        If target = List(Middle) Then      ' We found it.
            InterpSearch = Middle
            Exit Function
        ElseIf target < List(Middle) Then ' Search the left half.
            Max = Middle - 1
        Else                              ' Search the right half.
            Min = Middle + 1
        End If
    Loop

    ' If we got to this point, the item is not in the list.
    InterpSearch = 0
End Function
```

While binary search is very fast, interpolation search is much faster. In one set of tests, binary search took between three and six times as long to locate values in a list of 32,000 items. The difference would have been even greater if the data had been stored on a hard disk or other relatively slow device. While interpolation search spends more time calculating than binary search does, that time would be more than made up by the reduced number of disk accesses.

The exact performance you will get depends on the distribution of your data. When the data values are evenly distributed, interpolation search is quite fast. If the values are not so evenly distributed, like in the list 0, 1, 2, 199, 200 from the example above, the algorithm will not perform as well.

String Data

If the data items in your list are strings, you have a couple of options. The easiest thing to do is use a binary search. Binary search compares items to each other directly and there is no reason why it cannot compare strings.

Interpolation search, on the other hand, uses the numeric data values to compute the index where the target item should be. If the items to be sorted are strings, the algorithm cannot use the data values directly to compute the target item's location.

If the strings are short enough, you can encode them as integers, longs, or doubles using techniques discussed in Chapter 8 (see pages 214–217). For example, the string "FAST" would be encoded as 27^3 * ("F" – "A" + 1) + 27^2 * ("A" – "A") + 27 * ("S" – "A" + 1) + ("T" – "A" + 1) = 19,683 * 6 + 729 * 1 + 27 * 19 + 20 = 119,360. Using this technique you can encode strings of length up to three as integers, strings of length up to six as longs, and strings of length up to ten as doubles. Once you have encoded your strings, you can use a normal interpolation search to locate items within the list.

If your strings are too long to encode as doubles, you can still use the string values for interpolation. Begin by finding the first character at which List(Min) and List(Max) differ. Next encode the three following characters of each string and the corresponding three characters of the target value using the techniques from Chapter 8. Then use those values for the interpolation.

For example, suppose you are searching for the string "TARGET" in the list: TABULATE, TANTRUM, TARGET, TATTERED, TAXATION. When Min = 1 and Max = 5, you examine the values TABULATE and THEATER. These values first differ at the second character so you consider the three characters starting with character two. These characters are "ABU" for List(1), "AXA" for List(5), and "ARG" for the target string.

Encoding each of these strings you get 804, 1378, and 1222 respectively. Plugging these values into the calculation of Middle in the interpolation search algorithm, you get:

```
Middle = Min + (target - List(Min)) * ((Max - Min) / (List(Max) - List(Min)))
       = 1 + (1222 - 804) * ((5 - 1) / (1378 - 804))
       = 2.91
```

This rounds to 3 so the next value for Middle is 3. This happens to be the location of TARGET in the list so the search ends.

Hunting and Searching

If you know you will need to locate many items within a list and you suspect that each item will be close to the previous one, a hunting technique can make your search faster. Instead of starting the search by considering the entire list, you can use the value from the previous search to begin searching close to the target's correct position in the list.

Binary Hunt and Search

To begin a binary hunt, compare the target value from the previous search to the new target value. If the new target value is smaller, begin hunting to the left. If the new target is larger, begin hunting to the right.

To hunt to the left, set Min and Max equal to the index returned by the previous search. Then set Min equal to Min − 1 and compare the target value to List(Min). If the target is smaller than List(Min), set Max = Min and Min = Min − 2, and try again. If the target is still smaller, set Max = Min and Min = Min − 4. If that fails, set Max = Min and Min = Min − 8, and so on. Continue setting Max equal to Min and subtracting the next power of 2 from Min until you find a value for Min where List(Min) is less than the target.

Be sure you do not run off the end of the array with Min smaller than the lower array bound. If you reach a point where Min is smaller, set Min equal to the lower array bound. If List(Min) is still larger than the target item, the target is not in the list. Figure 9.3 shows a hunt to the left from the previous target value 44, looking for the new target 17.

A hunt to the right is similar to a hunt to the left. Start by setting Min and Max equal to the index returned by the previous search. Then set Min = Max and Max + 1, Min = Max and Max = Max + 2, Min = Max and Max = Max + 4, and so on until you come to a point where List(Max) is greater than the target. Once again be sure you do not run past the end of the array.

Once you have finished the hunt phase, you will know that the target has index between Min and Max. You can then use a normal binary search to find the target's exact location.

If the new target is close to the old target, a hunt will quickly find the correct values for Min and Max. If the indexes of the new and old targets are P positions apart, the hunt will take roughly log(P) steps to find the correct values for Min and Max.

Suppose you started a normal binary search for the target without a hunt phase. It would take that search about log(NumItems) − log(P) steps to narrow the search down to the point where Min and Max were within P positions of each other.

That means a hunt and search will be faster than a normal binary search if log(P) < log(NumItems) − log(P). Adding log(P) to both sides you get 2 * log(P) < log(NumItems). If you now exponentiate both sides, you have $2^{2 * \log(P)} < 2^{\log(NumItems)}$ or $(2^{\log(P)})^2 <$ NumItems. This simplifies to $P^2 <$ NumItems.

This shows that a hunt and search will be faster if you are pretty sure that the distance between two consecutive searches will be less than the square root of the number of items in the list. If consecutive searches will be for targets that are farther apart, you will probably be better off using a normal binary search.

Interpolative Hunt and Search

You can build upon the techniques of the previous section to perform a hunt using interpolation. Begin as before by comparing the target value from the previous search to the

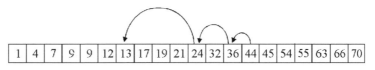

Figure 9.3 Binary hunt for value 17 from value 44.

new target value. If the new target value is smaller, begin a hunt to the left. If the new target is larger, begin a hunt to the right.

To hunt to the left, you would now use interpolation to guess where the value is between the previous target and List(1). But this is the same as a normal interpolation search where Min = 1 and Max is the index returned by the previous search. After a single step the hunt phase is over and you can proceed with a normal interpolation search.

A hunt to the right is similar. Simply set Max = NumItems and Min to the index returned by the previous search. Then continue with a normal interpolation search.

Figure 9.4 shows an interpolation search starting from the previous target value 44, looking for the new target 17.

If the data values are fairly evenly distributed, interpolation search always picks a value near the target in its first step or in any later step. That means starting from a previous value does not improve the algorithm too much. In its first step, without using the result of the previous search, interpolation search will probably pick an index close to the target's true location anyway.

On the other hand, using the previous target value may help protect against unevenness in the data. Since the new target's value is close to the old target's value, an interpolation starting from the previous search's value will have to give a value near the old target's location. This means using the old target as a starting point may provide some benefit.

The previous search's result also bounds the new target's location a little more tightly than the range 1 to NumItems, so the algorithm might save a step or two. This is especially important if the list is stored on a hard disk or other slow device where every disk access counts. If you can save the results of the previous search in memory, you can at least compare the new target to the previous target without an extra disk access.

In summary, using the previous result to start an interpolation search is probably a good idea if you think consecutive targets will be near each other. While you may only save a step or two, you have nothing to lose.

Summary of Search Techniques

If you need to search a list containing a dozen or so items, use an exhaustive search. This will not only be easier to debug and maintain than a more complicated search technique, it will also be faster for such a small list.

If you need to search a larger list, use an interpolation search. As long as your data values are fairly evenly distributed, interpolation search will give you the best performance. If your list is on a hard disk or other slow storage device, the difference between an interpolation search and a different search technique will be quite large.

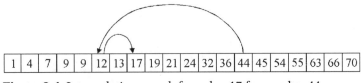

| 1 | 4 | 7 | 9 | 9 | 12 | 13 | 17 | 19 | 21 | 24 | 32 | 36 | 44 | 45 | 54 | 55 | 63 | 66 | 70 |

Figure 9.4 Interpolation search for value 17 from value 44.

Table 9.1 Advantages and Disadvantages of Search Techniques

Technique	*Advantages*	*Disadvantages*
Exhaustive	Simple. Fast for small lists (15 items).	Slow for large lists.
Binary	Fast for large lists. Not dependent on data distribution. Easily handles string data.	More complicated.
Interpolation	Fast for very large lists. Fast for lists on slow devices.	Very complicated. Data must be evenly distributed. Difficult to handle string data.

If the data values are strings, try to encode the values as integers, longs, or doubles. Then you can use an interpolation search to locate items within the list. If the data values are too long to fit in doubles, it may be easiest to use a binary search.

Table 9.1 summarizes the advantages and disadvantages of each of the different search techniques.

Using binary search or interpolation search, you can locate items within a huge list extremely quickly. If the data is evenly distributed, interpolation search would allow you to locate an item in a list containing millions of items with only a few searches.

Such a large list would still be difficult to manage, however, if you need to make changes to the list. Inserting or removing an item from a sorted list requires O(N) time. If the item is at the beginning of the list, this could be quite time consuming, especially if the list is stored on a slow storage device.

If you need to add and remove items from a large list, you should consider using a different data structure. The balanced trees discussed in Chapter 6 allow you to add and remove items in only O(log(N)) time. The drawback to these methods is that they require extra storage space. In a B-tree, for example, as much as half of the tree's entries might be empty.

Hashing schemes, discussed in Chapter 10, allow you to add items even more quickly but they, too, require extra storage space. Hash tables also do not provide information about the ordering of the data. You can add, locate, and remove items from a hash table, but you cannot easily list the items in the table in order.

If your list will never change, a sorted list using interpolation search may be your best choice. If you need to add and remove items from the list, a hash table may provide good performance with a minimum of unused space. If you will need to list the items in order, you might want to consider using a balanced tree. By examining which operations you will need to perform, you can select the algorithm that best suits your needs.

10

Hashing

Basic Concepts

In interpolation search, described in Chapter 9, you use interpolation to quickly locate an item within a list. By comparing a target value with values at known locations in the list, you can guess at what position the target item should be. You essentially create a function that maps the target value to the index where you think the item lies. If your first guess proves incorrect, you use the function again to make a new guess. You continue in this manner until you find the target item.

Hashing uses a similar concept to map items into a *hash table*. Using the value of the target item, you decide where in the table the item should lie.

Suppose you need to store several records that each have unique keys with values between 1 and 100. You could create an array of records with 100 entries and then initialize the keys of each entry to zero. To add a new record to the array, you would simply copy its data into the corresponding position. To add a record with key value 37, for example, you would copy the record into the 37th position in the array. To locate a record with a particular key, you would examine the corresponding array entry. To remove a record you would just reset the corresponding array entry's key value to zero. Using this scheme you can add, locate, and remove items from the array in a single step.

Unfortunately, in real applications the key values do not always fit in nice ranges like 1 to 100. Usually the possible key values span a very wide range. An employee database might use Social Security number as a key. There are 1 billion possible values for nine digit numbers like Social Security numbers. While in theory you could allocate an array with one entry for every possible nine digit number, in reality you probably do not have enough memory or disk space. If each employee record required 1 kilobyte of memory, the array would occupy 1 terabyte (1 million megabytes) of memory. Even if you could allocate this much storage, this scheme would be quite wasteful. Unless your company hired more than 1 million employees, the array would always be more than 99 percent empty.

To work around these problems, hashing schemes map a potentially large number of possible keys into a relatively small hash table. If your company employed 700 workers, you might allocate a hash table with 1,000 entries. Then the hashing scheme would map the 700 employee records into the 1,000 positions in the hash table. The hashing function might map records into entries according to the first three digits of the employees' Social Security numbers. An employee with Social Security number 123-45-6789 would map to table position 123.

Of course if there are more possible key values than there are table entries, some key values must map to the same position in the hash table. For example, the values 123-45-6789 and 123-99-9999 would both map to table position 123. If there are 1 billion possible Social Security numbers and you only have 1,000 positions in the table, then on the average 1 million Social Security numbers must map to each table position.

To handle this potential problem, a hashing scheme must have a *collision resolution policy* that tells what to do when a key maps to a position that is already occupied by another record. The following sections discuss several different methods for handling collisions.

All of the methods discussed follow a similar approach to collision resolution. They first map a record's key to a position in the hash table. If that position is already occupied, the key is mapped to a new position. If that position is also occupied, the key is remapped again until the algorithm finally locates an empty table position. The sequence of positions examined while locating or inserting an item in a hash table is called a *probe sequence*.

To summarize, you need three things to implement hashing:

- A data structure (hash table) to hold the data.
- A hashing function to map key values into table entries.
- A collision resolution policy that tells you what to do when keys map to the same position.

The sections that follow describe several different data structures you can use to store the hash table entries. Each has a corresponding hashing function and one or more possible collision resolution policies. As is the case with most computer algorithms, each method has its strengths and weaknesses. The final section in the chapter summarizes these so you can pick the best hashing technique for your situation.

Chaining

One method for collision resolution is to store records that map to the same table position in linked lists. To add a new record to the table, you use a hash function to decide in which linked list it belongs. You then add the record to that linked list.

Figure 10.1 shows an example of chaining in a hash table that contains ten entries. The hashing function maps a key K into array position K Mod 10. Each position in the array contains a pointer to the first item in a linked list. To add an item to the table, you add it to the appropriate linked list.

To implement this hashing scheme in Visual Basic, you begin much as you would to create any linked list as described in Chapter 2. First you declare a user-defined data type to hold the cells in the linked lists. Then you define an array of these cells. You can write a subroutine NewCell to allocate a new cell from this array when you need it (see Chapter 2 for more details on linked lists).

```
Type HashCell
    Value As Long
    Next As Integer
End Type
Global NumCells As Integer       ' # cells allocated.
Global HashCells() As HashCell   ' The cells.
Global TopGarbage As Integer     ' Top of the garbage list.
```

To initially create the hash table, redimension the HashCells array using a **ReDim** statement. If you want NumLists linked lists in the hash table, you should dimension the HashCells array with the statement **ReDim HashCells(0 To NumLists – 1).** These first NumLists entries will be used as sentinels for the linked lists. This method follows the fixed list top strategy described in Chapter 2.

Initially each of the linked lists is empty so you should initialize the Next fields in these entries to END_OF_LIST.

```
Sub CreateTable (size As Integer)
Dim i As Integer

    NumLists = size
    NumCells = NumLists
    ReDim HashCells (0 To NumLists - 1)
    For i = 0 To NumLists - 1
        HashCells(i).Next = END_OF_LIST
    Next i
    TopGarbage = END_OF_LIST
End Sub
```

To locate an item with key K in the hash table, first compute its hash table entry K Mod NumLists. This gives the index of the sentinel of the linked list in which the item may lie. Then look through this linked list until you find the item or you reach the end of the list.

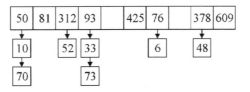

Figure 10.1 Chaining.

```
' Find the item. Return its location or END_OF_LIST
' if it is not present.
Function LocateItem (Value As Long) As Integer
Dim list As Integer
Dim cell As Integer

    ' Get the hash table entry.
    list = Value Mod NumLists

    ' Look through the corresponding linked list.
    cell = HashCells(list).Next
    Do While cell <> END_OF_LIST
        If HashCells(cell).Value = Value Then Exit Do
        cell = HashCells(cell).Next
    Loop
    LocateItem = cell
End Function
```

Functions to add and remove items from the linked lists are similar to the functions described in Chapter 2 (see Chapter 2 for more details).

Advantages and Disadvantages of Chaining

One advantage of chaining is that it is relatively easy to insert or locate items in the table even if the table is completely full. In some of the hashing techniques described in later sections, performance drops drastically when the table is almost full.

You can also easily remove items from a hash table that uses chaining. Simply remove the item's cell from its linked list and add it to the garbage list. In some of the hashing schemes presented in the following sections, it is difficult or impossible to remove items.

One disadvantage of chaining is that, unless the number of linked lists is relatively large, the chains can grow long. Then to insert or locate an item, you will need to search down a fairly long chain. If a hash table contained 10 linked lists and you added 1,000 items to the table, the linked lists would have an average length of 100. Whenever you needed to locate an item in the table, you might have to search through 100 or more linked list entries.

One way you can make the search a little faster is to keep the linked lists in sorted order. Then you can use the techniques presented in Chapter 9 to search for items in a sorted linked list. This allows you to stop searching for a target value if you encounter an item with value larger than the target. On the average, you will need to search only half of a linked list before you either find the item or you can conclude that it is not present.

```
' Find the item. Return its location or END_OF_LIST
' if it is not present.
Function LocateItem (Value As Long) As Integer
Dim list As Integer
Dim cell As Integer

    ' Get the hash table entry.
    list = Value Mod NumLists

    ' Look through the corresponding linked list.
    cell = HashCells(list).Next
```

```
        Do While cell <> END_OF_LIST
            If HashCells(cell).Value >= Value Then Exit Do
            cell = HashCells(cell).Next
        Loop


        ' See if we found the item.
        If cell = END_OF_LIST Then
            LocateItem = END_OF_LIST
        ElseIf Cells(cell).Value <> target Then
            LocateItem = END_OF_LIST
        Else
            LocateItem = cell
        End If
End Function
```

While keeping the lists sorted makes searches a little faster, it does not address the real problem. The reason the chains are long is that the table is too full. A better, though more time consuming solution, is to create a larger hash table and rehash the items into the new table so the new linked lists are smaller. This can be a lot of work, particularly if the lists are stored on a hard disk or other slow device rather than in memory.

Example program CHAIN implements a hash table with chaining. Enter the number of lists you want in the Table Creation area on the form. Check the Sort Lists box if you want the program to use sorted chains. Then press the Create Table button to create the hash table. You can enter new values in this section and press the Create Table button at any time to create a new hash table.

Since hash tables are often most interesting when they contain lots of items, program CHAIN allows you to create many random items at the same time. Fill in the number of items you want to create and the maximum value those items should have in the Random Items area. Then press the Create Items button and the program will add the random items to the hash table.

Finally, enter a value in the Search area. If you then press the Add button, the program will insert the item in the hash table if it is not already there. If you press the Find button, the program will locate the item in the table.

After finishing an add or find operation, the program displays the status of the operation in a status label at the bottom of the form. This label tells whether or not the operation succeeded and shows the number of items the program examined during the operation.

The status label also tells you the current average length of a successful probe sequence (when the item is in the table) and an unsuccessful probe sequence (when the item is not in the table). The program calculates this average by searching for every number between one and the largest number currently in the hash table, and computing the average probe sequence length.

Buckets

Another way to handle collisions is to allocate a number of buckets, each of which can hold several data items. To add an item to the table, you map the item into a bucket and then insert the item in that bucket. If the bucket is full, use an overflow policy to deal with the new item.

Probably the simplest overflow policy is to place all overflowed items into overflow buckets at the end of the array of "normal" buckets. This makes it easy to extend the hash table when necessary. When you need more overflow buckets, you simply redimension the array of buckets to make it larger and create new overflow buckets at the end.

To add a new item K to a hash table containing five buckets, first try to place it in bucket number K Mod 5. If that bucket is full, place it in an overflow bucket.

To locate an item K in the table, calculate K Mod 5 to see which bucket the item belongs in. Then search that bucket. If the item does not appear in the bucket and the bucket is not full, then the item is not present in the hash table. If the item does not appear in the bucket and the bucket is full, search the overflow buckets.

Figure 10.2 shows five buckets numbered 0 through 4 and one overflow bucket. Each of the buckets can hold five items. In this example the following items have been added to the hash table in order: 50, 13, 10, 72, 25, 46, 68, 30, 99, 85, 93, 65, 70. When items 65 and 70 were added, the buckets in which they belonged were already full so they were placed in the first overflow bucket.

To implement a bucket hashing scheme in Visual Basic, you can use a 2-dimensional array to hold the buckets. If you want NumBuckets buckets of size BucketSize, allocate the buckets with the statement **ReDim TheBuckets(0 To BucketSize − 1, 0 To Num-Buckets − 1).** The second dimension is the one that indicates the bucket number. It may seem more natural to use the first dimension to hold the bucket number, but you may need to change the number of buckets later to add overflow buckets. Visual Basic's **ReDim** statement only allows you to change the size of the last dimension in an array, so the bucket number must come last.

To locate an item K, calculate the bucket number K Mod NumBuckets. Then search that bucket until you find the item, an empty bucket entry, or the end of the bucket. If you find the item, you are done. If you find an unused entry, you know the item is not in the hash table and you are also done. If you search the entire bucket and do not find the item or an unused entry, search the overflow buckets.

```
Global Const HASH_FOUND = 0
Global Const HASH_NOT_FOUND = 1


' Locate the item. Return:
'       HASH_FOUND      The item was found
'       HASH_NOT_FOUND  The item is not in the tableFunction
LocateItem (Value As Long, bucket As Integer, pos As Integer) As _
Integer
    ' See what bucket it belongs in.
```

Buckets

0	1	2	3	4		Overflow
50	46	72	13	99		65
10			68			70
25			93			
30						
85						

Figure 10.2 Hashing with buckets.

```
    bucket = (Value Mod NumBuckets)

    ' Look for the item or an empty position.
    For pos = 0 To BucketSize - 1
        If TheBuckets(pos, bucket).Value = empty Then
            LocateItem = HASH_NOT_FOUND ' Not here.
            Exit Function
        End If
        If TheBuckets(pos, bucket).Value = Value Then
            LocateItem = HASH_FOUND    ' We found it.
            Exit Function
        End If
    Next pos

    ' Check the overflow buckets
    For bucket = NumBuckets To MaxOverflow
        For pos = 0 To BucketSize - 1
            If TheBuckets(pos, bucket).Value = empty Then
                LocateItem = HASH_NOT_FOUND ' Not here.
                Exit Function
            End If
            If TheBuckets(pos, bucket).Value = Value Then
                LocateItem = HASH_FOUND     ' We found it.
                Exit Function
            End If
        Next pos
    Next bucket

    ' We still haven't found the item.
    LocateItem = HASH_NOT_FOUND
End Function
```

Example program BUCKET demonstrates this sort of scheme. This program is very similar to program CHAIN except it uses hashing with buckets instead of chaining.

Hash Tables on Disk

Most storage devices, like tape drives, floppy drives, and hard disks, can retrieve large chunks of data a block at a time. Usually this block is 512 or 1,024 bytes long. It takes the disk drive no more time to read one of these blocks of data than it takes it to read a single byte.

If you have a large hash table stored on a hard disk, you can use this fact to improve performance. Accessing data on a disk takes much longer than accessing data in memory. If you load all of the items in a bucket at once, you may be able to read them all in a single disk access. Once the items are loaded into memory, you can examine them much more quickly than you could if you had to read them one at a time from the disk.

If you use a **For** loop to read each item from the disk one at a time, Visual Basic will need to access the disk separately for each item. If you use a **Get** statement to read the entire bucket at once, Visual Basic can read the data one bucket at a time. This may require only a single disk access so it will be much faster.

The **Get** statement cannot read array variables, however, so you need to rearrange the data structure a bit. The **Get** statement can read user-defined types, so you can create a user-defined type to represent a bucket. This type will contain an array of data items. Since you cannot redimension an array within a user-defined type at run time, you will need to decide how many items will be in the bucket ahead of time. This gives you a little less flexibility than you had before in sizing the buckets.

```
Global Const BucketSize = 10      ' Items per bucket.
Global Const MaxItem = 9          ' BucketSize - 1.

Type ItemType
    Value As Long
End Type
Global Const ITEM_SIZE = 4           ' Size of this type.

Type BucketType
    Item(0 To MaxItem) As ItemType
End Type
Global Const BUCKET_SIZE = BucketSize * ITEM_SIZE
```

Before you read data from the hash file, open the data file in **Random** mode.

```
Open filename For Random As #DataFile
```

For convenience you can write functions to read and write buckets. These functions read and write data from a global variable TheBucket which holds the data for a single bucket. Once you have loaded the data into this variable, you can search the items within the bucket in memory.

Since random access files start numbering records at one not zero, these functions must add one to the hash table's bucket number before reading data from the file. The hash table's bucket number zero, for example, is stored in file record number one.

```
Sub GetBucket (num As Integer)
    Get #DataFile, num + 1, TheBucket
End Sub

Sub PutBucket (num As Integer)
    Put #DataFile, num + 1, TheBucket
End Sub
```

Using functions GetBucket and PutBucket, you can rewrite the hash table search routine to read records from a file.

```
Function LocateItem (Value As Long, bucket As Integer, pos As _
Integer) As Integer
Dim new_value As Long

    ' See what bucket it belongs in.
    bucket = (Value Mod NumBuckets)
    GetBucket bucket

    ' Look for the item or an empty position.
    For pos = 0 To MaxItem
        new_value = TheBucket.Item(pos).Value
        If new_value = UNUSED Then
            LocateItem = HASH_NOT_FOUND ' Not here.
            Exit Function
        End If
        If new_value = Value Then
```

```
            LocateItem = HASH_FOUND      ' We found it.
            Exit Function
        End If
    Next pos


    ' Check the overflow buckets
    For bucket = NumBuckets To MaxOverflow
        GetBucket bucket

        For pos = 0 To MaxItem
            new_value = TheBucket.Item(pos).Value
            If new_value = UNUSED Then
                LocateItem = HASH_NOT_FOUND ' Not here.
                Exit Function
            End If
            If new_value = Value Then
                LocateItem = HASH_FOUND      ' We found it.
                Exit Function
            End If
        Next pos
    Next bucket


    ' We still haven't found the item.
    LocateItem = HASH_NOT_FOUND
End Function
```

Example program BUCKET2 demonstrates a bucket hashing scheme where all of the items are stored on disk. This program is similar to program BUCKET. In addition to the status information presented by program BUCKET, this program also tells you how many buckets it examines each time it adds or locates an item. Since bucket accesses occur on disk while item accesses occur in memory, the number of buckets accessed is much more important in determining the program's run time than the number of items examined.

Each bucket in program BUCKET2 can hold up to ten items. This makes it easy for you to fill the buckets until they overflow. In a real program you should try to fit as many items as possible into a bucket while keeping the bucket size a multiple of your disk drive's natural block size.

For example, you might decide to read and write data in blocks of 1,024 bytes. If your data items had a size of 44 bytes, you could fit 23 data items into one bucket while keeping the bucket size under 1,024 bytes.

```
Global Const BucketSize = 23     ' Items per bucket.
Global Const MaxItem = 22        ' BucketSize - 1.

Type ItemType
    LastName As String * 20          ' 20 bytes.
    FirstName As String * 20         ' 20 bytes.
    EmployeeId As Integer            ' 2 bytes (this is the key).
End Type
Global Const ITEM_SIZE = 44          ' Size of this type.


Type BucketType
    Item(0 To MaxItem) As ItemType
End Type
Global Const BUCKET_SIZE = BucketSize * ITEM_SIZE
```

Putting more items in each bucket allows you to read more data in a single disk access. It also allows the table to hold more items before you need to use overflow buckets. Since accessing overflow buckets requires extra disk accesses, you should try to avoid using them whenever possible.

On the other hand, if the buckets are large they may contain a lot of unused entries. If the data items are not evenly distributed among the buckets, some buckets may overflow while others are nearly empty. A different arrangement with more buckets that were smaller might reduce this problem. While some data items would still overflow and some buckets would be nearly empty, the nearly empty buckets would be smaller so they would not contain as many unused entries.

Figure 10.3 shows two bucket arrangements holding the same data. The arrangement on the top uses five buckets containing five items each. It holds all of the data with no overflow buckets and 12 unused item entries. The arrangement on the bottom uses ten buckets containing two items each. It holds the items with one overflow bucket and contains nine unused item entries.

This is an example of a space versus time tradeoff. In the first arrangement, all of the items are located in normal (non-overflow) buckets so you can locate them all quickly. The second arrangement saves space but places some of the items in overflow buckets which take longer to access.

Bucket Chaining

A slightly different way to manage full buckets is to chain them to overflow buckets. Each full bucket gets its own set of overflow buckets rather than having all of the overflow buckets shared. When you search for an item in a full bucket, you will not need to examine any items that have overflowed from other buckets. If many buckets have overflowed, this could save quite a bit of time.

Figure 10.4 shows the same data in two different hashing schemes. In the top arrangement, items that overflow are added to common overflow buckets. Notice that to locate the items 32 or 30 you would need to access three buckets. First you would exam-

Buckets

0	1	2	3	4
50	46	72	18	
10		57	68	
25			93	
35			28	
65			73	

Buckets

0	1	2	3	4	5	6	7	8	9	Overflow
50		72	93		25	46	57	18		28
10			73		35			68		65

Figure 10.3 Two different bucket arrangements.

ine the bucket in which the item normally belongs. When you did not find the item in that bucket, you would examine the first overflow bucket. When you still did not locate the item, you would examine the second overflow bucket where you would finally find the item.

In the bottom arrangement, full buckets are linked to their own overflow buckets. In this arrangement you can locate every item after accessing at most two buckets. As before, you start by examining the bucket in which the item normally belongs. If you do not find the item there, you examine that bucket's linked list of overflow buckets. In this example you would only need to check one overflow bucket to find the item you wanted.

If the hash table contains many items in its overflow buckets, chaining the overflow buckets may save you a lot of time. For example, suppose you have a moderately large hash table containing 1,000 buckets holding 10 items each. Suppose also that you have 1,000 items in overflow buckets. To hold all of those overflow items, you would need 100 overflow buckets. To locate one of the last items in the overflow buckets you would have to examine 101 buckets.

Even worse, suppose you wanted to locate an item K that is not in the table but which maps to a bucket that is full. You would need to search all 100 overflow buckets before you learned that the item was not in the table. If your program often searches for items that are not in the table, it will spend a huge amount of time looking through the overflow buckets.

If you chain overflow buckets, and if the data keys are reasonably distributed, you will be able to locate items much more quickly. If the largest number of items that have overflowed out of any single bucket is ten, you will be able to store all of the overflow for each bucket in a single overflow bucket. In that case you will be able to locate any item, or determine that an item is not in the table, by examining at most two buckets.

On the other hand, if the hash table is just a little too full, many buckets may have overflow buckets containing only one or two items. To continue this example, suppose 11 items mapped into each bucket. Since each bucket can hold only ten items, every regular bucket would need an overflow bucket. In this case you would need 1,000 overflow buckets, each containing a single item. Between them all, these overflow buckets would contain 900 unused entries.

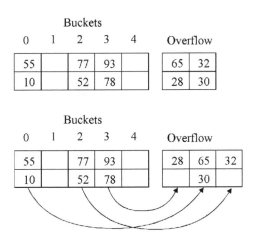

Figure 10.4 Linked overflow buckets.

This is another example of a space versus time tradeoff. Chaining buckets can allow you to add and locate items more quickly, but it may also fill the hash table with unused space. Of course you could probably avoid the problem completely by creating a new, larger hash table and rehashing all of the table entries.

Removing Items

While it is not as easy to remove items from buckets as it is to remove them from chains, it is still possible. First, locate the item you want to remove in the hash table. Then, if the bucket it is in is not full, replace the target item with the last item in the bucket. This will ensure that all of the non-empty bucket entries are stored at the front of the bucket. Later, when you are searching for an item in the bucket, if you find an unused item you can assume that the item is not in the table.

If the bucket containing the target item is full, you must search the overflow buckets to find an item that can replace the target item in this bucket. If none of the items in the overflow buckets belong in this bucket, replace the target item with the last item in the bucket, leaving the bucket's last entry empty.

Otherwise, if there is an item in the overflow buckets that belongs in this bucket, move the chosen overflow item into the target bucket in place of the target item. That will leave a hole in the overflow bucket, but that is easy to fix. Just take the last item from the last overflow bucket and move it to fill in the hole.

Figure 10.5 illustrates the process of removing an item from a full bucket. First the item 24 is removed from bucket 0.

Since bucket 0 was full, you must look for an item in the overflow buckets that you could move into bucket 0. In this case bucket 0 holds all of the even items so any even item in the overflow buckets will do. The first even item in the overflow buckets is item 14 so you should replace item 24 in bucket 0 with item 14.

That leaves a hole in the third position in the first overflow bucket. Fill in the hole by replacing item 14 with the last item in the last overflow bucket, in this case item 79. At this point the hash table is up to date.

An alternative method for removing an item is to mark the item as having been removed but to leave it in its bucket. To locate items in that bucket, you should ignore the removed item and go on to examine the other items in the bucket. Later, when you are adding a new item to that bucket, you can reuse the removed item's position.

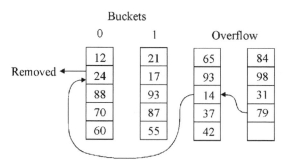

Figure 10.5 Removing an item from a bucket.

Marking an item as removed is faster and easier than actually removing it from the hash table, but eventually the table might become full of unused entries. If you add a bunch of items to the hash table and then remove most of them in first-in-first-out order, the buckets will become "bottom heavy." Most of the real data will be in the bottom of the buckets and in the overflow buckets. While it will be easy to add new items to the table, you will waste a fair amount of time skipping removed entries when you search for an item.

As a compromise, when you remove an item from a bucket, you can move the last item in the bucket into the emptied position and then mark the last item in the bucket as removed. Then when you search a bucket, you can stop looking through that bucket if you encounter an item that has been marked as removed. You would then search the overflow buckets if there are any.

Figure 10.6 shows the same data as Figure 10.5 after the item 24 has been removed. In this case the item 24 has been replaced with item 60, the last item in the bucket. The last position in the bucket has been marked as removed.

Advantages and Disadvantages of Buckets

Adding or locating an item in a hash table with buckets is relatively fast, even when the table is completely full. In fact, a hash table using buckets will usually be faster than a hash table using chaining (chaining from the previous section—not bucket chaining). If the hash table is stored on a hard disk, a bucket scheme can read an entire bucket of data in one disk access. With chaining, the next item in a chain may not be anywhere near the previous one on the disk. You would need one disk access every time you needed to examine an item.

Removing an item from a table using buckets is harder than removing an item from a table that uses chaining. To remove an item from a bucket that is full, you may need to examine all of the overflow buckets to find a suitable replacement item.

A final advantage to a hash table that uses buckets is that it is easy to extend the table when it becomes full. When all of the overflow buckets are full, you simply redimension the bucket array and create a new overflow bucket at the end.

If you extend the table in this way too many times, a large fraction of the data will eventually be stored in the overflow buckets. Then to find or insert an item, you will need to examine many buckets and performance will suffer. In that case it may be better to create a new hash table with more initial data buckets and rehash the items than to expand the overfull table.

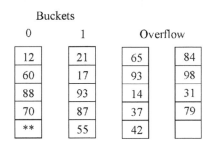

Figure 10.6 Marking an item as removed.

Open Addressing

Sometimes the data items you need to store will be too big to fit conveniently in buckets. If you needed a list of 1,000 items, each occupying 1Mb of disk space, it would be difficult to use buckets that could hold more than one or two items. If the buckets only hold one or two items, you will need to examine many buckets to add or locate an item.

In open addressing you use a hashing function to map data items individually into positions in an array. For example, you could use an array with dimensions 0 to 99 for a hash table. Then for a hashing function you could map item K to array position K Mod 100. You would insert the item 1,723 in the table at position 23. Later, if you wanted to locate item 1,723, you would look for it at position 23.

Different open addressing schemes use different methods for generating probe sequences. The following sections examine three of the more important methods: linear probing, quadratic probing, and pseudo-random probing.

Linear Probing

When you map a new item into an array position that is already in use, you could simply look through the array from that point until you came to an unoccupied position. This collision resolution policy is called *linear probing* because you search through the table in a linear fashion.

Consider again the example where you have an array dimensioned 0 to 99 and the hashing function maps K to position K Mod 100. To insert the item 1,723, you would first examine array position 23. If that position was in use, you would try position 24. If it, too, was in use you would try positions 25, 26, 27, and so on until you found an array entry that was not yet occupied.

To insert a new item into a hash table, you follow that item's probe sequence using linear probing until you find an unused entry. To locate an item in the table, you follow the item's probe sequence until you find the item or you find an unused entry. If you find an unused entry first, you know that the item is not in the hash table.

You could write a combined hashing and probing function as:

```
Hash(K, P) = (K + P) Mod 100        where P = 0, 1, 2, ...
```

Here P is the number of the item in the probe sequence for K. In other words, to hash item K you would try the entries Hash(K, 0), Hash(K, 1), Hash(K, 2), . . . until you found an empty position in the table.

You can generalize this idea to build a table of size N using an array dimensioned from 0 to N – 1 and then hash items into the table using the function:

```
Hash(K, P) = (K + P) Mod N        where P = 0, 1, 2, ...
```

The Visual Basic source code for locating an item using linear probing is:

```
Function LocateItem (Value As Long, position As Integer) As _
Integer
Dim num_probes As Integer

    num_probes = 1
    position = (Value Mod NumEntries)
```

```
    Do
        ' We found it.
        If HashTable(position) = Value Then
            LocateItem = HASH_FOUND
            Exit Function
        End If


        ' The item's not here.
        If HashTable(position) = UNUSED Or num_probes >= _
NumEntries Then
            LocateItem = HASH_NOT_FOUND
            Exit Function
        End If


        position = (position + 1) Mod NumEntries
        num_probes = num_probes + 1
    Loop
End Function
```

Example program LINEAR demonstrates a linear probing hash scheme. By filling in the Table Size field and pressing the Create Table button, you can create hash tables of different sizes. You can then enter the value of an item and press the Add or Find button to insert or locate the item in the table.

To add several random values to the table all at once, enter the number of items you want to add and the maximum value they should have in the Random Items area. Then press the Create Items button and the program will add the items to the table.

After the program completes each operation, it displays the status of the operation (whether it succeeded or not) and the length of the probe sequence it just followed. The program also displays the average lengths of a successful and an unsuccessful probe sequence. The program computes the average probe sequence lengths by searching for every value between 1 and the largest value in the table at that time.

Table 10.1 shows the average lengths of successful and unsuccessful probe sequences produced by program LINEAR for a table with 100 entries and items in the range 1 to 1,000. The table shows that the algorithm's performance degrades as the table becomes full. Whether the performance is acceptable to you depends on how you use the table. If your program spends most of its time searching for values that are in the table, performance will be reasonably good even when the table is quite full. If your program often searches for values that are not in the table, performance will be poor if the table is too full.

As a rule, hashing provides reasonable performance without too much wasted space when the table is 50 to 75 percent full. If the table is more than 75 percent full, performance suffers. If the table is less than 50 percent full, the table occupies more space than it really needs. This makes hashing a good example of a space versus time tradeoff. By making a hash table larger, you can decrease the time needed to insert and locate items.

Linear probing has an unfortunate *primary clustering* property. After you have inserted many items into the table, the items will tend to cluster together to form large groups. When you add more items, the new items will tend to collide with the clusters. Then you will need to search over the length of the cluster before you find an empty position in the table.

To see how clusters form, suppose you begin with an empty hash table that can hold N entries. If you pick a number at random and insert it into the table, there will be a 1/N chance that the item will end up in any given position P in the table.

Table 10.1 Lengths of Successful and Unsuccessful Probe Sequences

Entries Used	Successful	Unsuccessful
10	1.10	1.12
20	1.15	1.26
30	1.20	1.50
40	1.35	1.83
50	1.92	2.64
60	2.03	3.35
70	2.61	5.17
80	3.41	8.00
90	3.81	10.74
100	6.51	100.00

When you insert a second randomly chosen item, there is a 1/N chance that the item will map to the same position P. This collision will force you to put the item in position P + 1. There is also a 1/N chance that the item will map directly to position P + 1 and a 1/N chance that the item will map to position P − 1. In all three of these cases, the new item will end up next to the previously inserted item. There is a total chance of 3/N that the new item will wind up next to the previous one, starting a small cluster. These odds are slightly greater than the 1/N odds that the item will end up in any other particular position.

Once a cluster starts to grow, the chances of subsequent items landing on or next to the cluster increase. When a cluster contains 2 items, there will be a 4/N chance that the next item will add to the cluster. When it contains 4 items, there will be a 6/N chance that the cluster will grow, and so on.

Worse still, once a cluster starts to grow it will continue to grow until it bumps into the next cluster. The two clusters will join to form an even larger cluster that will grow even faster, meet other clusters, and form still larger clusters.

Ideally if a hash table is half full, the items in the table will occupy every other array position. Then there would be a 50 percent chance that the next item added would immediately find an empty position. There would also be a 50 percent chance that it would find an empty position after examining only two table positions. The average probe sequence length would be 0.5 * 1 + 0.5 * 2 = 1.5.

In the worst case all of the items in the table will be grouped together in one giant cluster. Then there would still be a 50 percent chance that the next item added would immediately find an unused position. When it did not, however, it would take a much longer time to find an open position. If the item landed on the first position in the cluster, it would have to move over all of the entries in the cluster before it found an open position. It would take much longer to insert an item in this arrangement than it would if the items were evenly spaced throughout the hash table.

In practice the amount of clustering will be somewhere between these extremes. You can use program LINEAR to see the clustering effect. Run the program and build a hash table with 100 entries. Then randomly add 50 items with values up to 1,000. You should notice that several clusters have formed. In one test 38 of the 50 items were part of clusters.

If you add another 25 items to the table, most of the items should be part of clusters. In another test 70 of the 75 items were grouped in clusters.

Ordered Linear Probing

When you perform an exhaustive search of a sorted list, you can stop whenever you find an item with value greater than the target value. Since you have passed the position where the target item would be if it were in the list, the item must not be present.

You can use a similar idea when searching a hash table. Suppose you can arrange the items in the hash table so the values along every probe sequence are arranged in increasing order. Then as you follow a probe sequence looking for an item, you can stop if you ever find an item with value greater than the target value. In that case you would have passed the position where the item belongs in the table so you know the item is not there.

```
Function LocateItem (Value As Long, position As Integer) As _
Integer
Dim num_probes As Integer

    num_probes = 1
    position = (Value Mod NumEntries)
    Do
        ' We either found it or it's not here.
        If HashTable(position) >= Value Then Exit Do

        position = (position + 1) Mod NumEntries
        num_probes = num_probes + 1

        ' The item's not here.
        If num_probes > NumEntries Then Exit Do
    Loop
    If HashTable(position) = Value Then
        LocateItem = HASH_FOUND
    Else
        LocateItem = HASH_NOT_FOUND
    End If
End Function
```

For this method to work, you must arrange the items in the hash table so you encounter them in increasing order whenever you follow a probe sequence. There is a fairly simple method for inserting items into the hash table that guarantees this arrangement.

When you insert a new item into the table, follow its probe sequence. If you find an empty position, insert the item at that position and you are done. If you come to an item with value larger than the item you are inserting, swap the two items. Then follow the probe sequence for the larger item to find a new location for it in the table. As you search for a new position for the larger item, you may come to another item that is larger still. You would then swap those items and go on to find a new location for the new, larger item. Continue this process, possibly swapping several items, until you eventually find an empty position to hold the item you are currently placing. The Visual Basic code for inserting an item in an ordered hash table is:

```
' Insert the item into the table. Return:
'       HASH_FOUND      if the item was already there
```

```
'       HASH_INSERTED   if we inserted the item
'       HASH_TABLE_FULL if the table was full
Function InsertItem (Value As Long, position As Integer) As _
Integer
Dim num_probes As Integer
Dim new_value As Long

    num_probes = 1
    position = (Value Mod NumEntries)
    Do
        new_value = HashTable(position)
        ' If we found the value, we're done.
        If new_value = Value Then
            InsertItem = HASH_FOUND
            Exit Function
        End If

        ' If the entry is empty, this is where it belongs.
        If new_value = UNUSED Then
            HashTable(position) = Value
            InsertItem = HASH_INSERTED
            Exit Function
        End If

        ' If the table entry is larger than the value, swap
        ' them and continue.
        If new_value > Value Then
            HashTable(position) = Value
            Value = new_value
        End If

        position = (position + 1) Mod NumEntries
        num_probes = num_probes + 1

        If num_probes > NumEntries Then
            ' The entry is not there and the table is full.
            position = -1
            InsertItem = HASH_TABLE_FULL
            Exit Function
        End If
    Loop
End Function
```

Example program ORDERED manages a hash table using ordered linear probing. It is identical to program LINEAR except it uses an ordered hash table.

Table 10.2 shows average probe sequence lengths of successful and unsuccessful searches using linear and ordered linear probing. The average lengths of successful searches are similar for the two methods. For unsuccessful searches, however, ordered probing is significantly faster. The difference is particularly noticeable when the hash table is more than about 70 percent full.

Both methods require the same number of steps to insert a new item. To add item K to the table, each method starts at position (K Mod NumEntries) and moves through the hash table until it finds an empty position. During ordered hashing you may need to swap the item you are inserting with others in its probe sequence. If the items are large records, this may be quite time consuming, particularly if the records are stored on a disk or other slow storage device.

Table 10.2 Lengths of Searches Using Linear and Ordered Linear Probing

Entries Used	Linear Successful	Linear Unsuccessful	Ordered Successful	Ordered Unsuccessful
10	1.10	1.12	1.10	1.04
20	1.15	1.26	1.10	1.09
30	1.20	1.50	1.23	1.13
40	1.35	1.83	1.38	1.23
50	1.92	2.64	1.36	1.35
60	2.03	3.35	1.53	1.56
70	2.61	5.17	1.64	1.76
80	3.41	8.00	2.04	2.18
90	3.81	10.74	3.42	3.88
100	6.51	100.00	6.16	6.20

Ordered linear probing is definitely a better choice if you expect your program to make many unsuccessful searches. If your program will usually search for items that are in the hash table, or if the items in the table are large and difficult to move, you may get better performance using unordered linear probing.

Quadratic Probing

One way to reduce primary clustering is to use a hashing function like this:

```
Hash(K, P) = (K + P²) Mod N        where P = 0, 1, 2, ...
```

Suppose, while inserting an item into a hash table, you map the item into a cluster of other items. If the item maps to a position near the beginning of the cluster, you will have several more collisions before you find an empty position for the item. As the parameter P in the probe function grows, the value of this function changes quickly. That means the final position where you place the item will probably not be adjacent to the cluster.

Figure 10.7 shows a hash table containing a large cluster of items. It also shows the probe sequences that result when you try to insert two different items into positions occupied by the cluster. Both of these probe sequences end in a final position that is not adjacent to the cluster, so the cluster does not grow when you insert these items.

The Visual Basic code for locating an item using quadratic probing is:

```
Function LocateItem (value As Long, position As Integer) As _
Integer
```

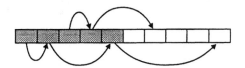

Figure 10.7 Quadratic probing.

```
Dim num_probes As Integer

    num_probes = 1
    position = (value Mod NumEntries)
    Do
        ' We found it.
        If HashTable(position) = value Then
            LocateItem = HASH_FOUND
            Exit Function
        End If


        ' The item's not here.
        If HashTable(position) = UNUSED Or num_probes >= _
NumEntries Then
            LocateItem = HASH_NOT_FOUND
            Exit Function
        End If


        position = (value + num_probes * CLng(num_probes)) Mod _
NumEntries
        num_probes = num_probes + 1
    Loop
End Function
```

Example program QUAD demonstrates quadratic probing. It is similar to program LINEAR except it uses quadratic rather than linear probing.

Table 10.3 shows average probe sequence lengths produced by programs LINEAR and QUAD for a hash table with 100 entries and items ranging in value from 1 to 1,000. Quadratic probing generally gives better results than linear probing.

Quadratic probing does have its disadvantages. Because of the way in which the probe sequence is generated, you cannot guarantee that the probe sequence will visit every item in the table. That means you may sometimes be unable to insert an item into a hash table even though the table is not completely full.

Consider a small example where the hash table holds only 6 entries. The probe sequence for the number 3 would be:

Table 10.3 Lengths of Searches Using Linear and Quadratic Probing

Entries Used	*Linear Successful*	*Linear Unsuccessful*	*Quadratic Successful*	*Quadratic Unsuccessful*
10	1.10	1.12	1.00	1.11
20	1.15	1.26	1.10	1.21
30	1.20	1.50	1.33	1.44
40	1.35	1.83	1.77	1.75
50	1.92	2.64	1.80	2.14
60	2.03	3.35	1.88	2.67
70	2.61	5.17	2.09	3.43
80	3.41	8.00	2.30	5.05
90	3.81	10.74	2.77	15.03
100	6.51	100.00	3.79	101.00

```
3
3 +  1² =    4 = 4 (Mod 6)
3 +  2² =    7 = 1 (Mod 6)
3 +  3² =   12 = 0 (Mod 6)
3 +  4² =   19 = 1 (Mod 6)
3 +  5² =   28 = 4 (Mod 6)
3 +  6² =   39 = 3 (Mod 6)
3 +  7² =   52 = 4 (Mod 6)
3 +  8² =   67 = 1 (Mod 6)
3 +  9² =   84 = 0 (Mod 6)
3 + 10² =  103 = 1 (Mod 6)
Etc.
```

In this probe sequence you visit the positions 1 and 4 twice each before you visit the position 3, and you never visit positions 2 and 5. To see this effect, create a 6 entry hash table using program QUAD. Then add the items 1, 3, 4, 6, and 9. The program will tell you that the table is full even though there are two unused entries. The probe sequence for the item 9 does not visit positions 2 and 5 so the program cannot insert the new item in the table.

It can be shown that a quadratic probe sequence will visit at least N/2 of the table entries if the size of the table N is prime. While this guarantees some level of performance, it may still become a problem when the table is almost full. Since performance drops when the table is almost full anyway, you would probably be better off enlarging the hash table rather than worrying about not being able to find the last empty entries.

A more subtle problem with quadratic probing is that, while it eliminates primary clustering, it allows a similar problem called *secondary clustering*. If two items initially hash to the same location, they will follow the same probe sequence. If many items initially map to the same table location, they will form a secondary cluster that is spread out within the hash table. When a new item with the same value appears, it will have to follow a long probe sequence before it gets past the other items in the secondary cluster.

Figure 10.8 shows a hash table that can hold 10 entries. The table contains the items 2, 12, 22, and 32, all of which map initially to position 2. If you now try to add the item 42 to the table, you will need to follow a long probe sequence that visits each of these other items' positions before you find an empty position.

Pseudo-Random Probing

Clustering occurs when items that hit a cluster join the cluster. Secondary clustering occurs when items that initially collide at the same location follow the same probe sequence to form a secondary cluster spread through the hash table. You can eliminate both of these effects if you can make different items follow different probe sequences even if they initially map to the same position.

One simple way to do this is to use a pseudo-random number generator to provide the probe sequence. To compute the probe sequence of an item, use the item's value to ini-

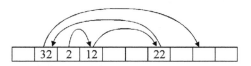

Figure 10.8 Secondary clustering.

tialize a random number generator. Then use the successive numbers produced by the random number generator to build the probe sequence. This is called *pseudo-random probing*.

Later, when you want to locate an item in the hash table, reinitialize the random number generator using the item's value. Then the random number generator will produce the same sequence of numbers that you used to insert the item into the table. You can use this sequence of random numbers to follow the same probe sequence and find the item.

If your random number generator is good, different item values will produce different random numbers and therefore different probe sequences. Even if two item values initially map to the same position, the next positions in their probe sequences will probably be different. In this case your hash table will not suffer from clustering or secondary clustering.

In Visual Basic the **Randomize** statement initializes the random number generator **Rnd.** Unfortunately it does not initialize the random number generator to the same state whenever you pass it the same parameter. You can pass an item's value to **Randomize** and insert the item into the hash table. Later, when you pass the item's value to **Randomize** again, **Rnd** produces a different set of random numbers so you get a different probe sequence and you cannot find the number in the table.

The easiest way to solve this problem is to write a simple random number generator of your own:

```
Global Const UNUSED = -2147483648


' Set seed <> UNUSED to initialize the generator.
'
' Set seed = UNUSED to produce the next pseudo-random
' number in the sequence.
Function SimpleRand (ByVal seed As Long) As Double
Const MODULUS = 714025#
Const MULTIPLIER = 1366#
Const INCREMENT = 150889#


Static prev_value As Long

    ' Initialize/reinitialize
    If seed <> UNUSED Then prev_value = seed
    prev_value = (MULTIPLIER * prev_value + INCREMENT) Mod MODULUS
    SimpleRand = CDbl(prev_value) / MODULUS
End Function
```

When you want to insert or find an item in the hash table, pass the item's value into SimpleRand to initialize the random number generator. To get random values once the generator has been initialized, pass the value UNUSED to the routine.

The Visual Basic code for locating an item using pseudo-random probing is:

```
Function LocateItem (value As Long, position As Integer) As _
Integer
Dim num_probes As Integer

    num_probes = 1
    position = Int(SimpleRand(value) * NumEntries)
    Do
```

```
      ' We found it.
      If HashTable(position) = value Then
          LocateItem = HASH_FOUND
          Exit Function
      End If

      ' The item's not here.
      If HashTable(position) = UNUSED Or num_probes >= _
NumEntries Then
          LocateItem = HASH_NOT_FOUND
          Exit Function
      End If

      position = Int(SimpleRand(UNUSED) * NumEntries)
      num_probes = num_probes + 1
    Loop
End Function
```

Example program RAND demonstrates pseudo-random probing. It is the same as programs LINEAR and QUAD except it uses pseudo-random rather than linear or quadratic probing.

Table 10.4 shows approximate average probe sequence lengths produced by programs QUAD and RAND for a hash table with 100 entries and items ranging from 1 to 1,000. Pseudo-random probing generally gives the best results though the difference between quadratic and pseudo-random probing is not as great as the difference between linear and quadratic probing.

Pseudo-random probing also has its drawbacks. Since the probe sequence is chosen pseudo-randomly, you cannot be certain how quickly the algorithm will visit every item in the table. If the table is small compared to the number of possible pseudo-random values, there is a chance that the probe sequence will visit the same value repeatedly before it visits other values in the table. It is also possible that a probe sequence will completely miss a table entry so it will be unable to insert an item even when the table has room.

As was the case with quadratic probing, these effects only cause trouble when the table is mostly full. When the table is almost full, enlarging it will provide a much greater performance improvement than worrying about finding the last unused table entries.

Table 10.4 Lengths of Searches Using Quadratic and Pseudo-Random Probing

Entries Used	Quadratic Successful	Quadratic Unsuccessful	Pseudo-Random Successful	Pseudo-Random Unsuccessful
10	1.00	1.11	1.00	1.10
20	1.10	1.21	1.15	1.24
30	1.33	1.44	1.13	1.41
40	1.77	1.75	1.23	1.63
50	1.80	2.14	1.36	1.91
60	1.88	2.67	1.47	2.37
70	2.09	3.43	1.70	3.17
80	2.30	5.05	1.90	4.70
90	2.77	15.03	2.30	9.69
100	3.79	101.00	3.79	101.00

Removing Items

Removing items from a hash table that uses open addressing is not as easy as removing items from a table that uses chains or buckets. You cannot simply remove an item from the table because that item may lie in the probe sequence for some other item.

Suppose item A is in the probe sequence for item B. If you remove A from the table, you will no longer be able to find item B. When you search for B, you will find the empty position left by the removal of item A so you will incorrectly conclude that item B is not in the table.

Instead of removing the item from the hash table, you can mark it as removed. If you later find a position that is marked as removed while you are adding a new item to the table, you can reuse that position. If you encounter a marked item while you are searching for another item, ignore the removed item and continue examining other items in the probe sequence.

After you have marked many items as removed, the hash table may become full of removed items. When you search for items, you may spend a great deal of time skipping over these removed items. Eventually you may need to rehash the table to remove the unused items.

Rehashing

As is mentioned above, if the table becomes full of items that have been marked as removed, you might want to rehash the table to make locating items faster. If you do not also want to resize the table at the same time, you can rehash the table in place.

For this algorithm to work, you must have some way to tell whether or not an item has already been rehashed. The easiest way to do this is to assume that the items are user-defined structures that contain an IsRehashed field.

```
Type ItemType
    IsRehashed As Integer
    Value As Long
End Type
```

Begin by initializing all of the IsRehashed fields to false. Then pass through the table looking for entries that are not marked as removed and that have not yet been rehashed.

When you find such an item, remove it from the table and rehash it. Follow the normal probe sequence for the item. If you come to an entry that is empty or marked as removed, deposit the item there, mark it as rehashed, and continue moving through the table looking for other items that have not yet been rehashed.

While rehashing an item, if you find an item that is already marked as rehashed, continue following the item's probe sequence.

While rehashing an item, if you come to an item that has not yet been rehashed, swap the two items, mark the position as rehashed, and start the process over to rehash the new item.

If a hash table becomes too full, performance drops dramatically. In that case you might want to enlarge the table to improve performance and make room for more entries. Similarly if a hash table contains very few entries, you might want to make it smaller so you could free up some memory. Using techniques similar to those used to rehash a table in place, you can expand or shrink a hash table.

To expand the hash table, first make the table array larger using a **ReDim** statement. Then rehash the table allowing items to hash into the newly created space at the end of the table. When you are finished, the table will be ready for use.

To reduce the size of the hash table, first decide how many entries you want the smaller table array to contain. Then rehash the table allowing items to hash only into the reduced table array. When you have finished rehashing all of the items, redimension the array using the **ReDim** statement to make it smaller.

The Visual Basic code to rehash a table in place using linear probing is shown below. The code to rehash using quadratic or pseudo-random probing is similar.

```
Sub Rehash ()
Dim i As Integer
Dim position As Integer
Dim probes As Integer
Dim Value As Long
Dim new_value As Long

    ' Mark all items as not rehashed.
    For i = 0 To NumEntries - 1
        HashTable(i).IsRehashed = False
    Next i

    ' Look for unrehashed items.
    For i = 0 To NumEntries - 1
        If Not HashTable(i).IsRehashed Then
            Value = HashTable(i).Value
            HashTable(i).Value = UNUSED
            If Value < DELETED Then
                ' Follow this item's probe sequence until we
                ' find an empty, deleted, or unrehashed item.
                probes = 0
                Do
                    position = (Value + probes) Mod NumEntries

                    ' If empty or deleted, place the item here.
                    If HashTable(position).Value = UNUSED Or _
HashTable(position).Value = DELETED Then
                        HashTable(position).Value = Value
                        HashTable(position).IsRehashed = True
                        Exit Do
                    End If

                    ' If not rehashed, swap and continue.
                    If Not HashTable(position).IsRehashed Then
                        new_value = HashTable(position).Value
                        HashTable(position).Value = Value
                        HashTable(position).IsRehashed = True
                        Value = new_value
                        probes = 0
                    Else
                        probes = probes + 1
                    End If
                Loop
            End If
        End If
    Next i
End Sub
```

Example program REHASH uses linear probing to manage a hash table. It is similar to program LINEAR but it also allows you to mark objects as removed and to rehash the table.

Advantages and Disadvantages of Open Addressing

When a hash table using chaining or buckets becomes full, you can easily add more cells or buckets to the table simply by resizing the hash table array. While performance may suffer slightly, the program can continue to use the table.

As a hash table using open addressing becomes full, on the other hand, performance drops dramatically. If the table fills completely, there is no easy way to extend the table. You must redimension the table array and then rehash all of the table entries. Rehashing the table can be very time consuming, especially if the table array is stored on a disk drive or other slow storage device.

There is also no easy way to remove items from a hash table using open addressing. One alternative is to mark an item as removed but not actually remove it from the table. After many such removals, the hash table may become full of unused entries. This will make locating items in the table more time consuming. Eventually you may want to rehash the table in place to reclaim the unused entries and improve performance.

With all of these disadvantages, open addressing is still a valuable technique. Generally open addressing provides better performance than chaining or buckets. Even when a hash table is 90 percent full, you can usually locate an item in two or three attempts using open addressing. As long as you can determine beforehand roughly how large your hash table will need to be, open addressing will provide excellent performance.

Summary of Hashing Techniques

The different kinds of hash tables described in this chapter each have their strengths and weaknesses.

Hash tables that use chaining or buckets are easy to enlarge and allow easy removal of items. Buckets can also take advantage of disk behavior by loading many data items with a single disk access. Both of these methods are slower than open addressing techniques, however.

Linear probing is simple and allows you to insert and locate items in the hash table fairly quickly. Ordered linear probing allows you to determine that an item is not in the table more quickly than does unordered linear probing. On the other hand, it is more difficult to add items to the table using ordered linear probing.

Quadratic probing prevents clustering which affects linear probing, so it gives better performance. Pseudo-random probing avoids clustering and secondary clustering so it gives better performance still.

Table 10.5 shows a summary of the advantages and disadvantages of the various hashing methods.

Table 10.5 Advantages and Disadvantages of Hashing Methods

Method	*Advantages*	*Disadvantages*
Chaining	• Easy to enlarge • Easy to remove items • Does not contain unused entries	• Slows when lists grow long
Buckets	• Easy to enlarge • Fairly easy to remove items • Works naturally on disks	• Slows when there are many overflow buckets • May contain unused entries
Linear Probing	• Fast access	• Hard to enlarge • Hard to remove items • May contain unused entries
Ordered Linear Probing	• Fast access • Short unsuccessful probes	• Hard to enlarge • Hard to remove items • Takes longer to insert items • May contain unused entries
Quadratic Probing	• Faster access	• Hard to enlarge • Hard to remove items • May contain unused entries
Pseudo-Random Probing	• Fastest access	• Hard to enlarge • Hard to remove items • May contain unused entries

11

Network Algorithms

Overview

Chapters 5 and 6 discussed tree algorithms. This chapter covers the more general topic of networks. Networks play important roles in many applications. You can use them to model streets, telephone facilities, power lines, water pipes, sewers, storm drains, airline connections, railroad lines, etc. Networks are also used in less obvious ways to solve other problems such as districting, critical path scheduling, crew scheduling, and work assignment.

You can store networks using techniques similar to those discussed in Chapter 5 for storing trees (see pages 113–123), so this chapter will not spend a lot of time describing network storage. The sections in this chapter will assume that the network is stored in a forward star representation (see pages 118–122) unless indicated otherwise.

Definitions

Like a tree, a *network* or *graph* is a set of *nodes* connected by a set of *edges* or *links*. Unlike in a tree, there is no concept of parent or child nodes in a network.

The links in a network may each have an associated direction in which case the network is called a *directed network*. Each link may also have an associated *cost*. In a street network, for example, the cost might be the time it takes to drive across the section of road represented by the link. In a telephone network the cost might be the amount of electrical loss across the cable represented by the link. Figure 11.1 shows a small directed network where numbers next to the links show the links' costs.

A *path* between nodes A and B is a series of links in the network that connects the two nodes. If there is at most one link between any two nodes in the network, a path can be described uniquely by listing the nodes along the path. Since that is usually easier to visualize, paths are described in this way if possible. In Figure 11.1 the path containing the nodes B, E, F, G, E, and D is a path connecting nodes B and D.

A *cycle* is a path that connects a node to itself. The path E, F, G, E in Figure 11.1 is a cycle. A path is *simple* if it contains no cycles. The path B, E, F, G, E, D is not simple because it contains the cycle E, F, G, E.

If there is any path between two nodes, then there must be a simple path between the two nodes. You can find this path by removing any cycles from the original path. For example, if you replace the cycle E, F, G, E with the node E in the non-simple path B, E, F, G, E, D, you get the simple path B, E, D connecting nodes B and D.

A network is *connected* if there is at least one path from every node in the network to every other node. In a directed network, it is not always obvious whether or not the network is connected. In Figure 11.2 the network on the left is connected. The network on the right is not because, for example, there is no path from node E to node C.

Network Traversals

Traversing a network is similar to traversing a tree. You can traverse a network using either a depth first or breadth first traversal. Depth first traversals are generally similar

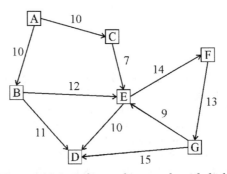

Figure 11.1 A directed network with link costs.

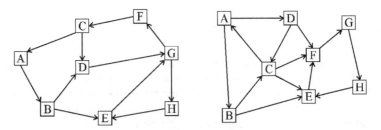

Figure 11.2 Connected (left) and unconnected (right) networks.

to preorder traversals in trees, though you could also define postorder and even inorder traversals for a network.

The algorithm for performing a preorder traversal for a binary tree is described in Chapter 5 (see page 124):

1. Visit the node.
2. Recursively traverse the left subtree in preorder.
3. Recursively traverse the right subtree in preorder.

In a tree there is a parent-child relationship between nodes that are connected. Since the algorithm starts at the root and always works downward through the child nodes, it will never visit a node twice.

In a network, on the other hand, nodes may be linked in any way. If you try to implement the preorder traversal shown above in a network, your program may find a cycle in the network and enter an infinite loop following the cycle.

To prevent this, when the algorithm reaches a node it can mark the node as visited. Then when the algorithm is searching the neighboring nodes, it visits only the nodes that are not yet marked. When the algorithm finishes, all of the nodes in the network will be marked as visited. The preorder network traversal algorithm is:

1. Mark the node.
2. Visit the node.
3. Recursively traverse the node's neighbors that are not yet marked.

To implement this algorithm in Visual Basic, you should allocate an array Marked to indicate which nodes have been visited. Assuming the network is stored in forward star format, you can write a Visual Basic routine to display a list of the indexes in a network using a preorder traversal like this:

```
Dim Marked() As Integer
    :
Sub PreorderPrint(node As Integer)
Dim link As Integer
    Marked(node) = True
    Print NodeLabel(node)
    ' Visit the node's unmarked neighbors.
    For link = FirstLink(node) To FirstLink(node + 1) - 1
        If Not Marked(ToNode(link)) Then
            PreorderPrint ToNode(link)
        End If
    Next link
End Sub
```

If the network is connected, the resulting traversal will visit every node in the network. Since no node is visited twice by the traversal algorithm, the collection of links traversed does not contain any cycles. That makes this collection a tree. Since the collection of links spans every node in the network, this tree is called a *spanning tree* for the network. Figure 11.3 shows a small network with a spanning tree rooted at node A drawn in bold lines.

Similarly you can use this node marking technique to convert the breadth first tree traversal algorithm into a network traversal algorithm. The tree traversal algorithm begins by placing the tree's root node in a queue. It then removes the first node from the queue, visits it, and places its children at the end of the queue. It repeats this process until the queue is empty.

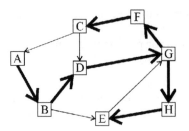

Figure 11.3 A spanning tree.

In the network traversal algorithm, you must make certain that a node is not placed in the queue if it has been visited before or if it is currently in the queue. To do this, mark each node as you place it in the queue. The network version of the algorithm is:

1. Mark the first node (this will be the root of the spanning tree) and add it to the end of the queue.
2. Repeat until the queue is empty:
   a) Remove the first node from the queue and visit it.
   b) For each of the node's neighbors that are not yet marked, mark the node and add it to the end of the queue.

A Visual Basic routine that displays a list of the indexes in a network in depth first order would look like this:

```
Sub BreadthFirstPrint ()
ReDim Marked(1 To NumNodes) As Integer

Dim node As Integer
Dim link As Integer

    ' Put the root in the queue.
    Marked(Root) = True
    EnterQueue Root

    ' Repeatedly process the top item in the queue until
    ' the queue is empty.
    Do While QueueBack - QueueFront > 0
        node = LeaveQueue()

        ' Visit the node
        Print NodeLabel(node)

        ' Add the node's unmarked neighbors to the queue.
        For link = FirstLink(node) To FirstLink(node + 1) - 1
            If Not Marked(ToNode(link)) Then
                EnterQueue ToNode(link)
            End If
        Next link
    Loop
End Sub
```

Minimal Spanning Trees

Given a network with a cost associated with each link, a *minimal spanning tree* is a spanning tree where the total cost of all of the links in the tree is as small as possible. You can use a minimal spanning tree to pick the least costly way to connect all of the nodes in a network.

For example, suppose you needed to design a telephone network to connect six cities. You could build a trunk between every pair of the cities but that would be needlessly expensive. A less costly solution would be to connect the cities along the links contained in a minimal spanning tree. Figure 11.4 shows six cities with a possible trunk drawn between each pair of cities. The minimal spanning tree is drawn in bold.

Notice that a network may contain more than one minimal spanning tree. Figure 11.5 shows two pictures of one network with two different minimal spanning trees drawn in bold. The total cost of both of these trees is 32.

There is a simple algorithm for finding a minimal spanning tree for a network. Start by placing any node in the spanning tree. Then find the smallest link that connects a node in the tree to a node that is not yet in the tree. Add that link and the corresponding node to the tree. Repeat this procedure until you have added all of the nodes to the tree.

In a way this algorithm is similar to the hill climbing heuristic described in Chapter 7 (see pages 193–194). At each step both algorithms modify the solution to improve it as much as possible. At each step the spanning tree algorithm selects the smallest link that adds a new node to the tree. Unlike the hill climbing heuristic, which does not always find an optimal solution, this algorithm is guaranteed to find a minimal spanning tree.

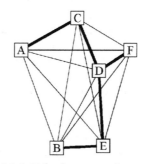

Figure 11.4 Telephone trunks connecting six cities.

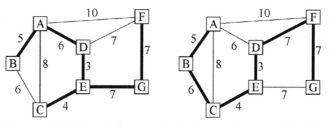

Figure 11.5 Two different minimal spanning trees for the same network.

Algorithms like this, that reach globally optimal solutions by making locally optimal decisions, are called *greedy algorithms*. You can think of greedy algorithms as hill climbing algorithms that are not heuristics—they are guaranteed to find the best solution possible.

To implement this algorithm in Visual Basic, create an array LinkInTree. This array will indicate whether or not a given link is in the spanning tree during a particular stage of the algorithm. In other words, LinkInTree(I) will be true if link number I is in the spanning tree. Initialize this array so all of its entries have the value false.

Similarly create an array NodeInTree. This array will indicate whether a node is in the spanning tree as the tree grows during the course of the algorithm. When the algorithm is finished, all of the nodes will be part of the spanning tree. Initialize this array so all of its entries have the value false.

Now add a single node to the spanning tree. If the network is connected, it does not matter much which node you start with since they will all eventually be added to the tree. For convenience you can start by adding the first node in the network. Set this node's NodeInTree entry to be true.

To keep track of the links which you might add to the spanning tree, use a heap-based priority queue like the one described in Chapter 8 (see pages 236–237). This priority queue should use the cost of the links as their priorities, with smaller costs having higher priority. The queue will need to store each link's index along with its cost so you can tell which link you are examining as you remove the links from the queue.

Since the tree initially contains the first node in the network, add the links that leave the first node to the link priority queue.

At this point the initialization phase of the algorithm is complete.

Now find the least costly link in the priority queue that connects a node in the tree to a node not yet in the tree. Add that link to the tree. Repeat this process until you have added all of the nodes to the tree.

Use the priority queue's LeavePQueue function to remove the link with the highest priority (smallest cost). Since this link is in the priority queue, it must start at a node that is already in the spanning tree. You only need to check to see if the link ends at a node that is not yet in the spanning tree.

If the link ends at a node that is already in the spanning tree, discard the link and get another one from the queue.

If the link ends at a node that is not yet in the spanning tree, add the link to the tree by setting its LinkInTree entry to true. Also set the NodeInTree entry for the corresponding node ToNode(link) to be true. Finally, examine all of the links leaving the new node and add any that end at nodes not yet in the tree to the priority queue.

Continue removing links from the priority queue until you have added all of the nodes to the spanning tree. If you keep track of the number of nodes you have added, you can stop when they are all part of the tree.

It is possible that the priority queue will empty completely before you have added all of the nodes to the spanning tree. In that case the network is not connected. There is no path from the first node you added to the tree to at least one other node in the network.

```
Sub FindMinSpanningTree ()
Dim NodeInTree() As Integer
Dim node As Integer
Dim link As Integer
Dim to_node As Integer
Dim link_cost As Integer
```

```
' Pick a good size for the initial priority queue.
PreallocatePQueue NumLinks


' We can have at most NumNodes nodes in the tree.
ReDim NodeInTree(1 To NumNodes)
' Start with nothing in the tree.
For node = 1 To NumNodes
    NodeInTree(node) = False
Next node
For link = 1 To NumLinks
    LinkInTree(link) = False
Next link


' Add node 1 to the tree.
NodeInTree(1) = True
For link = FirstLink(1) To FirstLink(1 + 1) - 1
    EnterPQueue link, Cost(link)
Next link


' The tree starts with cost 0.
TreeCost = 0


' We are done when we have added NumNodes to the tree.
For node = 1 To NumNodes
    ' Repeat until we find a link that connects a node
    ' in the tree to a node not in the tree.
    Do
        ' Remove the least cost link from the queue.
        LeavePQueue link, link_cost


        ' If there are no more links in the queue,
        ' we're stuck. This may happen if the network
        ' is not completely connected.
        If link < 1 Then Exit For
        ' See if the link connects a node in the tree
        ' to a node not in the tree.
        If Not NodeInTree(ToNode(link)) Then Exit Do
    Loop


    ' Add the link to the tree.
    LinkInTree(link) = True
    TreeCost = TreeCost + link_cost
    to_node = ToNode(link)
    NodeInTree(to_node) = True


    ' Add the links leaving the new node to the queue.
    For link = FirstLink(to_node) To FirstLink(to_node + 1) - 1
        If Not NodeInTree(ToNode(link)) Then
            EnterPQueue link, Cost(link)
        End If
    Next link
Next node
End Sub
```

While building a minimal spanning tree, this algorithm examines each link at most once. As each link is examined, it is added and then later removed from the priority queue. Since it takes O(log(N)) time to add or remove an item from a heap-based priority queue, the total run time for the algorithm is O(N * log(N)).

Example program SPAN uses this algorithm to find minimal spanning trees. Use the File menu's Load . . . command to load a network. File NET1.SPN contains a network with 8 nodes and 26 links. File NET2.SPN contains a larger network with 24 nodes and 86 links. These files are stored in forward star format. When you load one of these files, the program will find and display a minimal spanning tree.

Shortest Paths

The types of shortest path algorithms discussed in the following sections find all of the shortest paths from a single point, called the *root,* to every other point in the network. The collection of links used by all of the shortest paths in the network forms a tree. Figure 11.6 shows a network where the shortest path tree rooted at node A is drawn in bold. This tree shows the shortest path from node A to every other node in the network. The shortest path from node A to node F, for example, follows the path through the tree: A, C, E, F.

Most shortest path algorithms start with an empty shortest path tree and then add links one at a time to the tree until the tree is complete. These algorithms can be divided into two categories according to how they select the next link to add to the growing shortest path tree.

Label setting algorithms always select a link that is guaranteed to be part of the final shortest path tree. Once a link has been added to the tree, it will not be removed later.

Label correcting algorithms add links that may or may not be part of the final shortest path tree. As the algorithm progresses, it may discover a different link should have been added instead of one that it has already placed in the tree. In that case the algorithm replaces the old link with the new one and continues. Replacing a link in the tree may make new paths possible that were not possible before. To check for these paths, the algorithm must reexamine any paths it previously added to the tree using the link that was removed.

The label setting and the label correcting algorithms described below use similar data structures to store the growing shortest path tree.

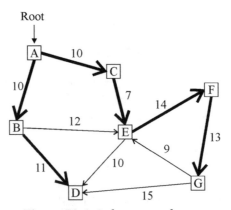

Figure 11.6 A shortest path tree.

The Dist array holds the current distance from the root to each node in the network. Initially the algorithms set Dist(Root) = 0 and Dist(I) = INFINITY for all other nodes I. As the algorithm progresses, it updates the Dist array when it adds new shortest paths to the tree. When the algorithm is finished, Dist(I) will be the shortest distance from the root to node I.

The Parent array holds the parent of each node in the shortest path tree. Using this array you can list the nodes in the path from the root to node I in reverse order: I, Parent(I), Parent(Parent(I)), etc. The parent of the root node is assigned the value 0 so you can tell where the paths end. Visual Basic code to list the path from the root to node I in reverse order might look like this:

```
J = I
Do While J <> 0
    Print J
    J = Parent(J)
Loop
```

The CL array is used as a slightly unusual linked list holding a queue of candidate nodes which could be added to the shortest path tree. The entry CL(I) will hold the value NOT_IN_LIST if node I is not currently in the candidate list. Otherwise CL(I) will be the index of the next node in the candidate list, or the value END_OF_LIST if the node is the last item in the list. By checking whether CL(I) equals NOT_IN_LIST, it is easy to tell if an item is currently in the candidate list.

The variable next_cl holds the index of the first node on the candidate list. Using this array you could print out the complete list using code like this:

```
node = next_cl
Do While node <> END_OF_LIST
    Print node            ' Print the index of a candidate.
    node = CL(node)       ' Move on to the next candidate.
Loop
```

Label setting and label correcting algorithms differ in the ways in which they manage the candidate list. Label setting algorithms always select a candidate from the list that is guaranteed to be part of the shortest path tree. The label correcting algorithm examined here selects whatever item is at the top of the candidate list.

Label Setting

This algorithm begins by setting Dist(Root) = 0 and by placing the root node in the candidate list.

It then searches the candidate list for the node with the smallest Dist value. Initially that will be the root node since the root is the only node in the list.

The algorithm removes the selected node from the candidate list. It then sets the node's CL entry to the value WAS_IN_LIST to indicate that the node is now a permanent part of the shortest path tree. Its Dist and Parent entries have their correct final values. For the root node, Parent(Root) = 0 and Dist(Root) = 0.

Next the algorithm examines each of the neighbors of the selected node. These are the nodes directly connected to it by a link. If a neighbor has never been on the candidate list before, its CL(I) entry will be the value NOT_IN_LIST. In that case the algorithm adds the neighbor to the candidate list. Otherwise the neighbor either has already been added to the shortest path tree or it is currently in the candidate list.

If the neighbor's CL entry is not WAS_IN_LIST, the algorithm also checks whether the distance from the root to the selected node plus the cost of the link is less than the current best distance to the neighbor node. If it is, the algorithm updates that neighbor's Dist and Parent entries so the best path to the neighbor now goes through the selected node.

The algorithm repeats this process, removing nodes from the candidate list, examining their neighbors, and adding neighbors to the candidate list, until the list is empty.

Figure 11.7 shows a partial shortest path tree. At this point the algorithm has considered nodes A and B, removed them from the candidate list, and has examined their links. It has added nodes A and B to the shortest path tree and the candidate list now contains nodes C, D, and E. The bold arrows in Figure 11.7 indicate the Parent array entries at this point. For example, the Parent entry for node E is currently node B.

The algorithm searches the candidate list to find the node with the smallest current distance. The distances to the nodes C, D, and E are currently 10, 21, and 22 respectively, so the algorithm selects node C. It removes node C from the candidate list and sets the node's CL entry to WAS_IN_LIST. At this point the node is part of the shortest path tree and its Dist and Parent entries have their final values.

The algorithm then examines the links leaving node C. The only link leaving node C goes to node E. Node E is currently in the candidate list so the algorithm does not add it to the list again.

The current shortest path from the root to node E is the path A, B, E which has a total cost of 22. But the path A, C, E has a cost of only 17. This is lower than the current cost of 22, so the algorithm changes the Parent entry for node E to node C and updates node E's Dist entry to 17.

The heart of the algorithm is subroutine FindPathTree shown below.

```
Sub FindPathTree (root As Integer)
Const INFINITY = 32767

Const END_OF_LIST = 0
Const NOT_IN_LIST = -1
Const WAS_IN_LIST = -2
```

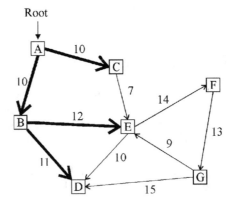

Figure 11.7 An incomplete shortest path tree.

```
Dim CL() As Integer
Dim next_cl As Integer ' First item in the list.
Dim node As Integer
Dim best_dist As Integer
Dim best_node As Integer
Dim link As Integer
Dim to_node As Integer

    ' We can have at most NumNodes nodes in the list.
    ReDim CL(1 To NumNodes)

    ' Initialize Dist and Parent arrays.
    For node = 1 To NumNodes
        Parent(node) = 0          ' Not in the tree.
        Dist(node) = INFINITY     ' Best distance infinite.
        CL(node) = NOT_IN_LIST    ' Not in candidate list.
    Next node
    Dist(root) = 0               ' The root gets distance 0.

    ' Put the Root on the candidate list.
    next_cl = root
    CL(root) = END_OF_LIST

    ' Repeat until the candidate list is empty.
    Do While next_cl <> END_OF_LIST
        ' Find the node in the candidate list for which
        ' Dist(node) is smallest.
        best_dist = Dist(next_cl)
        best_node = next_cl
        node = CL(best_node)
        Do While node <> END_OF_LIST
            If Dist(node) < best_dist Then
                best_dist = Dist(node)
                best_node = node
            End If
            node = CL(node)
        Loop

        ' Remove the node from the candidate list.
        If best_node = next_cl Then
            next_cl = CL(best_node)
        Else
            node = next_cl
            Do While CL(node) <> best_node
                node = CL(node)
            Loop
            CL(node) = CL(best_node)
        End If
        CL(best_node) = WAS_IN_LIST

        ' Examine the links out of this node.
        For link = FirstLink(best_node) To FirstLink(best_node + 1) - 1
            to_node = ToNode(link)

            ' If the node has never been on the
            ' candidate list, add it now.
            If CL(to_node) = NOT_IN_LIST Then
                CL(to_node) = next_cl
```

```
                next_cl = to_node
          End If


          ' If the node is currently in the candidate
          ' list and this is an improvement, update
          ' its Parent and Dist entries.
          If CL(to_node) >= END_OF_LIST And Dist(to_node) > _
Dist(best_node) + Cost(link) Then
                Dist(to_node) = Dist(best_node) + Cost(link)
                Parent(to_node) = best_node
          End If
      Next link
  Loop
End Sub
```

It is important that the algorithm update the Parent and Dist entries only for nodes that are on the candidate list at the time. For many networks there will be no improvement possible for a node unless it is in the candidate list. If the network contains a cycle of negative length, however, the algorithm will find that it can improve the distances to some nodes that it has already placed in the shortest path tree. This will connect two branches of the shortest path tree so it will no longer be a tree.

Figure 11.8 shows a network with a negative cycle and the shortest path "tree" that would result if the algorithm did not make this check. As the algorithm is written, it will not update nodes that have been removed from the candidate list so it will always produce a tree.

Example program PATH_S uses this label setting algorithm to compute shortest paths. Use the File menu's Load . . . command to load a network. File NET1.PTH contains the network shown in Figure 11.1. File NET2.PTH contains a larger network with 24 nodes and 37 links. File NET3.PTH contains the network shown in Figure 11.8 which has a negative length cycle. These files are stored in forward star format.

If you click on a node with the left mouse button, the program will compute and display the shortest path tree rooted at that node. If you click on node A using NET1.PTH, you should see a picture similar to Figure 11.6.

If you then click on another node with the right mouse button, the program will highlight the shortest path from the root to that node.

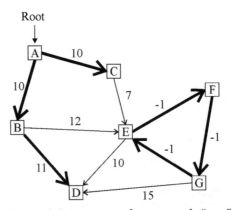

Figure 11.8 Incorrect shortest path "tree" for a network with a negative cost cycle.

Label Setting Variations

The main bottleneck in this algorithm is in locating the node in the candidate list that has the smallest Dist value. There are several variations of this algorithm that use different data structures for storing the candidate list. For example, you could store the candidate list as a sorted linked list. Using this method it would take only a single step to find the next node to add to the shortest path tree. Since the list would always be sorted, the node at the top would always be the one to add.

While this would make finding the correct node in the list easier, it would also make adding a node to the list harder. Instead of placing the node at the beginning of the list, you would need to add it at the appropriate position in the list.

You would also sometimes need to move nodes around in the list. If, by adding a node to the shortest path tree, you reduced the best distance to another node that was already in the list, you would need to move that node closer to the top of the list.

The previous algorithm and this new variation represent two extremes for managing the candidate list. The first stores the list in a totally unordered way and spends a lot of time looking for nodes in the list. The second spends a lot of effort maintaining a sorted linked list and then can select nodes very quickly. Other variations use intermediate strategies.

You could store the candidate list in a heap. Then it would be easy to select the next node from the top of the heap. Adding a new node to the heap and rearranging the heap would be easier than performing the same operations on a sorted linked list. Other strategies use clever arrangements of buckets to keep the best candidates easy to find.

Some of these variations are quite complicated. The extra complication slows these algorithms down, so they are often slower than simpler algorithms for small networks. For very large networks or networks where each node has a very large number of links, these algorithms may be worth the extra complication.

Label Correcting

Like the label setting algorithm, this algorithm begins by setting Dist(Root) = 0 and by placing the root node in the candidate list. It then selects the first node in the candidate list to add to the shortest path tree.

Next the algorithm examines each of the neighbors of the selected node. These are the nodes that are connected to the selected node by a link. It checks whether the distance from the root to the selected node plus the cost of the link is less than the current best cost to the neighbor node. If it is, the algorithm updates that node's Dist and Parent entries so the best path to the neighbor node goes through the selected node. If the neighbor is not already in the candidate list, the algorithm also adds it. Notice that this algorithm does not check whether or not the item has already been on the list before. If there is improvement in the path from the root to the neighbor, it is always added to the list.

The algorithm continues removing nodes from the candidate list, examining their neighbors, and adding neighbors to the candidate list until the list is empty.

If you compare the label setting and label correcting algorithms carefully, you will find that they are very similar. The only difference is in how each selects a node from the candidate list to add to the shortest path tree.

The label setting algorithm always picks a link that is guaranteed to belong in the shortest path tree. Once it removes a node from the candidate list, that node has been permanently added to the tree and will not be placed in the candidate list again.

The label correcting algorithm always selects the first node from the candidate list. That node may not always be the best choice. The node's Dist and Parent entries may not hold the best possible values. In that case the algorithm will eventually examine a node in the candidate list that is a better Parent entry than the one that was originally chosen. The algorithm will then update the incorrect node's Dist and Parent entries, and will place the updated node back in the candidate list.

The algorithm may be able to use the new path to form other paths that it might have missed earlier. By placing the updated node back in the candidate list, the algorithm ensures that it will consider the node again and find any such paths.

The Visual Basic code for this algorithm is shown below.

```
Sub FindPathTree (root As Integer)
Const INFINITY = 32767

Const END_OF_LIST = 0
Const NOT_IN_LIST = -1

Dim CL() As Integer
Dim last_cl As Integer   ' Last item in the list.
Dim next_cl As Integer   ' First item in the list.
Dim node As Integer
Dim link As Integer
Dim to_node As Integer

    ' We can have at most NumNodes nodes in the list.
    ReDim CL(1 To NumNodes)

    ' Initialize Dist and Parent arrays.
    For node = 1 To NumNodes
        Parent(node) = 0           ' Not in the tree.
        Dist(node) = INFINITY      ' Best distance infinite.
        CL(node) = NOT_IN_LIST     ' Not in candidate list.
    Next node
    Dist(root) = 0                 ' The root gets distance 0.

    ' Put the Root on the candidate list.
    next_cl = root                 ' Oldest item in the list.
    last_cl = root                 ' Newest item in the list.
    CL(root) = END_OF_LIST

    ' Repeat until the candidate list is empty.
    Do While next_cl <> END_OF_LIST
        node = next_cl

        ' Check the links out of this node.
        For link = FirstLink(node) To FirstLink(node + 1) - 1
            to_node = ToNode(link)

            ' If this is an improvement for to_node,
            ' update its Dist and Parent entries.
            If Dist(to_node) > Dist(node) + Cost(link) Then
                Dist(to_node) = Dist(node) + Cost(link)
                Parent(to_node) = node

                ' If the node is not already in the
                ' candidate list, add it to the list.
```

```
                    If CL(to_node) = NOT_IN_LIST Then
                        CL(last_cl) = to_node
                        last_cl = to_node
                        CL(to_node) = END_OF_LIST
                    End If
                End If
            Next link

            ' Remove the node from the candidate list.
            next_cl = CL(node)
            CL(node) = NOT_IN_LIST
        Loop
    End Sub
```

Unlike the label setting algorithm, this algorithm cannot handle networks that contain negative length cycles. If the network contains a negative length cycle, the algorithm will enter an infinite loop following the links in the cycle. Each time it passes through the cycle, it will be able to reduce the distances to the nodes it is examining. As it reduces their distances, it will place these nodes back in the candidate list so it can update other paths using the nodes. When it examines the nodes in the cycle again, it will reduce their distances further. This process will continue until the distances to these nodes underflow with values less than –32,768.

If you know that your network contains negative cycles, the easiest thing to do is to use a label setting algorithm instead of a label correcting algorithm.

Example program PATH_C uses this label correcting algorithm to compute shortest paths. It is similar to PATH_S except it uses a label correcting algorithm rather than a label setting algorithm. As with program PATH_S, you can use the program's File . . . menu to load the networks contained in the data files NET1.PTH and NET2.PTH.

File NET3.PTH contains a network that has a negative length cycle. If you load this network and click on any node other than node D, the program will enter an infinite loop examining the nodes in the cycle and will eventually stop with an Overflow error.

Label Correcting Variations

This label correcting algorithm can select a node from the candidate list very quickly. It can also add a node to the list in only one or two steps. The trouble with this algorithm is that, when it selects a node from the candidate list, it may not make a very good choice. If the algorithm selects a node before that node's Dist and Parent entries reach their final values, it will need to correct the entries later and place the node back in the candidate list. The more often the algorithm places nodes back in the candidate list, the longer the algorithm will take.

Variations on this algorithm try to improve the quality of the node selections without creating a lot of additional work. One technique which works well in practice is to add nodes to both the front and back of the candidate list. If a node has never been on the candidate list before, the algorithm adds it at the back of the list as usual. If the node has previously been on the candidate list but is not now, the algorithm adds it at the front of the list. This will make the algorithm revisit that node quite soon, probably the next time it selects a node.

The idea behind this approach is that, if the algorithm has made a mistake, it should fix the mistake as soon as possible. If the mistake is left uncorrected, the algorithm may use the incorrect information to build long false paths that will need to be corrected later. By reexamining the node quickly, the algorithm may be able to reduce the number of incorrect paths it must rebuild. In the best case, if the node's neighbors are still in the candidate list, reexamining this node before examining the neighbors prevents any incorrect paths from starting.

In Visual Basic the differences between this version and the previous one are in the ways in which nodes are added and removed from the candidate list. When removing a node from the list, the new algorithm sets the node's CL entry to WAS_IN_LIST to indicate that the item was on the list before. Then when adding a node to the list, the algorithm checks the value of CL to see if it should add the node at the front or the back of the list.

```
Sub FindPathTree (root As Integer)
Const INFINITY = 32767

Const END_OF_LIST = 0
Const NOT_IN_LIST = -1
Const WAS_IN_LIST = -2

Dim CL() As Integer
Dim last_cl As Integer    ' Last item in the list.
Dim next_cl As Integer    ' First item in the list.
Dim node As Integer
Dim link As Integer
Dim to_node As Integer

    ' We can have at most NumNodes nodes in the list.
    ReDim CL(1 To NumNodes)

    ' Initialize Dist and Parent arrays.
    For node = 1 To NumNodes
        Parent(node) = 0          ' Not in the tree.
        Dist(node) = INFINITY     ' Best distance infinite.
        CL(node) = NOT_IN_LIST    ' Not in candidate list.
    Next node
    Dist(root) = 0                ' The root gets distance 0.
    ' Put the Root on the candidate list.
    next_cl = root                ' Oldest item in the list.
    last_cl = root                ' Newest item in the list.
    CL(root) = END_OF_LIST

    ' Repeat until the candidate list is empty.
    Do While next_cl <> END_OF_LIST
        node = next_cl

        ' Check the links out of this node.
        For link = FirstLink(node) To FirstLink(node + 1) - 1
            to_node = ToNode(link)

            ' If this is an improvement for to_node,
            ' update its Dist and Parent entries.
            If Dist(to_node) > Dist(node) + Cost(link) Then
                Dist(to_node) = Dist(node) + Cost(link)
                Parent(to_node) = node
                ' If the node is not already in the
                ' candidate list, add it to the list.
```

```
                    If CL(to_node) = NOT_IN_LIST Then
                        ' The node has not been on the list before.
                        ' Add it at the back of the list.
                        CL(last_cl) = to_node
                        last_cl = to_node
                        CL(to_node) = END_OF_LIST
                    ElseIf
                        ' The node was in the list before.
                        ' Add it to the front of the list.
                        CL(to_node) = CL(next_cl)
                        CL(next_cl) = to_node
                    End If
                End If
            Next link

            ' Remove the node from the candidate list.
            next_cl = CL(node)
            CL(node) = NOT_IN_LIST
        Loop
    End Sub
```

Shortest Path Variations

The previous shortest path algorithms compute all of the shortest paths from a single root node to all of the other nodes in the network. There are many other types of shortest path problems. This section examines three: point-to-point shortest paths, all pairs shortest paths, and shortest paths with turn penalties.

Point-to-Point Shortest Path

In some applications you may want to find the shortest path between two points but you may not care about all of the other shortest paths stored in a complete shortest path tree. One easy way you can find a point-to-point shortest path is to compute the complete shortest path tree using either a label setting or label correcting algorithm. Then use the shortest path tree to find the shortest path between the two points.

Another method is to use a label setting algorithm that stops when it finds a path to the destination node. A label setting algorithm never adds links to the shortest path tree that do not belong there. When it adds the destination node to the shortest path tree, the algorithm will have found a correct shortest path. In the algorithm described earlier, this occurs when the algorithm removes the destination node from the candidate list.

The only change you need to make in the label setting algorithm comes right after the algorithm has found the node in the candidate list with the smallest distance value Dist(best_node). Before removing the node from the candidate list, the algorithm should check whether the node is the destination node. If so, the shortest path tree already holds a correct path from the start node to the destination node so the algorithm can stop early.

```
' Find the node in the candidate list for which
' Dist(node) is smallest.
    :

' See if this is the destination node.
If best_node = destination Then Exit Do
```

```
' Remove the node from the candidate list.
    :
```

In practice if the two points are far apart in the network, this algorithm will usually take longer than computing the entire shortest path tree. Checking for the destination node each time the loop executes slows the algorithm down. On the other hand, if the nodes are close together in the network, this algorithm may be much faster than building a complete shortest path tree.

For some networks, like street networks, you may be able to guess how far apart the two points are and then decide which version of the algorithm to use for those points. If your network contains all the streets in southern California and the two points are ten miles apart, you should use the version that stops when it removes the destination from the candidate list. If the points are 800 miles apart, it will probably be faster to compute the complete shortest path tree.

All Pairs Shortest Paths

Some applications may require you to quickly find the shortest path between any pair of nodes in the network. If the application requires you to compute a large fraction of the possible N^2 paths in the network, it may be faster for you to precompute all of the possible shortest paths rather than finding each as you need it.

You can store the shortest paths in two 2-dimensional arrays Dist and Prev. Dist(I, J) holds the shortest distance from node I to node J. Prev(I, J) holds the node that comes before node J in the path from node I to node J. This array is similar to the Parent array in the previous algorithms. You could print out the path from node I to node J backwards using code like this:

```
node = J
Do While node <> I
    Print node
    node = Prev(I, node)
Loop
```

At this point the easiest way to find the shortest path information is to build the shortest path tree rooted at each node in the network using one of the previous algorithms. Then save the results in the Dist and Prev arrays.

```
Sub FindAllPaths ()
Dim i As Integer
Dim j As Integer
Dim node As Integer

    ' Start from scratch.
    ReDim AllDist(1 To NumNodes, 1 To NumNodes)
    ReDim AllPrev(1 To NumNodes, 1 To NumNodes)
    For i = 1 To NumNodes
        For j = 1 To NumNodes
            AllDist(i, j) = INFINITY
            AllPrev(i, j) = 0
        Next j
    Next i
```

```
    ' Fill in the direct links.
    For i = 1 To NumNodes
        For j = FirstLink(i) To FirstLink(i + 1) - 1
            AllPrev(i, ToNode(j)) = i
            AllDist(i, ToNode(j)) = Cost(j)
        Next j
    Next i

    ' Compute shortest path trees.
    For i = 1 To NumNodes
        ' Build the shortest path tree rooted at node i.
        FindPathTree i

        ' Save the results.
        For j = 1 To NumNodes
            node = j
            Do While node <> 0
                ' If we find a node that already has an
                ' AllPrev entry, then the rest of this path
                ' is already saved.
                If AllPrev(i, node) <> 0 Then Exit Do

                AllPrev(i, node) = Parent(node)
                AllDist(i, node) = Dist(node)
                node = Parent(node)
            Loop
        Next j
    Next i
End Sub
```

Another method for computing all of the shortest paths successively constructs paths through the network using more and more nodes. First the algorithm finds all of the shortest paths that use only the first node plus the end nodes in the path. In other words, for nodes J and K the algorithm finds the shortest path between nodes J and K that uses only node number 1 plus nodes J and K, if any such paths exist.

Next the algorithm finds all of the shortest paths that use only the first two nodes. It then builds paths using the first three nodes, then the first four nodes, and so on until it has built all of the shortest paths using all of the nodes. At this point, since the shortest paths can use any node, the algorithm has found all of the shortest paths in the network.

Notice that the shortest path from node J to node K, using only the first I nodes, will include the node I only if Dist(J, K) > Dist(J, I) + Dist(I, K). Otherwise the shortest path will be whatever path was shortest using only the first I − 1 nodes. That means when the algorithm adds the node I into consideration, it only needs to check whether Dist(J, K) > Dist(J, I) + Dist(I, K). If so, the algorithm updates the shortest path from node J to node K. Otherwise the old shortest path between these two nodes is still the shortest.

```
Sub FindAllPaths ()
Dim i As Integer
Dim j As Integer
Dim k As Integer

    ' Start from scratch.
    ReDim AllDist(1 To NumNodes, 1 To NumNodes)
    ReDim AllPrev(1 To NumNodes, 1 To NumNodes)
```

```
            For i = 1 To NumNodes
                For j = 1 To NumNodes
                    AllDist(i, j) = INFINITY
                    AllPrev(i, j) = 0
                Next j
            Next i

            ' Fill in the direct links.
            For i = 1 To NumNodes
                For j = FirstLink(i) To FirstLink(i + 1) - 1
                    AllPrev(i, ToNode(j)) = i
                    AllDist(i, ToNode(j)) = Cost(j)
                Next j
                AllDist(i, i) = 0
        Next i

        ' Compute shortest path trees.
        For i = 1 To NumNodes
            For j = 1 To NumNodes
                For k = 1 To NumNodes
                        ' See if i-->j-->k is better than i-->k.
                        If AllDist(j, k) > AllDist(j, i) + AllDist(i, k) _
        Then
                            AllDist(j, k) = AllDist(j, i) + AllDist(i, k)
                            AllPrev(j, k) = AllPrev(i, k)
                        End If
                    Next k
                Next j
            Next i
        End Sub
```

Turn Penalties

Some networks, particularly street networks, are more useful if you add turn penalties and prohibitions. In a street network a car must slow down before it turns. It may also take longer to turn left than to turn right or to go straight. At some intersections certain turns may be illegal or impossible due to a center median. You can handle these details by adding turn penalties to the network.

Few Turn Penalties

Often only a few key turn penalties are important. You might like to prevent illegal or impossible turns and place turn penalties on a few key intersections, without placing turn penalties on every intersection in the network. In that case you can break the node that should have turn penalties into subnodes that implicitly take the penalties into account.

Suppose you want to add a turn penalty for entering an intersection and turning left, and a different penalty for entering the intersection and turning right. Figure 11.9 shows an intersection where you might like to place these penalties. The numbers next to each link are the link's cost. You want to place penalties for entering node A along link L_1 and then leaving along the links L_2 or L_3.

To add turn penalties to node A, break the node into one subnode for each of the links leaving it. In this example there are two links leaving node A so you should break node A into two subnodes A_1 and A_2. Replace the links leaving node A with correspond-

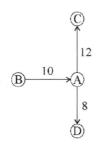

Figure 11.9 An intersection.

ing links leaving these subnodes. You can think of the subnodes as representing the action of entering node A and turning onto the corresponding link.

Next replace the link L_1 entering node A with links entering each of the subnodes. These links should have costs equal to the original cost of link L_1, plus any turn penalty you want to assign to the corresponding turn. Figure 11.10 shows the intersection with turn penalties added. In this figure a turn penalty of 5 has been added for the left turn out of node A and a turn penalty of 2 has been added for a right turn.

By placing turn penalty information directly in the network, you avoid the need to modify previous shortest path algorithms. Those algorithms will correctly find shortest paths taking the turn penalties into account.

You will still need to modify your programs slightly to deal with the fact that some nodes have been split into subnodes. Suppose you want to find the shortest path between nodes I and J but node I has been split into subnodes. Assuming you are allowed to leave node I along any link, you can create a dummy node to use as the root node in the shortest path tree. Connect that node to each of the subnodes of node I using zero cost links. Then when you build the shortest path tree rooted at the dummy node, you will have found all of the shortest paths that use any of the subnodes. Figure 11.11 shows the intersection from Figure 11.10 connected to a dummy root node.

It is easier to deal with the case of finding a path to a node that has been split into subnodes. If you want to find the shortest path between nodes I and J and node J has been split into subnodes, first find the shortest path tree rooted at node I as usual. Then check each of the subnodes of node J to see which is closest to the tree's root. The path to that subnode is the shortest path to the original node J.

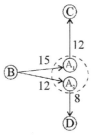

Figure 11.10 An intersection with turn penalties.

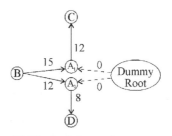

Figure 11.11 An intersection connected to a dummy root.

Many Turn Penalties

If you want to add turn penalties to most of the nodes in your network, the previous method is not very efficient. A better method is to create a completely new network to include the turn penalty information.

For each link in the original network connecting nodes A and B, create a node AB in the new network.

Create a link between two nodes if the corresponding links were connected in the original network. For example, suppose in the original network one link connects nodes A and B and another link connects nodes B and C. Then you should make a link in the new network connecting the node AB to the node BC.

Set the cost of the new link to be the cost of the second link in the original network plus the turn penalty. In this example the cost of the link from node AB to node BC should be the cost of the link connecting nodes B and C in the original network plus the turn penalty for moving from node A to B to C.

Figure 11.12 shows a small network and the corresponding new network representing the turn penalties. Here left turns carry a penalty of 3, right turns carry a penalty of 2, and straight "turns" carry no penalty. Since the turn from node B to E to F in the original network is a left turn, for example, the link between nodes BE and EF in the new network carries a turn penalty of three. The cost of the link connecting nodes E and F in the original network is 3, so the total cost of the link is $3 + 3 = 6$.

Now suppose you wanted to find the shortest path tree rooted at node D in the original network. To do this in the new network, create a dummy root node. Create links connecting that node to all of the links that leave node D in the original network. Give these links the same costs as the corresponding links in the original network. Figure 11.13 shows the new network from Figure 11.12 with the dummy root node corresponding to node D. The shortest path tree through this network is drawn in bold lines.

To find the shortest path from node D to node C, examine all of the nodes in the new network that correspond to links ending at node C. In this example, those are the nodes BC and FC. The node that is closest to the dummy root gives the shortest path to node C in the original network. The nodes in the shortest path in the new network correspond to the links in the shortest path in the original network.

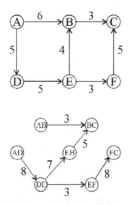

Figure 11.12 A network and corresponding turn penalty network.

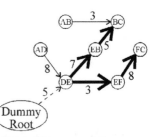

Figure 11.13 Shortest path tree in a turn penalty network.

In Figure 11.13 the best path goes from the dummy root node, to node DE, to node EF, to node FC and has a total cost of 16. This path corresponds to the path D, E, F, C in the original network. Counting the one left turn penalty for the E, F, C turn, this path also has a cost of 16 in the original network.

Notice that you would not have found this path if you had built a shortest path tree in the original network. Without turn penalties the shortest path from node D to node C would be D, E, B, C which has a total cost of 12. With turn penalties that path has a cost of 17.

Shortest Path Applications

Shortest path calculations are used in many applications. Finding the shortest route between two points in a street network is an obvious example. There are many other applications that use shortest paths through networks in less obvious ways. The following sections describe a few of these applications.

Districting

Suppose you have the map of a city that shows the locations of all of the fire stations. You might want to determine, for every point in the city, which is the closest fire station. At first glance this might seem like a difficult problem. You might try computing the shortest path tree rooted at every node in the network to see which fire stations were closest to each node. You might compute the shortest path tree rooted at each fire station and record how close each node is to each fire station. There is a much faster method.

Create a dummy root node and connect it with zero cost links to each of the fire stations. Then find the shortest path tree rooted at this dummy node. For each point in the network, the shortest path from the root node to the point will pass through the fire station that is closest to that point. To find the fire station closest to a point, simply follow the shortest path from that point towards the root until it reaches one of the fire stations. By building a single shortest path tree, you can find the closest fire station to every point in the network.

Figure 11.14 shows a small street network with two fire stations indicated by dark circles. The zero cost links connecting the dummy root to the fire stations are drawn in dashed lines. Bold lines show the shortest path tree for this network.

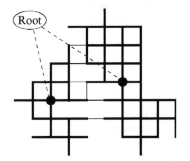

Figure 11.14 Districting using a shortest path tree.

Critical Path Scheduling

In many projects, including large programming projects, certain tasks must be completed before certain others can begin. When building a house, for example, the land must be graded before the foundation is poured, the foundation must be dry before the framing can begin, the framing must be finished before the electrical, plumbing, and roofing work can start, and so on.

Some of these tasks can be performed at the same time while others must happen one after another. The electrical and plumbing work, for example, can be done at the same time.

A *critical path* is one of the longest sequences of tasks that must occur to finish the project. Items that lie along a critical path are important because a slip in any of their schedules will impact the completion time of the entire project. If the foundation is poured a week late, the house will be finished a week late. You can use a shortest path algorithm modified to find *longest* paths, to identify the critical path tasks.

First, create a network that represents the scheduling relationships among the project tasks. Create a node for each task. Create a link between task I and task J if task I must be completed before task J can begin. Set the cost of the link between task I and task J equal to the length of time it will take to complete task I.

Next, create two dummy nodes, one to represent the start of the project and one to represent the completion. Create zero cost links connecting the start node to every node in the project that has no links leading into it. These nodes correspond to tasks that can begin immediately without waiting for the completion of any other tasks.

Then create zero cost dummy links connecting every node that has no links leaving it to the finish node. These nodes represent tasks for which no other task must wait. Once all of these tasks have been finished, the entire project is completed.

Now by finding the longest path between the start and finish nodes in this network, you can find a critical path for the project. The tasks along this path are the critical tasks.

For example, consider a simplified sprinkler installation project with five tasks. The tasks and their precedence relationships are shown in Table 11.1. The network for this installation project is shown in Figure 11.15.

In this simple example it is easy to see that the longest path through the network follows the sequence of tasks: dig trenches, install pipe, bury pipe. Those are the critical tasks and if any of them is delayed, the project completion will be delayed.

The length of this critical path gives the expected completion time of the project. In this case, if all of the tasks are completed on schedule, the project will take 5 days. This also assumes that tasks are performed at the same time whenever possible. For example, one person should dig trenches while another buys pipe.

Table 11.1 Sprinkler Installation Tasks

Task	Time	Must start after:
A. Buy pipe	1 day	(nothing)
B. Dig trenches	2 days	(nothing)
C. Cut pipe	1 day	A
D. Install pipe	2 days	B, C
E. Bury pipe	1 day	D

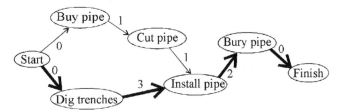

Figure 11.15 Sprinkler installation task network.

In a larger project, like building a skyscraper or producing a movie, there may be thousands of tasks and the critical paths may be much less obvious.

Crew Scheduling

Suppose you can hire any of several part-time contractors to answer your phone. Each has a certain number of available hours and each costs a different amount per hour. You want to hire the least expensive combination of contractors that can answer your phone between 9:00 AM and 5:00 PM. Table 11.2 lists the contractors' prices and hours of availability.

To build the corresponding network, create a node to represent each hour of the day. For each contractor, build links representing the hours that contractor is available. If a contractor is available between 9:00 and 11:00, make a link between the 9:00 node and the 11:00 node. Set the link's cost to the total cost for that contractor working during that period. If the contractor charges $6.50 per hour and the period is two hours long, the cost of the link would be $13.00. Figure 11.16 shows the network corresponding to the data in Table 11.2.

The shortest path from the first node to the last node gives the least expensive combination of contractors. Each link in the path corresponds to a contractor working a particular time period. In this case the shortest path from the 9:00 node to the 5:00 node passes through the 11:00, 12:00, and 3:00 nodes. The corresponding employment schedule is: A works 9:00–11:00, D works 11:00–12:00, A works 12:00–3:00, and E works 3:00 to 5:00. The total cost of this work schedule is $52.15.

Table 11.2 Employee Availability and Costs

Contractor	*Hours Available*	*Cost per hour*
A	9–11	$6.50
	12–3	
B	9–2	$6.75
C	2–5	$7.00
D	11–12	$6.25
E	9–12	$6.70
	3–5	

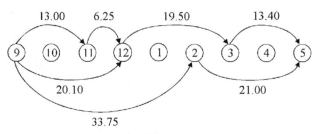

Figure 11.16 Crew scheduling network.

Maximum Flow

In many networks, links have *capacities* in addition to costs. Each link can carry a *flow* that is no greater than its capacity. For instance, the streets in a street network can only carry a certain number of cars per hour. If the number of cars on a link exceeds the link's capacity, the result is a traffic jam. A network with capacities on its links is called a *capacitated network*.

Given a capacitated network, the maximum flow problem is to determine the largest flow possible through the network from a specific *source* node to a specific *sink* node. Figure 11.17 shows a small capacitated network. The numbers next to the links in this network are the link capacities rather than the link costs. In this example the maximum flow is 4 and can be produced by flowing two units along the path A, B, E, F and two units along the path A, C, D, F.

The algorithm described here starts with no flows on the links and then incrementally modifies the flows to improve the solution it has found so far. When it can make no more improvements, the algorithm is finished.

To find ways to increase the total flow, the algorithm examines the *residual capacities* of the links. The residual capacity of the link between nodes I and J is the maximum additional net flow that you could send from node I to node J using the link between I and J and the link between J and I. This net flow can include additional flow across the I–J link if that link has unused capacity, and it can include removing flow from the J–I link if that link is carrying flow.

For example, suppose there is a flow of 2 on the link connecting nodes A and C in Figure 11.17. Since that link has a capacity of 3, you could add an additional flow of 1 to that link so its residual capacity is 1. Even though the network shown in Figure 11.17 does not have a C–A link, there is a residual capacity for the C–A link. In this example, since there is a flow of 2 units across the A–C link, you could remove up to 2 units of that flow. This would increase the net flow from node C to node A by 2. That means the residual capacity of the C–A link is 2.

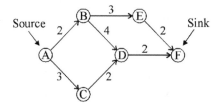

Figure 11.17 A capacitated network.

The network consisting of all of the links with positive residual capacities is called the *residual network*. Figure 11.18 shows the network in Figure 11.17 with flows assigned to each link. For each link, the first number is the flow across the link and the second is the link's capacity. The label "1/2," for example, means the link holds a flow of 1 and has capacity 2. The links carrying flows greater than zero are shown in bold.

Figure 11.19 shows the residual network corresponding to the flows shown in Figure 11.18. Only the links that might actually have residual capacity have been drawn. For example, no links between nodes A and D have been drawn. The original network does not contain an A–D link or a D–A link so those links will always have residual capacities equal to zero.

A key fact about residual networks is that any path using links with residual capacities greater than zero, that connects the source to the sink, shows a way to increase the flow in the network. Since this path shows how to increase or augment the flow, this type of path is called an *augmenting path*. Figure 11.20 shows the residual network in Figure 11.19 with an augmenting path drawn in bold.

To update the solution using an augmenting path, find the smallest residual capacity along the path. Then adjust the flows along the path by this amount. In Figure 11.20, for example, the smallest residual capacity of any link along the augmenting path is 2. To update the flows in the network, you would add a flow of 2 to any link I–J along the path. You would also subtract a flow of 2 from any link J–I where the reversed I–J link is in the path.

Rather than actually adjusting the flows and then rebuilding the residual network, it is easier to simply adjust the residual network. Then, when the algorithm is finished, you can use the residual network to compute the flows for each of the links. To adjust the residual network in this example, follow the augmenting path. Subtract 2 from the residual capacity of any link I–J along the path and add 2 to the residual capacity of the corresponding link J–I. Figure 11.21 shows the updated residual network for this example.

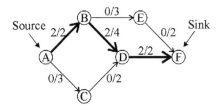

Figure 11.18 Network flows.

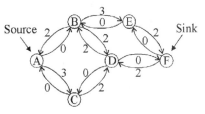

Figure 11.19 Residual network.

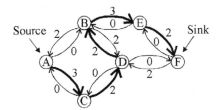

Figure 11.20 An augmenting path through a residual network.

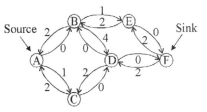

Figure 11.21 Updated residual network.

When you can find no more augmenting paths, you can use the residual network to compute the flows for the original network. For each link between nodes I and J, if the residual flow between nodes I and J is less than the capacity of the link, then the flow should equal the capacity minus the residual flow. Otherwise the flow should be zero.

For instance, in Figure 11.21 the residual flow from node A to node C is 1 and the capacity of the A, C link is 3. Since 1 is less than 3, the flow across this link should be $3 - 1 = 2$. Figure 11.22 shows the network flows corresponding to residual network in Figure 11.21.

So far the algorithm does not have a method for finding augmenting paths in the residual network. Perhaps the simplest method is similar to a label correcting shortest path algorithm. Start by placing the source node in a candidate list. Then, while the candidate list is not empty, remove an item from the list. Examine any neighboring nodes connected to the selected node by a link that has a remaining residual capacity greater than zero. If the neighbor has never yet been placed in the candidate list, add it to the list.

There are two ways in which this method differs from a label correcting shortest path algorithm. First, this method does not follow links with residual capacity zero. The shortest path algorithm will examine any link no matter what cost the link has.

Second, this algorithm examines each node at most once. The label correcting shortest path method will update a node and place it back in the candidate list if it later finds an improved path from the root to that node. In this algorithm you do not care how short the augmenting path is, so you do not need to update paths and place nodes back in the candidate list.

```
Sub FindMaxFlows (source As Integer, sink As Integer)
Const INFINITY = 32767

Dim CL() As Integer
Dim Residual() As Integer

Dim next_cl As Integer  ' First item in the list.
Dim last_cl As Integer  ' Last item in the list.
Dim i As Integer
Dim j As Integer
Dim min_residual As Integer

    ' Dimension key arrays.
    ReDim CL(1 To NumNodes)
    ReDim Residual(1 To NumNodes, 1 To NumNodes)

    ' Reset the flows.
    For i = 1 To NumNodes
```

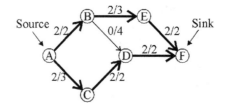

Figure 11.22 Maximum flows.

```
        For j = 1 To NumNodes
            LinkFlow(i, j) = 0
        Next j
    Next i


    ' Initially the residual values are the same as the
    ' capacities.
    For i = 1 To NumNodes
        For j = 1 To NumNodes
            Residual(i, j) = Capacity(i, j)
        Next j
    Next i


    ' Repeat until we can find no more augmenting paths.
    Do
        ' Find an augmenting path in the residual network.
        ' Initialize the Parent and CL arrays.
        For i = 1 To NumNodes
            CL(i) = 0
            Parent(i) = 0
        Next i
        Parent(source) = -1

        ' Put the source on the candidate list.
        next_cl = source
        last_cl = source

        ' Repeat until the candidate list is empty.
        Do While next_cl > 0
            i = next_cl

            ' Check the links out of this node.
            For j = 1 To NumNodes
                ' If the residual link > 0 and this node
                ' has never been on the candidate list,
                ' add it to the list.
                If Residual(i, j) > 0 And Parent(j) = 0 Then
                    Parent(j) = i
                    CL(last_cl) = j
                    last_cl = j
                End If
            Next j

            ' Remove the node from the candidate list.
            next_cl = CL(i)
            ' Stop if the sink has been labeled.
            If Parent(sink) <> 0 Then Exit Do
        Loop

        ' Stop if we found no augmenting path.
        If Parent(sink) = 0 Then Exit Do

        ' Find the smallest residual along the
        ' augmenting path.
        min_residual = INFINITY
        j = sink
        Do While j <> source
            i = Parent(j)
```

```
                    If min_residual > Residual(i, j) Then min_residual = _
    Residual(i, j)
                j = i
        Loop

        ' Update the flows using the augmenting path.
        j = sink
        Do While j <> source
            i = Parent(j)
            Residual(i, j) = Residual(i, j) - min_residual
            Residual(j, i) = Residual(j, i) + min_residual
            j = i
        Loop
    Loop

    ' Calculate the flows from the residuals.
    For i = 1 To NumNodes
        For j = 1 To NumNodes
            If Capacity(i, j) > Residual(i, j) Then
                LinkFlow(i, j) = Capacity(i, j) - Residual(i, j)
            Else
                LinkFlow(i, j) = 0
            End If
        Next j
    Next i
End Sub
```

Example program FLOW uses this augmenting path technique to compute maximal flows through a network. To keep things simple, this program stores network information in a 2-dimensional array. For example, Capacity(I, J) is the capacity on the link connecting node I to node J. While a forward star representation would save space for most networks, this version is easier to understand so it will allow you to concentrate on the maximum flow algorithm.

Use the File menu's Load . . . command to load a network. File NET1.FLO contains the network shown in Figure 11.17. File NET2.FLO contains a larger network with 16 nodes.

If you click on a node with the left mouse button, the program will use that node as a source. If you click on another node with the right mouse button, the program will use the second node as a sink. It will then compute and display the maximum flows between the source and sink nodes.

Maximum Flow Applications

Maximum flow calculations are used in many applications. While maximal flows may be directly useful for some networks, they are most often used indirectly to calculate results that may seem at first to have little relation to maximal flow.

Disjoint Paths

Redundancy is important in large communications networks. Given a network like the one shown in Figure 11.23, you might like to know how many disjoint paths there are between the source node and the sink node. If there are many paths between the two nodes that do not share a common link, then there will still be a path between the two nodes even if several links in the network fail.

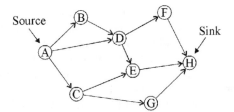

Figure 11.23 A communication network.

You can determine how many different paths there are using a maximum flow calculation. Create a network with nodes and links corresponding to those in the communications network. Set the capacity of each link to one.

Next perform a maximum flow calculation on the network. The maximal flow will be the same as the number of different paths from the source to the sink. Since each link can hold a flow of only one, none of the paths used by the maximum flow calculation can share a common link.

A stricter definition of redundancy might require that the different paths share no links or nodes. By modifying the previous network slightly, you can still use a maximum flow calculation to solve this problem.

Divide each node, except the source and sink nodes, into two subnodes connected by a single link with capacity one. Connect the first subnode to all of the links entering the original node. Connect all of the links leaving the original node to the second subnode. Figure 11.24 shows the network in Figure 11.23 with the nodes divided in this way. Now find the maximal flow for this new network.

If a path used by the maximal flow calculation passes through a node, it must use the link that connects that node's two subnodes. Since that link has a capacity of one, no two paths used by the maximum flow calculation can cross this connecting link, so no two paths can use the same node in the original network.

Work Assignment

Suppose you have a group of employees who each have certain skills. Suppose you also have a collection of jobs that require the attention of an employee who has a particular

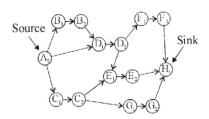

Figure 11.24 Transformed communication network.

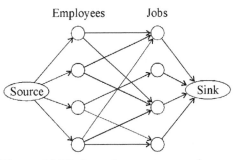

Figure 11.25 An assignment network.

set of skills. The assignment problem is to match the employees to the jobs so each job is assigned to an employee who has the skills to work that job.

To convert this problem into a maximum flow calculation, create a network with two columns of nodes. In the left column, place one node to represent each employee. In the right column, place one node to represent each job.

Next, compare the skills of each employee with the skills needed by each job. Create a link between each employee and every job that employee can work. Set the capacities of all of these links to one.

Create a source node and connect it to every employee with a link of capacity one. Then create a sink node and connect every job to it, again using links of capacity one. Figure 11.25 shows the assignment network for a four person, four job assignment problem.

Now find the maximum flow from the source node to the sink node. Each resulting unit of flow must pass through one employee node and one job node. That flow represents the assignment of that employee to that job.

If the employees have the proper skills to work all of the jobs, the maximum flow calculation will assign all of the jobs. If it is not possible to work all of the jobs, the maximum flow calculation will assign employees to jobs so as many jobs as possible are worked.

I N D E X

Integrated Spelling

GRADE 1

Harcourt Brace & Company

Orlando   Atlanta   Austin   Boston   San Francisco   Chicago   Dallas   New York   Toronto   London

Contents

Making Your Spelling Log

What's a Spelling Log?

It's a place to write words.

Take a look at my Spelling Log.

What words do you write?

I write words I like.

I write words I use a lot.

I write words I want to remember.

I write words I want to know

how to spell.

Grade 1 • Harcourt Brace School Publishers

Here's how you use it!

The Spelling Log is just for you.

Your Spelling Log is in the back of this book.

You will make your own list of words.

You will write words you want to remember.

Your Spelling Log has **two parts.**

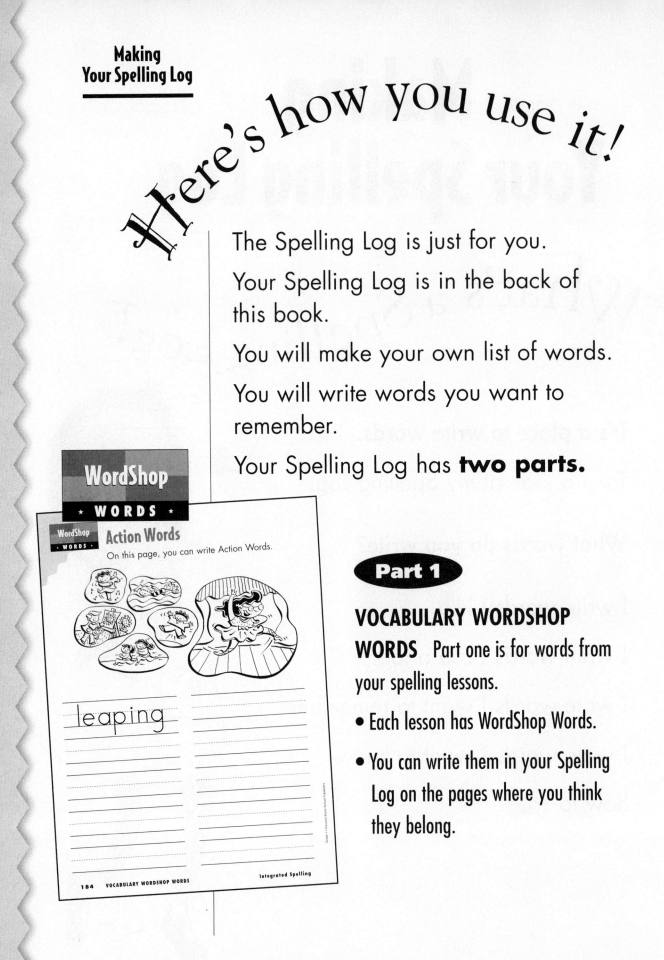

WordShop

★ WORDS ★

WordShop
· WORDS ·
Action Words
On this page, you can write Action Words.

leaping

184 VOCABULARY WORDSHOP WORDS

Integrated Spelling

Grade 1 • Harcourt Brace School Publishers

Part 1

**VOCABULARY WORDSHOP
WORDS** Part one is for words from your spelling lessons.

• Each lesson has WordShop Words.

• You can write them in your Spelling Log on the pages where you think they belong.

Grade 1 • Harcourt Brace School Publishers

These pages have some good ideas
about how to group my words.

My Own Word Collection

What's a word collection?

It's like a sticker collection. You choose words you like. Then you put them in groups with other words.

Weather Words
School Words
Sports Words
Story Words
Play Words

What kinds of groups?

Look at the pictures to get some ideas. Use your own ideas, too.

Group _____

Group _____

190   VOCABULARY WORDSHOP WORDS

Integrated Spelling

My Own Word Collection

Add words that you want to know how to spell. Then you can use them in your writing.

Food Words
Noise Words
Home Words
Math Words
Party Words

1+2=3

Group _____

Group _____

Integrated Spelling

VOCABULARY WORDSHOP WORDS   191

Part 2

MY OWN WORD COLLECTION

Part two is for you to write more words.

• You can add any words you want to write.

• You can also choose how to group the words.

This is going to be fun!

Study Steps to Learn a Word

▶ Follow these steps to learn to spell a word!

1

SAY

THE WORD.

Remember when you have heard it used. Think about what it means.

2

LOOK

AT THE WORD.

Think about words that rhyme with it or that look like it. Picture the word in your mind.

Grade 1 • Harcourt Brace School Publishers

3

SPELL
THE WORD TO YOURSELF.
Think about the letter or letters that stand for each sound.

4

WRITE
THE WORD WHILE YOU LOOK AT IT.
Check the way you wrote your letters. Did you write the word clearly and correctly? If not, write it again.

5

CHECK
WHAT YOU HAVE LEARNED.
Cover the word and write it again. Did you spell it correctly?

Initial Consonants

▶ Draw a line from the picture to the letter that stands for the beginning sound of its name.

PICTURE PERFECT "What I See" • Harcourt Brace School Publishers

Name _____

Strategy Workshop

| b | h | d | t |

▶ Name each picture. Listen for the beginning sound.
Write and trace the letter to spell the word.

1. __d__ og

2. __h__ at

3. __t__ ie

4. __b__ oy

5. a __d__ og and a __b__ oy

**A letter stands for the beginning
sound you hear in a word.**

PICTURE PERFECT "What I See" • Harcourt Brace School Publishers

Name _____

Vocabulary WordShop

Picnic
★ **WORDS** ★

pie
hat
bee

▶ Write the word from the box that names each thing.

1. _____

2. _____

3. _____

Plan a Picnic Draw a picture of things to bring on a picnic. Write words to go with your picture. Add these words to your Spelling Log.

PICTURE PERFECT "What I See" • Harcourt Brace School Publishers

Name _____

Vocabulary Adventures

▶ Write a word from the box that tells what each child sees.

1. _____

2. _____

3. _____

Words with -ap

▶ Circle the pictures whose names rhyme with **clap**.

PICTURE PERFECT "Down on the Farm" • Harcourt Brace School Publishers

Integrated Spelling

Strategy Workshop

| m | t | p | h |

▶ Name these pictures. Listen for rhyming words.
Write and trace the letters to spell the words.

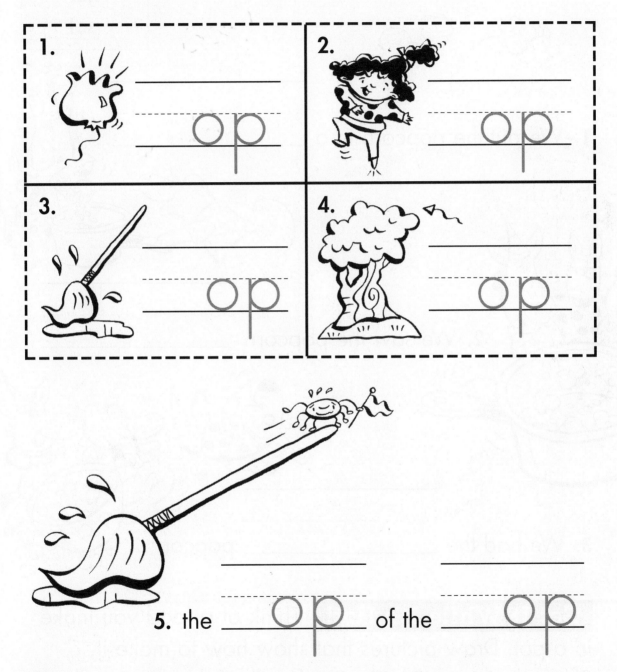

1. _____
o p

2. _____
o p

3. _____
o p

4. _____
o p

5. the _____ o p _____ of the _____ o p

**Words that rhyme with top and mop often end
with the letters op.**

Name _____

Vocabulary WordShop

▶ Use the words from the box to tell what the friends did.

_____

1. We put the popcorn in a _____ .

_____

2. We saw the popcorn _____ .

_____

3. We had the _____ popcorn.

Get It While It's Hot! Think of a food you make in a pot. Draw pictures that show how to make it. Share the pictures with your family. Ask them to help you cook the food.

Integrated Spelling

Vocabulary Adventures

▶ Write the words from the box to answer the riddle.

_____

1. Put it in a _____ .

2. It will get _____ .

3. It will _____ .

4. What is it? It is _____ !

▶ Draw a picture that shows the answer to the riddle.

Words with -et

▶ Circle the pictures whose names rhyme with **jet**.

Strategy Workshop

| w j n g v |

▶ Name these pictures. Listen for rhyming words.
Write and trace the letters to spell the words.

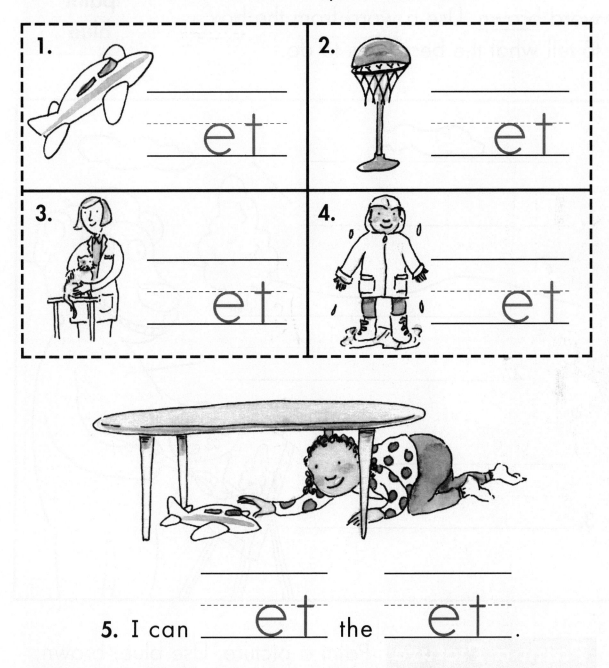

1. ___ et

2. ___ et

3. ___ et

4. ___ et

5. I can ___ et the ___ et.

**Words that rhyme with <u>get</u> and <u>jet</u> often end
with the letters <u>et</u>.**

Vocabulary WordShop

Painting
★ W O R D S ★
brown
paint
blue

▶ Paint the sky blue. Write the word <u>blue</u>. Paint the bear brown. Write the word <u>brown</u>. Use a word from the box to tell what the bear likes to do.

1. _____

2. _____

3. _____

Paint a Picture Paint a picture. Use blue, brown, and other colors. Then write the words that name the colors you used. Add these words to your Spelling Log.

BIG DREAMS "Big Brown Bear" • Harcourt Brace School Publishers

Vocabulary Adventures

▶ Follow the directions for each picture.

1. Draw a circle around the animals that like to <u>paint</u>.

2. Color the big animal <u>brown</u>.

3. Color the little animal's hat <u>blue</u>.

Name _____

Words with -ell

▶ Circle the pictures whose names rhyme with **sh<u>ell</u>**.

Strategy Workshop

▶ Name these pictures. Listen for rhyming words. Write and trace the letters to spell the words.

1. _____ ell

2. _____ ell

3. _____ ell

4. _____ ell

5. The baby _____ ell !

6. He gave a _____ ell !

Words that rhyme with fell and yell often end with the letters ell.

Name _____

Vocabulary WordShop

▶ Write a word from the box to complete each sentence.

1. The chick came out of the _____ .

2. The chick saw a_____ .

3. The chick is digging for a _____ .

Nature Flash Cards On separate cards, draw four things you see in nature. On the backs, label the pictures. Have a friend choose a card and name the picture.

BIG DREAMS "The Chick and the Duckling" • Harcourt Brace School Publishers

Name _____

Vocabulary Adventures

▶ Complete each picture. Then write the word that tells what you drew.

_____
- -

1. The _____ is big.

_____
- -

2. She is looking for a _____ .

_____
- -

3. He got one more _____ .

Integrated Spelling

Words with -en

▶ Circle the pictures whose names rhyme with **pen**.

Elephants
fed at 10

Integrated Spelling

Strategy Workshop

| t p m h |

▶ Name these pictures. Listen for rhyming words.
Write and trace the letters to spell the words.

1. ___ ___ en

2. ___ ___ en

3. ___ ___ en

4. ___ ___ en

5. It is as big as ___ ___ en ___ ___ en !

**Words that rhyme with <u>ten</u> and <u>men</u> often end
with the letters <u>en</u>.**

BIG DREAMS "Cloudy Day, Sunny Day" • Harcourt Brace School Publishers

Integrated Spelling

Name _____

Vocabulary WordShop

▶ Write the word from the box to complete the sentence about each picture.

_____
1. It is a _____ day.

_____
2. It is a _____ day.

_____
3. It is a _____ day.

Weather Report Draw a picture of today's weather. Show what the sky looks like. Write a sentence to go with your picture.

BIG DREAMS "Cloudy Day, Sunny Day" • Harcourt Brace School Publishers

Integrated Spelling

Vocabulary Adventures

▶ Read and follow the directions.

1. Draw a picture of a <u>sunny</u> day.

2. Draw a picture of a <u>cloudy</u> day.

3. Draw a picture. Show what you like to do on a <u>gray</u> day.

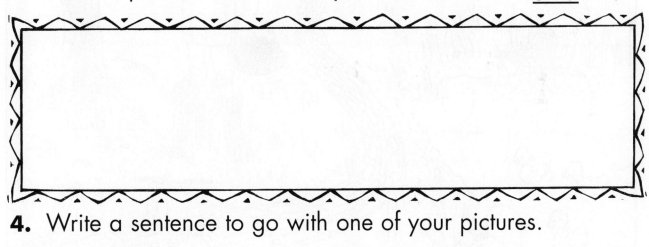

4. Write a sentence to go with one of your pictures.

_____

- - - - - - - - - - - - - - - - - -

_____

- - - - - - - - - - - - - - - - - -

_____

Name _____

Words with -ick

▶ Circle the pictures whose names rhyme with **ch<u>ick</u>**.

BIG DREAMS "Moving Day" • Harcourt Brace School Publishers

Integrated Spelling

Strategy Workshop

l s p k

▶ Name these pictures. Listen for rhyming words.
Write and trace the letters to spell the words.

1. ___ ick

2. ___ ick

3. ___ ick

4. ___ ick

5. The friends ___ ick and then ___ ick !

**Words that rhyme with pick and <u>kick</u> often end
with the letters <u>ick</u>.**

Vocabulary WordShop

▶ Write the words from the box to complete the story.

_____

1. It is _____ day.

_____

2. Let me put my dog in the _____ .

_____

3. He is _____, too!

Pack a Box   Imagine that you are moving. Make a picture of things you would pack in a box. Write the words that name the items. Add these words to your Spelling Log.

Integrated Spelling

Vocabulary Adventures

▶ Use the words from the pictures below. Write them in the puzzle.

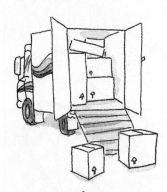

moving

dog

box

going

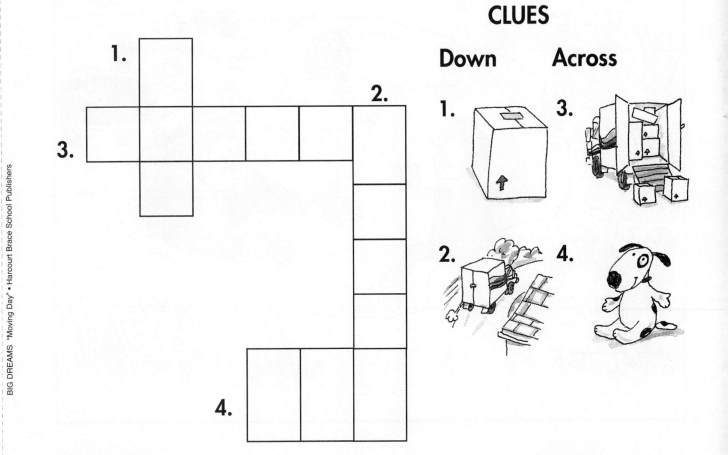

CLUES

Down   **Across**

1.   3.

2.   4.

Words with -ip

▶ Circle the pictures whose names rhyme with **flip**.

Integrated Spelling

Name _____

Strategy Workshop

$\boxed{l \quad z \quad t \quad r}$

▶ Name these pictures. Listen for rhyming words.
Write and trace the letters to spell the words.

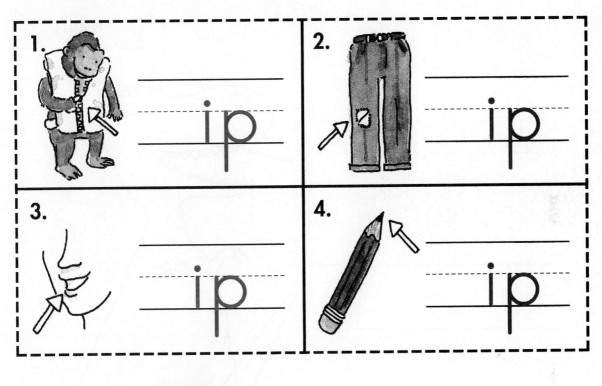

1. _____ ip

2. _____ ip

3. _____ ip

4. _____ ip

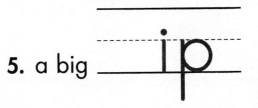

5. a big _____ ip

**Words that rhyme with rip and tip often end
with the letters ip.**

Integrated Spelling

Vocabulary WordShop

▶ Write the word from the box that names each body part of the .

Dinosaur
★ W O R D S ★
tail
feet
teeth

1. _____

2. _____

3. _____

Animal Body Parts Draw a picture of an animal. Write the words that name the animal's body parts.

Vocabulary Adventures

BIG DREAMS "Catch Me If You Can" • Harcourt Brace School Publishers

▶ Look at each picture. Write a word to tell about it.

tail
feet
teeth

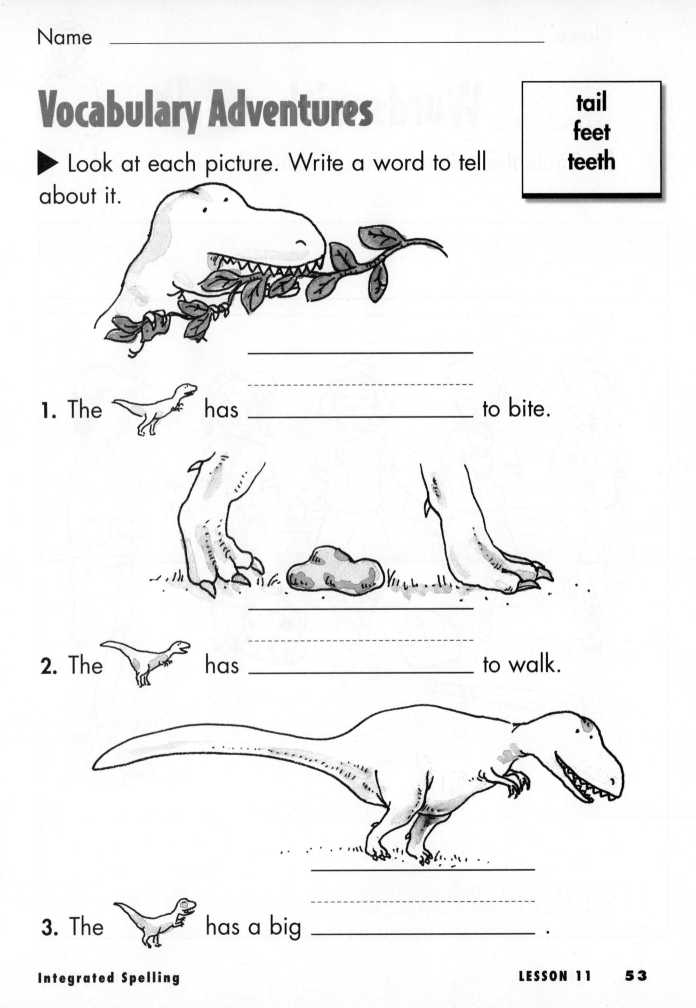

_____

_ _

1. The ____ has _____ to bite.

_____

_ _

2. The ____ has _____ to walk.

_____

_ _

3. The ____ has a big _____ .

Integrated Spelling

Name _____

Words with -ad

▶ Circle the pictures whose names rhyme with **dad**.

Strategy Workshop

m s p d

▶ Name these pictures. Listen for rhyming words.
Write and trace the letters to spell the words.

1. _____ ad

2. _____ ad

3. _____ ad

4. _____ ad

5. This _____ ad has a _____ ad.

**Words that rhyme with <u>dad</u> and pad often end
with the letters <u>ad</u>.**

Name _____

Vocabulary WordShop

▶ Use the words from the box to tell about the game.

Game
★ W O R D S ★

ran
caught
threw

1. She _____ the ball.

2. He hit it and_____ .

3. She _____ the ball.

Game Time Think of a game to play. Write sentences that tell how to play it. Then ask your friends to play the game with you.

BIG DREAMS "Later, Rover" • Harcourt Brace School Publishers

Integrated Spelling

Name _____

Vocabulary Adventures

ran
caught
threw

▶ Find and circle the hidden words.
Hint: Words can go across or down.
Then write the words on the lines below.

m	c	o	r	f
r	a	n	g	y
t	u	l	m	a
b	g	u	r	e
t	h	r	e	w
x	t	a	s	m

_____

1. _____

2. _____

3. _____

Name _____

Words with -in

▶ Circle the pictures whose names rhyme with **pin**.

FINISH LINE FINISH LINE FINIS

JUDGE

WARM FRIENDS "Hattie and the Fox" • Harcourt Brace School Publishers

Integrated Spelling

Name _____

Strategy Workshop

▶ Name these pictures. Listen for rhyming words.
Write and trace the letters to spell the words.

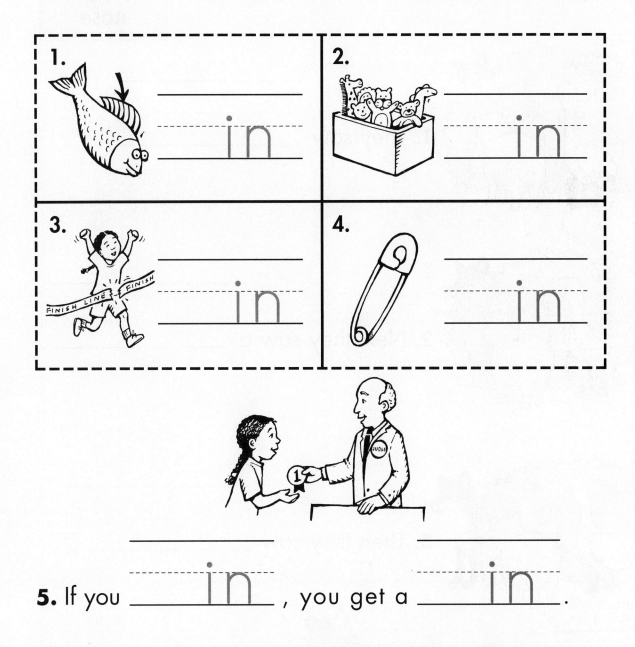

1. _____ in

2. _____ in

3. _____ in

4. _____ in

5. If you _____ in , you get a _____ in .

Words that rhyme with <u>win</u> and pin often end with the letters <u>in</u>.

Name _____

Vocabulary WordShop

▶ Write a word from the box in each sentence.

| Body |
| **★ WORDS ★** |
| legs |
| ears |
| nose |

_____
- -

1. They saw _____.

_____
- -

2. Next they saw a _____.

_____
- -

3. Then they saw _____.

They saw a _____.

60   LESSON 13

Integrated Spelling

WARM FRIENDS "Hattie and the Fox" • Harcourt Brace School Publishers

Vocabulary Adventures

▶ Use words from the box to tell about the picture.

legs
nose
ears

1. _____

2. _____

3. _____

Favorite Animals Make a picture of your favorite animal. Write the WordShop Words and other words to label your picture. Add these words to your Spelling Log.

Words with -ill

▶ Circle the pictures whose names rhyme with **hill**.

Integrated Spelling

Strategy Workshop

▶ Name these pictures. Listen for rhyming words.
Write and trace the letters to spell the words.

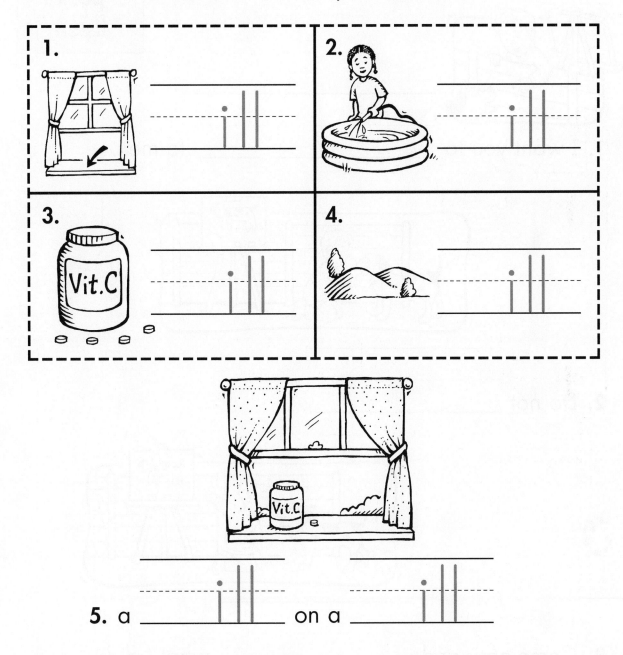

1.

2.

3. Vit.C

4.

5. a _____ill _____ on a _____ill

**Words that rhyme with pill and <u>sill</u> often end
with the letters <u>ill</u>.**

Name _____

Vocabulary WordShop

▶ What is the boy saying? Write words from the box to complete the sentences.

_____

----

1. I want you to _____ to me.

_____

- -

2. Do not _____.

_____

- -

3. Come now and _____ what I did.

WARM FRIENDS "And I Mean It, Stanley!" • Harcourt Brace School Publishers

Name _____

Vocabulary Adventures

▶ Write a word from the box to tell about each picture.

_____

1. _____

2. _____

3. _____

Act It Out Play this game with a partner. Act out a word from the box. See if your partner can guess which word it is.

Words with **-ug**

▶ Circle the pictures whose names rhyme with **hug**.

Integrated Spelling

Strategy Workshop

m	b	t	r

▶ Name these pictures. Listen for rhyming words.
Write and trace the letters to spell the words.

1. _____ ug

2. _____ ug

3. _____ ug

4. _____ ug

5. The _____ ug _____ is on the _____ ug _____.

**Words that rhyme with bug and rug often end
with the letters ug.**

Vocabulary WordShop

▶ Write a word from the box to complete each sentence.

_____

1. The friends _____.

_____

2. The friends _____.

_____

3. The friends _____.

Friends Together Work with a friend. Make up sentences using the WordShop Words. Act out your sentences.

WARM FRIENDS "Best of Friends" • Harcourt Brace School Publishers

Vocabulary Adventures

▶ Draw a picture to answer each question.

1. Where do you and a friend like to <u>swim</u>?

2. What do you and a friend like to <u>ride</u>?

3. What do you and a friend like to <u>paint</u>?

Name _____

Words with -ig

▶ Circle the pictures whose names rhyme with **pig**.

Strategy Workshop

▶ Name these pictures. Listen for rhyming words.
Write and trace the letters to spell the words.

1. _____ ig

2. _____ ig

3. _____ ig

4. _____ ig

5. The _____ ig puts on a _____ ig.

**Words that rhyme with pig and wig often end
with the letters ig.**

Vocabulary WordShop

▶ Write words from the box to tell about the pictures.

_____

1. She has a _____ house.

_____

2. They will take a _____ walk.

_____

3. She is a _____ hen.

Name _____

Vocabulary Adventures

▶ Read the word below each picture. Write the word that has the opposite meaning.

sad

_____

1. _____

big

_____

2. _____

short

_____

3. _____

Describe Something Draw a picture of a person, place, or thing. Write words that describe what you drew. Add these words to your Spelling Log.

Words with -un

▶ Circle the pictures whose names rhyme with **sun**.

Strategy Workshop

| f s r b |

▶ Name these pictures. Listen for rhyming words.
Write and trace the letters to spell the words.

1. _____ un

2. _____ un

3. _____ un

4. _____ un

5. The friends _____ un _____ in the _____ un _____.

Words that rhyme with <u>run</u> and <u>sun</u> often end with the letters <u>un</u>.

Name _____

Vocabulary WordShop

▶ Look at the pictures. Write a word from the box in each sentence.

1. It is time for _____.

2. She will _____ about bugs.

3. They think that _____ is fun.

Integrated Spelling

WARM FRIENDS "Making Friends, Keeping Friends" • Harcourt Brace School Publishers

Vocabulary Adventures

reading
math
learn

▶ Use the words from the box to tell about the friends.

1. It is a game.

_____

- -

The friends want to _____ it.

_____

- -

2. The friends know _____ .

1 + 2 =

_____

- -

3. The friends love _____ the best.

School Time Add words about school to your Spelling Log. Then draw or paint a picture about a favorite school day activity.

WARM FRIENDS "Making Friends, Keeping Friends" • Harcourt Brace School Publishers

Words with -ack

▶ Circle the pictures whose names rhyme with **sack**.

Integrated Spelling

Strategy Workshop

| p | s | j | b | t |

▶ Name these pictures. Listen for rhyming words.
Write and trace the letters to spell the words.

1. ___ack

2. ___ack

3. ___ack

4. ___ack

5. a ___ack in a ___ack

**Words that rhyme with pack and <u>sack</u> often end
with the letters <u>ack</u>.**

Name _____

Vocabulary WordShop

▶ Write a word from the box to complete each sentence.

Dancing
★ W O R D S ★

step
dance
music

1. We hear the _____.

2. We take a big _____.

3. We _____ all day.

WARM FRIENDS "Rex and Lilly Playtime" • Harcourt Brace School Publishers

Integrated Spelling

Vocabulary Adventures

▶ Complete the directions. Write words from the box.

| dance |
| step |
| music |

How to Dance

_____

1. Put on the _____.

_____

2. Say to a friend, "Let's _____."

_____

3. Take a _____ again and again.

SPELLING
★ **WORDS** ★

1. red

2. hen

3. help

4. went

Add Your Own ★ W O R D ★

5. _____

Words with Short e

▶ Read the Spelling Words out loud. Write them on the lines.

Where do you hear the short e sound in these words? Color the hen above the word that tells where you hear the short e sound.

| beginning | middle | end |

The short e sound is usually spelled e.

Integrated Spelling

Strategy Workshop

▶ Name each picture. Write a Spelling Word that rhymes with the picture name to complete the sentence.

pen

_____

- -

1. I have a _____ .

bed

_____

- -

2. My hen is _____ .

tent

_____

- -

3. She _____ to the garden.

Fun with Words   Write a Spelling Word to complete the sentence.

_____

- -

4. Who will _____ me?

Name _____

Vocabulary WordShop

▶ Use the best word from the box to
complete the sentence about each picture.

Talking
★ WORDS ★
asked
called
said

_____

----

1. The hen _____ to the animals.

_____

----

2. "Will you help me?" _____ the hen.

_____

----

3. The animals _____, "No!"

FULL SAILS "The Little Red Hen" • Harcourt Brace School Publishers

Name _____

Vocabulary Adventures

▶ Write answers to the boy's questions.

1. What did you do?

_____

I _____ my mother.

2. What did you say?

_____

I _____ her if I could go for a ride.

3. What did she say?

_____

She _____ to be back at two.

SPELLING
★ **WORDS** ★

1. but

2. must

3. just

4. run

Add Your Own ★ W O R D ★

5. _____

Words with Short **U**

▶ Read the Spelling Words out loud. Write them on the lines.

Where do you hear the short u sound in these words? Color the acorn above the word that tells where you hear the short u sound.

beginning   **middle**   **end**

The short u sound is usually spelled u.

FULL SAILS "Henny Penny" • Harcourt Brace School Publishers

Strategy Workshop

▶ Two of the Spelling Words rhyme.
Write them in the sentences.

1. I _____ woke up!

2. Now I _____ get up!

Fun with Words   Write Spelling Words in the
sentences.

3. The sky is not falling, _____ I am.

4. Everybody, _____! I can't fly!

Name _____

Vocabulary WordShop

▶ Draw a line to show where the hen
goes. Then write the name of each picture.

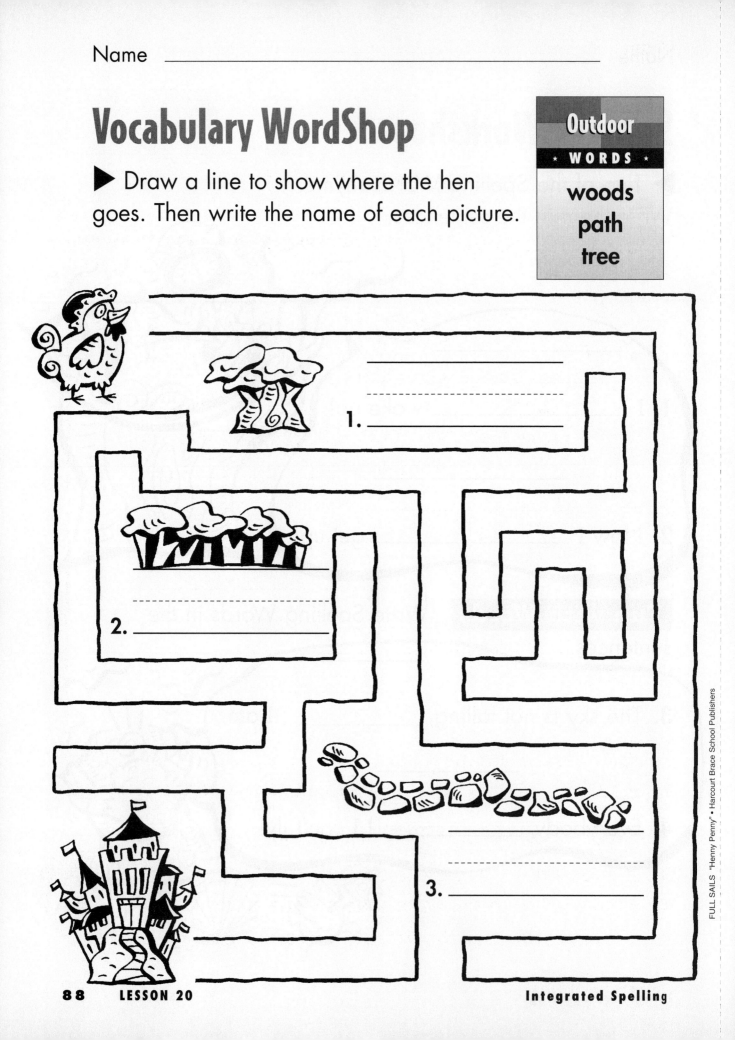

1. _____

2. _____

3. _____

Integrated Spelling

Vocabulary Adventures

woods
path
tree

▶ Look at the map. Then write words to complete the directions.

Come to My Birthday!

_____

----

1. Go down the _____.

_____

----

2. Walk into the _____.

_____

----

3. Stop at the big oak _____.

A Birthday Surprise Draw four pictures of birthday gifts. Write a Spelling Word on the back of each one. Have friends choose a gift. See if they can spell the words on the pictures.

FULL SAILS "Henny Penny" • Harcourt Brace School Publishers

SPELLING
★ WORDS ★

1. in

2. it

3. big

4. him

Add Your Own
★ W O R D ★

5. _____

Words with Short **i**

▶ Read the Spelling Words out loud. Write them on the wall.

For each word, color the stone that shows where you hear the short i sound.

beginning   middle

The short i sound is usually spelled i.

FULL SAILS "Little Lumpty" • Harcourt Brace School Publishers

Strategy Workshop

▶ Read each word that names a picture. Cross out the first letter. What Spelling Word do you see? Write it in the sentence.

kit

1. He will climb _____ .

pin

2. He will get _____ trouble.

Fun with Words Complete the sentences. Write the Spelling Words with the short i sound in the middle.

3. Can he make the _____ jump?

4. Will his friends catch _____?

Name _____

Vocabulary WordShop

▶ Look at the pictures. Write a word from the box in each sentence.

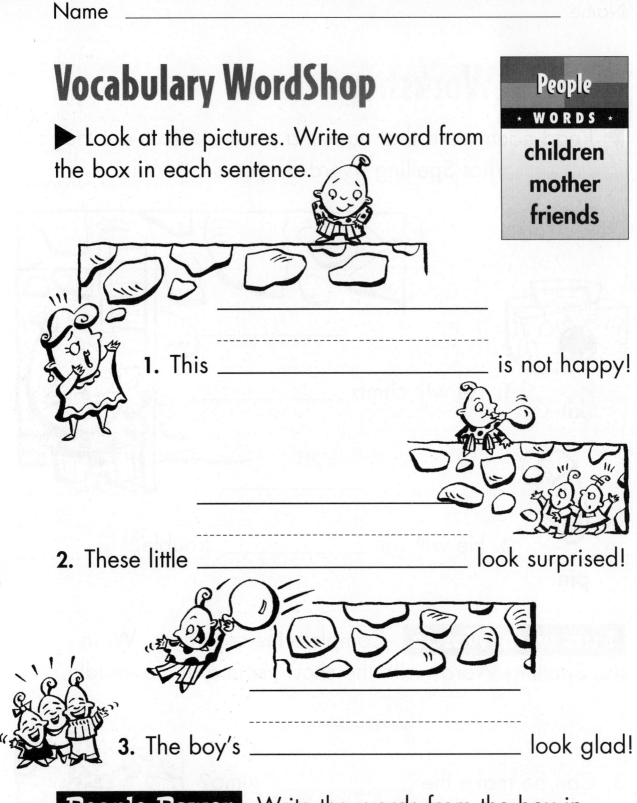

1. This _____ is not happy!

2. These little _____ look surprised!

3. The boy's _____ look glad!

People Power Write the words from the box in your Spelling Log. Then draw a picture of your friends. Share it with your family. Tell the names of the friends in your picture.

FULL SAILS "Little Lumpty" • Harcourt Brace School Publishers

Name _____

Vocabulary Adventures

▶ Color the pictures. Then write about them. Use these words.

_____

_____

_____

_____

_____

_____

_____

_____

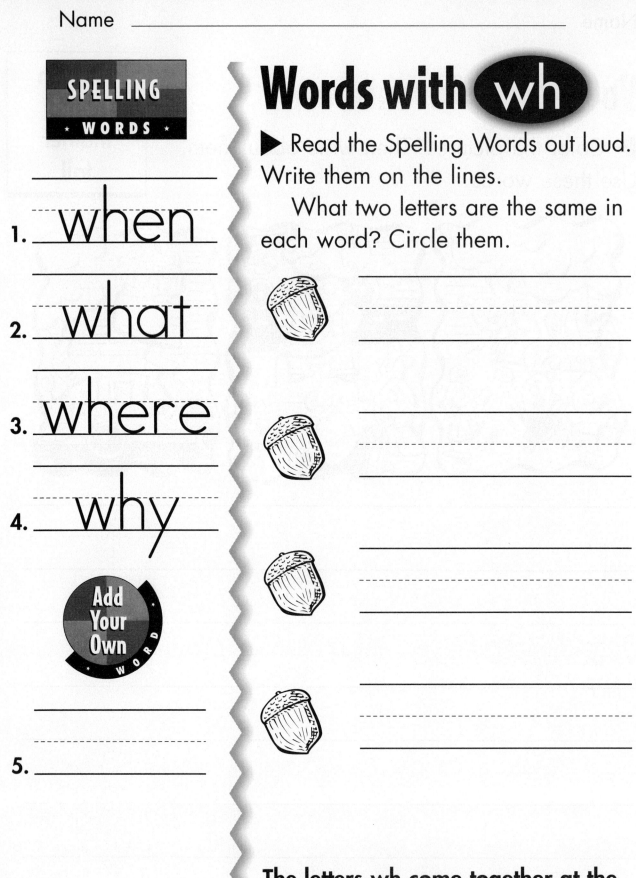

SPELLING
★ WORDS ★

1. **when**

2. **what**

3. **where**

4. **why**

Add Your Own WORD

5. _____

Words with wh

▶ Read the Spelling Words out loud. Write them on the lines.

What two letters are the same in each word? Circle them.

The letters wh come together at the beginning of some question words.

FULL SAILS "The Wild Woods" • Harcourt Brace School Publishers

Integrated Spelling

Strategy Workshop

▶ Look at each picture. What does it show?
Write <u>when</u>, <u>what</u>, or <u>where</u>. Think about the
shape of each word.

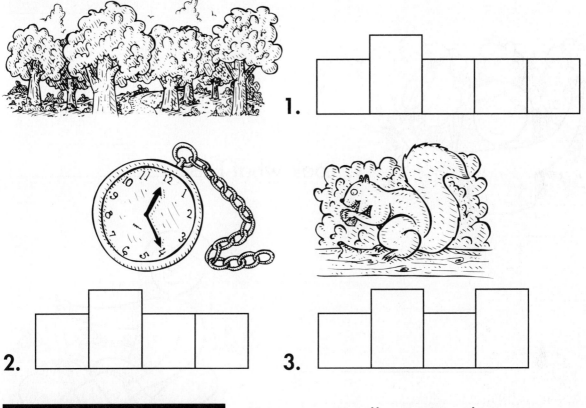

1.

2.

3.

Fun with Words Write a Spelling Word to
complete the sentence.

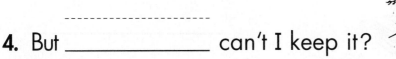

4. But _____ can't I keep it?

Name _____

Vocabulary WordShop

▶ Use the best word from the box to complete the sentence about each picture.

Action
★ WORDS ★
found
keep
take

_____

1. Look what I _____!

_____

2. I will _____ it home.

_____

3. I will always _____ it!

Integrated Spelling

FULL SAILS "The Wild Woods" • Harcourt Brace School Publishers

Name _____

Vocabulary Adventures

▶ Draw yourself in the picture. Then write a word in each sentence.

snow
scarf
snowman

_____

----

1. It is fun to play in the _____.

_____

----

2. We are making a _____.

_____

----

3. Let's put a _____ on him.

FULL SAILS "Lionel in the Winter" • Harcourt Brace School Publishers

SPELLING ★ WORDS ★

1. now

2. of

3. come

4. one

Add Your Own WORD

5. _____

Words to Remember with o

▶Read the Spelling Words out loud. Listen for the different sounds of the letter o. Write each word so that the letter o is in a star.

The letter o can stand for different sounds.

FULL SAILS "Jenny's Journey" • Harcourt Brace School Publishers

Strategy Workshop

▶ Write a Spelling Word to complete each sentence. Think about the shape of the word.

1. This is a wish ☐☐ mine.

2. I want to ☐☐☐☐ to see you.

Fun with Words Look at the picture. What are the girls saying? Write a Spelling Word in each sentence.

3. Here comes _____ of my best friends!

4. I feel so happy _____!

Name _____

Vocabulary WordShop

Boating
★ W O R D S ★
water
waves
sail

▶ Write the words from the box to tell about the picture.

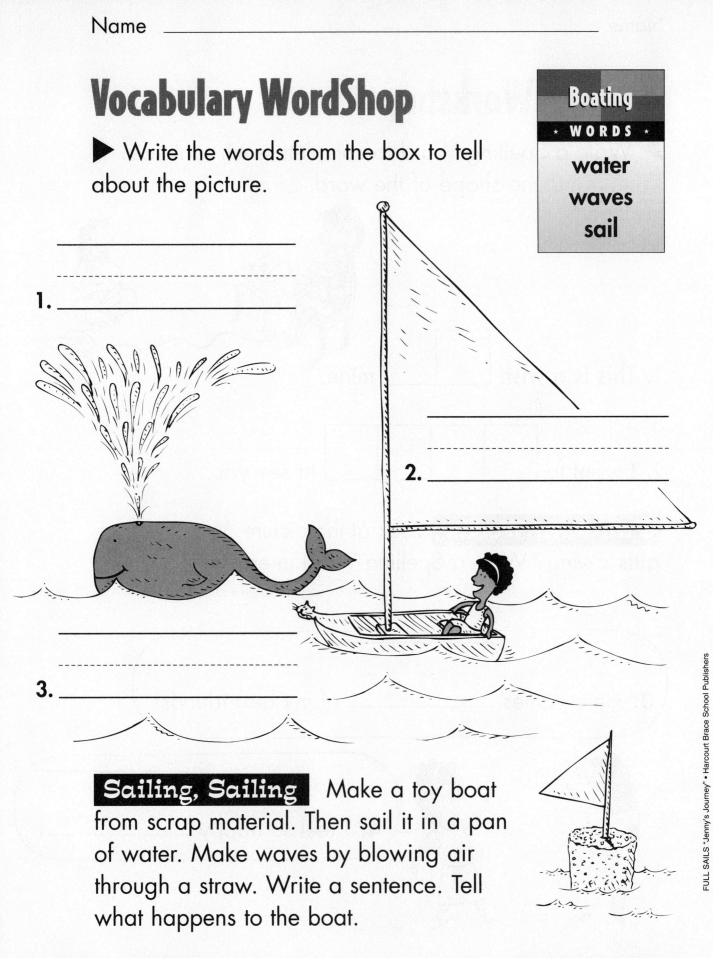

1. _____

2. _____

3. _____

Sailing, Sailing Make a toy boat from scrap material. Then sail it in a pan of water. Make waves by blowing air through a straw. Write a sentence. Tell what happens to the boat.

FULL SAILS "Jenny's Journey" • Harcourt Brace School Publishers

Integrated Spelling

Name _____

Vocabulary Adventures

► Complete the pictures. In each sentence, write the word that tells what you drew.

| water |
| waves |
| sail |

_____

1. The _____ are high.

2. She put up the _____.

3. My friend lives next to the _____.

Integrated Spelling

LESSON 26   113

FULL SAILS "Jenny's Journey" • Harcourt Brace School Publishers

Practice Test

Read each pair of sentences. Look at how the underlined words are spelled. Then fill in the circle next to the correct sentence.

SAMPLE: ○ I can't find my <u>hin</u>.
● I can't find my <u>hen</u>.

1. ○ She <u>must</u> be out.
   ○ She <u>mest</u> be out.

2. ○ She's not very <u>beg</u>.
   ○ She's not very <u>big</u>.

3. ○ She likes to <u>run</u> away.
   ○ She likes to <u>ren</u> away.

4. ○ She ran <u>in</u> the garden.
   ○ She ran <u>ine</u> the garden.

5. ○ I will <u>hulp</u> you catch her.
   ○ I will <u>help</u> you catch her.

ALL SMILES • Review • Harcourt Brace School Publishers

Name _____

Read each sentence. Look at how the two words are spelled.
Fill in the circle next to the correct word.

SAMPLE: A bee _____ a birthday.   ● had ○ hod

1. He asked a duck _____ a cow.   ○ und ○ and

2. He _____ a cake on the table.   ○ put ○ pute

3. He _____ birthday hats.   ○ got ○ gat

4. And _____ did his friends get him?   ○ wat ○ what

5. He got a bag _____ blocks.   ○ of ○ uf

Integrated Spelling

Review Activities

Story Rhyme Time

Sometimes a rhyme tells a story. Look at this
picture. Does it make you think of an old
rhyming story?

On another paper, write sentences
to go with the picture. Tell what
you think will happen next. You
may want to use the Helpful
Words from the box at the top
of the page.

Tips for Spelling Success

• Read your sentences.

• Make sure that names and special
words begin with capital letters.

• If you used any of the words from
the box, check that they are spelled
correctly.

Word Magic

Change one letter in each word to spell a new word.

How can something <u>big</u> turn into a little <u>bug</u>?

big   **bag**   **bug**

1. Turn a <u>hen</u> into a <u>pin</u>.

hen

2. Turn <u>him</u> into a <u>hut</u>.

him

SPELLING
★ WORDS ★

1. came

2. made

3. wait

4. play

Add Your Own WORD

5. _____

Words with Long **a**

▶ Read the Spelling Words out loud. Look at the letters that stand for the long **a** sound.

Write each word where it belongs.

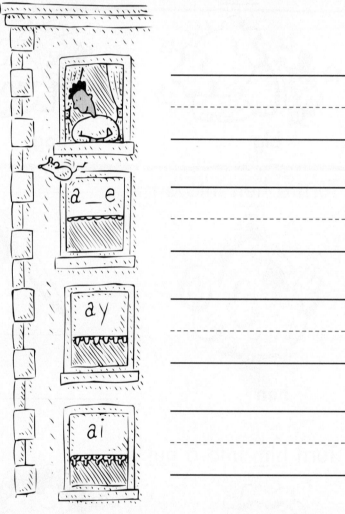

a _ e

a y

a i

The letters **ay** and **ai** often stand for the long **a** sound.
The letter **a** followed by a consonant and a silent **e** usually stands for the long **a** sound.

Integrated Spelling

Strategy Workshop

▶ Name each picture. Write a Spelling Word that rhymes with the picture name to complete the sentence.

wade

game

day

1. Look what I _____.

2. Dad _____ to watch.

3. We put on a _____.

Fun with Words Write the Spelling Word that tells about the picture. **Hint:** It has the letters <u>ai</u> that stand for the long <u>a</u> sound.

4. _____

Vocabulary WordShop

▶ Look at the pictures. Write a word from the box in each question. Then circle yes or no to answer.

Nighttime
★ WORDS ★
dream
asleep
bedtime

_____

- -

1. Is it _____?

yes   no

_____

- -

2. Will the boy fall _____?

yes   no

_____

- - - - - - - - - - - - - - - - - - -

3. Will his _____ make him happy?

yes   no

ALL SMILES "Dreams" • Harcourt Brace School Publishers

Vocabulary Adventures

| dream |
| asleep |
| bedtime |

▶ Read the story. Add words from the box to the story. Complete the picture at the bottom.

The boy was not happy.

_____

It was past his _____.

_____

He still could not fall _____.

His dad played for him.

_____

Soon he began to _____ about a surprise he had made at school.

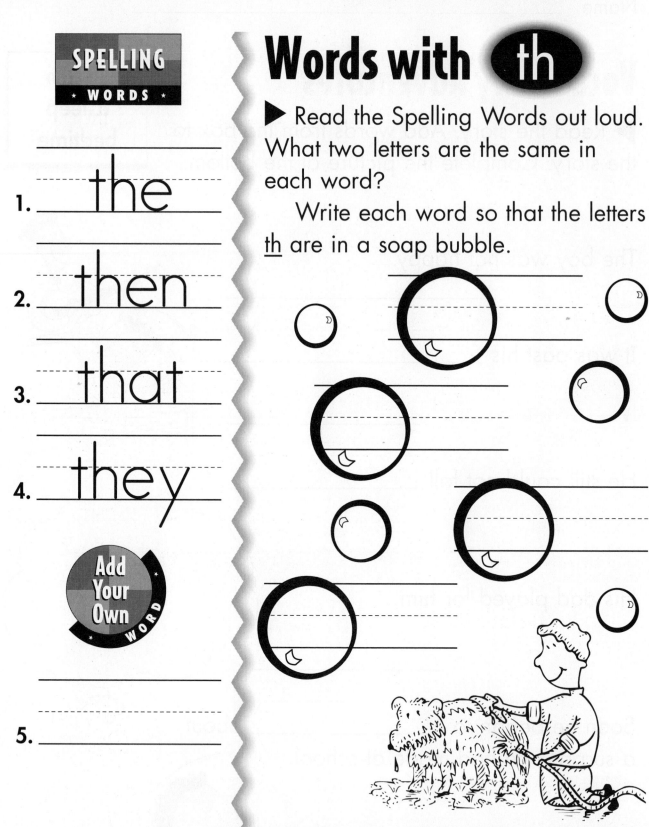

SPELLING WORDS

1. the
2. then
3. that
4. they

Add Your Own WORD

5. _____

Words with th

▶ Read the Spelling Words out loud. What two letters are the same in each word?

Write each word so that the letters th are in a soap bubble.

The letters th often stand for the sound you hear at the beginning of the.

Name _____

Strategy Workshop

▶ Complete each sentence. Write a Spelling Word that rhymes with the picture name.

cat

_____

----

1. He scrubbed _____ dog.

pen

_____

----

2. What did he do _____?

Fun with Words A Spelling Word is hiding in two other Spelling Words. Write all three words in the sentence.

_____

----

3. The word _____ hides in the words

_____   _____

---------------------------   ---------------------------

_____ and _____ .

Name _____

Vocabulary WordShop

▶ Write a word from the box to tell about each picture. You will use one word two times.

1. before a _____

2. after a _____

3. a _____ dog and a _____ boy

Vocabulary Adventures

▶ Follow the directions.

1. Color things used to make something wet.

2. Color things used to make something <u>dry</u>.

3. Draw things that you use to take a bath.

Name _____

More Words to Remember

▶ Read the Spelling Words out loud. Where do you hear the vowel sound? Write each word in the correct place.

1. have

2. live

3. do

4. some

Add Your Own WORD

5. _____

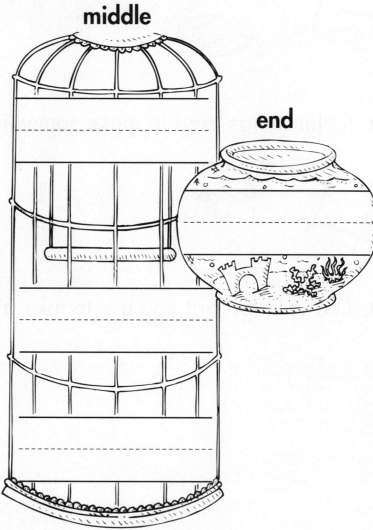

middle

end

Words you use often are words to remember.

Name _____

Strategy Workshop

▶ Write a Spelling Word to complete each question. Think about the shape of the word.

1. What do you ☐☐☐☐ in that box?

2. What does it like to ☐☐ ?

3. Where does it ☐☐☐☐ ?

Fun with Words Write a Spelling Word to tell about the picture.

4. It eats _____ garden greens!

Vocabulary WordShop

Animal
Body Part
★ W O R D S ★

paws
beaks
fins

▶ Look at each picture. Write the word that names the part of an animal that shows.

1. _____

2. _____

3. _____

Imagine That! Imagine an animal that has paws, fins, and a beak. What does it look like? Draw a picture of the animal. Make up a name for it. Tell a friend about the animal.

Integrated Spelling

Vocabulary Adventures

paws
beaks
fins

▶ Complete each picture. Then write the word that tells what you drew.

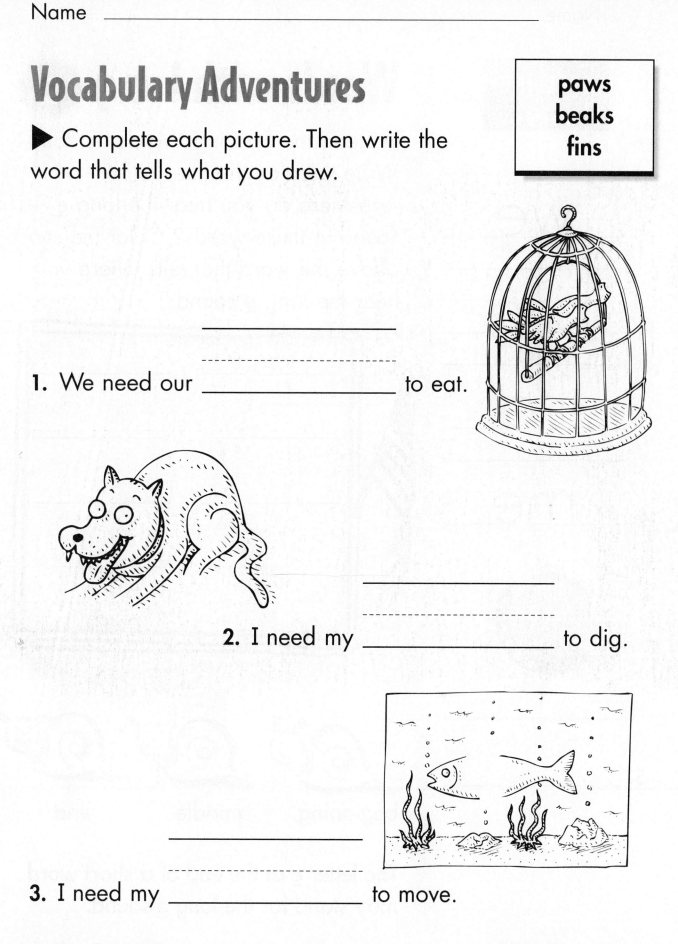

_____

- - - - - - - - - - - - - - - -

1. We need our _____ to eat.

_____

- - - - - - - - - - - - - - - -

2. I need my _____ to dig.

_____

- - - - - - - - - - - - - - - -

3. I need my _____ to move.

1. we

2. she

3. he

4. me

Add Your Own
WORD

5. _____

Words with Long **e**

▶ Read the Spelling Words out loud. Write them on the lines.

Where do you hear the long **e** sound in these words? Color the snail above the word that tells where you hear the long **e** sound.

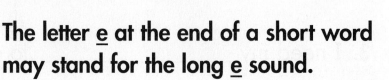

beginning   **middle**   **end**

The letter e at the end of a short word may stand for the long e sound.

Strategy Workshop

▶ Find the Spelling Words that rhyme with <u>be</u>. Color those parts of the picture yellow.

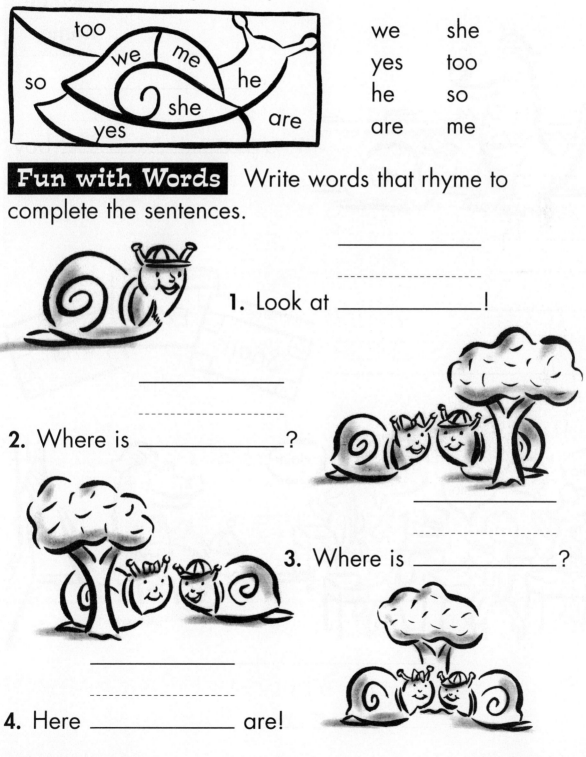

we	she
yes	too
he	so
are	me

Fun with Words Write words that rhyme to complete the sentences.

_____

1. Look at _____!

_____

2. Where is _____?

_____

3. Where is _____?

_____

4. Here _____ are!

Vocabulary **WordShop**

▶ Write words from the box to tell about the pictures.

_____

- -

1. a _____ boy

_____

- -

2. _____

_____

- -

3. _____

Name _____

Vocabulary Adventures

▶ Follow the directions.

1. Write your <u>name</u> on the tag.

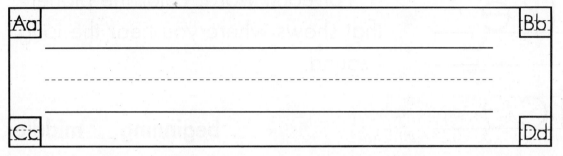

2. Write the name of someone <u>new</u> at your school.

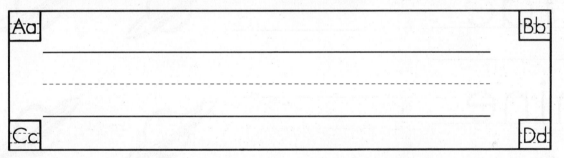

3. Draw a picture. Show how you <u>welcome</u> someone new to your school.

How Do You Do? Work with two friends. Pretend one friend is a new student. Practice introducing one friend to another.

Words with Long

▶ Read the Spelling Words out loud. Write them on the lines.

For each word, color the planet that shows where you hear the long i sound.

1. like

2. ice

3. ride

4. nine

Add Your Own WORD

5. _____

beginning   **middle**

_____

_____

_____

_____

The long i sound can be spelled i–consonant–e.

Strategy Workshop

▶ Write a Spelling Word that rhymes with the picture name to complete the sentence.

side

pine

bike

_____
- - - - - - - - - - - - - - - - -

1. He goes on a _____ .

_____
- - - - - - - - - - - - - - - - -

2. He visits _____ places.

_____
- - - - - - - - - - - - - - - - -

3. One is cold _____ snow!

Fun with Words   Find a Spelling Word that is hiding in the underlined word. Then write the Spelling Word to complete the sentence.

_____
- - - - - - - - - - - - - - - - -

Two <u>mice</u> played on the _____ .

Name _____

Vocabulary WordShop

▶ Write the words from the box to tell about the pictures.

1. the hot _____

2. a far-off _____

3. our home _____

Sky Time Add words about space to your Spelling Log. Then draw or paint a space picture. Write the names of the things in your picture.

Integrated Spelling

Vocabulary Adventures

▶ Use the words from the pictures below. Write them in the puzzle.

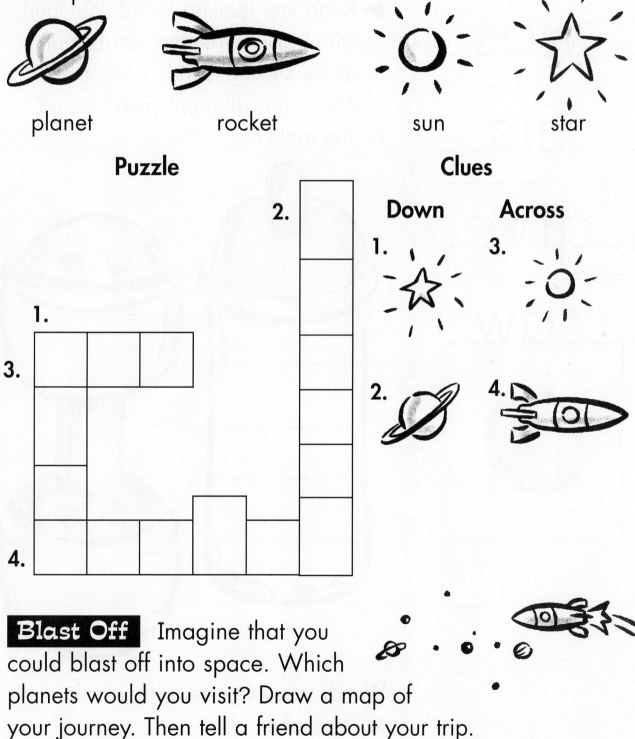

planet   rocket   sun   star

Puzzle

Clues

Down   **Across**

1.   3.

2.   4.

Blast Off Imagine that you could blast off into space. Which planets would you visit? Draw a map of your journey. Then tell a friend about your trip.

_____
1. was

2. his

3. give

4. saw

Add
Your
Own
★ W O R D ★

5. _____

More Words to Remember

▶ Read the Spelling Words out loud. On the bottle, write the words that have the short i sound. Write the words with a different vowel sound on the rattle.

Words you use often are words to remember.

Strategy Workshop

▶ Write a Spelling Word to complete each sentence. Think about the shape of the word.

1. The baby ☐☐☐ thinking about food.

2. Mother will ☐☐☐☐ him dinner.

3. Then he will close ☐☐☐ eyes.

Fun with Words   Two Spelling Words have the same letters. Write the words to complete the sentence.

_____   _____

She _____ he _____ happy!

Vocabulary WordShop

▶ Write a word from the box to tell about each picture.

_____
a _____ pig

_____
starts to _____

_____
his _____

Integrated Spelling

Name _____

Vocabulary Adventures

▶ Geraldine's mother left her directions.
Complete them. Write words from the box.

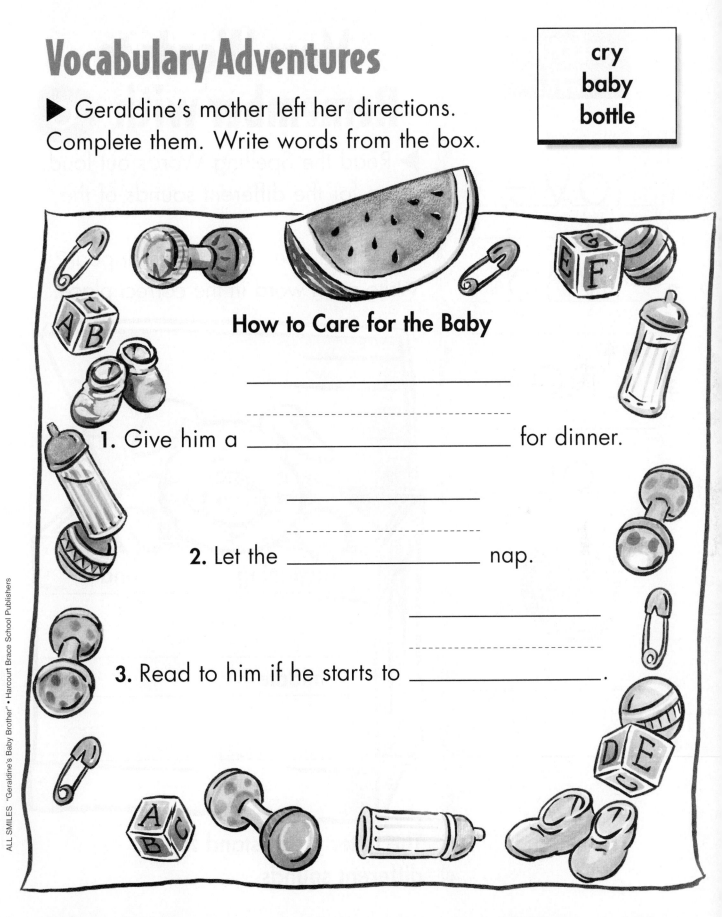

How to Care for the Baby

_____

1. Give him a _____ for dinner.

2. Let the _____ nap.

3. Read to him if he starts to _____.

SPELLING
★ WORDS ★

1. love

2. who

3. no

4. or

Add Your Own ★ WORD ★

5. _____

More Words to Remember with ⊙

▶ Read the Spelling Words out loud. Listen for the different sounds of the letter o.

Where does the letter o appear? Write each word in the correct place.

beginning   end

middle

The letter o can stand for different sounds.

ALL SMILES "Julius" • Harcourt Brace School Publishers

Strategy Workshop

▶ Name each small picture. Write a Spelling Word that rhymes with the picture to complete the sentence.

glove

1. Do you _____ my pig?

go

2. Father says a pig is _____ fun!

door

3. Do not say that, _____ I will cry!

Fun with Words Write a Spelling Word to complete the sentence.

But _____ says pigs can't dance!

Vocabulary WordShop

▶ Write a word from the box to complete each sentence.

"-thing" WORDS

anything
everything
something

_____

_____

1. He took _____ .

_____

_____

2. Will he take just _____ ?

_____

_____

3. Did he find _____ he likes?

Vocabulary Adventures

▶ Follow the directions below.

1. Find everything that grows.
   Color all these things.

2. Can you find anything to ride in?
   Color it.

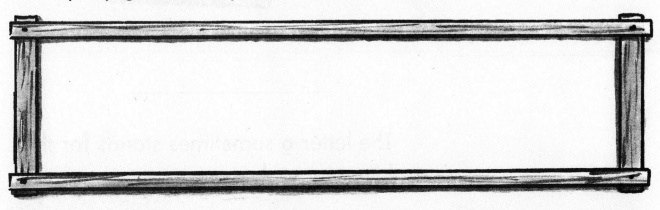

3. Think of something that you would like to do with
   a pet pig. Draw a picture to show what it is.

SPELLING
★ WORDS ★

1. old

2. rose

3. home

4. go

Add Your Own W O R D

5. _____

Words with Long O

▶ Read the Spelling Words out loud. Where do you hear the long o sound? Write each word where it belongs.

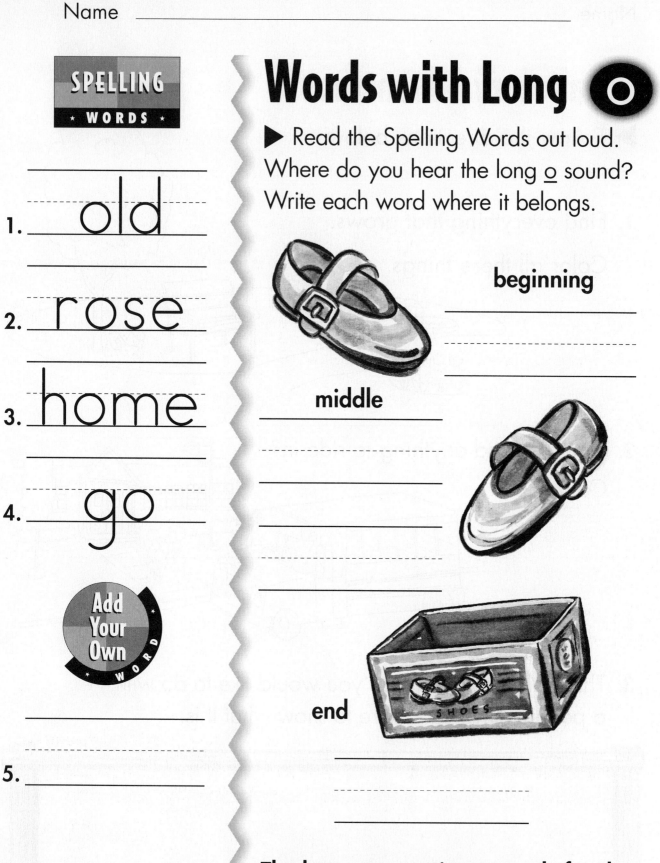

beginning
_____
_____

middle
_____
_____

end
_____
_____

The letter o sometimes stands for the long o sound.

Integrated Spelling

Strategy Workshop

▶ Name each small picture. Write a Spelling Word that rhymes with the picture to complete the sentence.

hose

cold

no

_____

----

1. What a pretty red _____ !

_____

----

2. I found it behind the _____ shed.

_____

----

3. Let's _____ look for another one.

Fun with Words Write a Spelling Word to tell about the picture.

_____

--- ---- ----- ----- ----- -----

_____

Vocabulary WordShop

▶ Write the words from the box to name the people in the pictures.

1. my _____

2. my _____ 3. my _____

Name _____

Vocabulary Adventures

▶ Look at the picture. Draw a line from each word to the person or people it names.

aunt   **baby**   **grandparents**   **father**

Write a sentence about your family.

_____

- -

_____

_____

- -

_____

Draw a picture to go with your sentence.

Name _____

Practice Test

Read each sentence. Look at how the two words are spelled. Fill in the circle next to the correct word.

SAMPLE: Let's _____ visit space. ○ goe ● go

1. How can _____ do it? ○ we ○ wea

2. We do not have a _____! ○ ride ○ riid

3. A story can _____ us a lift. ○ giv ○ give

4. We might see the stars _____ the sun. ○ ar ○ or

5. We will be _____ for dinner! ○ home ○ hom

ALL SMILES • Review • Harcourt Brace School Publishers

Name _____

Read each pair of sentences. Look at how the underlined words are spelled. Then fill in the circle next to the correct sentence.

SAMPLE: ● A pet could live here.
○ A pet could liv here.

1. ○ We maad a little home.
   ○ We made a little home.

2. ○ We put in sume water.
   ○ We put in some water.

3. ○ And theen we got a big rock.
   ○ And then we got a big rock.

4. ○ Do they like this home?
   ○ Do thay like this home?

5. ○ We think they do!
   ○ We think they doo!

Review Activities

made
maybe
open
could

Thanks So Much

Think about this school year. What new things did you learn? Who helped you?

Draw a picture of someone you would like to thank. Show what the person did to help you.

On another paper, write a thank-you letter. Tell the person what you learned and how he or she helped you. You may want to use the Helpful Words from the box at the top.

Tips for Spelling Success

- Make sure your letter is clear.
- Check that names and special words begin with capital letters.
- If you used any of the words from the box, check that they are spelled correctly.

Rhyme Time

Change a letter in the underlined word to make a rhyming word.

1. Change the <u>i</u> in <u>like</u> to make a word that rhymes with <u>make</u>.

_____
- - - - - - - - - - - - - - - - - - -
_____

2. Change the <u>s</u> in <u>rose</u> to make a word that rhymes with <u>hope</u>.

_____
- - - - - - - - - - - - - - - - - - -
_____

3. Change the <u>d</u> in <u>ride</u> to make a word that rhymes with <u>pipe</u>.

_____
- - - - - - - - - - - - - - - - - - -
_____

My Spelling Picture Dictionary

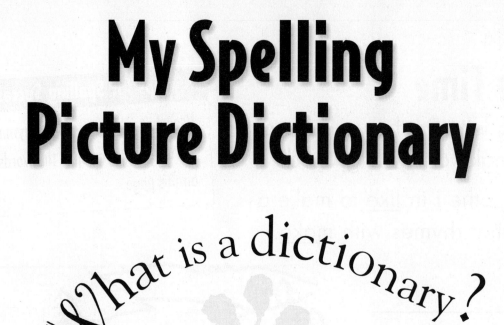

What is a dictionary?

A dictionary tells what words mean. It shows how words are spelled, too.

How can a dictionary help me when I am reading?

If you are not sure what a word means, you can find its meaning in a dictionary.

How can a dictionary help me when I am writing?

If you are not sure how to spell a word, you can find the correct spelling in a dictionary.

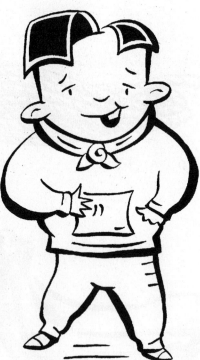

Grade 1 • Harcourt Brace School Publishers

hen
a big hen

him
See him dance!

his
his garden

home
my home

Grade 1 • Harcourt Brace School Publishers

nine

nine ducks

no

no more room

not

This cat is not scary.

now

The mouse will fly now, not later.

Grace 1 • Harcourt Brace School Publishers

O

of — part of a cake — a cube of ice

old — an old hat

on — A bee is on the hat.

one / **or** — You can get one hat or the other.

Grade 1 • Harcourt Brace School Publishers

O

P

play

Let's play tag.

You can watch our play.

put

Please put your blocks away.

red

red paint

ride

Let's go for a ride.

rose

a pretty rose

run

They run.

R

said

He <u>said</u>, "Go!"

saw

They <u>saw</u> a star.

she

What is <u>she</u> mixing?

some

We have <u>some</u> books.

stop

You must <u>stop</u>.

STOP

Grade 1 • Harcourt Brace School Publishers

that

He wants <u>that</u> one.

the

painting <u>the</u> boat

then

Let's play, and <u>then</u> we can eat.

they

Have <u>they</u> been here before?

Grade 1 • Harcourt Brace School Publishers

T

Action Words

Food Words

milk
sandwich
hamburger
juice
salad
spaghetti
bread
corn
cake
cookie
carrot
pie
apple
orange
banana
grapes

HAPPY BIRTHDAY!

Place Words

apartment

park

city

farm

lake

river

bridge

barn

town

house

road

Position Words

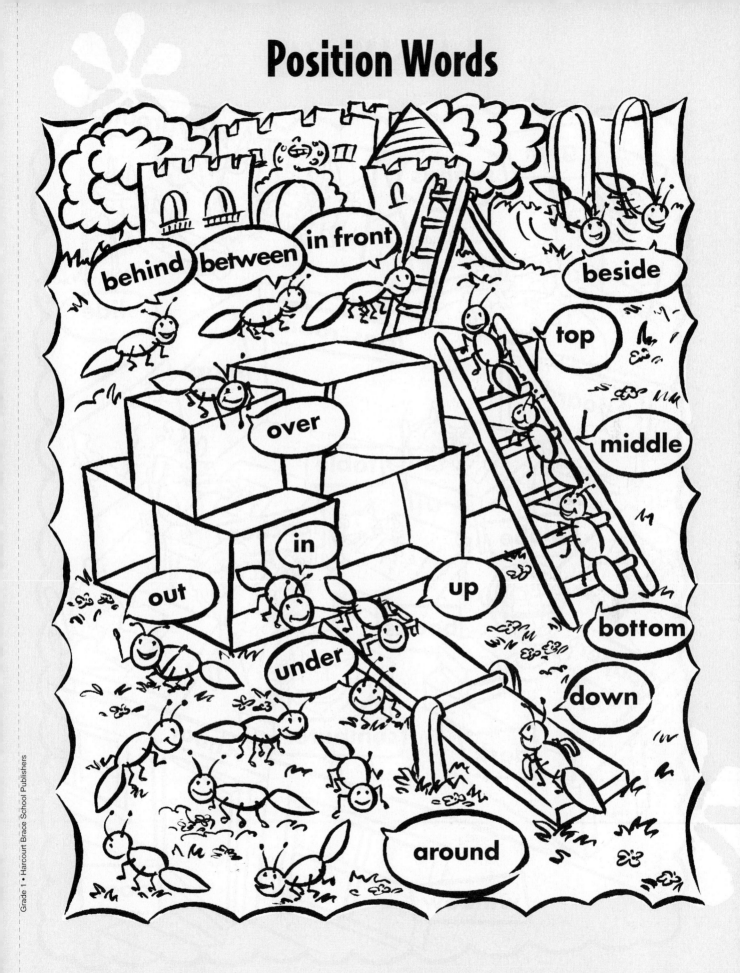

School Words

gym

swings

playground

slide

classroom

board

map

table

globe

teacher

books

paper

desk

computer

school

window

door

Integrated Spelling

Transportation Words

airport

helicopter

bike

plane

ship

train

boat

gas station

bus

truck

motorcycle

The Writing Process

When you write, follow the five steps of the Writing Process.

PREWRITE

When you prewrite, you decide what to write about. You could make a list or a web. You could also draw a picture.

Grade 1 • Harcourt Brace School Publishers

DRAFT

When you write a draft, you put your ideas on paper. Don't worry about making mistakes. Just write what you want to say.

REVISE

When you revise, you make changes in your writing. You can add or take out words or sentences. You can also move words or sentences. Ask others to read your work. Use their ideas to make your writing better.

We looked all over for our cat.

paper
She was in a ~~big~~ bag!

Integrated Spelling

PROOFREAD

When you proofread, you look for mistakes. Correct any mistakes you find.

Proofreading Checklist

✓ Did you spell words correctly?

✓ Did you form each letter correctly?

✓ Did you write complete sentences?

✓ Did you begin sentences with capital letters?

✓ Did you end sentences with the correct marks?

✓ Did you begin people's names with capital letters?

✓ Did you write <u>I</u> with a capital letter?

PUBLISH

When you publish your work, you share it with others. Make a neat copy so everyone can read it. Add pictures if you want. Be proud of what you have done!

Grade 1 • Harcourt Brace School Publishers

Spelling Strategies

Look for word families...

These words are a family.
- Words in a word family rhyme.
- The first letters are different.
- The other letters are the same.

> I want to spell ⬚.
> The letter **h** stands for the beginning sound.
> A word in the same family is **pen**.
> I'll add the letters **en** and write **hen**.

Word families can help you spell words.
- Think about the beginning sound of the word you want to spell.
- Write the letter that stands for this sound.
- Think of a word in the same word family.
- Write the letters that are the same.

Grade 1 • Harcourt Brace School Publishers

Look at word shapes...

Every word has its own shape.
Look at the shapes of these words.

Word shapes can help you spell words.

- Think about the shape of the word.
  Try to see the shape in your mind.
- Think about the letters that spell the word.

- Write the word. Look at the shape.
- Does the shape look right? If not, try a different spelling.

Grade 1 • Harcourt Brace School Publishers

My Spelling Log

What's a Spelling Log? It's a special place for words that are important to you. Here's what you'll find in this Spelling Log!

VOCABULARY WORDSHOP WORDS

Every spelling lesson has Vocabulary WordShop Words. List them where you think they belong on these special pages.

MY OWN WORD COLLECTION,
pages 190–192

Be a word collector. Keep your collection here! Group words you want to remember any way you please!

Action Words

On this page, you can write Action Words.

leaping

Grade 1 • Harcourt Brace School Publishers

Describing Words

This page is for Describing Words.
These words tell how things look,
feel, taste, smell, and
sound. They also
tell how many
or what color.

wet

People Words

You can write People Words on this page.

baby

Position Words

This page is for writing Position Words.

down

Integrated Spelling   **VOCABULARY WORDSHOP WORDS**   **187**

Science Words

You can write Science Words on this page.
Clues can help you remember a word. Your
clues can be words or pictures like this one.

web

Time and Place Words

Time and Place Words belong on this page.

day

Grade 1 • Harcourt Brace School Publishers

My Own Word Collection

What's a word collection?

It's like a sticker collection.
You choose words you like.
Then you put them in groups
with other words.

What kinds of groups?

Look at the pictures to get some
ideas. Use your own ideas, too.

Weather Words
School Words
Sports Words
Story Words
Play Words

_____   _____

Group _____   Group _____

_____   _____

_____   _____

_____   _____

_____   _____

_____   _____

_____   _____

Grade 1 • Harcourt Brace School Publishers

My Own Word Collection

Add words that you want to know how to spell. Then you can use them in your writing.

Food Words
Noise Words
Home Words
Math Words
Party Words

_____

Group _____

_____

_____

_____

_____

_____

Group _____

_____

_____

_____

_____

My Own Word Collection

Write more of your own words on this page.

Happy Words
Sad Words
Silly Words
Long Words
Short Words

Group _____

Group _____

Grade 1 • Harcourt Brace School Publishers